Human Perception of Visual Information

Bogdan Ionescu • Wilma A. Bainbridge
Naila Murray

Editors

Human Perception of Visual Information

Psychological and Computational Perspectives

 Springer

Editors
Bogdan Ionescu
Politehnica University of Bucharest
Bucharest, Romania

Wilma A. Bainbridge
University of Chicago
Chicago, IL, USA

Naila Murray
NAVER Labs Europe
Meylan, France

ISBN 978-3-030-81467-0   ISBN 978-3-030-81465-6   (eBook)
https://doi.org/10.1007/978-3-030-81465-6

This Springer imprint is published by the registered company Springer Nature Switzerland AG
The registered company address is: Gewerbestrasse 11, 6330 Cham, Switzerland

Preface

There is one thing the photograph must contain, the humanity of the moment.

—Robert Frank

Computational models of objective visual properties such as semantic content and geometric relationships have made significant breakthroughs using the latest achievements in machine learning and large-scale data collection. There has also been limited but important work exploiting these breakthroughs to improve computational modelling of subjective visual properties such as interestingness, affective values and emotions, aesthetic values, memorability, novelty, complexity, visual composition and stylistic attributes, and creativity. Researchers that apply machine learning to model these subjective properties are often motivated by the wide range of potential applications of such models, including for content retrieval and search, storytelling, targeted advertising, education and learning, and content filtering. The performance of such machine learning-based models leaves significant room for improvement and indicates a need for fundamental breakthroughs in our approach to understanding such highly complex phenomena.

Largely in parallel to these efforts in the machine learning community, recent years have witnessed important advancements in our understanding of the psychological underpinnings of these same subjective properties of visual stimuli. Early focuses in the vision sciences were on the processing of simple visual features like orientations, eccentricities, and edges. However, utilizing new neuroimaging techniques such as functional magnetic resonance imaging, breakthroughs through the 1990s and 2000s uncovered specialized processing in the brain for high-level visual information, such as image categories (e.g., faces, scenes, tools, objects) and more complex image properties (e.g., real-world object size, emotions, aesthetics). Recent work in the last decade has leveraged machine learning techniques to allow researchers to probe the specific content of visual representations in the brain. In parallel, the widespread advent of the Internet has allowed for large-scale crowd-sourced experiments, allowing psychologists to go beyond small samples with limited, controlled stimulus sets to study images at a large scale. With the combination of these advancements, psychology is now able to take a fresh look at age-old questions like what we find interesting, what we find beautiful, what drives our emotions, how we perceive spaces, or what we remember.

The field of machine learning, and Artificial Intelligence more broadly, enjoys a long tradition of seeking inspiration from investigations into the psychology and neuroscience of human and non-human intelligence. For example, deep learning neural networks in Computer Vision were originally inspired by the architecture of the human visual system, with its many layers of neurons thought to apply filters at each stage. Psychology and neuroscience also rely heavily on developments from Artificial Intelligence, both for parsing down the Big Data collected from the brain and behavior, as well as for understanding the underlying mechanisms. For example, now, object classification deep neural networks such as VGG-16 are frequently used as stand-ins for the human visual system to predict behavior or even activity in the brain. Given the progress made in machine learning and psychology towards more successfully modelling subjective visual properties, we believe that the time is ripe to explore how these advances can be mutually enriching and lead to further progress.

To that end, this book showcases complementary perspectives from psychology and machine learning on high-level perception of images and videos. It is an interdisciplinary volume that brings together experts from psychology and machine learning in an attempt to bring these two, at a first glance, different fields, into conversation, while at the same time providing an overview of the state of the art in both fields. The book contains 10 chapters arranged in 5 pairs, with each pair describing state-of-the-art psychological and computational approaches to describing and modelling a specific subjective perceptual phenomenon.

In Chap. 1, Lauer and Võ review recent studies that use diverse methodologies like psychophysics, eye tracking, and neurophysiology to help better capture human efficiency in real-world scene and object perception. The chapter focuses in particular on which contextual information humans take advantage of most and when. Further, they explore how these findings could be useful in advancing computer vision and how computer vision could mutually further understanding of human visual perception. In Chap. 2, Constantin et al. consider the related phenomenon of interestingness prediction from a computational point of view and present an overview of traditional fusion mechanisms, such as statistical fusion, weighted approaches, boosting, random forests, and randomized trees. They also include an investigation of a novel, deep learning-based system fusion method for enhancing performance of interestingness prediction systems.

In Chap. 3, Bradley et al. review recent research related to photographic images that depict affectively engaging events, with the goal of assessing the extent to which specific pictures reliably engage emotional reactions across individuals. In particular, they provide preliminary analyses that encourage future investigations aimed at constructing normative biological image databases that, in addition to evaluative reports, provide estimates of emotional reactions in the body and brain for use in studies of emotion and emotional dysfunction. On the computational side, in Chap. 4, Zhao et al. introduce image emotion analysis from a computational perspective with a focus on summarizing recent advances. They revisit key computational problems with emotion analysis and present in detail aspects such as emotion feature extraction, supervised classifier learning, and domain adaptation. Their discussion concludes with the presentation of the relevant datasets for evaluation and the identification of open research directions.

In Chap. 5, Chamberlain sets out the history of empirical aesthetics in cognitive science and the state of the research field at present. The chapter outlines recent work on inter-observer agreement in aesthetic preference before presenting empirical work that argues the importance of objective (characteristics of stimuli) and subjective (characteristics of context) factors in shaping aesthetic preference. Valenzise et al. explore machine learning approaches to modelling computational image aesthetics, in Chap. 6. They overview the several interpretations that aesthetics have received over time and introduce a taxonomy of aesthetics. They discuss computational advances in aesthetics prediction, from early methods to deep neural networks, and overview the most popular image datasets. Open challenges are identified and discussed, including dealing with the intrinsic subjectivity of aesthetic scores and providing explainable aesthetic predictions.

Bainbridge, in Chap. 7, draws from neuroimaging and other research to describe our current state-of-the-art understanding of memorability of visual information. Such research has revealed that the brain is sensitive to memorability both rapidly and automatically during late perception. These strong consistencies in memory across people may reflect the broad organizational principles of our sensory environment and may reveal how the brain prioritizes information before encoding items into memory. In Chap. 8, Bylinskii et al. examine the notion of memorability with a computational lens, detailing the state-of-the-art algorithms that accurately predict image memorability relative to human behavioral data, using image features at different scales from raw pixels to semantic labels. Beyond prediction, they show how recent Artificial Intelligence approaches can be used to create and modify visual memorability, and preview the computational applications that memorability can power, from filtering visual streams to enhancing augmented reality interfaces.

In Chap. 9, Akcelik et al. review recent research that aims to quantify visual characteristics and design qualities of built environments, in order to relate more abstract aspects of an urban space to quantifiable design features. Uncovering these relationships may provide the opportunity to establish a causal relationship between design features and psychological feelings such as walkability, preference, visual complexity, and disorder. Lastly, in Chap. 10, Medina Ríos et al. review research that uses machine learning approaches to study how people perceive urban environments according to subjective dimensions like beauty and danger. Then, with a specific focus on Global South cities, they present a study on perception of urban scenes by people and machines. They use their findings from this study to discuss implications for the design of systems that use crowd-sourced subjective labels for machine learning and inference on urban environments.

We have edited this book to appeal to undergraduate and graduate students, academic and industrial researchers, and practitioners who are broadly interested in cognitive underpinnings of subjective visual experiences, as well as computational approaches to modelling and predicting them. The authors of this book provide overviews of the current state of the art in their respective fields of study; therefore, chapters are largely accessible to researchers who may not be familiar with either prevailing computational, and particularly machine learning, practice, or with research practice in cognitive science. As such, we believe that researchers from both worlds will have much to learn from these chapters.

We are indebted to all the authors for their contributions, and hope that readers of this book will enjoy reading the fruits of their hard work as much as we have. Finally, we thank our editor, Springer, who gave us the opportunity to bring this project to life.

Bucharest, Romania   Bogdan Ionescu

Chicago, IL, USA   Wilma A. Bainbridge

Meylan, France   Naila Murray

Contents

The Ingredients of Scenes that Affect Object Search and Perception

Tim Lauer and Melissa L.-H. Võ

1 Introduction

What determines where we attend and what we perceive in a visually rich environment? Since we typically cannot process everything that is in our field of view at once, certain information needs to be selected for further processing. Models of attentional control often distinguish two aspects: Bottom-up attention (sometimes referred to as "exogenous attention") focuses on stimulus characteristics that may stand out to us, while top-down (or "endogenous") attention focuses on goal-driven influences and knowledge of the observer (e.g., Henderson et al., 2009; Itti & Koch, 2001). In this chapter, we focus on top-down guidance of attention and object perception in scene context; particularly, on top-down guidance that is rooted in generic scene knowledge—or *scene grammar* as we will elaborate on later—and is abstracted away from specific encounters with a scene, but stored in long-term memory.

Suppose that you are looking for cutlery in a rented accommodation. You would probably search in the kitchen or in the living room but certainly not in the bathroom. Once in the kitchen, you would probably readily direct your attention to the cabinets—it would not be worthwhile to inspect the fridge or the oven. Despite having a specific goal, certain items may attract your attention, such as a bowl of fruits or colorful flowers on the kitchen counter. If you found forks, you might expect to find the knives close by. While viewing the kitchen, you would probably not have a hard time recognizing various kitchen utensils, even if they were visually small, occluded or otherwise difficult to identify. In this example, one benefits from context information, from prior experience with kitchens of all sorts. That is, in the real

T. Lauer (✉) · M. L.-H. Võ
Goethe University Frankfurt, Frankfurt am Main, Germany
e-mail: tlauer@psych.uni-frankfurt.de

© The Author(s), under exclusive license to Springer Nature Switzerland AG 2022
B. Ionescu et al. (eds.), *Human Perception of Visual Information*,
https://doi.org/10.1007/978-3-030-81465-6_1

world, objects are hardly ever seen in isolation but typically in similar, repeating surroundings which allows us to make near-optimal predictions in perception and goal-directed behavior (Bar, 2004; Oliva & Torralba, 2007; Võ et al., 2019). Figure 1 provides an illustration: While it is difficult to recognize the isolated object in the left panel, the availability of scene context (right panel) probably helps in determining the identity of the object (here an electric water kettle).

In this chapter, we will first review how attention is allocated in the real world from a stimulus-driven perspective. We will then outline important aspects of attentional guidance during visual search, followed by a section on contextual influences on object recognition—an integral part of search. In particular, we focus on what types of contextual information or "ingredients" the visual system utilizes for object search and recognition, a question that has remained largely unexplored until recently. To this end, we refer to diverse methodologies (like psychophysics, eye tracking, neurophysiology, and computational modelling) used at different degrees of realism (ranging from on-screen experiments, via virtual reality to studies in the real world). Finally, we will bring the findings together, discussing the relative contributions of various context ingredients to object search and recognition, as well as future directions and mutual benefits of human and computer vision research.

2 Attentional Allocation in Real-World Scenes

2.1 The Role of Low-Level Features

The bowl of fruits in our introductory example (see Fig. 1) would be expected based on the semantic scene context, but might initially stand out to us in terms of low-level features (e.g., color) that differ from the surroundings (e.g., white kitchen

Fig. 1 While it is difficult to recognize the isolated object in the left panel, the kitchen context (right panel) may help in determining that the object is an electric water kettle. The kitchen scene was reproduced and adapted with permission from *Lignum Moebel*, Germany (https://lignum-moebel.de)

counter). Over the last two decades, several computational models of bottom-up, stimulus-driven attention have been put forth (for reviews, see Borji, 2019; Borji & Itti, 2013; Krasovskaya & Macinnes, 2019). A seminal early model of attention that inspired numerous other models is the saliency model by Itti and Koch (2000, 2001). Visual salience is defined as the "distinct subjective perceptual quality which makes some items in the world stand out from their neighbors and immediately grab our attention" (Itti, 2007). The model computes a salience map with regions that are likely attended by the observer based on low-level feature contrast (in intensity, orientation, and color) across spatial scales, motivated by receptive fields in the human visual system. Note that, as a proxy for *overt* visual attention, researchers often measure fixations and compare the empirical distributions to model predictions. However, visual attention is in principle not limited to the point of fixation and can be directed to regions outside of the fovea (commonly referred to as *covert* attention). Low-level saliency models have been shown to predict overt attention above chance under free viewing conditions (i.e., in the absence of a specific task), with highest predictability found for the first fixation (e.g., Parkhurst et al., 2002). Interestingly, these models capture where we direct our gaze merely based on low-level feature contrast, that is, without knowledge of image content or meaning (e.g., it is not known that the salient spot in the kitchen is a bowl of fruits or flowers).

2.2 The Role of Mid-Level Features and Objects

While low-level image features certainly play a decisive role for attentional allocation, it has been questioned whether attention is effectively attracted by such low-level features or rather higher-level features or objects that are not incorporated in low-level salience models (Einhäuser et al., 2008; Nuthmann & Henderson, 2010; Pajak & Nuthmann, 2013; Stoll et al., 2015). Objects often occur in locations that are salient (Spain & Perona, 2011)—oftentimes they make locations salient in the first place—and might thus be the driving force in attentional deployment (Schütt et al., 2019). Stoll et al. (2015) found that a state-of-the-art model of low-level salience and an object model predicted fixations equally well; however, when salience was reduced in regions that were relevant in terms of object content, the object model outperformed the salience model. Nuthmann and Einhäuser (2015) introduced a novel approach to investigate which image features influence gaze: Using mixed-effects models, they showed that mid-level features (e.g., edge density) and higher-level features (e.g., image clutter and segmentation) had a distinct contribution in gaze prediction as opposed to low-level features. Thus, many recent models incorporate mid to higher-level features in addition to low-level features to better predict fixation distributions in scene perception. To this end, deep neural networks (DNNs) have become increasingly popular and achieve benchmark performance in gaze prediction nowadays (Borji, 2019). One of the currently best-performing networks, *DeepGazeII*, utilizes high-level features from a DNN trained on object recognition (Kümmerer et al., 2016).

2.3   The Role of Meaning

The role of scene meaning (or semantic informativeness) in attentional deployment while viewing real-world scenes has been studied for decades, and was recently systematically assessed by Henderson and colleagues (Henderson et al., 2018, 2019; Peacock et al., 2019a, 2019b). For a large number of local scene patches derived from scene images, they collected ratings of meaningfulness based on how informative or recognizable the patches were to observers. The authors then generated meaning maps which represent the spatial distribution of semantic features across a scene, comparable to a salience map (though not rooted in image-computable features). Meaning was shown to predict gaze successfully, as was low-level salience, but salience did not have a unique contribution when controlling for its correlation with meaning (Henderson & Hayes, 2017). This finding was replicated when predicting fixation durations instead of fixation distributions (Henderson & Hayes, 2018), and held across different tasks (Henderson et al., 2018; Rehrig et al., 2020), even when low-level image salience was highly task-relevant and meaning was not (Peacock et al., 2019a). However, it has been argued that the success of the meaning maps approach could be due to high-level image features that are not captured in classic salience models and could have strongly influenced observer's ratings of meaningfulness: *DeepGazeII*, which incorporates high-level object features, is able to outperform meaning maps at predicting fixations (Pedziwiatr et al., 2019).

Further, deriving meaning from objects in scenes has been shown to guide attention such that gaze tends to transition from one object to another object if the items are semantically related (Hwang et al., 2011; Wu et al., 2014a; for a review, see Wu et al., 2014b; see also De Groot et al., 2016). Objects that violate the global meaning of a scene (e.g., a mixer in the bathroom) strongly engage attention; they are typically looked at longer and more often than consistent objects (e.g., Cornelissen & Võ, 2017; De Graef et al., 1990; Friedman, 1979; Henderson et al., 1999; Loftus & Mackworth, 1978; Võ & Henderson, 2009b). While it has been established that attention can be "stuck" on these inconsistencies once they are spotted—even when they are irrelevant to one's current goals (Cornelissen & Võ, 2017, p.1)—it is a matter of debate whether they attract attention before they are fixated. Some studies have found semantic inconsistencies to influence initial eye-movements (e.g., the critical object is fixated earlier than a consistent object) (Becker et al., 2007; Bonitz & Gordon, 2008; Coco et al., 2019; Loftus & Mackworth, 1978; Nuthmann et al., 2019; Underwood et al., 2007, 2008; Underwood & Foulsham, 2006), yet other studies did not find indication for attention capture by inconsistencies (Cornelissen & Võ, 2017; De Graef et al., 1990; Furtak et al., 2020; Henderson et al., 1999; Võ & Henderson, 2009b, 2011). These mixed results may be related to characteristics of the scene stimuli (e.g., line drawings, photographs, or 3D-rendered scenes with varying degrees of clutter) and/or more or less controlled characteristics of the critical objects (e.g., size, eccentricity, salience).

With the rise of fully labeled image databases like LabelMe (Russell et al., 2008) assessing the semantic relatedness between objects and their scene contexts as well as inter-object relatedness has become easier. For instance, using graph theory by treating objects as nodes and assigning different weights to their connections has provided new avenues to determine clusters of semantically related objects within scenes—which we have started to call "phrases"—or prominent objects therein that anchor predictions about the location and identity of other objects nearby (for more details, see Sect. 4.3; Boettcher et al., 2018; for reviews, see Võ, 2021; Võ et al., 2019). Objects that do not fit their context tend to be regarded as surprising or interesting and can affect where we attend to in scenes.

2.4 The Role of Interestingness and Surprise

While the role of image features has been studied extensively (for reviews, see Borji, 2019; Borji & Itti, 2013; Krasovskaya & Macinnes, 2019), relatively little is known about how other factors such as interestingness or surprise modulate attentional deployment. Elazary and Itti (2008) proposed that interesting objects are in fact visually salient: Observers who contributed to the LabelMe database—a large collection of scenes with object annotations (Russell et al., 2008) tended to label those objects that were salient even though they were free to choose which objects to label. In another study, when explicitly asked which scene locations are interesting, the choice of locations was largely similar across observers and correlated with fixation distributions of other observers (Masciocchi et al., 2009). Behavioral judgements and eye movements were also correlated with predictions of a salience model, yet not as highly as one would expect if salience was the only driving factor of interestingness. The authors concluded that there are both bottom-up and top-down influences on what we perceive as interesting and where we attend in an image (see also Borji et al., 2013; Onat et al., 2014). Other studies have shown that, beyond an influence of low-level salience, attentional allocation is modulated by the affective-motivational impact of objects or their importance for the scene ('t Hart et al., 2013; Schomaker et al., 2017), and that attention is attracted by surprising image locations in a Bayesian framework (e.g., Itti & Baldi, 2005). Moreover, some types of objects hold a special status: Text and faces, for instance, have been shown to greatly attract attention in scenes (see Wu et al., 2014b).

Taken together, inspired by early models of low-level salience, more recent research highlights the importance of higher-level features and indicates that attention in scenes is largely object-based—with some objects attracting and/or engaging attention more than others. While DNNs achieve benchmark performance in a variety of tasks nowadays and have become increasingly popular in fixation prediction, more research is needed to see how they will further our understanding of human attention mechanisms. Further, it will be crucial to shed more light on when during scene viewing various features exert influence on attentional allocation. Schütt et al. (2019) disentangled the contribution of low and higher-level features to fixation distributions over time, showing that the influence of low-level features is mostly limited to the first fixation and that higher-level features, as incorporated in *DeepGazeII*, predict fixations better starting 200 ms after stimulus onset. Despite the popularity of DNNs, a shortcoming of data-driven approaches is that they do not capture some aspects of human visual attention such as singleton (or "odd one out") detection in artificial stimuli (even when the training data is adjusted, e.g., Kotseruba et al., 2020).

3   Guidance of Attention during Real-World Search

While the processing of image features can certainly play a role in where we attend, especially when free-viewing scenes, we are rarely ever mindlessly looking around. Instead, we tend to be driven by various agendas and task demands, one of which is the need to locate something or somebody. The interplay of bottom-up image features and more cognitively based, top-down influences during search is complex. As Henderson (2007) put it: "In a sense, we can think of fixation as either being "pulled" to a particular scene location by the visual properties at that location, or "pushed" to a particular location by cognitive factors related to what we know and what we are trying to accomplish" (p. 219). However, it should be noted that it is not always straightforward to strictly delineate between bottom-up and top-down influences (Awh et al., 2012; see also Teufel & Fletcher, 2020); we are certainly not claiming that the aspects presented here are one *or* the other.

Traditionally, visual search was studied using simple artificial displays of randomly arranged targets and distractors (e.g., "find the letter T among several instances of the letter L"). The main measure was—and still is— reaction time (RT) as a function of set size (i.e., the number of items in the display). With increasing set size, RT is consistently longer in such a task, in equal steps, indicating that attention is serially deployed to one item after another (see Wolfe, 2020; Wolfe & Horowitz, 2017). However, in some cases, it is not necessary to inspect all items in the display: In "classic guided search" theory, a limited set of target features (e.g., color, motion, orientation, size) can guide attention in a top-down manner, narrowing down the number of possible items (for reviews, see Wolfe, 2020; Wolfe et al., 2011b; Wolfe & Horowitz, 2017). For instance, when looking for a red "T" among some red and some black "L"s one can disregard all black items. To this end, "feature binding" takes place: The shape and the color of the target are bound together in order to reject distractors as well as recognize the target(s). While the field has learned a lot from these types of experiments that mostly used meaningless stimuli, search in real-world scenes seems to be strongly influenced by other guiding factors.

Scenes are not random assemblies of features but most often structured and meaningful, which allows us to perform searches with remarkable efficiency. For instance, when looking for a teddy in the bedroom, fixations tend to cluster around the bed even if the target is not present and cannot guide attention by means of its features (see Võ et al., 2019). Search for objects in scenes appears to be much more efficient than search for isolated objects in random arrays, although it can be challenging to define a scene's set size adequately (see Wolfe et al., 2011a). As proposed in the *cognitive relevance framework,* search in scenes is mainly guided by cognitive factors such as prior knowledge and current goals (Henderson et al., 2009; for a review, see Wolfe et al., 2011b).

What makes search in the real world so efficient despite the wealth and complexity of information contained in the visual input? While no one would doubt that scene context aids object search, relatively little is known about which "ingredients" of real-world scenes effectively guide attention, what their relative contributions are, and when they contribute during the search. In the following, we attempt to shed more light on these ingredients.

3.1   The Role of Scene Gist

One line of work addressed the question of whether an initial brief glance at a scene influences attentional allocation. Within a fraction of a second, observers can obtain the "gist" of a scene, a coarse representation of its spatial properties and meaning that does not require the selection of individual objects (Greene & Oliva, 2009a, 2009b; Rousselet et al., 2005). While there is no universal account of scene gist, many definitions (including ours), state that gist allows the categorization of scenes at a basic level. For instance, one may categorize a scene as a kitchen and tell that it comprises something like a kitchen counter but not yet grasp that there are a toaster and a mixer resting on any of the surfaces. That is, one may "see the forest without representing the trees" (Greene & Oliva, 2009a). A brief glance in the range of milliseconds is too short to make a saccade and thus to foveate selected parts of the scene in order to perceive them with fine detail. In fact, scene gist recognition does not depend on the high visual acuity of the fovea; it can be achieved even when the scene is blurred or when only peripheral information is available (e.g., Loschky et al., 2019). One fundamental aspect of scene gist is spatial layout information. As demonstrated in the *spatial envelope model* and supported by behavioral studies, scenes can be categorized based on their global properties, such as the global shape, without the need to identify any objects in the scene (Oliva & Torralba, 2001, 2006). This way of processing the scene is considered to be largely feed-forward and, in terms of search guidance, is assumed to take place on a "nonselective pathway" that parallels a "selective pathway" which binds features and recognizes individual objects (Wolfe et al., 2011b). Note that objects can also be an important source of information for scene categorization (MacEvoy & Epstein, 2011), especially for indoor scenes that are not always easily distinguishable in terms of their global properties.

To investigate how a brief glance at a scene guides search behavior, researchers have used the flash-preview moving window paradigm (Castelhano & Henderson,

2007; Võ & Henderson, 2010, 2011; Võ & Schneider, 2010; Võ & Wolfe, 2015): It initiates with a brief preview of a scene, followed by a target word and a search phase in which observers look for the target object in the original scene but through a gaze-contingent window that only reveals a small area of the scene at the current point of fixation. Given that the scene as a whole is not perceived during the search phase, this paradigm allows experimenters to assess the contribution of the scene's initial global percept to visual search. Note, however, that this contribution may be weaker under more natural search conditions in which the entire scene can be processed online during the search as well (see Võ & Wolfe, 2015). A scene's preview has been shown to influence visual search consistently in these studies, even when it was as short as 50 ms (Võ & Henderson, 2010). Võ and Schneider (2010) manipulated the type of context information that was available in the scene preview, selectively preserving either the global scene background or local objects (for an illustration, see Fig. 2). The availability of the scene background, conveying the spatial layout of the scene, resulted in faster detection of the targets and required fewer fixations compared to a control condition, whereas a preview of local objects did not facilitate search. Thus, a coarse representation of a scene's structure and meaning appears to already guide visual search effectively. Interestingly, knowing only the category of the scene does not seem to be sufficient, as was shown when a searched scene was

Fig. 2 Illustration of a kitchen scene (top left) that can be divided into the background (top right), local objects (bottom left) as well as an anchor object (bottom right)

primed by a different scene exemplar from the same category or by a word label of the category. Yet, a scene that is semantically inconsistent with a target (e.g., a mug of paint brushes in a bedroom) can facilitate search given that the object occurs in a reasonable location (Castelhano & Heaven, 2011, for a review see Castelhano & Krzyś, 2020).

The spatial layout of a scene can provide us with important constraints regarding the location of objects. For example, the occurrence of objects is constrained by the laws of physics such that objects rest on surfaces rather than hovering in the air. Even when we do not fully grasp a scene's meaning, we may be able to tell where its major surfaces lie (e.g., kitchen counters, tables, etc.) (see Fig. 2) and/or where the sky and the horizon are located. Moreover, two objects usually do not occupy the same physical space (Biederman et al., 1982), and we know where certain objects typically occur (e.g., a rug is often located on the floor) (Kaiser & Cichy, 2018; Neider & Zelinsky, 2006). Incorporating likely vertical object locations in a low-level salience model can significantly improve gaze prediction, as was demonstrated in the *contextual guidance model* (see Oliva & Torralba, 2006). More recently, the *surface guidance framework* was introduced, proposing that attention is allocated to surfaces in the scene that are related to the target object (Castelhano & Heaven, 2011; Pereira & Castelhano, 2014, 2019; for a review, see Castelhano & Krzyś, 2020).

3.2 The Role of Local Objects

Another line of work investigated the influence that selected parts of the scene, specifically objects, have on attentional allocation. In a naturalistic search task, Mack and Eckstein (2011) instructed participants to search for objects on tables while wearing mobile eye tracking glasses. The target object (e.g., a fork) was either located near a so-called cue object with which it would likely co-occur in natural scenes (e.g., a plate) or elsewhere (close to other objects). Targets were found faster if they were located near cue objects, and cue objects were fixated more frequently than other objects surrounding the targets, suggesting that object co-occurrence in the real world can boost search performance. In another study, in which participants inspected scene images or searched for targets therein, the LabelMe database of scenes with object annotations was used to determine the semantic relatedness of the currently fixated object to other objects in the scene or to the search target (Hwang et al., 2011). Gaze was shown to transition more likely to objects that are semantically related to the currently fixated object, even when the objects were not in close proximity. Moreover, the search data revealed that the influence of target-based semantic guidance increased throughout the trial. The finding of likely transitioning between related objects was replicated even when the objects were cropped (removed) from the scenes but not when discarding spatial dependencies among the cropped objects by re-arranging them (Wu et al., 2014a). When a preview of the original scene was added in order to provide gist information, there was no indication of increased semantic guidance. Moreover, there is evidence that the functional arrangement of objects influences gaze direction in the absence of scene context (e.g., a key that is arranged such that it can or cannot be inserted in a lock) (Clement et al., 2019). In object arrays, semantic information can be extracted extrafoveally and can guide even the first eye movement during search (Nuthmann et al., 2019). Taken together, both the semantic relation of objects as well as their spatial dependencies appear to be relevant for attentional allocation during search.

3.3   The Role of Anchor Objects

There seem to be certain objects that predict not only the occurrence, but particularly the location of other objects within a scene. Boettcher et al. (2018) explored the role of spatial predictions in object-based search guidance, introducing the concept of *anchor* objects. Anchors are typically large, static objects (i.e., they are rarely moved) that give rise to strong predictions regarding the identity and location of *local* objects clustering around them (e.g., the table may predict the position of a chair, a glass of water, and the salt). By contrast, local objects do not necessarily predict the location of other local objects (e.g., when searching for the salt, the location of a glass might not be that informative) (see Fig. 2). Using the LabelMe database, the concept of anchor objects was operationalized through four factors: variance of spatial location, frequency of co-occurrence, object-to-object distance, and clustering of objects (see Boettcher et al., 2018; c.f. Võ et al., 2019). In a series of eye tracking experiments, observers searched for target objects in images of 3D-rendered scenes (e.g., bathroom) that were manipulated to either contain a target-relevant anchor (e.g., shower) or a substitute object that was chosen to also be semantically consistent with the scene and of similar size (e.g., cabinet). Compared to the substitute objects, relevant anchors affected search performance such that there was a reduction in reaction time, scene coverage, and the time to transition from the anchor to the target. In line with this, in a recent virtual reality experiment, participants were slower at locating target objects when anchors were concealed by grey cuboids of similar dimensions compared to when they were fully visible (Helbing et al., 2020). Randomly re-arranging the anchors (or cuboids) resulted in an opposite effect, that is, targets were located faster in the cuboid condition, suggesting that both the identity and spatial predictions of anchors are crucial for their ability to guide search. Note that these inherent spatial predictions distinguish anchor objects from the notion of diagnostic objects (e.g., MacEvoy & Epstein, 2011) which may be important for conveying scene meaning and facilitating scene categorization, but need not yield precise predictions of the occurrence of other objects (Võ et al., 2019). It seems likely that anchor objects can be identified even in the periphery (see Koehler & Eckstein, 2017b, for a demonstration of peripheral extraction of object cues) and thus they might provide an effective way to locate smaller targets, building a bridge between the global scene and local objects.

3.4   Scene Grammar

Taken together, while scene gist yields an initial coarse representation of the scene's structure and meaning that can already effectively narrow down the search space, selected objects allow for a more fine-grained type of guidance (see also Wolfe et al., 2011b). Recent studies on the role of anchor objects showed that objects are not all equal in their ability to guide search. Rather, scenes appear to be hierarchically organized, with anchors being the core of so-called "phrases" that constitute meaningful subunits within a scene (e.g., the "shower phrase" versus the "toilet phrase"). Within these phrases, anchors hold stronger predictions about other local objects therein (e.g., the shampoo is *in* the shower and the toilet brush *next to* the toilet). When searching for the toilet paper in a bathroom, one can substantially reduce search time (and stress!) by outright avoiding to search the non-relevant shower and sink phrases.

While some of the regularities inherent in scenes have already been described decades ago (e.g., Biederman et al., 1982; Boyce & Pollatsek, 1992; Palmer, 1975), they are nowadays directly measurable using large-scale annotated databases and descriptive statistics (Greene, 2013, 2016; Russell et al., 2008). In analogy to the language domain, we have been referring to implicitly acquired knowledge of various regularities in scenes regarding *what* objects tend to be *where* as *scene grammar* (for reviews, see Võ, 2021; Võ et al., 2019; Võ & Wolfe, 2015). In language, semantics refers to conceptual relations between words while syntax describes the rules of sentence structure. Accordingly, we have used the terms scene semantics and syntax to describe the meaningfulness of object-scene relations (e.g., a pot belongs in the kitchen, not in the bathroom) or structural nature of these relations (the pot belongs on top of the stove, not on the floor), respectively (Võ & Henderson, 2009b). Violations of scene grammar have been shown to impede search performance and strongly influence eye-movements (e.g., Võ & Henderson, 2011). For instance, both semantic and syntactic violations are typically fixated longer and more often than their consistent counterparts (e.g., Võ & Henderson, 2009a). When objects are positioned inconsistently in a scene, it also takes longer to decide whether an object is the target or not once it is fixated (e.g., Võ & Wolfe, 2013b). Thus, contextual regularities may not only affect search guidance but also object recognition at various stages of the search.

4   Object Recognition in Scene Context

Object recognition is an integral part of search: Distractors need to be evaluated as to whether they are target candidates or not, and eventually the target needs to be identified and matched against the search template (for more details, see Sect. 5). In the following, we will outline how scene context affects object perception. Contextual influences on object perception were studied extensively for decades—

though mostly isolated from visual search—using behavioral measures, and more recently also neurophysiological methods. One of the core questions of this line of work has been at what stage(s) of object processing contextual modulation occurs.

4.1 Behavioral Work

Traditionally, the influence of scene context on object processing was studied using line drawings (Biederman et al., 1982; Boyce et al., 1989; Boyce & Pollatsek, 1992; Hollingworth & Henderson, 1998, 1999; Palmer, 1975). In Biederman's et al. (1982) influential object detection paradigm, observers were shown a target word (e.g., fire hydrant), followed by a briefly presented line drawing of a scene and a pattern mask with a location cue. Observers were asked if they had or had not seen the target object in the cued location. Target objects that were consistent with the scene context (e.g., a fire hydrant on the street) were detected faster and more accurately than semantically or syntactically inconsistent objects (e.g., a fire hydrant in the kitchen or a fire hydrant positioned in the air above a street, respectively) (see also Boyce et al., 1989), or other forms of violations (objects in unlikely rather than impossible locations, or objects with abnormal sizes). However, the consistency advantage was not replicated when taking response bias into account (Hollingworth & Henderson, 1998, 1999), which lent support to the *functional isolation model*, proposing that there is no interaction of scene and object processing on a perceptual level.

More recently, researchers have used color or grayscale photographs of scenes and an object naming task to probe the role of context in object recognition (Davenport & Potter, 2004; Lauer et al., 2018; Lauer et al., 2020a; Munneke et al., 2013; Sastyin et al., 2015). Observers were briefly presented with a scene containing a consistent or inconsistent object cutout in the foreground (or an isolated object superimposed on a scene; Lauer et al., 2018, 2020a, 2020b), followed by a perceptual mask and a response window, where they typed in the name of the object. In this paradigm, which is not prone to response bias and overcomes some limitations of early behavioral work (see Davenport & Potter, 2004), consistent objects were named more accurately than inconsistent objects across studies. Here, we refer to this effect as *scene-to-object consistency effect*. Moreover, scenes are named more accurately if they contain a consistent versus inconsistent object in the foreground (*object-to-scene consistency effect*), suggesting that objects and scenes are processed interactively (Davenport & Potter, 2004; see also Davenport, 2007; Leroy et al., 2020). The scene-to-object consistency effect cannot be explained by mere low-level feature overlap between the context and the target, nor does it depend on overt attention being directed to the object (Leroy et al., 2020; Munneke et al., 2013). Interestingly, the magnitude of the scene-to-object consistency effect is modulated by viewpoint: Objects that are seen from a canonical (easy) angle evoke a weaker effect than objects seen from a non-canonical (difficult) angle (Sastyin et al., 2015). Contextual modulation also depends on the displayed size of the target, with stronger effects seen for smaller objects that are more difficult to interpret (Zhang et al., 2020).

In the *model of contextual facilitation* (Bar, 2004), the gist of a scene rapidly activates scene schemata and yields predictions of associated objects that are matched against incoming information of the target, boosting its identification. We have recently probed if the scene-to-object consistency effect reflects such facilitation of object processing on a perceptual level by contrasting accuracy for isolated objects superimposed on scenes with accuracy for objects on unrecognizable scrambled scenes (baseline) (Lauer et al., 2020a). Consistent objects on scenes were named more accurately than consistent objects on scrambled scenes, suggesting that scene context indeed facilitated object recognition. Moreover, inconsistent objects on scenes were named less accurately than inconsistent objects on scrambled scenes, suggesting that the consistency manipulation also interfered with performance, either on a perceptual stage (e.g., by yielding misleading predictions) or a post-perceptual stage (e.g., through a mismatch detection that interfered with performance). It should be noted, however, that some other studies did not find facilitation of object recognition when the scene context was present versus absent (Davenport & Potter, 2004; Lauer et al., 2018; Roux-Sibilon et al., 2019). Possibly, facilitation effects are not always robust in the case of salient foreground objects or isolated objects for which figure-ground segmentation is arguably easy. In some paradigms, a strong segmentation advantage in the baseline (no-context condition) may also contribute to the absence of facilitation effects (see Davenport & Potter, 2004). Under more natural conditions—when objects are embedded in scenes and segmentation demands are also present in the baseline (e.g., by providing minimal context around the target)—facilitation was repeatedly shown, particularly pronounced for smaller targets that are more difficult to interpret (for extensive demonstrations, see Zhang et al., 2020; see also Brandman & Peelen, 2017). Besides distinct segmentation demands in the case of embedded objects, these objects also differ from isolated objects such that the context can yield spatial predictions and estimates of the target's size, potentially increasing the magnitude of contextual facilitation of object recognition.

In another recent study, objects were either presented within a scene or outside of it on the same horizontal or vertical plane (either unilateral or bilateral) (Leroy et al., 2020). Across manipulations, consistent objects and consistent scenes were named more accurately than inconsistent objects and scenes, respectively, confirming the reciprocal nature of the object-scene consistency effect. Given that contextual modulation was robust even when objects and scenes were not embedded in the same percept, these findings also suggest that, rather than arising at the earliest stages of object processing, scene context effects may occur at the stage of matching visual information with prior knowledge.

4.2   Neurophysiological Work

Context effects on object processing have also been investigated in neurophysiological studies, using electroencephalography. Specifically, event-related potentials
(ERPs) provide a temporally precise measure that can track context effects online
during stimulus exposure. The most widely studied context-sensitive ERP component is the N400—a negative deflection that peaks about 400 ms post stimulus
onset—which was originally reported in the language domain: Sentences with
a semantically inconsistent versus consistent word typically evoke a centrally
distributed N400 effect, suggesting an impedance of semantic access (Kutas &
Hillyard, 1980, 1983; for a review, see Kutas & Federmeier, 2011). In the scene
perception domain, consistent versus inconsistent objects in (or superimposed on)
scenes have been shown to evoke an N400 response with a comparable time
course and topography (Draschkow et al., 2018; Ganis & Kutas, 2003; Lauer et
al., 2018; Lauer et al., 2020a; Mudrik et al., 2010, 2014; Truman & Mudrik,
2018; Võ & Wolfe, 2013a; Zucker & Mudrik, 2019), indicating impeded access
or integration of an object in a semantically inconsistent scene context (Mudrik et
al., 2010, 2014). Moreover, across those studies that used scene stimuli, semantic
consistency manipulations evoked an earlier negativity with a sometimes more
frontal maximum known as N300 (but see Ganis & Kutas, 2003). This component
has been suggested to reflect context effects on a more perceptual level, before
object identification is completed (e.g., Mudrik et al., 2010, 2014). Specifically,
it may reflect the difficulty of matching incoming information of the target with
(misleading) predictions yielded by the inconsistent scene context. While it has
been established that scene context can modulate object processing before object
identification is completed (Lauer et al., 2020; Leroy et al., 2020; Truman & Mudrik,
2018; see also Brandman & Peelen, 2017), it is still debated whether the N300/N400
components are actually distinguishable in terms of the underlying processes or
not: In a recent study from our laboratory, the two components were found to
widely share neuronal activity patterns in a time-generalized decoding analysis
(Draschkow et al., 2018). As opposed to semantic violations in scenes, syntactic
violations (e.g., a towel on the bathroom floor) do not evoke N300/N400 effects but
a later positivity that is comparable to the P600 frequently reported for grammatical
violations in language (Võ & Wolfe, 2013a). A differential response to structural,
"syntactic" inconsistencies has also been found in comic strips (Cohn et al., 2014)
and action sequences (Maffongelli et al., 2015). Thus, the brain seems to distinguish
the processing of object-scene relations in terms of their meaning and structural
nature.

Where is scene meaning processed in the brain, and where does it influence
object perception? In a functional magnetic resonance imaging (fMRI) experiment,
Brandman and Peelen (2017) presented observers with isolated degraded (i.e.
pixelated) objects, degraded objects in scenes, or scenes without any target objects,
and found indication of contextual facilitation in the visual cortex (specifically
in regions lateral occipital and posterior fusiform sulcus): Decoding accuracy for

degraded objects in scenes exceeded accuracies for the other two conditions in a supra-additive manner, that is, it was greater than the sum of accuracies for these conditions. Interestingly, the effect of contextual facilitation was correlated with activity in regions that are crucial for scene processing (e.g., the parahippocampal place area and the retrosplenial cortex) (for a review on scene-selective regions and their functions, see Epstein & Baker, 2019). Magnetencephalography (MEG) data revealed that supra-additive facilitation emerged around 320 ms post stimulus onset, which is relatively late compared to a feedforward type of object processing in the absence of scene context influences (Cichy et al., 2014). It should be noted that the magnitude of contextual facilitation appears to depend on the visual characteristics of the target: On the behavioral level, facilitation of object detection was correlated with object ambiguity, with reduced facilitation seen for easier to identify, intact objects. In line with previous studies, these findings suggest that contextual modulation can arise on a perceptual level, and point to separate scene and object processing pathways that may interact in the visual cortex. Another recent study complemented these findings by showing signs of contextual facilitation in scene-selective areas when presenting degraded scenes with intact objects (Brandman & Peelen, 2019). Besides a reciprocal type of object-scene facilitation, there is also evidence of multimodal facilitation of object processing through auditory and semantic cues (Brandman et al., 2019).

Taken together, recent behavioral and neurophysiological work suggests that scene and object processing are not functionally isolated but that there are reciprocal influences facilitating perception, especially when the target stimulus is difficult to interpret.

4.3   Which Scene Ingredients Affect Object Processing?

Over the last few decades, numerous studies have demonstrated that scene context influences object perception, however, it was hardly ever asked which context ingredients the visual system actually utilizes, and at which time points they are relevant. The few studies that have probed individual scene properties are outlined below, grouped as studies employing *global* or *local* manipulations (affecting the context as a whole or parts of it, respectively).

Global influences on object processing. In a behavioral study, Brady et al. (2017) briefly presented observers with an object primed by either a grayscale scene or a texturized scene with a similar spatial distribution of orientations and spatial frequencies, preserving the global shape of the scene but no recognizable objects (Oliva & Torralba, 2006) (see Fig. 3). Objects primed by a semantically consistent scene were named more accurately than objects primed by an inconsistent scene. Critically, a similar but weaker scene-to-object consistency effect was found for texturized scenes, indicating that global scene properties—specifically spatial layout information—can modulate object recognition even in the absence of semantic object information. This finding is in line with studies highlighting the importance of

Fig. 3 Illustration of global context manipulations. From top left to bottom right: original scene, inverted scene, blurred scene, context area, jigsaw 4 × 4, material, layout texture (Brady et al., 2017), scene texture (Lauer et al., 2018), phase-scrambled scene. Note that the images only serve for illustration purposes; they are not a reproduction of the stimuli and parameters used in original studies

global scene properties for rapid scene understanding and categorization (Greene & Oliva, 2009a, 2009b; Joubert et al., 2007; Oliva & Torralba, 2001, 2006; Rousselet et al., 2005).

In a related study from our group, we presented consistent and inconsistent thumbnail objects superimposed on colored scenes, scene textures, or scrambled scenes (color controls) (Lauer et al., 2018). Our way of texturizing the scenes was different such that we preserved global scene summary statistics (including first to second order statistics as well as magnitude and phase correlation; see Portilla & Simoncelli, 2000) while discarding object semantics *and* spatial layout information (see Fig. 3). For scenes, we found a consistency effect at the behavioral level as well as an N300/N400 effect in ERPs. For textures, we found a non-significant trend in the same direction at the behavioral level as well as a significant N300/N400 response with a comparable time course, though less pronounced. Scrambled scenes, that retained color characteristics of the original scenes, did not show such effects. Thus, low-level scene statistics, as preserved in the textures, may modulate object processing even in the absence of spatial layout information while mere color information appears to be insufficient. It should be noted, however, that there was no indication of facilitation at the behavioral level, neither for scenes nor for textures, suggesting that the context effects may have been driven by interference in this study. By contrast, Zhang et al. (2020) found strong facilitation for objects embedded in scenes but still no facilitation for object cutouts on textures: Accuracy was even slightly higher in the baseline (minimal texture context) compared to a condition with full-size texture context. Note that there was no consistency manipulation in this study. A computer vision model (for more detail, see Sect. 5.2) was able to achieve higher accuracy for objects on textures than in the baseline, yet only when the target objects were small, and the facilitation effect was considerably weaker than the one found for original scenes.

Moreover, recent unpublished data from our laboratory suggests that objects in the context of global material backgrounds (e.g., a chair on wood vs. chair on water) (see Fig. 3) but not in the context of scrambled materials (color controls) yield a marginal consistency effect on the behavioral level as well as N300/N400 responses that are comparable to those found for scenes albeit weaker. In another study, we explored the role of object and scene orientation in the scene consistency effect (Lauer et al., 2020a). Specifically, we used inversion, a global manipulation that preserves low-level image properties (except for phase) but may interfere with semantic processing (see Fig. 3). Behaviorally and in ERPs, we found indication that upright scenes modulate the processing of both upright and inverted objects but that inverted scenes only modulate the processing of inverted objects. Corroborated by a later occurrence of ERP effects for inverted versus upright scenes, we argued that scene inversion may interfere with rapid scene gist-recognition, resulting in a later emergence of contextual influences on object processing.

Further, the amount of visual context that is available to the observer (quantified as revealed image area without the target divided by the target's size) was shown to strongly influence object recognition performance (illustrated in Fig. 3); facilitation was particularly strong in the case of small, difficult to perceive targets (Zhang et al., 2020). Moreover, contextual modulation by full scenes was robust even when the image was moderately blurred (Gaussian with $M = 0$, $SD \leq 8$, image size $= 1024 \times 1280$ pixels) (see Fig. 3 for an illustration) but not when it was blurred more strongly ($SD > 8$, see Zhang et al., 2020), suggesting that context effects do not depend on fine detail conveyed by high spatial frequencies. In addition, the role of global spatial configuration of scene parts was investigated. To this end, full scenes were divided in equal parts (2×2, 4×4 or 8×8 "jigsaw") that were randomly re-arranged while the part that contained the target remained in its original position (see Fig. 3). Intact configuration facilitated object recognition compared to a minimal context (control) condition. There was also an increase in accuracy compared to the inconsistent 4×4 and 8×8 configurations; however, the inconsistent 2×2 configuration resulted in a similar performance, possibly indicating that large scene parts already convey sufficient context information even when the global configuration of the scene is inconsistent.

The role of peripheral vision in foveal object recognition was explored by Roux-Sibilon et al. (2019). Objects surrounded by a semantically consistent peripheral scene context (beyond 6 or 8 degrees) were categorized faster than those surrounded by an inconsistent context when there was a preview of the peripheral scene. Moreover, altering the phase coherence of the targets resulted in a lower visibility threshold for consistent objects than for inconsistent ones. The context effects were not observed in the case of phase-scrambled peripheral scenes, maintaining the power spectrum but no scene summary statistics or shape information (see Brady et al., 2017; Lauer et al., 2018).

Taken together, these studies indicate that there are global influences of context on object processing which do not depend on selected parts of the context but rather on a coarse representation of context as a whole. In the following, we will explore the role of more local influences on object processing.

Local influences on object processing. One type of local information that may be relevant for object processing is the presence of other objects. A number of studies have manipulated semantic object-to-object relation in the absence of scene context, for example, by priming a target object with a related or unrelated object, or by simultaneously presenting a target with surrounding object(s). An influence of relatedness was frequently found on the behavioral level (e.g., Auckland et al., 2007; Henderson et al., 1987) as well as on the neuronal level (e.g., Barrett & Rugg, 1990; Kovalenko et al., 2012; Li et al., 2019; McPherson & Holcomb, 1999). Besides semantic relatedness, spatial object-to-object relation has been shown to modulate object processing. For instance, two related objects are named more accurately or classified faster if their spatial arrangement is typical compared to atypical (e.g., a lamp on a desk vs. a lamp under a desk, respectively), given that both objects are attended (Gronau & Shachar, 2014; Roberts & Humphreys, 2011; see also Gronau, 2020). Moreover, there is electrophysiological evidence that semantic relatedness and spatial relation interacts in object processing (Quek & Peelen, 2020). However, the role of these object-to-object effects in the presence of scene context—in the presence of other visual information—is yet to be explored.

Only two behavioral studies, to our knowledge, have jointly investigated the influence of scene background and objects. One study found an influence of scene background on object detection but no influence of relatedness among the (five) objects in the scene (Boyce et al., 1989). However, the absence of a local context effect in this study may have been due to characteristics of the stimuli (e.g., line drawings of scenes with small objects), as pointed out by Davenport (2007). In a more recent object naming experiment, observers were presented with two foreground objects, either related or unrelated, in a scene that was either consistent with both objects, one object, or neither. Scene-to-object consistency resulted in higher accuracy, as did object-to-object relatedness, without interaction of the two variables (Davenport, 2007). In a related study from our laboratory, we explored the temporal dynamics of these types of context effects using EEG (Lauer et al., 2020b). We only found N300/N400 ERP responses when both objects were unrelated and inconsistent with the scene in comparison to all other conditions; all other possible comparisons were not significant, indicating that one congruent relation of an object with either the scene or the neighboring object is sufficient to eliminate the N300/N400 inconsistency effect in this type of paradigm. Thus, we found some indication of both global and local context effects, with no apparent difference in the timeline, in accordance with an interactive view of scene perception (Davenport & Potter, 2004). It should be noted that in these studies, the background scenes contained objects that may have contributed to the context effects. Moreover, in our study, the critical objects were salient and close to the point of fixation. Future studies might want to assess the influence of other local scene properties and viewing conditions.

5 Concluding Remarks and Future Directions

Although visual search and object recognition are typically two distinct research areas with varying experimental setups, in the following, we attempt to bring the findings outlined in this chapter together, pointing out some similarities and apparent differences between the two domains. Further, we will discuss the question of relative contributions of context ingredients, and conclude with a section on reciprocal benefits of human and computer vision research.

To begin with, visual search usually includes object recognition at various stages. For instance, every distractor needs to be evaluated as to whether it is a target candidate or not. Once the target is foveated this critical object needs to be identified and matched against the search template. Thus, benefits of scene context are not only due to more efficient guidance by scene grammar, but likely also due to improved object recognition leading to faster disengagement of distractors and target identification—the latter is usually measured as decision time (i.e., the time from initial target fixation to button press indicating the termination of search). Figure 4 provides an illustration of a search for a toaster in the kitchen.

Accordingly, evidence from both literatures suggests that scene gist, which can be inferred from the spatial layout of a scene (c.f. Võ & Wolfe, 2015), can readily modulate both search performance and object processing. This type of context information is available very rapidly and allows narrowing down search space (e.g., we would search for a toaster on that large horizontal surface in what appears to be a kitchen) or the number of possible object identities (e.g., the item is probably an electronic device, not a rock), respectively. In fact, even 50 ms of exposure to context is sufficient to affect search (Võ & Henderson, 2010) as well as object recognition (Zhang et al., 2020)—this number can even be lower in the absence of backward masking (e.g., 25 ms in the case of object recognition, Zhang et al., 2020).

Moreover, it has been established that local properties of a scene, specifically co-occurring objects, are an important source of information for target localization as well as identification. To this end, both the semantic relatedness of co-occurring local objects as well as their spatial dependencies are utilized. In a recent virtual reality study from our laboratory, anchor objects in scenes not only guided search but also significantly reduced the decision time once the target object was fixated, compared to a condition in which the anchors were concealed by gray cuboids (Helbing et al., 2020).

Fig. 4 Illustration of a search for a toaster in the kitchen which not only benefits from contextual guidance of eye-movements but also from faster disengagement of distractors as well as enhanced recognition of the target. Blue arrows and circles illustrate an exemplary scan path and fixations, respectively. Thought bubbles indicate successful object identification and matching against the search template

5.1 Relative Contributions of Context Ingredients

While several context ingredients that modulate search and/or object processing have been identified, relatively little is known about the relative contributions of these ingredients, especially over time. Some work has focused on assessing the relative importance of scene background and object content in visual search, as outlined below. While a brief glance at a scene background without objects was shown to facilitate search, no facilitation was found when local objects were briefly shown instead of the scene background (Võ & Schneider, 2010). Moreover, there is evidence that search performance is higher when scene background versus object content is available throughout the search; yet, both types of information were shown to interact such that scene context provides coarse guidance to relevant regions while object content yields guidance to specific areas (Pereira & Castelhano, 2014). Together, these findings may suggest that global scene properties have a stronger contribution overall, and that they are utilized more readily than local properties—the latter presumably first need to be parsed through a "selective pathway" that binds features into objects (Wolfe et al., 2011b). However, in some other studies, the influence of objects was arguably stronger: Koehler and Eckstein (2017a, 2017b) found scene background to affect search and perceptual decisions less than object content which was divided into a co-occurring object (in close proximity to the target) and multiple object configuration (encompassing all other objects in the scene). While the influence of multiple object configuration was already present in early eye-movements, co-occurring object information was utilized later for a more fine-grained type of guidance. These findings are in line with work showing that object content yields semantic guidance in the absence of scene gist information—but only when the spatial configuration of objects is intact—while scene gist does not enhance the utilization of semantic information when object content is available (Wu et al., 2014a).

One explanation of the mixed results as to the relative importance of scene background could be that scene background is not equally informative of the target's location across studies. Interestingly, Koehler and Eckstein (2017a, 2017b) found that judgments of expected target locations per context ingredient predicted the magnitude of eye-movement guidance for that particular ingredient—the inferior contribution of scene background was related to the finding that scene background was the least informative of the target's location. In other studies, scene background may have been more informative, possibly related to the way that scene background and object content was defined. For instance, larger elements (e.g., a bed) are sometimes considered as objects, given that they can plausibly be moved (Koehler & Eckstein, 2017a, 2017b), whereas they are assumed to belong to the background in other cases (Võ & Schneider, 2010; see also Pereira & Castelhano, 2014). These larger objects may not only provide surfaces for local objects (Castelhano & Krzyś, 2020; Pereira & Castelhano, 2019) but also constitute meaningful subunits in scenes: It has recently been established that anchor objects distinctly contribute to search guidance, yielding stronger facilitation than other semantically related objects (Boettcher et al., 2018) or meaningless cuboids of similar sizes (Helbing et al., 2020). Thus, the relative contributions of context ingredients may strongly depend on the precision of the spatial predictions they yield (see also Eckstein, 2017), which may vary across studies and conceptualizations. In other words, the goal of visual search is to locate something, and we may utilize most those properties that precisely "tell us where to look". Naturally, there are constraints with respect to what information is available when/where in the visual system, and at what cost. That is, a property may be very informative but not yet selected and processed to the extent that it can guide search (Wolfe et al., 2011b).

While there is no doubt that spatial predictions are also utilized in object recognition, they are naturally not a prerequisite for contextual modulation of object processing. For instance, facilitation of object recognition is seen even when the target's location is entirely uninformative with respect to its identity (see Lauer et al., 2020a). While the object recognition literature provides clear evidence of contextual modulation in the absence of any recognizable objects in the scene (e.g., Brady et al., 2017), the *relative* contribution of such scene-based (vs. object-based) ingredients has not been assessed in the absence of object content. Currently, there is some indication that both scene context (including objects) and object co-occurrence can yield context effects of a comparable magnitude (Davenport, 2007; Lauer et al., 2020b) and timeline (Lauer et al., 2020b).

Taken together, future work could aim at further teasing apart the relative contributions of distinct global scene properties on the one hand and more local information in the form of various types of co-occurring objects on the other while also assessing how informative they are of the target. It will be especially crucial to test how the various types of scene ingredients exert influence over time.

5.2   Context in Human and Computer Vision

Many of the recent advances in better capturing human efficiency in object search and perception in the real world have been facilitated by large-scale databases and computational models (e.g., Boettcher et al., 2018; Greene, 2013, 2016; Rosenholtz et al., 2012)—inspired by a wide range of psychophysical, eye tracking, and neurophysiological studies. Interestingly, in recent years, computer vision algorithms have reached (or even surpassed) human performance levels in a number of tasks. Studying how computational solutions accomplish these tasks may be quite useful for understanding the mechanisms of human visual perception even better in the future. That is, computational models inspired by the visual system can, if validated, be used to test hypotheses about human vision in a highly controlled manner (for a review, see Lindsay, 2020). Despite several challenges, researchers have recently begun to compare and relate DNNs (specifically convolutional neuronal networks, CNNs) to human perception across the hierarchy of the visual system. Activity in the ventral stream has been shown to be generally well predicted by CNNs, with outputs from higher artificial layers better predicting activity in higher visual areas (see Lindsay, 2020). A network trained on scene recognition was able to predict activity in occipital place area, providing insights into the processing of navigational affordances (Bonner & Epstein, 2018; c.f. Lindsay, 2020). There is also electrophysiological evidence of shared spatiotemporal scene category information in humans and DNNs (Greene & Hansen, 2018). On the behavioral level, one cannot only compare benchmark classification accuracy (for which DNNs are commonly optimized) but also error patterns that humans and DNNs might share—or not share (Wichmann et al., 2017). For example, why is it that humans unlike DNNs sometimes fail to notice giant targets in scenes even when they are salient and fixated (Eckstein et al., 2017)? These and other assessments may provide further insights into the mechanisms of search and object perception in scene context. To test or to generate new hypotheses, biologically inspired artificial networks can be altered in many ways, for instance by manipulating their architectures, training sets, or training procedures (see Lindsay, 2020). Of course, careful comparisons and interpretations are important; humans and neuronal networks may achieve a very similar task outcome but accomplish it in an entirely different way computationally.

On the other hand, for large parts of the computer vision community, neuronal networks need not be biologically plausible; they are commonly intended to achieve the highest possible performance in a given tasks such as object recognition. An understanding of human efficiency in object perception, however, may help in further optimizing computer vision algorithms. A key difference between state-of-the-art DNNs and the human visual machinery is that DNNs still require massive quantities of labeled training data, while humans can learn new object concepts from a very small number of examples (Morgenstern et al., 2019; Spiegel & Halberda, 2011). Moreover, while DNNs achieve benchmark performance under certain controlled conditions, they sometimes fail under slightly changing conditions (e.g., image degradation or contrast reduction; Geirhos et al., 2018; Wichmann et al., 2017) and may thus lack the robustness and flexibility of human vision. Intriguingly, misclassification can even occur when the target is altered in a way that is unnoticeable for the human eye (see "adversarial examples", e.g., Goodfellow et al., 2014). In many algorithms for object recognition, context information is utilized only indirectly (Zhang et al., 2020): For instance, DNNs trained on object recognition in natural scenes typically represent some contextual features implicitly, which becomes apparent when they are fooled by a target-incongruent scene context (see Fig. 5). Recently, Zhang et al. (2020) introduced a biologically-inspired model that builds on feature extraction of a state-of-the-art DNN for object recognition (VGG16), yet incorporates scene context more explicitly; target and context features are processed in parallel using a dual stream architecture, with an attention mechanism selecting informative parts of the context. Performance of the

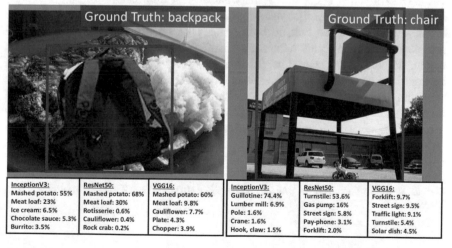

Fig. 5 DNNs for object recognition do not yield an accurate label when the scene context is inconsistent with the target, as seen in the top-five labels and corresponding confidence levels for three state-of-the art models. This indicates that DNNs represent some contextual features even though they are usually not specifically designed to do so. Figure reproduced from Zhang et al. (2020) with permission

Context aware Two-stream Attention network (CATNet) was highly correlated with human performance across various object recognition experiments (manipulating the quantity, quality and dynamics of context) while also outperforming other models overall. However, it should be noted that all tested models, including CATNet, performed considerably worse than humans when the targets were small. That is, variable object size in natural images still remains a challenge in computer vision (Zhang et al., 2020). Another recent dual pathway model, *GistNet*, was designed such that it would utilize coarse global features of the context, inspired by human scene gist perception (Wu et al., 2018). GistNet was shown to outperform VGG16, even when the scene context was significantly blurred which strongly reduced recognizable objects. The authors also visualized what features the two streams actually utilized and concluded that the foveal pathway employs "local edges and lines", while the global pathway finds "more holistic scene information corresponding to gist-like features" (p. 5).

Taken together, similar to exploring the influence of various context ingredients in human perception, these same ingredients could also be put to a test in computer vision applications furthering the reciprocal benefit when combining methods and theory of both research areas.

6   Conclusion

The way we search for, identify, and interact with objects in the real world is substantially shaped by the scene context in which they occur. In this chapter, we outline recent endeavors to determine what context information (or "ingredients") are actually utilized by the visual system for efficient object localization and identification. We argue that, in both domains, a rapidly acquired coarse global representation of the scene, which can be inferred from spatial layout information, can already lead to contextual modulation. Moreover, at least indoor scenes tend to be organized hierarchically with various levels of context exerting strong influence on both object search and perception. While we have begun to understand which ingredients of a scene matter, there is still much work to be done to more precisely assess the relative contributions of various context ingredients, especially as they unfold over space and time.

Acknowledgments This work was funded by the Deutsche Forschungsgemeinschaft (DFG, German Research Foundation)—project number 222641018—SFB/TRR 135, sub-project C7 to MLV.

References

Auckland, M. E., Cave, K. R., & Donnelly, N. (2007). Nontarget objects can influence perceptual processes during object recognition. *Psychonomic Bulletin & Review, 14*(2), 332–337. https://doi.org/10.3758/BF03194073

Awh, E., Belopolsky, A. V., & Theeuwes, J. (2012). Top-down versus bottom-up attentional control: A failed theoretical dichotomy. *Trends in Cognitive Sciences, 16*(8), 437–443. https://doi.org/10.1016/j.tics.2012.06.010

Bar, M. (2004). Visual objects in context. *Nature Reviews. Neuroscience, 5*, 617–629. https://doi.org/10.1038/nrn1476

Barrett, S. E., & Rugg, M. D. (1990). Event-related potentials and the semantic matching of pictures. *Brain and Cognition, 14*(2), 201–212. https://doi.org/10.1016/0278-2626(90)90029-N

Becker, M. W., Pashler, H., & Lubin, J. (2007). Object-intrinsic oddities draw early saccades. *Journal of Experimental Psychology: Human Perception and Performance, 33*(1), 20–30. https://doi.org/10.1037/0096-1523.33.1.20

Biederman, I., Mezzanotte, R. J., & Rabinowitz, J. C. (1982). Scene perception: Detecting and judging objects undergoing relational violations. *Cognitive Psychology, 14*, 143–177. https://doi.org/10.1016/0010-0285(82)90007-X

Boettcher, S. E. P., Draschkow, D., Dienhart, E., & Võ, M. L.-H. (2018). Anchoring visual search in scenes: Assessing the role of anchor objects on eye movements during visual search. *Journal of Vision, 18*(13), 1–13. https://doi.org/10.1167/18.13.11

Bonitz, V. S., & Gordon, R. D. (2008). Attention to smoking-related and incongruous objects during scene viewing. *Acta Psychologica, 129*(2), 255–263. https://doi.org/10.1016/j.actpsy.2008.08.006

Bonner, M. F., & Epstein, R. A. (2018). Computational mechanisms underlying cortical responses to the affordance properties of visual scenes. *PLoS Computational Biology, 14*(4), 1–31. https://doi.org/10.1371/journal.pcbi.1006111

Borji, A. (2019). Saliency prediction in the deep learning era: Successes and limitations. *IEEE Transactions on Pattern Analysis and Machine Intelligence*, 1–44. https://doi.org/10.1109/tpami.2019.2935715

Borji, A., & Itti, L. (2013). State-of-the-art in visual attention modeling. *IEEE Transactions on Pattern Analysis and Machine Intelligence, 35*(1), 185–207. https://doi.org/10.1109/TPAMI.2012.89

Borji, A., Sihite, D. N., & Itti, L. (2013). What stands out in a scene? A study of human explicit saliency judgment. *Vision Research, 91*, 62–77. https://doi.org/10.1016/j.visres.2013.07.016

Boyce, S. J., & Pollatsek, A. (1992). Identification of objects in scenes: The role of scene background in object naming. *Journal of Experimental Psychology, Learning, Memory, and Cognition, 18*(3), 531–543. https://doi.org/10.1037/0278-7393.18.3.531

Boyce, S. J., Pollatsek, A., & Rayner, K. (1989). Effect of background information on object identification. *Journal of Experimental Psychology: Human Perception and Performance, 15*(3), 556–566. https://doi.org/10.1037/0096-1523.15.3.556

Brady, T. F., Shafer-Skelton, A., & Alvarez, G. A. (2017). Global ensemble texture representations are critical to rapid scene perception. *Journal of Experimental Psychology: Human Perception and Performance, 43*(6), 1160–1176. https://doi.org/10.1037/xhp0000399

Brandman, T., Avancini, C., Leticevscaia, O., & Peelen, M. V. (2019). Auditory and semantic cues facilitate decoding of visual object category in MEG. *Cerebral Cortex*, 1–28. https://doi.org/10.1093/cercor/bhz110

Brandman, T., & Peelen, M. V. (2017). Interaction between scene and object processing revealed by human fMRI and MEG decoding. *The Journal of Neuroscience, 37*(32), 7700–7710. https://doi.org/10.1523/jneurosci.0582-17.2017

Brandman, T., & Peelen, M. V. (2019). Signposts in the fog: Objects facilitate scene representations in left scene-selective cortex. *Journal of Cognitive Neuroscience, 31*(3), 390–400. https://doi.org/10.1162/jocn_a_01258

Castelhano, M. S., & Heaven, C. (2011). Scene context influences without scene gist: Eye movements guided by spatial associations in visual search. *Psychonomic Bulletin and Review, 18*(5), 890–896. https://doi.org/10.3758/s13423-011-0107-8

Castelhano, M. S., & Henderson, J. M. (2007). Initial scene representations facilitate eye movement guidance in visual search. *Journal of Experimental Psychology: Human Perception and Performance, 33*(4), 753–763. https://doi.org/10.1037/0096-1523.33.4.753

Castelhano, M. S., & Krzyś, K. (2020). Rethinking space: A review of perception, attention, and memory in scene processing. *Annual Review of Vision Science, 6*, 563–586. https://doi.org/10.1146/annurev-vision-121219-081745

Cichy, R. M., Pantazis, D., & Oliva, A. (2014). Resolving human object recognition in space and time. *Nature Neuroscience, 17*(3), 455–462. https://doi.org/10.1038/nn.3635

Clement, A., O'Donnell, R. E., & Brockmole, J. R. (2019). The functional arrangement of objects biases gaze direction. *Psychonomic Bulletin and Review, 26*(4), 1266–1272. https://doi.org/10.3758/s13423-019-01607-8

Coco, M. I., Nuthmann, A., & Dimigen, O. (2019). Fixation-related brain potentials during semantic integration of object–scene information. *Journal of Cognitive Neuroscience, 32*(4), 571–589. https://doi.org/10.1162/jocn_a_01504

Cohn, N., Jackendoff, R., Holcomb, P. J., & Kuperberg, G. R. (2014). The grammar of visual narrative: Neural evidence for constituent structure in sequential image comprehension. *Neuropsychologia, 64*, 63–70. https://doi.org/10.1016/j.neuropsychologia.2014.09.018

Cornelissen, T. H. W., & Võ, M. L.-H. (2017). Stuck on semantics: Processing of irrelevant object-scene inconsistencies modulates ongoing gaze behavior. *Attention, Perception, & Psychophysics, 79*(1), 154–168. https://doi.org/10.3758/s13414-016-1203-7

Davenport, J. L. (2007). Consistency effects between objects in scenes. *Memory & Cognition, 35*(3), 393–401. https://doi.org/10.3758/BF03193280

Davenport, J. L., & Potter, M. C. (2004). Scene consistency in object and background perception. *Psychological Science, 15*, 559–564. https://doi.org/10.1111/j.0956-7976.2004.00719.x

De Graef, P., Christiaens, D., & Ydewalle, G. (1990). Perceptual effect of scene context on object identification. *Psychological Research*, 317–329. https://doi.org/10.1007/BF00868064

De Groot, F., Huettig, F., & Olivers, C. N. L. (2016). When meaning matters: The temporal dynamics of semantic influences on visual attention. *Journal of Experimental Psychology: Human Perception and Performance, 42*(2), 180–196. https://doi.org/10.1037/xhp0000102

Draschkow, D., Heikel, E., Võ, M. L.-H., Fiebach, C. J., & Sassenhagen, J. (2018). No evidence from MVPA for different processes underlying the N300 and N400 incongruity effects in object-scene processing. *Neuropsychologia, 120*, 9–17. https://doi.org/10.1016/j.neuropsychologia.2018.09.016

Eckstein, M. P. (2017). Probabilistic computations for attention, eye movements, and search. *Annual Review of Vision Science, 3*, 319–342. https://doi.org/10.1146/annurev-vision-102016-061220

Eckstein, M. P., Koehler, K., Welbourne, L. E., & Akbas, E. (2017). Humans, but not deep neural networks, often miss Giant targets in scenes. *Current Biology, 27*(18), 2827–2832.e3. https://doi.org/10.1016/j.cub.2017.07.068

Einhäuser, W., Spain, M., & Perona, P. (2008). Objects predict fixations better than early saliency. *Journal of Vision, 8*(14), 1–26. https://doi.org/10.1167/8.14.18

Elazary, L., & Itti, L. (2008). Interesting objects are visually salient. *Journal of Vision, 8*(3), 1–15. https://doi.org/10.1167/8.3.3

Epstein, R. A., & Baker, C. I. (2019). Scene perception in the human brain. *Annual Review of Vision Science, 5*(1), 373–397. https://doi.org/10.1146/annurev-vision-091718-014809

Friedman, A. (1979). Framing pictures: The role of knowledge in automatized encoding and memory for gist. *Journal of Experimental Psychology: General, 108*(3), 316–355. https://doi.org/10.1037//0096-3445.108.3.316

Furtak, M., Doradzińska, Ł., Ptashynska, A., Mudrik, L., Nowicka, A., & Bola, M. (2020). Automatic attention capture by threatening, but not by semantically incongruent natural scene images. *Cerebral Cortex, 30*(7), 4158–4168. https://doi.org/10.1093/cercor/bhaa040

Ganis, G., & Kutas, M. (2003). An electrophysiological study of scene effects on object identification. *Cognitive Brain Research, 16*, 123–144. https://doi.org/10.1016/s0926-6410(02)00244-6

Geirhos, R., Rubisch, P., Michaelis, C., Bethge, M., Wichmann, F. A., & Brendel, W. (2018). ImageNet-trained CNNs are biased towards texture; increasing shape bias improves accuracy and robustness. *ICLR*, 1–20. https://zhuanlan.zhihu.com/p/81257789%0Ahttps://github.com/rgeirhos/texture-vs-shape%0Ahttps://github.com/rgeirhos/Stylized-ImageNet 3.

Goodfellow, I. J., Shlens, J., & Szegedy, C. (2014). Explaining and harnessing adversarial examples. In *3rd international conference on learning representations, ICLR 2015 – conference track proceedings* (pp. 1–11) http://arxiv.org/abs/1412.6572

Greene, M. R. (2013). Statistics of high-level scene context. *Frontiers in Psychology, 4*, 1–31. https://doi.org/10.3389/fpsyg.2013.00777

Greene, M. R. (2016). Estimations of object frequency are frequently overestimated. *Cognition, 149*, 6–10. https://doi.org/10.1016/j.cognition.2015.12.011

Greene, M. R., & Hansen, B. C. (2018). Shared spatiotemporal category representations in biological and artificial deep neural networks. *PLoS Computational Biology, 14*(7), 1–17. https://doi.org/10.1371/journal.pcbi.1006327

Greene, M. R., & Oliva, A. (2009a). Recognition of natural scenes from global properties: Seeing the forest without representing the trees. *Cognitive Psychology, 58*, 137–176. https://doi.org/10.1016/j.cogpsych.2008.06.001

Greene, M. R., & Oliva, A. (2009b). The briefest of glances: The time course of natural scene understanding. *Psychological Science, 20*, 464–472. https://doi.org/10.1111/j.1467-9280.2009.02316.x

Gronau, N. (2020). Vision at a glance: The role of attention in processing object-to-object categorical relations. *Attention, Perception, and Psychophysics, 82*(2), 671–688. https://doi.org/10.3758/s13414-019-01940-z

Gronau, N., & Shachar, M. (2014). Contextual integration of visual objects necessitates attention. *Attention, Perception, and Psychophysics, 76*(3), 695–714. https://doi.org/10.3758/s13414-013-0617-8

Helbing, J., Draschkow, D., & Võ, M. L.-H. (2020). Semantic and syntactic anchor object information interact to make visual search in immersive scenes efficient. *Journal of Vision, 20*(11), 573. https://doi.org/10.1167/jov.20.11.573

Henderson, J. M. (2007). Regarding scenes. *Current Directions in Psychological Science, 16*(4), 219–222. https://doi.org/10.1111/j.1467-8721.2007.00507.x

Henderson, J. M., & Hayes, T. R. (2017). Meaning-based guidance of attention in scenes as revealed by meaning maps. *Nature Human Behaviour, 1*(10), 743–747. https://doi.org/10.1038/s41562-017-0208-0

Henderson, J. M., & Hayes, T. R. (2018). Meaning guides attention in real-world scene images: Evidence from eye movements and meaning maps. *Journal of Vision, 18*(6), 1–18. https://doi.org/10.1167/18.6.10

Henderson, J. M., Hayes, T. R., Peacock, C. E., & Rehrig, G. (2019). Meaning and attentional guidance in scenes: A review of the meaning map approach. *Vision, 3*(2), 1–10. https://doi.org/10.3390/vision3020019

Henderson, J. M., Hayes, T. R., Rehrig, G., & Ferreira, F. (2018). Meaning guides attention during real-world scene description. *Scientific Reports, 8*(1), 1–9. https://doi.org/10.1038/s41598-018-31894-5

Henderson, J. M., Malcolm, G. L., & Schandl, C. (2009). Searching in the dark: Cognitive relevance drives attention in real-world scenes. *Psychonomic Bulletin and Review, 16*(5), 850–856. https://doi.org/10.3758/PBR.16.5.850

Henderson, J. M., Pollatsek, A., & Rayner, K. (1987). Effects of foveal priming and Extrafoveal preview on object identification. *Journal of Experimental Psychology: Human Perception and Performance, 13*(3), 449–463. https://doi.org/10.1037/0096-1523.13.3.449

Henderson, J. M., Weeks, P. A. J., & Hollingworth, A. (1999). The effects of semantic consistency on eye movements during complex scene viewing. *Journal of Experimental Psychology: Human Perception and Performance, 25*(1), 210–228. https://doi.org/10.1037/0096-1523.25.1.210

Hollingworth, A., & Henderson, J. M. (1998). Does consistent scene context facilitate object perception? *Journal of Experimental Psychology: General, 127*(4), 398–415. https://doi.org/10.1037/0096-3445.127.4.398

Hollingworth, A., & Henderson, J. M. (1999). Object identification is isolated from scene semantic constraint: Evidence from object type and token discrimination. *Acta Psychologica, 102*(2–3), 319–343. https://doi.org/10.1016/S0001-6918(98)00053-5

Hwang, A. D., Wang, H. C., & Pomplun, M. (2011). Semantic guidance of eye movements in real-world scenes. *Vision Research, 51*(10), 1192–1205. https://doi.org/10.1016/j.visres.2011.03.010

Itti, L. (2007). Visual salience. *Scholarpedia, 2*(9), 3327. https://doi.org/10.4249/scholarpedia.3327

Itti, L., & Baldi, P. (2005). Bayesian surprise attracts human attention. *Advances in Neural Information Processing Systems*, 547–554. https://doi.org/10.1016/j.visres.2008.09.007

Itti, L., & Koch, C. (2000). A saliency-based search mechanism for overt and covert shifts of visual attention. *Vision Research, 40*(10–12), 1489–1506. https://doi.org/10.1016/S0042-6989(99)00163-7

Itti, L., & Koch, C. (2001). Computational modelling of visual attention. *Nature Reviews Neuroscience, 2*(3), 194–203. https://doi.org/10.1038/35058500

Joubert, O. R., Rousselet, G. A., Fize, D., & Fabre-Thorpe, M. (2007). Processing scene context: Fast categorization and object interference. *Vision Research, 47*(26), 3286–3297. https://doi.org/10.1016/j.visres.2007.09.013

Kaiser, D., & Cichy, R. M. (2018). Typical visual-field locations enhance processing in object-selective channels of human occipital cortex. *Journal of Neurophysiology, 120*(2), 848–853. https://doi.org/10.1152/jn.00229.2018

Koehler, K., & Eckstein, M. P. (2017a). Beyond scene gist: Objects guide search more than scene background. *Journal of Experimental Psychology: Human Perception and Performance, 43*(6), 1177–1193. https://doi.org/10.1037/xhp0000363

Koehler, K., & Eckstein, M. P. (2017b). Temporal and peripheral extraction of contextual cues from scenes during visual search. *Journal of Vision, 17*(2), 1–32. https://doi.org/10.1167/17.2.16

Kotseruba, I., Wloka, C., Rasouli, A., & Tsotsos, J. K. (2020). Do saliency models detect odd-one-out targets? *New Datasets and Evaluations*, 1–14. http://arxiv.org/abs/2005.06583

Kovalenko, L. Y., Chaumon, M., & Busch, N. A. (2012). A pool of pairs of related objects (POPORO) for investigating visual semantic integration: Behavioral and electrophysiological validation. *Brain Topography, 25*(3), 272–284. https://doi.org/10.1007/s10548-011-0216-8

Krasovskaya, S., & Macinnes, W. J. (2019). Salience models: A computational cognitive neuroscience review. *Vision, 3*(4). https://doi.org/10.3390/vision3040056

Kümmerer, M., Wallis, T. S. A., & Bethge, M. (2016). DeepGaze II: Reading fixations from deep features trained on object recognition. *ArXiv*, 1–16. http://arxiv.org/abs/1610.01563

Kutas, M., & Federmeier, K. D. (2011). Thirty years and counting: Finding meaning in the N400 component of the event-related brain potential (ERP). *Annual Review of Psychology, 62*, 621–647. https://doi.org/10.1146/annurev.psych.093008.131123

Kutas, M., & Hillyard, S. A. (1980). Reading senseless sentences: Brain potentials reflect semantic incongruity. *Science, 207*, 203–205. https://doi.org/10.1126/science.7350657

Kutas, M., & Hillyard, S. A. (1983). Event-related brain potentials to grammatical errors and semantic anomalies. *Memory & Cognition, 11*(5), 539–550. https://doi.org/10.3758/BF03196991

Lauer, T., Boettcher, S. E. P., Kollenda, D., Draschkow, D., & Võ, M. L.-H. (2020b). Manipulating semantic consistency between two objects and a scene: An ERP paradigm. *Journal of Vision, 20*(11), 1078. https://doi.org/10.1167/jov.20.11.1078

Lauer, T., Cornelissen, T. H. W., Draschkow, D., Willenbockel, V., & Võ, M. L.-H. (2018). The role of scene summary statistics in object recognition. *Scientific Reports, 8*(1), 1–12. https://doi.org/10.1038/s41598-018-32991-1

Lauer, T., Willenbockel, V., Maffongelli, L., & Võ, M. L.-H. (2020a). The influence of scene and object orientation on the scene consistency effect. *Behavioural Brain Research, 394*, 1–13. https://doi.org/10.1016/j.bbr.2020.112812

Leroy, A., Faure, S., & Spotorno, S. (2020). Reciprocal semantic predictions drive categorization of scene contexts and objects even when they are separate. *Scientific Reports, 10*(1), 1–13. https://doi.org/10.1038/s41598-020-65158-y

Li, B., Gao, C., & Wang, J. (2019). Electrophysiological correlates of masked repetition and conceptual priming for visual objects. *Brain and Behavior, 9*(10), 1–8. https://doi.org/10.1002/brb3.1415

Lindsay, G. W. (2020). Convolutional neural networks as a model of the visual system: Past, present, and future. *Journal of Cognitive Neuroscience*, 1–15. https://doi.org/10.1162/jocn_a_01544

Loftus, G. R., & Mackworth, N. H. (1978). Cognitive determinants of fixation location during picture viewing. *Journal of Experimental Psychology: Human Perception and Performance, 4*(4), 565–572. https://doi.org/10.1037/0096-1523.4.4.565

Loschky, L. C., Szaffarczyk, S., Beugnet, C., Young, M. E., & Boucart, M. (2019). The contributions of central and peripheral vision to scenegist recognition with a 180° visual field. *Journal of Vision, 19*(5), 1–21. https://doi.org/10.1167/19.5.15

MacEvoy, S. P., & Epstein, R. A. (2011). Constructing scenes from objects in human occipitotemporal cortex. *Nature Neuroscience, 14*(10), 1323–1329. https://doi.org/10.1038/nn.2903

Mack, S. C., & Eckstein, M. P. (2011). Object co-occurrence serves as a contextual cue to guide and facilitate visual search in a natural viewing environment. *Journal of Vision, 11*(9), 1–16. https://doi.org/10.1167/11.9.9

Maffongelli, L., Bartoli, E., Sammler, D., Kölsch, S., Campus, C., Olivier, E., Fadiga, L., & D'Ausilio, A. (2015). Distinct brain signatures of content and structure violation during action observation. *Neuropsychologia, 75*, 30–39. https://doi.org/10.1016/j.neuropsychologia.2015.05.020

Masciocchi, C. M., Mihalas, S., Parkhurst, D., & Niebur, E. (2009). Everyone knows what is interesting: Salient locations which should be fixated. *Journal of Vision, 9*(11), 1–22. https://doi.org/10.1167/9.11.1

McPherson, W. B., & Holcomb, P. J. (1999). An electrophysiological investigation of semantic priming with pictures of real objects. *Psychophysiology, 36*(1), 53–65. https://doi.org/10.1017/S0048577299971196

Morgenstern, Y., Schmidt, F., & Fleming, R. W. (2019). One-shot categorization of novel object classes in humans. *Vision Research, 165*, 98–108. https://doi.org/10.1016/j.visres.2019.09.005

Mudrik, L., Lamy, D., & Deouell, L. Y. (2010). ERP evidence for context congruity effects during simultaneous object-scene processing. *Neuropsychologia, 48*, 507–517. https://doi.org/10.1016/j.neuropsychologia.2009.10.011

Mudrik, L., Shalgi, S., Lamy, D., & Deouell, L. Y. (2014). Synchronous contextual irregularities affect early scene processing: Replication and extension. *Neuropsychologia, 56*, 447–458. https://doi.org/10.1016/j.neuropsychologia.2014.02.020

Munneke, J., Brentari, V., & Peelen, M. V. (2013). The influence of scene context on object recognition is independent of attentional focus. *Frontiers in Psychology, 4*, 1–10. https://doi.org/10.3389/fpsyg.2013.00552

Neider, M. B., & Zelinsky, G. J. (2006). Scene context guides eye movements during visual search. *Vision Research, 46*(5), 614–621. https://doi.org/10.1016/j.visres.2005.08.025

Nuthmann, A., De Groot, F., Huettig, F., & Olivers, C. N. L. (2019). Extrafoveal attentional capture by object semantics. *PLoS One, 14*(5), 1–19. https://doi.org/10.1371/journal.pone.0217051

Nuthmann, A., & Einhäuser, W. (2015). A new approach to modeling the influence of image features on fixation selection in scenes. *Annals of the New York Academy of Sciences, 1339*(1), 82–96. https://doi.org/10.1111/nyas.12705

Nuthmann, A., & Henderson, J. M. (2010). Object-based attentional selection in scene viewing. *Journal of Vision, 10*(8), 1–19. https://doi.org/10.1167/10.8.20

Oliva, A., & Torralba, A. (2001). Modeling the shape of the scene: A holistic representation of the spatial envelope. *International Journal of Computer Vision, 42,* 145–175. https://doi.org/10.1023/A:1011139631724

Oliva, A., & Torralba, A. (2006). Building the gist of a scene: The role of global image features in recognition. *Progress in Brain Research, 155,* 23–36. https://doi.org/10.1016/S0079-6123(06)55002-2

Oliva, A., & Torralba, A. (2007). The role of context in object recognition. *Trends in Cognitive Sciences, 11*(12), 520–527. https://doi.org/10.1016/j.tics.2007.09.009

Onat, S., Açik, A., Schumann, F., & König, P. (2014). The contributions of image content and behavioral relevancy to overt attention. *PLoS One, 9*(4). https://doi.org/10.1371/journal.pone.0093254

Pajak, M., & Nuthmann, A. (2013). Object-based saccadic selection during scene perception: Evidence from viewing position effects. *Journal of Vision, 13*(5), 1–21. https://doi.org/10.1167/13.5.2

Palmer, T. E. (1975). The effects of contextual scenes on the identification of objects. *Memory & Cognition, 3*(5), 519–526. https://doi.org/10.3758/BF03197524

Parkhurst, D., Law, K., & Niebur, E. (2002). Modeling the role of salience in the allocation of overt visual attention. *Vision Research, 42*(1), 107–123. https://doi.org/10.1016/S0042-6989(01)00250-4

Peacock, C. E., Hayes, T. R., & Henderson, J. M. (2019a). Meaning guides attention during scene viewing, even when it is irrelevant. *Attention, Perception, and Psychophysics, 81*(1), 20–34. https://doi.org/10.3758/s13414-018-1607-7

Peacock, C. E., Hayes, T. R., & Henderson, J. M. (2019b). The role of meaning in attentional guidance during free viewing of real-world scenes. *Acta Psychologica, 198*(July). https://doi.org/10.1016/j.actpsy.2019.102889

Pedziwiatr, M. A., Wallis, T. S. A., Kümmerer, M., & Teufel, C. (2019). Meaning maps and deep neural networks are insensitive to meaning when predicting human fixations. *Journal of Vision, 19*(10), 253c. https://doi.org/10.1101/840256.

Pereira, E. J., & Castelhano, M. S. (2014). Peripheral guidance in scenes: The interaction of scene context and object content. *Journal of Experimental Psychology: Human Perception and Performance, 40*(5), 2056–2072. https://doi.org/10.1037/a0037524

Pereira, E. J., & Castelhano, M. S. (2019). Attentional capture is contingent on scene region: Using surface guidance framework to explore attentional mechanisms during search. *Psychonomic Bulletin and Review, 26*(4), 1273–1281. https://doi.org/10.3758/s13423-019-01610-z

Portilla, J., & Simoncelli, E. P. (2000). A parametric texture model based on joint statistics of complex wavelet coefficients. *International Journal of Computer Vision, 40,* 49–71. https://doi.org/10.1023/A:1026553619983

Quek, G. L., & Peelen, M. V. (2020). Contextual and spatial associations between objects interactively modulate visual processing. *Cerebral Cortex,* 1–14. https://doi.org/10.1093/cercor/bhaa197

Rehrig, G., Hayes, T. R., Henderson, J. M., & Ferreira, F. (2020). When scenes speak louder than words: Verbal encoding does not mediate the relationship between scene meaning and visual attention. *Memory and Cognition, 48*(7), 1181–1195. https://doi.org/10.3758/s13421-020-01050-4

Roberts, K. L., & Humphreys, G. W. (2011). Action relations facilitate the identification of briefly-presented objects. *Attention, Perception, and Psychophysics, 73*(2), 597–612. https://doi.org/10.3758/s13414-010-0043-0

Rosenholtz, R., Huang, J., & Ehinger, K. (2012). Rethinking the role of top-down attention in vision: Effects attributable to a lossy representation in peripheral vision. *Frontiers in Psychology, 3*(FEB), 1–15. https://doi.org/10.3389/fpsyg.2012.00013

Rousselet, G. A., Joubert, O. R., & Fabre-Thorpe, M. (2005). How long to get to the "gist" of real-world natural scenes? *Visual Cognition, 12*(6), 852–877. https://doi.org/10.1080/13506280444000553

Roux-Sibilon, A., Trouilloud, A., Kauffmann, L., Guyader, N., Mermillod, M., & Peyrin, C. (2019). Influence of peripheral vision on object categorization in central vision. *Journal of Vision, 19*(14), 1–16. https://doi.org/10.1167/19.14.7

Russell, B. C., Torralba, A., Murphy, K. P., & Freeman, W. T. (2008). LabelMe: A database and web-based tool for image annotation. *International Journal of Computer Vision, 77*, 157–173. https://doi.org/10.1007/s11263-007-0090-8

Sastyin, G., Niimi, R., & Yokosawa, K. (2015). Does object view influence the scene consistency effect? *Attention, Perception, & Psychophysics, 77*, 856–866. https://doi.org/10.3758/s13414-014-0817-x

Schomaker, J., Walper, D., Wittmann, B. C., & Einhäuser, W. (2017). Attention in natural scenes: Affective-motivational factors guide gaze independently of visual salience. *Vision Research, 133*, 161–175. https://doi.org/10.1016/j.visres.2017.02.003

Schütt, H. H., Rothkegel, L. O. M., Trukenbrod, H. A., Engbert, R., & Wichmann, F. A. (2019). Disentangling bottom-up versus top-down and low-level versus high-level influences on eye movements over time. *Journal of Vision, 19*(3), 1–23. https://doi.org/10.1167/19.3.1

Spain, M., & Perona, P. (2011). Measuring and predicting object importance. *International Journal of Computer Vision, 91*(1), 59–76. https://doi.org/10.1007/s11263-010-0376-0

Spiegel, C., & Halberda, J. (2011). Rapid fast-mapping abilities in 2-year-olds. *Journal of Experimental Child Psychology, 109*(1), 132–140. https://doi.org/10.1016/j.jecp.2010.10.013

Stoll, J., Thrun, M., Nuthmann, A., & Einhäuser, W. (2015). Overt attention in natural scenes: Objects dominate features. *Vision Research, 107*, 36–48. https://doi.org/10.1016/j.visres.2014.11.006

t'Hart, B. M., Schmidt, H. C. E. F., Roth, C., & Einhäuser, W. (2013). Fixations on objects in natural scenes: Dissociating importance from salience. *Frontiers in Psychology, 4*, 1–9. https://doi.org/10.3389/fpsyg.2013.00455

Teufel, C., & Fletcher, P. C. (2020). Forms of prediction in the nervous system. *Nature reviews neuroscience, 21*(4), 231–242. https://doi.org/10.1038/s41583-020-0275-5

Truman, A., & Mudrik, L. (2018). Are incongruent objects harder to identify? The functional significance of the N300 component. *Neuropsychologia, 117*, 222–232. https://doi.org/10.1016/j.neuropsychologia.2018.06.004

Underwood, G., & Foulsham, T. (2006). Visual saliency and semantic incongruency influence eye movements when inspecting pictures. *Quarterly Journal of Experimental Psychology, 59*(11), 1931–1949. https://doi.org/10.1080/17470210500416342

Underwood, G., Humphreys, L., & Cross, E. (2007). Congruency, saliency and gist in the inspection of objects in natural scenes. In R. P. G. van Gompel, M. H. Fischer, W. S. Murray, & R. L. Hill (Eds.), *Eye movements: A window on mind and brain* (pp. 563–579). Elsevier. https://doi.org/10.1016/B978-008044980-7/50028-8

Underwood, G., Templeman, E., Lamming, L., & Foulsham, T. (2008). Is attention necessary for object identification? Evidence from eye movements during the inspection of real-world scenes. *Consciousness and Cognition, 17*(1), 159–170. https://doi.org/10.1016/j.concog.2006.11.008

Võ, M. L.-H. (2021). The meaning and structure of scenes. *Vision Research, 181*, 10–20. https://doi.org/10.1016/j.visres.2020.11.003

Võ, M. L.-H., Boettcher, S. E., & Draschkow, D. (2019). Reading scenes: How scene grammar guides attention and aids perception in real-world environments. *Current Opinion in Psychology, 29*, 205–210. https://doi.org/10.1016/j.copsyc.2019.03.009

Võ, M. L.-H., & Henderson, J. M. (2009a). Does gravity matter? Effects of semantic and syntactic inconsistencies on the allocation of attention during scene perception. *Journal of Vision, 9*(3), 1–15. https://doi.org/10.1167/9.3.24

Võ, M. L.-H., & Henderson, J. M. (2009b). Does gravity matter? Effects of semantic and syntactic inconsistencies on the allocation of attention during scene perception. *Journal of Vision, 9*(3), 1–15. https://doi.org/10.1167/9.3.24

Võ, M. L.-H., & Henderson, J. M. (2010). The time course of initial scene processing for eye movement guidance in natural scene search. *Journal of Vision, 10*(3), 1–13. https://doi.org/10.1167/10.3.14

Võ, M. L.-H., & Henderson, J. M. (2011). Object-scene inconsistencies do not capture gaze: Evidence from the flash-preview moving-window paradigm. *Attention, Perception, and Psychophysics, 73*(6), 1742–1753. https://doi.org/10.3758/s13414-011-0150-6

Võ, M. L.-H., & Schneider, W. X. (2010). A glimpse is not a glimpse: Differential processing of flashed scene previews leads to differential target search benefits. *Visual Cognition, 18*(2), 171–200. https://doi.org/10.1080/13506280802547901

Võ, M. L.-H., & Wolfe, J. M. (2013a). Differential electrophysiological signatures of semantic and syntactic scene processing. *Psychological Science, 24*, 1816–1823. https://doi.org/10.1177/0956797613476955

Võ, M. L.-H., & Wolfe, J. M. (2013b). The interplay of episodic and semantic memory in guiding repeated search in scenes. *Cognition, 126*(2), 198–212. https://doi.org/10.1016/j.cognition.2012.09.017

Võ, M. L.-H., & Wolfe, J. M. (2015). The role of memory for visual search in scenes. *Annals of the New York Academy of Sciences, 1339*(1), 72–81. https://doi.org/10.1111/nyas.12667

Wichmann, F. A., Janssen, D. H. J., Geirhos, R., Aguilar, G., Schütt, H. H., Maertens, M., & Bethge, M. (2017). Methods and measurements to compare men against machines. *Electronic Imaging, 2017*(14), 36–45. https://doi.org/10.2352/ISSN.2470-1173.2017.14.HVEI-113

Wolfe, J. M. (2020). Visual search: How do we find what we are looking for? *Annual Review of Vision Science, 6*, 539–562. https://doi.org/10.1146/annurev-vision-091718-015048

Wolfe, J. M., Alvarez, G. A., Rosenholtz, R., Kuzmova, Y. I., & Sherman, A. M. (2011a). Visual search for arbitrary objects in real scenes. *Attention, Perception, and Psychophysics, 73*(6), 1650–1671. https://doi.org/10.3758/s13414-011-0153-3

Wolfe, J. M., & Horowitz, T. S. (2017). Five factors that guide attention in visual search. *Nature Human Behaviour, 1*(3), 1–8. https://doi.org/10.1038/s41562-017-0058

Wolfe, J. M., Võ, M. L.-H., Evans, K. K., & Greene, M. R. (2011b). Visual search in scenes involves selective and nonselective pathways. *Trends in Cognitive Sciences, 15*(2), 77–84. https://doi.org/10.1016/j.tics.2010.12.001

Wu, C. C., Wang, H. C., & Pomplun, M. (2014a). The roles of scene gist and spatial dependency among objects in the semantic guidance of attention in real-world scenes. *Vision Research, 105*, 10–20. https://doi.org/10.1016/j.visres.2014.08.019

Wu, C. C., Wick, F. A., & Pomplun, M. (2014b). Guidance of visual attention by semantic information in real-world scenes. *Frontiers in Psychology, 5*, 1–13. https://doi.org/10.3389/fpsyg.2014.00054

Wu, K., Wu, E., & Kreiman, G. (2018). Learning scene gist with convolutional neural networks to improve object recognition. *ArXiv*, 1–6. http://arxiv.org/abs/1803.01967

Zhang, M., Tseng, C., & Kreiman, G. (2020). Putting visual object recognition in context. *IEEE/CVF Conference on Computer Vision and Pattern Recognition (CVPR), 2020*, 12982–12991. https://doi.org/10.1109/CVPR42600.2020.01300

Zucker, L., & Mudrik, L. (2019). Understanding associative vs. abstract pictorial relations: An ERP study. *Neuropsychologia, 133*, 1–16. https://doi.org/10.1016/j.neuropsychologia.2019.107127

Exploring Deep Fusion Ensembling for Automatic Visual Interestingness Prediction

Mihai Gabriel Constantin, Liviu-Daniel Ştefan, and Bogdan Ionescu

1 Introduction

Given the prevalence of multimedia data associated with the current online environment and the immense quantity of data uploaded by both amateur and professional content creators, the need for in-depth understanding of the uploaded data has emerged. Automatic classification and recommendation systems are needed in order to help users navigate online platforms that are able to correctly understand both user preferences and the quality of the multimedia content hosted on the platforms. The research and development communities are currently giving increasing attention to the study of subjective content properties, therefore seeking to understand how visual content affects viewers and tune their algorithms accordingly. This represents a shift in research focus from previous directions, such as understanding the content of images and videos via objective properties such as object detection (He et al. 2017) and scene classification (Yalniz et al. 2019).

Visual interestingness represents one of the most popular concepts currently being studied, being defined as the capacity of "holding or catching attention" in the Oxford Dictionary of English (Stevenson 2010). Berlyne's initial studies in psychology (Berlyne 1949) show that interest heavily influences human behaviour and motivation, while more recent works that study the interestingness of images (Chamaret et al. 2016) show that interest and the willingness to view and study a media sample are positively correlated. Many researchers also point out the importance of other factors in creating and maintaining interest (Silvia 2005; Hidi & Anderson 1992), like novelty, coping potential, arousal and aesthetic quality. From an emotional perspective, Silvia (2005, 2009) includes interest among the class of

M. G. Constantin (✉) · L.-D. Ştefan · B. Ionescu
Politehnica University of Bucharest, Bucharest, Romania
e-mail: mihai.constantin84@upb.ro; lstefan@imag.pub.ro; bogdan.ionescu@upb.ro

© The Author(s), under exclusive license to Springer Nature Switzerland AG 2022
B. Ionescu et al. (eds.), *Human Perception of Visual Information*,
https://doi.org/10.1007/978-3-030-81465-6_2

emotions that relate to comprehension, exploration and learning. In this context, it is easy to understand why researchers and developers are starting to focus their efforts on the prediction of multimedia interestingness. An interestingness value assigned to each media item can represent the difference between a video being recommended to users if it fits their viewing profile and being forgotten, and the accurate assessment of this subjective concept can generate more user engagement and satisfaction. On the other hand, it would represent an useful tool for content creators, be they online creators, professors selecting their media samples for classes or advertising agencies, as it could select the most appropriate media samples for distribution out of a large collection of images and videos. Finally, it is important to note that in the current literature the notion of "interestingness" is used to describe two different concepts: *social interestingness* which is usually related to social media concepts like popularity and virality, and *visual interestingness* which is defined as the capacity of media samples to attract and maintain viewer attention. Previous work in this domain have shown these concepts to be both positively Gygli and Soleymani (2016) and negatively Hsieh et al. (2014) correlated, therefore the link between the concepts is still an opened research direction. However, throughout the rest of this chapter, we will use "interestingness" as a synonym for visual interestingness.

In this chapter we explore the possibility of employing a set of ensembling methods for interestingness prediction, by implementing deep neural networks as the primary ensembling function. To the best of our knowledge, this type of approach presents a high degree of novelty, as deep neural networks are used as inducers in the current state-of-the-art literature, not as the primary ensemble function. Our approach consists of several architectures that include dense, attention, convolutional and the novel cross-space-fusion layers, as well as two input decoration methods that help analyze correlations between similar inducers. Our methods are tested on the publicly available Interestingness10k dataset (Constantin et al. 2021a), validated during the 2017 MediaEval.[1] Predicting Media Interestingness task (Demarty et al. 2017a). With regards to media interestingness, Constantin et al. (2019) represents an in-depth literature review of interestingness and covariate concepts, analyzing these concepts and their correlations from psychological, user-centric and computer vision perspectives, while (Constantin et al. 2021a) represents a review of the MediaEval Predicting Media Interestingness task, analyzing the best practices, methods, user annotation statistics and the data itself. From an ensembling perspective, three papers introduce some of the deep neural network architectures that we will deploy in this work: (Ştefan et al. 2020; Constantin et al. 2021a, 2021b). The code corresponding to the proposed methods we will present is available online,[2] developed in Python 3 using the Keras 2.2.4 and Tensorflow 1.12 libraries.

---

[1] https://multimediaeval.github.io/.
[2] https://github.com/cmihaigabriel/DeepFusionSystem_v2.

The rest of this chapter is organized as follows. Section 2 analyzes the current state-of-the-art, with regards to both interestingness prediction and late fusion systems. In Sect. 3 we present the methods we propose for media interestingness prediction. Section 4 presents the results and their analysis, pointing out trends and general suggestions with regards to system performance. Finally, Sect. 5 concludes the paper and discusses future developments.

2 Previous Work

This section discusses and analyzes the current state-of-the-art with regards to two main topics: the advances in the prediction and classification of media interestingness and the most important late fusion methods currently used in the literature, while also presenting some arguments that advocate the deployment of late fusion schemes for interestingness prediction.

2.1 Media Interestingness

From a computer vision perspective, media interestingness prediction, usually referring to prediction in image or video samples, is gaining considerable traction in the community, with a significant increase in the number of papers published on this subject in recent years (Constantin et al. 2021a). However, this is still considered an opened research direction, as methods that improve results are constantly being published. One of the main difficulties in predicting interestingness comes from the subjectivity of interest among human annotators. Consequently, lower annotator agreement and a lesser degree of separation between interesting and non-interesting samples may be expected when designing a media interestingness dataset or computer vision methods that tackle this issue. Several methods of measuring interest in humans have been used. For example, for the Interestingness10k (Constantin et al. 2021a) dataset, annotators are shown pairs of images or videos and are asked to select which of the two samples are more interesting for them, and asked to also consider that "the selected video excerpts/key-frames should be suitable in terms of helping a user to make his/her decision about whether he/she is interested in watching a movie" (Demarty et al. 2017b).

Early works in interestingness prediction employ several types of traditional visual features. Gygli et al. (2013) use novelty, aesthetics and general preference as cues for image interestingness. Novelty is encoded with the help of a Local Outlier Factor approach, aesthetics via a set of descriptors that encode colorfulness, arousal, complexity, contrast and edge distribution, and general preference is computed by analyzing raw RGB (Red-Green-Blue color space) values, SIFT (Lowe 1999) and GIST (Oliva & Torralba 2001) features and color histograms. For the prediction of video interestingness (Jiang et al. 2013) use visual, audio and high-level attributes in a Ranking-SVM (Support-Vector Machine) approach. The authors show that the multi-modal fusion of audio and visual features, consisting of color histograms, SIFT, GIST, MFCC (Stein & Stanford 2008), Self-Similarities (Shechtman & Irani 2007), and Spectrogram SIFT (Ke et al. 2005), obtains the best result, with a prediction accuracy of 71.4%. Similar methods, that calculate different concepts with the help of traditional descriptors are also used by Grabner et al. (2013). The performance of Sentiment features (Jou et al. 2015) and C3D models (Tran et al. 2015) are compared by Gygli and Soleymani (2016), and, interestingly sentiment features achieve better results, with a Spearman's correlation rank of $\rho = 0.53$. Another interesting conclusion comes from Fan et al. (2016), showing that the fusion of several sources of data improves system performance.

While these studies present interesting approaches, it is difficult to compare them and propose a set of ideas that would increase the chances for a good performance, given their use of different datasets, splits and development conditions. In this context, the MediaEval 2016 and 2017 Predicting Media Interestingness competitions (Demarty et al. 2016, 2017a) address this problem, by creating a common evaluation framework, consisting of a dataset of images and videos with human-annotated interestingness values, common splits and evaluation metrics for the participating teams and open availability for the data. A large number of systems were submitted to the two editions of the benchmarking competition, 60 systems for the image tasks and 69 for the video tasks, but also outside of the competition, in state-of-the-art papers, 17 image processing systems and 46 video processing systems (Constantin et al. 2021a). While there are many diverse approaches, one noteworthy aspect is that the top results for both tasks can be considered rather low, especially when compared with other more traditional and objective tasks such as object detection or scene classification. For example, the best results achieved during the benchmarking competitions with regards to the official metric, Mean Average Precision (MAP), are $MAP = 0.3075$ in the image prediction task, by Permadi et al. (2017), and $MAP = 0.2094$ in the video prediction task, by Ben-Ahmed et al. (2017). These results are further improved outside of the competition, Parekh et al. (2018) obtaining a result of $MAP = 0.3125$ for the image task and Wang et al. (2018) obtaining a $MAP = 0.2228$. However, a study on the annotation process published by Constantin et al. (2021a) shows that human annotators also do not achieve near-perfect scores, considering that the best performing annotators never scored above $MAP = 0.7$. This further enforces the idea that the subjectivity of such a task represents one of its main challenges. While the approaches are diverse and a large number of systems are used for image and video predictions in the context of the MediaEval competition, one of the noticeable trends is that many of the top performing systems use some sort of fusion scheme. In general fusion is defined as "a technology to enable combining information from several sources in order to form a unified picture" (Khaleghi et al. 2013), therefore it involves combining the power of multiple detection systems in order to create a better final system. For the methods analyzed in this context, fusion is applied at feature level (also called *early fusion*), at decision level (also called *late fusion* or *ensemble learning*) or a combination of the two.

2.2 Ensembling Systems

Late fusion, also knows as ensembling systems or decision-level fusion, consist of a set of initial predictors, called *inducers*, that are trained and tested on the dataset, whose prediction outputs are combined in the final step in order to create a new and improved set of predictions. These systems have a long history and are shown to be particularly useful in scenarios where the performance of single-system approaches is not considered satisfactory. While their usefulness is proven even in some traditional tasks, such as video action recognition (Sudhakaran et al. 2020b), recently there is a noticeable trend of employing such approaches in subjective tasks, that seek to analyze the human perception of multimedia data. Some examples for this trend would include the prediction of media memorability (Azcona et al. 2020), violence detection in videos (Dai et al. 2015), emotional content analysis (Sun et al. 2018), and media interestingness prediction (Wang et al. 2018).

One important theoretical aspect of ensembling systems is formulated by Wolpert (2002), stating that, given an ensemble of N inducers, trained in a similar way, it is improbable that the prediction outputs of these inducers are completely uncorrelated. Thus, promoting a high level of diversity in the inducer set may improve the final result of the ensemble. Recently, Liu et al. (2019) show that ensemble error may decrease as the inducer error decreases and inducer diversity increases. These aspects and many more are analyzed in depth in several ensembling literature review papers (Gomes et al. 2017; Sagi and Rokach 2018).

Regarding the *ensembling functions*, the methods that are used in combining inducer prediction outputs, while there is a high variety among them, deep neural networks still represent a novelty for this domain. To the best of our knowledge, our works in using deep neural networks as the primary ensembling function is one of the first attempts in this direction. So far ensembling functions are dominated by simple statistical methods (Kittler et al. 1998), such as late fusion via weighted arithmetic mean calculation, voting systems, etc. Other more complex approaches employ methods that require an initial learning step, including Boosting approaches such as AdaBoost (Freund et al. 1999), Gradient Boosting (Friedman 2001) or XGBoost (Chen & Guestrin 2016), Bagging (Breiman 1996) or Random Forests (Breiman 2001). While these approaches have been successfully implemented in several tasks, our assumption is that, with the introduction of deep neural networks as the main ensembling function, late fusion results will significantly improve. In our work we will use two approaches as comparison baseline for our proposed prediction method, namely statistical methods and boosting.

One example of a statistical approach is the *weighted late fusion*. Under this scheme, given a set of N inducer methods, $A = [a_1, a_2, \ldots, a_N]$ that create a set of prediction outputs denoted $Y = [y_1, y_2, \ldots, y_N]$, the goal of a weighted late fusion approach is to create a set of weights, $W = [w_1, w_2, \ldots, w_N]$, that, once applied to the prediction outputs Y, represent better predictors for the dataset that is being studied. In other words, weighted late fusion creates a new prediction output denoted y_w, that is calculated as follows:

$$y_w = \frac{y_1 \cdot w_1 + y_2 \cdot w_2 + \ldots + y_N \cdot w_N}{N} \tag{1}$$

The goal of this approach is to minimize the prediction error ϵ, so that the new prediction output $\epsilon_w < \epsilon_i, i \in [1, N]$. Several types of strategies can be employed in choosing the values of W. The most common strategy involves ordering the Y vector according to inducer performance, i.e., $\epsilon_1 < \epsilon_2 < \ldots < \epsilon_N$. This would allow systems to assign higher weights for better inducers, thus making sure that the top performing inducers dictate the final result. Working under the assumption that the vector is ordered, some such schemes would be:

$$\begin{cases} w_i = \frac{1}{i}, i \in [1, N] \\ w_i = \frac{1}{e^i}, i \in [0, N-1] \\ w_i = 1 - (\epsilon_i - \epsilon_1), i \in [1, N] \end{cases} \tag{2}$$

Boosting approaches represent another important class of ensemble learning techniques. In general, boosting can be defined as an iterative way of adding inducers into a final ensemble system, while updating the weights assigned to each inducer as more inducers are added in the system. While there are major differences between different boosting approaches, such as AdaBoost and Gradient Boosting, the overarching idea is the sequential training of inducer weights, i.e., trying to adjust the learning process so that it can correct preceding errors.

AdaBoost identifies weaknesses in the inducers in each learning step, represented by miss-classified data points, and assigns higher internal weights for those points, under the assumption that this will allow the next classifiers in the ensembling scheme to correct these errors. Therefore, given a set of data points, $x_i, i \in [1, M]$, initially all the weights for these data points are set to $w_i = 1/M$. The total error can be calculated for each individual inducer $a_j, j \in [1, N]$ as :

$$err_j = \frac{\sum_{i=1}^{M} w_i \cdot \mathcal{I}(C(x_i) \neq y_{j,i})}{\sum_{i=1}^{M} w_i} \tag{3}$$

where $\mathcal{I}$ is a function that outputs 1 for a true positive or negative prediction and 0 for a false positive or negative one and C represents the new classification rule created by the ensembling scheme. Also, given the α factor for each inducer, the system will update the w_i weights accordingly:

$$\alpha_j = \ln \frac{1 - err_j}{err_j} \tag{4}$$

$$w_i = w_i \cdot e^{\alpha_j \cdot \mathcal{I}(C(x_i) \neq y_{j,i})} \tag{5}$$

Thus, considering k as the set of the possible prediction classes associated with the prediction task, the new output can be expressed as:

$$C(x) = \max_k \sum_{i=1}^{M} \alpha_i \cdot \mathcal{I}(y_i(x) = k) \tag{6}$$

Gradient boosting, on the other hand, does not focus on individual data points, but on finding the difference between prediction sets and ground truth data. Therefore, the goal of this method is the minimization of the loss function $L(g, y)$, where y represents the prediction output of the method, while g represents the ground truth values for the given samples. Practically, the goal is to create a new ensembling function $\hat{F}$ that best approximates the ground truth of the dataset:

$$\hat{F} = \min_y \sum_{i=1}^{N} L(g, y) \tag{7}$$

While going through consecutive calls of the training loop, gradient boosting methods seek to apply gradient descent for optimizing the ensembling result. The final version of the ensembling function $\hat{F}$ can therefore be expressed as a weighted sum computed over a set of approximation functions h, starting from the initial version F_0 for this function:

$$\hat{F} = \sum_{i=1}^{M} w_i \cdot h_i + F_0 \tag{8}$$

where M represents the number of training steps. The function is then updated, based on its previous values, as follows:

$$w_m = \min_w \sum_{i=1}^{N} L(g, w \cdot h_m) \tag{9}$$

$$F_m = F_{m-1} + w_m \cdot h_m \tag{10}$$

3 Deep Ensembling

In a general sense, ensembling systems are represented by an algorithm or function $\mathcal{F}$, that, given a set of M dataset samples denoted S and a series of N algorithms denoted A, uses the classification or regression outputs of all the N algorithms, called *inducers*, and by combining them can create a new output for each of the M samples. Individual elements of the sample set can be represented as $s_i, i \in$

[1, M], representing a vector $S = [s_1, s_2, \ldots, s_M]$, while the series of algorithms can be represented by a set of functions $a_j, j \in [1, N]$, representing a vector $A = [a_1, a_2, \ldots, a_N]$.

Therefore, a matrix Y (see Eq. 11) that contains elements $y_{i,j}, i \in [1, M]$ and $j \in [1, N]$ can be constructed, containing the prediction outputs of each inducer for each individual sample, where each row represents inducer outputs for a certain sample.

$$
Y = \begin{bmatrix} y_{1,1} & \cdots & y_{1,N} \\ \cdot & \cdot & \cdot \\ \cdot & \cdot & \cdot \\ \cdot & \cdot & \cdot \\ y_{M,1} & \cdots & y_{M,N} \end{bmatrix} \tag{11}
$$

Obtaining the final ensembled prediction output for a single sample i consists of using the $[y_{i,1}, y_{i,2}, \ldots, y_{i,N}]$ inducer output vector as inputs for the ensembling function $\mathcal{F}$, thus obtaining the final prediction value o_i. This entire process is presented in Fig. 1. While some variants of the ensembling methods can be represented by simple mathematical functions, i.e., calculating the average value

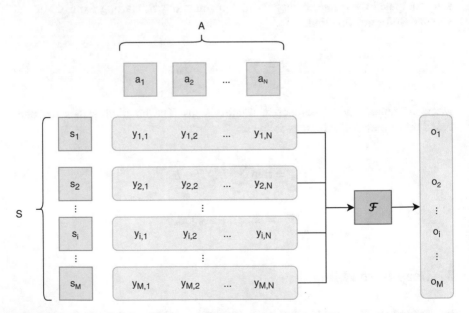

Fig. 1 General presentation of ensembling systems. The sample dataset, denoted S contains M elements, the set of inducers A contains N elements, while the inducer outputs for the samples are denoted as $y_{i,j}, i \in [1, M], j \in [1, N]$. The ensembling algorithm is denoted $\mathcal{F}$ and it produces a set of M prediction outputs, corresponding to each sample, denoted $o_i, i \in [1, M]$. Samples are represented with blue color, inducer algorithms with green, prediction outputs with yellow and the ensembling function with red

of the inducer output vector, other functions can be more complex and can require a preliminary learning stage, such as boosting methods, as shown in Sect. 2.2. We propose a different perspective in which the ensembling function is represented by deep neural networks that will process inducer prediction output values.

It is also interesting to note that, while in more complex cases, such as multi-label regression, the predictions created by the inducers do not represent a single value, as one output probability is assigned to each of the possible labels, in our case inducers output a single value, representing the degree of interestingness assigned to each image or video sample. Therefore the $y_{i,j}$ values are uni-dimensional.

With this general framework in mind, we will present in the following sections some new perspectives, consisting of several types of deep neural networks that are used as ensembling functions for the task of predicting media interestingness. Our assumption in this case is that DNNs are able to better understand the patterns and biases that individual inducers have towards the samples in the dataset. Our proposed DNN models will only use the inducer outputs in determining the final prediction score, so image and video samples will not be fed into the ensemble algorithm.

We investigate four types of DNN architectures as follows: (i) a dense layer-based approach, that is the augmented with (ii) attention layers, (iii) convolutional layers, and finally, (iv) Cross-Space-Fusion layer (CSF), a novel approach designed for parsing inducer vectors. While the first two types of network do not need any special data pre-processing, the latter two, namely convolutional and CSF, are designed to process data based on the spatial arrangement of data and understand how adjacent elements in a matrix can be interpreted in order to obtain a prediction. While this is heavily exploited in images and videos by convolutional layers, inducer output vectors have no intrinsic spatial arrangement and correlation, and therefore, some data pre-processing and decoration schemes that create spatial information are necessary for these two final types of neural networks, which we will present along with the implementation of the respective DNN models. One of the main reasons we theorize that such structures are able to create better ensembling systems is the ability of neural networks to accurately use various types of input data and classify this data into output predictions. While not directly attempting to model human behaviour and understanding of visual interestingness, we believe these models are able to model inducer behaviour and understanding, thus being able to learn the positive and negative biases of inducers towards visual samples. Thus, while the approaches presented here are centered around the prediction of visual interestingness, they are domain-independent and are useful in other tasks as well (Constantin et al. 2021b).

3.1 Dense Networks

Dense networks composed of fully connected (or dense) layers arguably represent one of the most popular DNN implementations. Given the innate ability of dense layers to correctly detect patterns in the input data and accurately classify samples, we theorize that, by using a set of connected dense layers, our proposed method will be able to accurately learn the correlation between inducer biases (Mitchell 1980), allowing combinations of inducers to support or dismiss their predictions, based on the patterns the networks learns. Another component of the final network is represented by the addition of batch normalization layers (Ioffe & Szegedy 2015), between the individual dense layers, with the role of helping the improving the network's learning process and speeding it up. Several variations of the dense network setup are tested, in order to ensure optimal performance. We present the optimal network architecture search method in Algorithm 1. We therefore change the depth of the network, by testing various numbers of layers in the network (5, 10, 15, 20, 25) and the width of the network by changing the number of neurons per layer (25, 50, 500, 1000, 2000). The third parameter in this search algorithm is represented by the presence or absence of batch normalization layers. Also, in Algorithm 1, the *process Dense* function has the role of both creating the network according to the three variable parameters and the role of training and testing the created network. A schematic view of the dense network architecture is presented in Fig. 2.

Algorithm 1: Optimal dense network parameter search method

Output : settings for optimal Dense network *best neuron, best layer, best bn*
begin
  //initiate the parameter options for the search algorithm
  $neurons \leftarrow [25, 50, 500, 1000, 2000, 5000]$;
  $layers \leftarrow [5, 10, 15, 20, 25]$;
  $bn \leftarrow [False, True]$ $bestmetric = 0.0$;

  //start searching for the best architecture
  for $i \leftarrow 0$ **to** 5 **do**
    for $j \leftarrow 0$ **to** 4 **do**
      for $k \leftarrow 0$ **to** 1 **do**
        //compute metric for current settings
        $metric \leftarrow processDense(neurons[i], layers[j], bn[k])$;

        //save these settings if they perform better
        if $metric > bestmetric$ **then**
          $bestneuron \leftarrow neurons[i]$;
          $bestlayer \leftarrow layers[j]$;
          $bestbn \leftarrow bn[k]$;
          $bestmetric \leftarrow metric$;
        end
      end
    end
  end
end

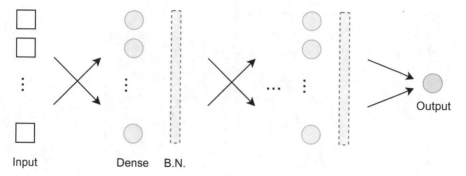

Input   Dense   B.N.

Fig. 2 A schematic presentation of the Dense architecture, presenting the variable width and depth of the network, as well as the presence or absence of the batch normalization layers

3.2 Attention Augmented Dense Networks

Though computational attention mechanisms (Bahdanau et al. 2014) were initially predominantly used in works that dealt with text processing and translation, it was quickly adopted in other domains, including computer vision (Xu et al. 2015). In a general sense, attention mechanisms have the role of understanding and detecting the parts in the input space that are most important for the final prediction stage and assigning higher weights for the important parts. While in a general computer vision these mechanisms would infer the most important parts in images or videos, the intuition in our ensembling system is that the attention layer will create a set of weights w that will indicate the relevance of each of the values from the inducer output vector $[y_{i,1}, y_{i,2}, \ldots, y_{i,N}]$. The implementation we choose for our experiments consists of a soft attention layer inserted into the dense architecture presented in Sect. 3.1, as presented in Fig. 3. Using the notation in Eq. 12 that represents the network input space for a single sample i, and the soft attention vector as $attn_i$, with values between 0 and 1, the system will create an appropriate attention mask $\widehat{attn}_i$, computed as the element wise product of the input vector and the attention vector, as shown in Eq. 13. The learning process for the attention mechanism is based on a supervised back-propagation approach:

$$\overline{y_i} = [y_{i,1}, y_{i,2}, \ldots, y_{i,N}] \tag{12}$$

$$\widehat{attn}_i = attn_i \odot \overline{y_i} \tag{13}$$

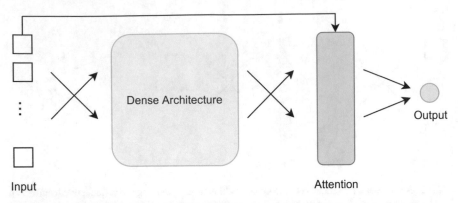

Fig. 3 A schematic presentation of the Attention augmented Dense networks. The attention mechanism, represented by an attention layer, is inserted into a Dense architecture

3.3   *Convolutional Augmented Dense Networks*

Convolutional networks represented a big step forward for deep learning in the field of computer vision, aided by the advancement of hardware processing power and software libraries that allow such networks to be easily deployed and lower the processing time, starting with AlexNet's performance at the ILSVRC 2012 benchmarking competition (Krizhevsky et al. 2012). While the shape of the input space is not important, as one, two or three dimensional convolutional networks have been implemented, they all rely on detecting and learning local correlations between adjacent elements in the input space. More to the point, convolutions can be represented by a set of filters of pre-determined shape that cover and process the entire input space. While this approach performs well for images and videos, that intrinsically have a spatial arrangement and correlation in the input space, in our particular case the order of the inducer prediction outputs in the $\overline{y_i}$ vectors does not have any intrinsic spatial correlation, and, furthermore, at this stage no relationships between individual inducers are calculated. Therefore, we must create these correlations and relationships, via a process we call *input decoration*. Our assumption in this case is that, by creating the decorated input vector for convolutional processing $\overline{dc_i}$ for each sample i and applying convolutional filters to this new input, we would be able create a system where similar inducers can be arranged in close spatial proximity and can support or revoke their prediction decisions based on their spatial relations. Two problems must therefore be solved in order to introduce convolutions into the ensemble networks: (i) find a criterion for detecting similarity between inducers, and (ii) create a spatial arrangement based on the similarity.

For the first problem, similarity between individual inducers can be calculated with the help of the official metric used for measuring system performance in the task. While in the case of interestingness mean average precision at 10 elements is used (mAP@10), in a generalized approach the metric can be expressed as a function $\mathcal{M}$, that takes two vectors as input (either ground truth data and prediction data or two prediction vectors from two separate systems), and outputs a value of similarity between them, denoted r. In other words, given a general form for a prediction vector $p_j = [y_{1,j}, y_{2,j}, \ldots, y_{M,j}]$, that represents the prediction vector created by inducer j for all the M samples in the dataset, the similarity value between two inducers m and n can be calculated as presented in Eq. 14. Finally, by ordering the vector of similarity scores between an inducer m and all other inducers, we can create a list of the most similar inducers for each of the N inducers.

$$r_{m,n} = \mathcal{M}(p_m, p_n) \tag{14}$$

The second problem involves using the similarity values calculated at the previous step, and decorating the predictions for each sample based on the r values. The decorated input vector for a sample i is presented in Eq. 15, and is composed of centroids built around the initial inducer prediction output values, denoted $s_1, s_2, \ldots, s_N$. The elements in each centroid, are as follows: (i) the central element, s_j, represents the initial value, (ii) the similarity scores for the first four most similar inducers, denoted $r_{1,j}, \ldots r_{4,j}$, and (iii) the prediction outputs for sample i extracted from the first four most similar inducers, denoted $c_{1,j}, \ldots c_{4,j}$. This decoration process for a single sample i is presented in Algorithm 2, and can easily be generalized to all the samples in the dataset.

$$\overline{dc_i} = \begin{bmatrix} r_{4,1} & c_{1,1} & r_{1,1} & \cdots & r_{4,N} & c_{1,N} & r_{1,N} \\ c_{4,1} & s_1 & c_{2,1} & \cdots & c_{4,N} & s_N & c_{2,N} \\ r_{3,1} & c_{3,1} & r_{2,1} & \cdots & r_{3,N} & c_{3,N} & r_{2,N} \end{bmatrix} \tag{15}$$

The decorated $\overline{dc_i}$ array will represent the new input for the convolutional ensembling system, as presented in Fig. 4. Finally, the $\overline{dc_i}$ array in processed by the convolutional layers, centroid by centroid. Equation 16 shows this process for a single centroid i, where the centroid is element-wise multiplied with the weights in the convolutional filter. The final step involves, in our case, an average pooling layer that will output a single element for the convolutional step that represents the average value of the element-wise multiplication result matrix. In a simple case where only one convolutional filter is employed, the input to the dense layers will practically be similar as the initial input, where each inducer output value is basically replaced by the result of the convolution process for the inducer's centroid. Finally, several setups will be tested for the convolutional architecture, that include different number of convolutional filters: 1, 5 or 10 filters. This would allow the network to assess more than one type of correlation between the inducers.

$$\begin{bmatrix} r_{4,i} & c_{1,i} & r_{1,i} \\ c_{4,i} & s_i & c_{2,i} \\ r_{3,i} & c_{3,i} & r_{2,i} \end{bmatrix} \odot \begin{bmatrix} w_1 & w_2 & w_3 \\ w_4 & w_5 & w_6 \\ w_7 & w_8 & w_9 \end{bmatrix} \tag{16}$$

Algorithm 2: Input decoration algorithm for convolutional networks for sample
i

Input : vector of inducer predictions $\begin{bmatrix} p_1 & p_2 & \dots & p_N \end{bmatrix}$

        vector of predictions for sample i $\begin{bmatrix} s_1 & s_2 & \dots & s_N \end{bmatrix}$

        similarity (and metric) function $\mathcal{M}$

Output : decorated input $\overline{dc_i}$

begin

    //initialize the $\overline{dc_i}$ vector

    $\overline{dc_i} \leftarrow zeros(3 \times N, 3)$;

    //compute the similarity between inducers

    for $j \leftarrow 1$ **to** N **do**

        $sim[j] \leftarrow zeros(N)$;

        for $k \leftarrow 1$ **to** N **do**

          | $sim[j][k] \leftarrow \mathcal{M}(p_j, p_k)$

        end

        //order the sim_j vectors

        $sim[j] \leftarrow Order\,Descending(sim[j])$;

    end

    //decorate the input

    for $i \leftarrow 1$ **to** N **do**

        //initialize centroid

        $cent_i \leftarrow zeros(3, 3)$;

        for $j \leftarrow 1$ **to** 4 **do**

          //insert elements into the centroid according to their proper placement based

          on the similarity measure, as presented in Eq. 15

          | $cent_i \leftarrow Insert\,Elems(sim[i, j])$

        end

        //insert the centroid in the decorated input vector $\overline{dc_i} \leftarrow Insert\,Centroid(cent_i)$

    end

end

3.4 Cross-Space-Fusion Augmented Dense Networks

With the introduction of convolutional layers in the network a method that can process the similarities between inducers has been created. However, convolutional networks are created with image processing as their main objective and use the same filters for processing the entire image and therefore would, in the case of ensembling systems, share the same weights between different centroids. While this does represent a step forward in processing inducer correlation, our assumption is that correlation between inducers are different for each individual inducer, and therefore weights should not be shared between centroids. Given this assumption, we propose the creation of a novel type of DNN layer, which we name *"Cross-Space-Fusion"*, or *CSF* layer. The implementation of the CSF layer is based on creating a new input decoration method and the creation of the layer itself.

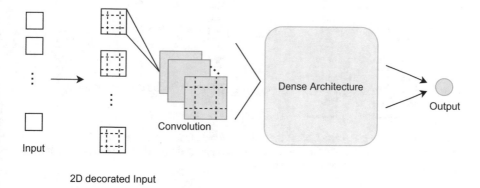

Fig. 4 A schematic presentation of the Convolutional augmented Dense networks. The convolutional layer, presented here with a varying number of filters, is preceded by the input decoration stage and inserted into the dense architecture

A few architectural decisions must be taken in order to fully exploit the correlation data we generate and overcome the possible limitations of convolutional processing. First of all, as shown in Eq. 16, inducer outputs and similarity scores are not processed together, each one of them being multiplied separately with its corespondent convolutional weight. This may break the correlation between the two elements and make it harder to process and learn in the neural network. Secondly, the same possible issue would appear no matter what type of convolutional layer we would use, as three-dimensional convolutional layers do not process correlations inter-dimensionally. Therefore, we propose a novel input decoration method, that would create an additional, third dimension, that would separately memorize similar inducer outputs and similarity scores. Also the CSF layer would need to process these details across the third dimension of the array, processing inducer outputs and corespondent similarity scores together, while using the same M presented in Eq. 14 function for calculating similarity scores. Finally, as previously mentioned, we must take into account that regular convolutional filters may not be the optimal for learning correlations, as they may be different from centroid to centroid. Thus a larger number of parameters must be designed into the CSF layer and, while this may represent a strain on the neural network, the number of added parameters is still small, especially when compared with the depth and width of the dense architecture.

Given the particularities of this approach, Eq. 17 presents the new version of the decorated input, where C_i represents the matrix of prediction outputs from the 8 most similar inducers for an inducer i, while R_i represents their respective similarity score, calculated with the help of the M function. These two matrices create the third dimension of the decorated input, as shown in Fig. 5. Similar to the convolutional approach, in this example, the $c_{1,i}$ and $r_{1,i}$ pair represents the prediction output and similarity score of the most similar system with inducer i, $c_{2,i}$ and $r_{2,i}$ the second most similar, and so on. While it is obvious that by using this decoration scheme more similar inducers can be added to the system that in a similar convolutional

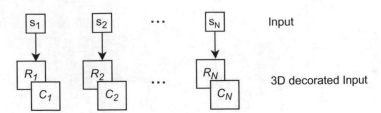

Fig. 5 A schematic presentation of the three-dimensional input decoration result. For each inducer output s_i, we create a pair of centroids C_i and R_i, containing the prediction outputs and similarity scores for similar inducers, as presented in Eq. 17

approach, the question of their utility for this task still remains and will be analyzed, as it may be possible that the new data inserted into the system is noisy or little real correlation exists between the systems.

$$C_i = \begin{bmatrix} c_{1,i} & c_{2,i} & c_{3,i} \\ c_{8,i} & s_i & c_{4,i} \\ c_{7,i} & c_{6,i} & c_{5,i} \end{bmatrix}, R_i = \begin{bmatrix} r_{1,i} & r_{2,i} & r_{3,i} \\ r_{8,i} & 1 & r_{4,i} \\ r_{7,i} & r_{6,i} & r_{5,i} \end{bmatrix} \quad (17)$$

Algorithm 3 presents this input decoration algorithm. It is worth to note that, in the case of the CSF approach, the shape of the $\overline{dc_i}$ decorated input array changes once more, from $(3 \times N, 3)$ in the convolutional approach to $(3 \times N, 3, 2)$, doubling in size. After the decoration step, the input is fed into the CSF layer. For each (c_i, r_i) group of centroids, the network must create and learn a set of weights that can combine the initial inducer prediction with the prediction outputs and similarity scores grouped in the centroids. Thus, the CSF layer contains a set of α and β parameters that must be learned. Equation 18 describes the operations that are performed by the CSF layer, where α are used for controlling the prediction output of each inducer i and β parameters are used for controlling the prediction outputs and similarity scores for the inducers similar to i.

$$\begin{bmatrix} \frac{\alpha_{1,i} \cdot s_i + \beta_{1,i} \cdot c_{1,i} \cdot r_{1,i}}{2} & \frac{\alpha_{2,i} \cdot s_i + \beta_{2,i} \cdot c_{2,i} \cdot r_{2,i}}{2} & \frac{\alpha_{3,i} \cdot s_i + \beta_{3,i} \cdot c_{3,i} \cdot r_{3,i}}{2} \\ \frac{\alpha_{8,i} \cdot s_i + \beta_{8,i} \cdot c_{8,i} \cdot r_{8,i}}{2} & s_i & \frac{\alpha_{4,i} \cdot s_i + \beta_{4,i} \cdot c_{4,i} \cdot r_{4,i}}{2} \\ \frac{\alpha_{7,i} \cdot s_i + \beta_{7,i} \cdot c_{7,i} \cdot r_{7,i}}{2} & \frac{\alpha_{6,i} \cdot s_i + \beta_{6,i} \cdot c_{6,i} \cdot r_{6,i}}{2} & \frac{\alpha_{5,i} \cdot s_i + \beta_{5,i} \cdot c_{7,i} \cdot r_{5,i}}{2} \end{bmatrix} \quad (18)$$

Figure 6 presents an outline of this approach. As presented, the final step in the CSF augmentation part of the method is represented by the addition of an average pooling layer, thus obtaining an input of equal dimensions as the initial one for the dense architecture. Also, given the number of inducers N, the final number of parameters in the CSF layer is $16 \times N$, with $8 \times N$ α and β parameters. As previously mentioned, we must also take into account the possibility that the addition of so many similar inducers in the centroid could add noise to the input and damage the final result. Thus, we decide to test two different setups for the CSF architecture: $4S$, where we

---

Algorithm 3: Input decoration algorithm for Cross-Space-Fusion networks for sample i

---

Input : vector of inducer predictions $\left[p_1 \; p_2 \; ... \; p_N\right]$
vector of predictions for sample i $\left[s_1 \; s_2 \; ... \; s_N\right]$
similarity (and metric) function $\mathcal{M}$
Output : decorated input $\overline{dc_i}$
begin

$\quad$ //initialize the $\overline{dc_i}$ vector
$\quad$ $\overline{dc_i} \leftarrow zeros(3 \times N, 3, 2)$;

$\quad$ //compute the similarity between inducers
$\quad$ **for** $j \leftarrow 1$ **to** N **do**
$\quad\quad$ $sim[j] \leftarrow zeros(N)$;
$\quad\quad$ **for** $k \leftarrow 1$ **to** N **do**
$\quad\quad\quad$ | $sim[j][k] \leftarrow \mathcal{M}(p_j, p_k)$
$\quad\quad$ **end**
$\quad\quad$ //order the sim_j vectors
$\quad\quad$ $sim[j] \leftarrow OrderDescending(sim[j])$;
$\quad$ **end**

$\quad$ //decorate the input
$\quad$ **for** $i \leftarrow 1$ **to** N **do**
$\quad\quad$ //initialize centroid pair c_i, r_i
$\quad\quad$ $c_i \leftarrow zeros(3, 3)$;
$\quad\quad$ $r_i \leftarrow zeros(3, 3)$;
$\quad\quad$ **for** $j \leftarrow 1$ **to** 4 **do**
$\quad\quad\quad$ //insert elements into the centroid pairs according to their proper placement based on the similarity measure, as presented in Eq. 17
$\quad\quad\quad$ | $(c_i, r_i) \leftarrow InsertElems(sim[i, j])$
$\quad\quad$ **end**

$\quad\quad$ //insert the centroid in the decorated input vector $\overline{dc_i} \leftarrow InsertCentroid(c_i, r_i)$
$\quad$ **end**
end

---

only populate the (c_i, r_i) centroid pairs with the top-4 most similar inducers, and $8S$, where the centroid pairs are completely populated with 8 inducers. It is important to note that, while our experiments may show a preference for one of the two setups, in other experiments that may use other datasets or inducers these results may be opposed, or other setups using a different number of populated similar inducers may produce better results.

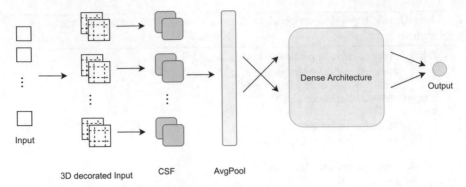

Fig. 6 A schematic presentation of the Cross-Space-Fusion augmented Dense networks. The CSF layer is preceded by the input decoration stage and inserted into the dense architecture

4 Experimental Setup

This section will present the main components of the experiment and how these components interact. We will describe the training protocol employed for the experiments, the dataset and the evaluation protocol used for obtaining the results.

4.1 Training Protocol

The common component in all the methods presented in Sect. 3 is represented by the dense architecture deep neural network. Our experiments will therefore start with finding an optimal dense architecture with regards to the depth and width of the network and the positive or negative influence of batch normalization layers, using the values presented in Sect. 3.1. This is done by collecting the prediction outputs of the entire set of inducers and feeding them into the different variations of the dense architecture networks. This step is described with Algorithm 1. In the following steps, the optimal dense network is augmented with attention, convolutional and CSF layers. As special implementations of the convolutional and CSF layers, the input, consisting of the prediction outputs, is decorated, according to Algorithm 2 for the convolutional approach and Algorithm 3 for the CSF approach.

The training process is performed for 50 epochs, for each variation of the network, using a batch size of 64 samples, mean squared error loss function and an Adam (Kingma & Ba 2014) optimizer featuring a learning rate of 0.01. We are interested in pointing out the optimal dense architecture, given the set of search parameters, as well as the effect of augmenting the dense network with the three types of layers: attention, convolutional and CSF.

4.2 Dataset

For our experiments we are using the latest version of the Interestingness10k (Constantin et al. 2021a) dataset, validated and used during the MediaEval 2017 Predicting Media Interestingness task (Demarty et al. 2017a). The dataset is composed of 9831 images and videos, split between 7396 samples included in the development set (devset) and 2435 samples in the testing set (testset). Participants to the benchmarking competition were tasked with developing and training their media interestingness prediction methods on the devset, running the systems on the testset samples and submitting their testset predictions to the task organizers for performance calculation.

Given the high number of systems submitted at the benchmarking competition, i.e., 33 for the image task and 42 for the video task, and the considerable amount of research and work that went into creating them, we consider these systems as ideal candidates for being used as inducers in our proposed method. With the help and collaboration of the task organizers, we gathered participant submission files and used them as input into our systems. However, given the fact that participants only submitted predictions for the testset samples and the inherent problems in recreating such a large number of diverse systems, we are bound to only use those predictions and create a new evaluation protocol that will be used in training our systems, based only on the samples that are featured in the testset.

We therefore have to create a new set of data splits, and choose to use two protocols for this: (i) RSKF75, featuring a random stratified k-fold that uses 75% of the samples for training and 25% for testing, and (ii) RSKF50, generating 50% training samples and 50% testing. It is important to note that, in order to avoid any "lucky" data splits that would create an unfair advantage for our approach, the split samples are randomized, and experiments are repeated with different random splits, generating 100 partitions for each network architecture variation. Therefore, the results we present in Sect. 6 are average values calculated over the 100 partitions. System performance is calculated by using the official metric of the MediaEval benchmarking competition, i.e., MAP@10.

5 Experimental Results

This section presents the experimental results, featuring a comparison with a set of baseline systems, a set of baseline ensembling approaches and identifying the best performing architectures.

5.1 Baseline Systems

In order to correctly position and analyze the results of the proposed methods, we compare them with a few methods from the literature, including (i) the best performers at the MediaEval competition, (ii) the best overall performers on the Interestingness10k dataset, and (iii) a set of traditional ensembling methods.

The best performers from the MediaEval competition also represent inducers for our systems, and an important target for the proposed systems. For the image prediction task we have the system developed by Permadi et al. (2017), with a MAP@10 performance of 0.1385, while for video prediction we have the system developed by Ben-Ahmed et al. (2017), with a MAP@10 performance of 0.0827. The overall performers consist of methods that are published outside the MediaEval venue, but used the same benchmarking protocol and metrics. For the image task we have the work of Parekh et al. (2018), with a performance of $MAP@10 = 0.156$, while for the video task, Wang et al. (2018) achieve a $MAP@10 = 0.093$.

The final set of baseline systems consists of a set of traditional ensembling methods, that we created using the same protocol and set of inducers as used by our proposed methods. Several types of ensembling methods are tested, starting with simple strategies (Kittler et al. 1998) like taking the maximum value of inducer prediction outputs (*LFMax*), average and mean values (*LFAvg* and *LFMean*), and weighted average (*LFWeight*), but also more complex approaches that involve learning steps, like AdaBoost (Freund et al. 1999) (*BAda*) and Gradient Boosting (Friedman 2001) (*BGrad*).

5.2 Results

The results are presented in Table 1. At a first glance, it is important to note that the proposed systems surpasses every baseline system, including the best performing baseline ensembling system, which for both images and videos is the AdaBoost approach. Furthermore, the best performing variant of the proposed systems increased performance by a large margin. Taking into account the RSKF75 split, the increase is as follows: for the image subtask an increase of 148.08% over the best MediaEval system, 73.09% over the best overall system and 105.25% over the best traditional ensembling system, while for the video subtask these values are 241.59%, 203.76% and 150.22% respectively.

With regards to the overall best performing proposed method, results vary, as the convolutional approach has the best results on the image task using the RSKF75 split (MAP@10 = 0.3436) and in the video task using the RSKF50 split (MAP@10 = 0.1692), while the CSF approach has the best results using the other two variants, obtaining a MAP@10 value of 0.2403 for image prediction under the RSKF50 setup and 0.2825 for video prediction under the RSKF75 setup.

It is also important to note the architecture variations that led to these results, i.e., the optimal dense, convolutional, and CSF architecture setups. For image prediction, the optimal dense architecture uses 10 layers with 1000 neurons per layer, and no batch normalization, achieving MAP@10 values of 0.2316 for RSKF50 and 0.3355 for RSKF75, while the best performing convolutional architecture uses 5 filters. Also, the best performing CSF setup in this case is 4*S*. For video prediction, the

Table 1 Results on the two interestingness prediction tasks: image and video. Systems are divided into baseline best performers from MediaEval and from the literature (b), best baseline ensembling performance (e) and proposed systems (p), and according to the split the systems employ (original or RSKF50 and RSKF75). The best results with regards to the official metric (MAP@10) are presented in bold

System type	Image			Video		
	System	Split	MAP@10	System	Split	MAP@10
(b)	Permadi et al. (2017)	Original	0.1385	Ben-Ahmed et al. (2017)	Original	0.0827
	Parekh et al. (2018)	Original	0.1985	Wang et al. (2018)	Original	0.093
(e)	BAda Freund et al. (1999)	RSKF50	0.1523	BAda Freund et al. (1999)	RSKF50	0.0961
		RSKF75	0.1674		RSKF75	0.1129
(p)	Dense	RSKF50	0.2316	Dense	RSKF50	0.1563
		RSKF75	0.3355		RSKF75	0.2677
	Attention	RSKF50	0.2399	Attention	RSKF50	0.1668
		RSKF75	0.3389		RSKF75	0.2750
	Convolutional	RSKF50	0.2293	Convolutional	RSKF50	**0.1692**
		RSKF75	**0.3436**		RSKF75	0.2799
	CSF	RSKF50	**0.2403**	CSF	RSKF50	0.1664
		RSKF75	0.3403		RSKF75	**0.2825**

Table 2 Progressive analysis of network setup for the video task, under RSKF75 setup with batch normalization layers activated. The left side of the table shows results when the number of neurons increases, while the right side shows results when the number of layers increases

Layers	5	5	5	5	5	5	10	15	20	25
Neurons	25	50	500	1000	2000	5000	25	25	25	25
MAP@10	0.2414	0.2410	0.2493	**0.2529**	0.2506	0.2094	0.2529	0.2650	**0.2660**	0.2646

optimal dense setup is composed of 25 layers with 2000 neurons per layer and features batch normalization, achieving MAP@10 values of 0.1563 for RSKF50 and 0.2677 for RSKF75. With regards to the convolutional architecture, the best setup again features 5 convolutional filters, while $4S$ again represents the best setup for the CSF layer. While the dense network performance is very good, the augmentation process with attention and especially convolutional and CSF layers further improves the results.

One final observation with regards to network setup is presented in Table 2. During our experiments, we observed that there are certain points when the network stops learning and achieves saturation. While Table 2 presents a particular setup, for the video task with batch normalization layers and RSKF75 split, the same behaviour is observable regardless of the task, of the presence of batch normalization layers or of the split. In the example presented, increasing the number of neurons past 1000 while keeping the number of layers constant at 5 only decreases the performance, while the same is true when increasing the number of layers past 20 when maintaining a constant number of 25 neurons per layer. Most importantly, this seems to indicate that the optimal network setup is not outside the set of values we tested in our experiments. Another important point to make here is that the proposed method have a high performance even when looking at the values for the most basic setup (5 layers, 25 neurons per layer), scoring a MAP@10 value of 0.2414, 9.82% lower than the best performing dense architecture, but still significantly better than all the selected baseline methods.

6 Conclusions

This work presents the creation and deployment of a series of deep neural network based ensemble systems, used in the prediction of image and video interestingness. The latest Interestingness10k dataset is used in our experiments, a dataset that was previously used and validated during the MediaEval 2017 Predicting Media Interestingness task. Though a large number of systems use this dataset, both during the MediaEval benchmarking competition and outside it, in different journals and conferences, system performance is generally low when compared with other tasks, i.e., a maximum MAP@10 performance of 0.1985 for image interestingness prediction and 0.093 for video prediction.

While very high, near-perfect performance is not necessarily expected for such tasks, where annotator subjectivity plays an important role, we theorize that the implementation of ensemble systems can increase overall performance. Furthermore, the exploration of deep neural networks as ensembling functions presents a high degree of novelty in the current literature, as current literature shows that they are only employed as inducers and not as ensembling functions. Different network setups are presented and tested, including architectures based on dense, attention, convolutional and CSF layers, presenting the theoretical background of implementing these architectures as ensemble functions and the introduction of input decoration algorithms that allow inducer prediction output data to be used and inducer correlations learned with the help of these architectures.

Experimental results show a significant increase in performance over state-of-the-art systems. Our proposed methods show a 148.08% increase in performance in the image prediction task over the best MediaEval system and 73.09% over the best state-of-the-art system, while in the video prediction task the increase is even higher: 241.59% and 203.76%. Furthermore, the proposed ensemble methods are compared with some traditional ensembling methods implemented under the same conditions, having a significantly better performance, i.e., 105.25% for the image task and 150.22% for the video task. While it is certainly possible that better results could be achieved with other network setups, featuring different number of layers or neurons, or different architectures, we believe the advantages of deep fusion systems to be thoroughly demonstrated. Given the results, it is still unclear which of the two inducer correlation based architectures (convolutional or CSF) perform better for this task, with top results being split between them. However it is important to note that inducer correlation processing did indeed improve the results of both the dense networks and the attention-based networks, thus indicating the validity of inducer correlation calculation, input decoration and correlation processing.

Finally, another important point, not only for our proposed methods, but for ensembling systems in general, is the analysis of the deployability of the proposed systems. While using a late fusion approach can be cost intensive, considering that inducers must be trained, tested and run individually, and a final ensembling step performed before the final prediction is provided, there are cases where developing a late fusion system can become a necessity. Critical infrastructure applications, where very accurate prediction results are a constant need, represent a good example, but, closer to the domain of interestingness prediction, applications where single-method approaches do not perform well, due to inherent multi-modality or complexity of the concept that is being predicted, represent another good example. While deploying an ensembling method may prove to be more costly, it may also be one of the only methods that achieves market-level performance, allowing the introduction of new features that can greatly increase user satisfaction. In this case we also consider the possibility that lowering the number of inducers may not affect system performance to a high degree, therefore trading an insignificant amount of performance for higher execution speed and lower hardware demands. While the creation of an inducer selection method is still an open question for our approach, we propose that future developments could address this problem by analyzing inducer correlations or by testing performance in a recursive leave-one-out scenario.

Acknowledgments This work was funded under project AI4Media "A European Excellence Centre for Media, Society and Democracy", grant #951911, H2020 ICT-48-2020.

References

Azcona, D., Moreu, E., Hu, F., Ward, T. E., & Smeaton, A. F. (2020). Predicting media memorability using ensemble models. In *Proceedings of the MediaEval Workshop*.

Bahdanau, D., Cho, K., & Bengio, Y. (2014). Neural machine translation by jointly learning to align and translate. arXiv preprint arXiv:1409.0473.

Ben-Ahmed, O., Wacker, J., Gaballo, A., & Huet, B. (2017). Eurecom@ mediaeval 2017: Media genre inference for predicting media interestingness. In *Proceedings of the MediaEval 2017 Workshop*, Dublin, Ireland.

Berlyne, D. E. (1949). Interest as a psychological concept. *British Journal of Psychology, 39*(4), 184.

Breiman, L. (1996). Bagging predictors. *Machine Learning, 24*(2), 123–140.

Breiman, L. (2001). Random forests. *Machine Learning, 45*(1), 5–32.

Chamaret, C., Demarty, C. H., Demoulin, V., & Marquant, G. (2016). Experiencing the interestingness concept within and between pictures. *Electronic Imaging, 2016*(16), 1–12.

Chen, T., & Guestrin, C. (2016). Xgboost: A scalable tree boosting system. In *Proceedings of the 22nd ACM SIGKDD International Conference on Knowledge Discovery and Data Mining* (pp. 785–794).

Constantin, M. G., Redi, M., Zen, G., Ionescu, B. (2019). Computational understanding of visual interestingness beyond semantics: literature survey and analysis of covariates. *ACM Computing Surveys (CSUR), 52*(2), 1–37.

Constantin, M. G., ştefan, L. D., Ionescu, B., Duong, N. Q., Demarty, C. H., & Sjöberg, M. (2021a). Visual interestingness prediction: A benchmark framework and literature review. *International Journal of Computer Vision.* https://doi.org/10.1007/s11263-021-01443-1

Constantin, M. G., Stefan, L. D., & Ionescu, B. (2021b). DeepFusion: Deep ensembles for domain independent system fusion. In *Proceedings of the 27th International Conference on Multimedia Modeling*, Prague, Czech Republic.

Dai, Q., Zhao, R. W., Wu, Z., Wang, X., Gu, Z., Wu, W., & Jiang, Y. G. (2015). Fudan-Huawei at MediaEval 2015: Detecting violent scenes and affective impact in movies with deep learning. In *Proceedings of the MediaEval 2015 Workshop, Wurzen, Germany.*

Demarty, C. H., Sjöberg, M., Ionescu, B., Do, T. T., Wang, H., Duong, N. Q., Lefebvre, F., & MediaEval. (2016). Predicting media interestingness task. In *MediaEval Workshop*, Hilversum, The Netherlands, October 20–21, 2016.

Demarty, C. H., Sjöberg, M., Ionescu, B., Do, T. T., Gygli, M., & Duong, N. (2017a). Mediaeval 2017 predicting media interestingness task. In *MediaEval Workshop*, Dublin, Ireland, September 13–15, 2017.

Demarty, C. H., Sjöberg, M., Constantin, M. G., Duong, N. Q., Ionescu, B., Do, T. T., & Wang, H. (2017b). Predicting interestingness of visual content. In *Visual Content Indexing and Retrieval with Psycho-Visual Models* (pp. 233–265). Cham: Springer.

Fan, S., Ng, T. T., Koenig, B. L., Jiang, M., & Zhao, Q. (2016). A paradigm for building generalized models of human image perception through data fusion. In *Proceedings of the IEEE Conference on Computer Vision and Pattern Recognition* (pp. 5762–5771).

Freund, Y., Schapire, R., & Abe, N. (1999). A short introduction to boosting. *Journal-Japanese Society For Artificial Intelligence, 14*(771–780), 1612.

Friedman, J. H. (2001). Greedy function approximation: A gradient boosting machine. *Annals of Statistics, 29*(5), 1189–1232.

Gomes, H. M., Barddal, J. P., Enembreck, F., & Bifet, A. (2017). A survey on ensemble learning for data stream classification. *ACM Computing Surveys, 50*(2), 1–36.

Grabner, H., Nater, F., Druey, M., & Van Gool, L. (2013). Visual interestingness in image sequences. In *Proceedings of the 21st ACM International Conference on Multimedia* (pp. 1017–1026).

Gygli, M., & Soleymani, M. (2016). Analyzing and predicting GIF interestingness. In *Proceedings of the 24th ACM International Conference on Multimedia* (pp. 122–126).

Gygli, M., Grabner, H., Riemenschneider, H., Nater, F., & Van Gool, L. (2013). The interestingness of images. In *Proceedings of the IEEE International Conference on Computer Vision* (pp. 1633–1640).

He, K., Gkioxari, G., Dollár, P., & Girshick, R. (2017). Mask R-CNN. In *Proceedings of the IEEE International Conference on Computer Vision* (pp. 2961–2969).

Hidi, S., Anderson, V. (1992). Situational interest and its impact on reading and expository writing. *The Role of Interest in Learning and Development, 11*, 213–214.

Hsieh, L. C., Hsu, W. H., & Wang, H. C. (2014). Investigating and predicting social and visual image interestingness on social media by crowdsourcing. In *2014 IEEE International Conference on Acoustics, Speech and Signal Processing (ICASSP)* (pp. 4309–4313). IEEE.

Ioffe, S., & Szegedy, C. (2015). Batch normalization: Accelerating deep network training by reducing internal covariate shift. In *International Conference on Machine Learning* (pp. 448–456). PMLR.

Jiang, Y. G., Wang, Y., Feng, R., Xue, X., Zheng, Y., & Yang, H. (2013). Understanding and predicting interestingness of videos. In *Proceedings of the AAAI Conference on Artificial Intelligence* (Vol. 27, No. 1).

Jou, B., Chen, T., Pappas, N., Redi, M., Topkara, M., & Chang, S. F. (2015). Visual affect around the world: A large-scale multilingual visual sentiment ontology. In *Proceedings of the 23rd ACM International Conference on Multimedia* (pp. 159–168).

Ke, Y., Hoiem, D., & Sukthankar, R. (2005). Computer vision for music identification. In *2005 IEEE Computer Society Conference on Computer Vision and Pattern Recognition (CVPR'05)* (Vol. 1, pp. 597–604). IEEE.

Khaleghi, B., Khamis, A., Karray, F. O., & Razavi, S. N. (2013). Multisensor data fusion: A review of the state-of-the-art. *Information Fusion, 14*(1), 28–44.

Kingma, D. P., & Ba, J. (2014). Adam: A method for stochastic optimization. arXiv preprint arXiv:1412.6980.

Kittler, J., Hatef, M., Duin, R. P., & Matas, J. (1998). On combining classifiers. *IEEE Transactions on Pattern Analysis and Machine Intelligence, 20*(3), 226–239.

Krizhevsky, A., Sutskever, I., & Hinton, G. E. (2012). Imagenet classification with deep convolutional neural networks. *Advances in Neural Information Processing Systems, 25*, 1097–1105.

Liu, L., Wei, W., Chow, K. H., Loper, M., Gursoy, E., Truex, S., & Wu, Y. (2019). Deep neural network ensembles against deception: Ensemble diversity, accuracy and robustness. In *2019 IEEE 16th International Conference on Mobile Ad Hoc and Sensor Systems (MASS)* (pp. 274–282). IEEE.

Lowe, D. G. (1999). Object recognition from local scale-invariant features. In *Proceedings of the Seventh IEEE International Conference on Computer Vision* (Vol. 2, pp. 1150–1157).

Mitchell, T. M. (1980). *The need for biases in learning generalizations* (pp. 184–191). New Jersey: Department of Computer Science, Laboratory for Computer Science Research, Rutgers Univ.

Oliva, A., & Torralba, A. (2001). Modeling the shape of the scene: A holistic representation of the spatial envelope. *International Journal of Computer Vision, 42*(3), 145–175.

Parekh, J., Tibrewal, H., & Parekh, S. (2018). Deep pairwise classification and ranking for predicting media interestingness. In *Proceedings of the 2018 ACM on International Conference on Multimedia Retrieval* (pp. 428–433).

Permadi, R. A., Putra, S. G. P., Helmiriawan, C., & Liem, C. C. (2017). DUT-MMSR at MediaEval 2017: Predicting media interestingness task. In *Proceedings of the MediaEval 2017 Workshop*, Dublin, Ireland.

Sagi, O., & Rokach, L. (2018). Ensemble learning: A survey. *Wiley Interdisciplinary Reviews: Data Mining and Knowledge Discovery, 8*(4), e1249.

Shechtman, E., & Irani, M. (2007). Matching local self-similarities across images and videos. In *2007 IEEE Conference on Computer Vision and Pattern Recognition* (pp. 1–8). IEEE.

Silvia, P. J. (2005). What is interesting? Exploring the appraisal structure of interest. *Emotion, 5*(1), 89.

Silvia, P. J. (2009). Looking past pleasure: anger, confusion, disgust, pride, surprise, and other unusual aesthetic emotions. *Psychology of Aesthetics, Creativity, and the Arts, 3*(1), 48.

Stein, B. E., & Stanford, T. R. (2008). Multisensory integration: current issues from the perspective of the single neuron. *Nature Reviews Neuroscience, 9*(4), 255–266.

Ştefan, L. D., Constantin, M. G., & Ionescu, B. (2020). System fusion with deep ensembles. In *Proceedings of the 2020 International Conference on Multimedia Retrieval* (pp. 256–260).

Stevenson, A. (Ed.). (2010). *Oxford dictionary of English*. Oxford University Press.

Sudhakaran, S., Escalera, S., & Lanz, O. (2020b). Gate-shift networks for video action recognition. In *Proceedings of the IEEE/CVF Conference on Computer Vision and Pattern Recognition* (pp. 1102–1111).

Sun, J. J., Liu, T., Prasad, G. (2018). Gla in mediaeval 2018 emotional impact of movies task. In *Proceedings of the MediaEval 2018 Workshop, Sophia Antipolis, France*.

Tran, D., Bourdev, L., Fergus, R., Torresani, L., & Paluri, M. (2015). Learning spatiotemporal features with 3d convolutional networks. In *Proceedings of the IEEE International Conference on Computer Vision* (pp. 4489–4497).

Wang, S., Chen, S., Zhao, J., & Jin, Q. (2018). Video interestingness prediction based on ranking model. In *Proceedings of the Joint Workshop of the 4th Workshop on Affective Social Multimedia Computing and first Multi-Modal Affective Computing of Large-Scale Multimedia Data* (pp. 55–61).

Wolpert, D. H. (2002). The supervised learning no-free-lunch theorems. Soft computing and industry, 25–42.

Xu, K., Ba, J., Kiros, R., Cho, K., Courville, A., Salakhudinov, R., Zemel, R.S., & Bengio, Y. (2015). Show, attend and tell: Neural image caption generation with visual attention. In *International Conference on Machine Learning* (pp. 2048–2057). PMLR.

Yalniz, I. Z., Jégou, H., Chen, K., Paluri, M., & Mahajan, D. (2019). Billion-scale semi-supervised learning for image classification. arXiv preprint arXiv:1905.00546.

Affective Perception: The Power Is in the Picture

Margaret M. Bradley, Nicola Sambuco, and Peter J. Lang

1 Introduction

Since the invention of the camera, photographers have exploited the power of pictures to elicit emotional reactions in the viewer. Photojournalists capture scenes of warfare and violence that excite and horrify; marketing agencies seek images that prompt consumers to attend and purchase; public health campaigns use photographs to target and encourage safer behaviors; charitable organizations mail images to solicit aid and assistance; a variety of media present scenes intended to titilate and arouse. From a basic science view, photographic images (because they are excellent perceptual matches to the events portrayed) act as salient retrieval cues that activate existing mental representations with associative links to the subcortical and cortical regions mediating emotional experience. Emotional scene perception has therefore proved to be an effective methodology in the basic study of emotion as well as emotional dysfunction in a variety of neurological, psychiatric and other mental health disorders (e.g., de Tommaso et al. 2009; De Zorzi et al. 2021; Hermanns et al. 2003; Huijbers et al. 2011; Ihssen et al. 2011; Renfroe et al. 2016).

In this chapter, we briefly review our prior research on emotional scene perception, and conduct new picture-based analyses utilizing existing databases to assess the extent to which individual scenes reliably engage emotional responses across individuals. We begin by briefly considering a motivational view of emotion (1.2), and then describe the existing databases (1.3) and analytic strategy (1.4) for assessing picture reliability. Scene reliability is then computed for evaluative reports of emotional experience (1.5.1), skin conductance (1.5.2), pupil diameter

M. M. Bradley (✉) · N. Sambuco · P. J. Lang
University of Florida Center for the Study of Emotion and Attention (CSEA), Gainesville, FL, USA
e-mail: bradley@ufl.edu; nsambuco@phhp.ufl.edu; langp@phhp.ufl.edu

(1.5.3), facial EMG (1.5.4), heart rate (1.5.5), functional amygdala activity (1.5.6) and free recall memory (1.5.7). We conclude (1.6) that, across measures, specific images reliably elicit emotional reactions, and discuss similarities and differences in emotional reactions as they vary with hedonic content and dependent measure.

2 Motivation and Emotion

There are hundreds of words in the English language describing the varieties of human emotional experience (e.g., anger, fear, happy, sad, etc.), and for decades, scientists have proposed different lists of labels that are held to be fundamental in the study of emotion (e.g., Ekman 1971; Plutchik 1980). Based on animal research and theory (e.g., Dickinson & Dearing 1979; Konorski 1967), we begin with a simpler approach in which two motivational systems are considered to be the foundations of emotional experience. These two systems—defensive and appetitive—are implemented in neural circuits that are evolutionarily old, shared across mammalian species, and have evolved to mediate a variety of behaviors that sustain and protect life. The defense system is primarily activated in contexts involving threat to life, with a primitive behavioral repertoire built on withdrawal, escape, and attack; the appetitive system is activated in contexts that promote survival, including sustenance, procreation, and nurturance, with a basic behavioral repertoire of ingestion, copulation, and care-giving.

In this view, emotional experience is characterized fundamentally by the intensity of defensive or appetitive activation, which we consider a strategic aspect of emotional experience (Lang & Bradley 2010; Lang et al. 1997; Löw et al. 2008), often having similar goals of directing attention and preparing for action, regardless of motivational context (Bradley 2009). And, although basic bidirectional actions of approach and withdrawal typify the behavioral repertoire of simpler species (e.g., aplysia, Schneirla 1959), a vast repertoire of coping behaviors have evolved in more complex organisms to defend life and permit its propagation. This tactical aspect of emotion can prompt similar actions in different motivational contexts, as well as different actions in the same motivational context (Lang & Bradley 2013).

From the layperson's perspective, emotion most centrally involves internal feeling states, which are not accessible to scientific measurement. Rather, as Lang (1968, 2010; Lang & Bradley 2018, see also Hugdahl 1981) originally proposed, emotional experience can be measured in three systems of: (1) subjective reports/expressive language, (2) biological and physiological reactivity, and (3) overt action. No single response system has a one-to-one relationship with the hypothesized conscious feeling state—one person can report high fear, with no other measurable indices of defensive activation, whereas another reports no distress in the context of measurable defensive activation. Rather than understanding conscious emotional experience, the empirical study of emotion instead simply aims to characterize and describe 3-system responses as they vary in specific emotional induction contexts (Lang 2010; Bradley 2000).

3 Emotional Reactivity Database

One goal of our emotion research over the past many years has been to characterize emotional reactions in the context of scene perception. From an experimental perspective, the static nature of photographic images is ideal, as a number of biological and physiological measures of emotional reactivity (e.g., heart rate, skin conductance, etc.) are sensitive to dynamic stimulus changes such as cuts, pans, zooms, etc., which can interfere with detecting reactions specific to affective content (see Detenber & Lang 2010 for an overview). To begin, we collected a set of emotionally evocative and neutral photographs from a variety of available sources, and collected reports of pleasure and arousal from a large group of participants (International Affective Picture System, IAPS: Lang et al. 2008). Judgments of pleasure and arousal are considered two parameters of motivational activation, with reports of pleasure indexing which motivational system is engaged (i.e., defensive or appetitive), and judgments of arousal indexing its intensity.

Initial studies (see Bradley & Lang 2007; Lang 2010 for overviews) presented emotional and neutral scenes for 6s in a free viewing context, finding that pleasant and unpleasant scenes elicit heightened skin conductance and pupil diameter changes, enhanced activation of the amygdala (a key subcortical node in both the appetitive and defensive motivational system), as well as better free recall. On the other hand, heart rate changes, startle reflexes, and facial EMG activity differed for pleasant and unpleasant scenes. Later studies, however, found that, despite similar ratings of pleasure and/or arousal, specific scene content plays an important role in the magnitude of emotional reactions, suggesting that evaluative ratings, although highly reliable, are not a direct readout of emotional engagement (see Bradley et al. 2001a, 2017a).

Data from a number of previously published and unpublished studies in our laboratory were used in the analyses conducted in the current chapter, and include evaluative reports of pleasure and arousal, change scores (from a baseline immediately preceding picture onset) for each participant and scene for skin conductance, heart rate, facial corrugator and zygomatic EMG activity (72 pictures; Bradley et al. 2001a), pupil diameter (60 pictures; Bradley et al. 2017b), functional activity in the amygdala (50 pictures; unpublished data) and free recall (360 pictures; Bradley et al. 2017a).

In all studies, each picture was novel and viewed only once by each participant; each study also included a set of neutral scenes. The order in which a specific scene was presented was counterbalanced across participants, reducing differences in emotional reactivity simply due to input serial position. Across studies, we focused on specific contents depicting erotic, romance, adventure, sports, family, food, nature, contamination (e.g., disgust), threat, and mutilation scenes (see Fig. 1).

| Erotic | Adventure | Family | Food | Nature | Contamination | Threat | Mutilation |

Fig. 1 Examples of the type of scenes in different content categories

4   Analytic Plan

Of central interest in the current analyses is how reliably specific scenes induce
emotional reactions across participants, for a variety of different 3-system measures
of emotion. Whereas previous analyses averaged emotional reactions over pictures
for each participant, in the current analyses we instead average emotional reactions
over participants for each picture. One possibility is that, in general, participants
react idiosyncratically to different exemplars of specific content (e.g., threat),
with little commonality in the induced emotional response across individuals,
which predicts low overall scene reliability. On the other hand, specific scenes
may uniformly tend to elicit heightened (or reduced) emotional reactions across
individuals, leading to high scene reliability. Moreover, for some measures of
emotional reactivity, reliability as a function of specific scene may be higher than
for other measures.

Single trial (picture) analysis requires a measure-free metric of emotional reactivity that indexes the extent to which each scene, for each participant, is emotionally
engaging, regardless of the measured emotional reaction. To accomplish this, on
each trial, the participant's response (separately for each measure) was standardized
based on the mean and standard deviation of the individual's response to a set
of neutral scenes. These emotional reactivity (z) scores (expressed in metric free
units of standard deviation), index the extent to which reactivity is greater (positive
z-score) or less (negative z-score) than that elicited by neutral scenes for each
individual, and are averaged across individuals to produce an emotional reactivity
score for each scene.

To assess image reliability, permutation analyses were conducted for each dependent measure in which participants were randomly divided into two subgroups and
the mean emotional reactivity (z) score calculated for each picture in each subgroup.
Then, the Pearson product moment correlation (r) was computed, indexing the
degree to which the same pictures were associated with more or less emotional
reactivity across cohorts. For each measure, the permutation analysis was conducted
500 times, and the resulting mean and distribution of these correlations was used to
estimate the extent to which specific scenes reliably engage emotional reactions
across individuals for each measure of emotional reactivity. Mean emotional
reactivity (z) scores were also averaged across exemplars in each picture content
and analyzed in a univariate ANOVA to assess overall effects of specific scene
content, and followed up by LSD comparison tests to assess differences between
scene contents.

In a second reliability analysis, the number of exemplars in each content category prompting strong emotional engagement was assessed by computing the proportion of scenes that appeared in the upper half of the emotional reactivity (z) distributions for each measure. To the extent that scene content is a significant factor to consider in emotional engagement, the proportion of scenes consistently eliciting emotional reactivity should be higher.

5 Affective Scene Perception

5.1 Evaluative Reports

To measure reports of pleasure and arousal, Lang (1980) developed the self-assessment manikin (SAM; see Fig. 2a) a graphic rating scale that provides a language-free, culture-free, age-free measure of evaluative reports that prompts equivalent results to administering the much longer semantic differential (Bradley

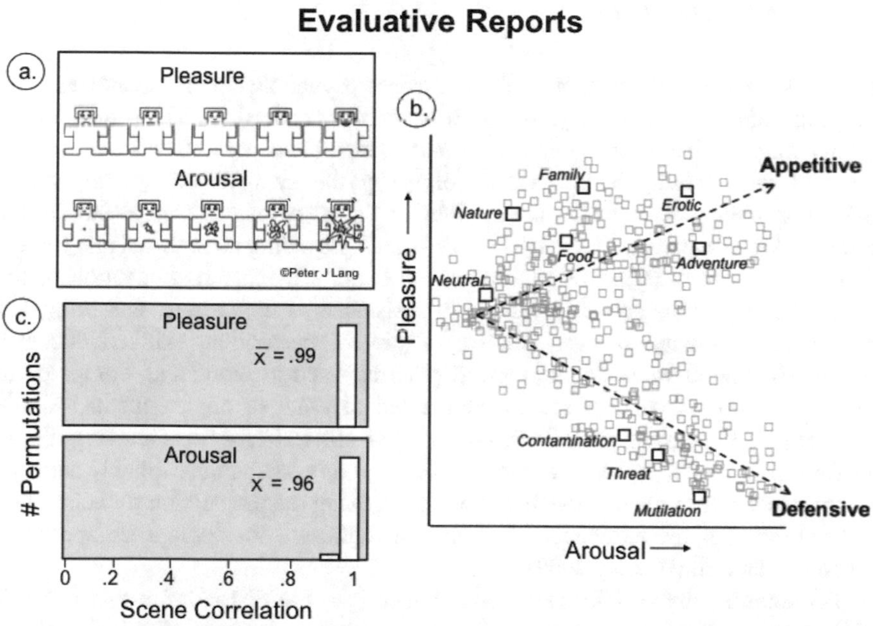

Fig. 2 (**a**) The Self-Assessment Manikin (SAM: Lang 1980) measures reports of pleasure and arousal. (**b**) The affective space that results when each picture is plotted in a 2-dimensional space defined by its mean pleasure and arousal rating; the underlying appetitive and defensive motivational systems are depicted by the dotted lines. (**c**) The distribution (and mean) of the correlations of emotional reactivity (z) scores for scenes for pleasure (upper panel) and arousal (lower panel) ratings resulting from permutation analyses

& Lang 1994). Figure 2b illustrates the affective space that results when pictures are rated in terms of evoked pleasure and arousal: Scenes rated highly pleasant or highly unpleasant are associated with higher arousal ratings, prompting a significant quadratic relationship between pleasure and arousal. The relationship of rated pleasure and arousal to the hypothesized underlying appetitive and defensive motivational systems is illustrated by the dotted lines in Fig. 2c, with separate appetitive and defensive motivational systems that vary in the intensity of activation.

Figure 2c illustrates the results of permutation analyses for emotional reactivity (z) rating scores. Evaluative reports of pleasure and arousal are highly reliable across cohorts, with a mean scene correlation of 0.99 for rated pleasure, and 0.96 for rated arousal, both of which are highly significant. Not surprisingly, then, although some minor differences exist, the shape of affective space is consistent for men and women (Bradley et al. 2001a), across the lifespan (Ferrari et al. 2017) and cultures (e.g., Molto et al. 1999; Lasaitis et al. 2008; Verschuere et al. 2001), and identical to the shape of affective space for other emotional cues, including sounds, words, and texts (Bradley & Lang 2007).

5.2 Skin Conductance

Electrodermal activity was one of the earliest psychophysiological indices used to gauge emotional reactivity. Whereas a variety of physiological responses are dually innervated by parasympathetic and sympathetic nervous system activity, electrodermal activity is innervated solely by the sympathetic system, whose activation mediates the well-known "fight or flight" response. One electrodermal index—skin conductance activity—is measured by sending an undetectable current across two sensors (typically placed on the hand, see Fig. 3a). Activation of the sympathetic nervous system lowers skin resistance to the current, elevating skin conductance activity. In early studies of picture perception, skin conductance reliably increased when people viewed pictures rated as emotional, compared to neutral, regardless whether scenes were rated pleasant or unpleasant in hedonic valence (e.g. Greenwald et al. 1989; Winton et al. 1984). Rather than reacting simply to aversive stimulation then, the sympathetic nervous system is also reliably engaged by intense appetitive activation, presumably indexing the preparation for action that not only readies the individual for fight and flight, but for appropriate appetitive behaviors as well (Bradley 2009).

Permutation analyses for skin conductance (see Fig. 3b) indicate that the reliability of specific scenes in eliciting electrodermal activity is quite high, with a mean scene correlation across random cohorts of 0.71 ($p < 0.05$). When averaged over exemplars in specific categories (see Fig. 3c), all emotional contents elicited skin conductance responses significantly greater than found for neutral scenes (i.e., $z = 0$; one-tailed $p < 0.05$), with erotica, threat, and mutilation scenes prompting significantly heightened responses compared to other scene contents. Moreover, as depicted in Fig. 3d, whereas no exemplars for family, food or nature are among the

Skin Conductance

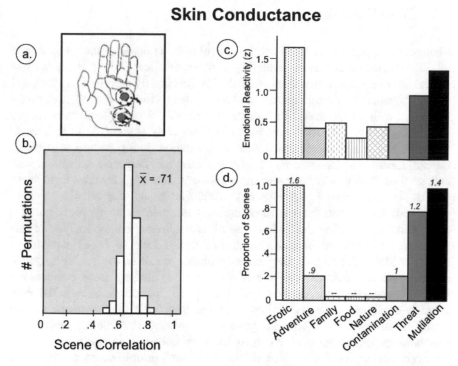

Fig. 3 (**a**) Placement of sensors for measuring skin conductance activity. (**b**) The distribution (and mean) of correlations of emotional reactivity (z) scores for scenes resulting from permutation analyses. (**c**) The mean emotional reactivity (z) score (relative to responses when viewing neutral scenes) averaged over exemplars for each scene content. (**d**) The proportion of exemplars in each scene content among the most reactive (upper half of distribution), and the mean emotional reactivity (z) score for these exemplars (listed above each bar)

most reactive scenes, more than 80% of the erotic, mutilation and threat exemplars elicited emotional reactivity scores in the upper half of the distribution. Although a small proportion of adventure and contamination exemplars appear among the most reactive scenes, the mean emotional reactivity (z) scores for these exemplars (see numbers above bars in Fig. 3d) is consistent with the overall lower emotional reactivity elicited by these scene contents.

Although specific scenes reliably elicit skin conductance activity across individuals, this measure may not be an optimal index of emotional reactivity. It has long been known that a significant proportion of participants (~40%) are non-responders—showing no measurable changes in electrodermal activity across an experiment (Venables and Mitchell 1996). Moreover, skin conductance is highly sensitive to novelty (Bradley 2009), habituating rapidly across the experiment, resulting in many zero trials. A different measure of sympathetic nervous system activation—pupil diameter—holds more promise.

5.3   *Pupil Diameter*

Changes in pupil diameter are under the control of dual muscles—the sphincter and dilator—that are separately innervated by parasympathetic and sympathetic nervous system activity, respectively. Hess and Polt (1960) famously proposed that the pupil dilated ("opened") for positive scenes and constricted ("closed") for negative scenes, consistent with a hypothesis of approach or avoidance for pupillary reactions, but methodological and measurement issues in these early studies led to failures to replicate. Our early studies found that pupil dilation during picture viewing is, instead, sensitive to the intensity of both appetitive and defensive activation, with enhanced pupil dilation for pleasant and unpleasant scenes that covaries highly with skin conductance reactivity (Bradley et al. 2008; Henderson et al. 2014).

The pupillary waveform measured during scene perception typically consists of an initial constriction that is followed by later dilation. Factor analysis of this waveform identifies two independent factors that include an initial constriction that is modulated by scene brightness (probably mediated by parasympathetic nervous system activation) and a later dilation modulated by scene emotionality that is sympathetically mediated (Bradley et al. 2017b). Because the initial light reflex primarily responds to differences in scene brightness and luminance, careful control of these variables during image viewing is critical. Possible controls include matching specific scenes of each content by brightness; equating the brightness for all scenes, and/or controlling the diameter of the pupil prior to scene viewing (e.g., matching upcoming scene brightness).

Despite these controls, however, we found that pupil diameter can also be affected by the brightness of the local region at fixation. A scene of clouds, for instance, prompts overall smaller pupil diameter throughout picture viewing because the foreground information (cloud) is brighter than the background (sky), despite the fact that overall scene brightness is identical to other stimuli. One solution is to present each scene so that the entire image (e.g., all brightness levels) is available at each fixation by reducing the image size, although this manipulation can affect apprehension of emotional content (e.g., De Cesarei & Codispoti 2010). Instead, we presented scenes (equated for overall brightness) in a 5×5 matrix in which the same scene was repeated in all 25 cells (see Fig. 4a). Scene content was not only easy to perceive, but this manipulation was highly effective in removing differences in pupil diameter due to differences in picture brightness at fixation (Bradley et al. 2017b).

Figure 4b illustrates that the reliability of late pupil dilation is quite high, with a mean scene correlation across random cohorts of 0.71 ($p < 0.05$). As found for skin conductance, viewing any emotional content elicited significantly greater pupil dilation than when viewing neutral scenes (see Fig. 4c). Heightened pupil dilation found when viewing erotic scenes was equivalent to that found when viewing scenes of threat and mutilation, and was also elevated and of similar magnitude for scenes of contamination. Erotic and mutilation scenes elicited significantly greater dilation, compared to all other scene contents, with a high proportion of exemplars in each of these contents among the most reactive (see Fig. 4d).

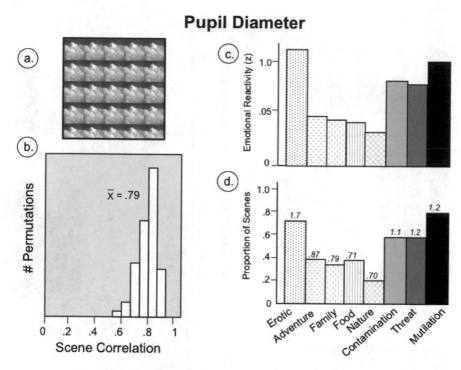

Fig. 4 (a) Example of a 5 × 5 matrix repeating the same image in each cell that is used to control effects of brightness at fixation. (b) The distribution (and mean) of correlations of emotional reactivity (z) scores for scenes resulting from permutation analyses. (c) The mean emotional reactivity (z) score (relative to responses when viewing neutral scenes) averaged over exemplars for each scene content. (d) The proportion of exemplars in each scene content that among the most reactive (upper half of distribution), and the mean emotional reactivity (z) score for these exemplars (listed above each bar)

In general, compared to skin conductance, a larger proportion of exemplars across emotional categories were in the upper half of the distribution of late pupil dilation, suggesting this measure may be sensitive to more modest differences in sympathetic engagement. And although, unlike skin conductance, a sizable proportion of contamination exemplars are among the most reactive scenes (see Fig. 4d), the specific exemplars (and participants) differed for the two measures. Future studies that include both measures and the same exemplars in a within-subject design can address this issue.

5.4 Facial EMG

Facial reactions to emotional events, such as frowns and smiles, are overt actions that primarily serve a social communication role in the real world, but subtle changes in facial muscle activity can be detected by monitoring electromyographic

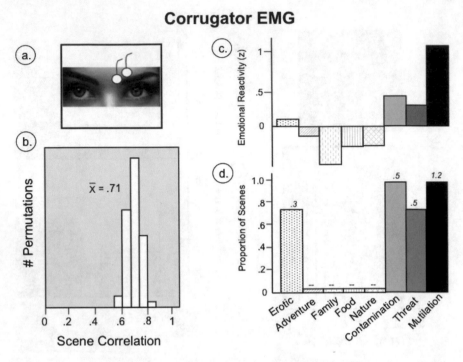

Fig. 5 (**a**) Placement of sensors for measuring corrugator supercili EMG activity. (**b**) The distribution (and mean) of correlations of emotional reactivity (z) scores for scenes resulting from permutation analyses. (**c**) The mean emotional reactivity (z) score (relative to responses when viewing neutral scenes) averaged over exemplars for each scene content. (**d**) The proportion of exemplars in each scene content that are among the most reactive (upper half of distribution), and the mean emotional reactivity (z) score for these exemplars (listed above each bar)

(EMG) activity using electrodes placed over appropriate facial muscles during solitary viewing. Most commonly, activity is measured by placing sensors over the corrugator supercili muscle which is active in facial expressions of frowning, and over the zygomaticus major muscle which is active during smiling. Initial studies found a significant increase in the activity of the corrugator muscle when viewing unpleasant, compared to neutral, pictures (Cacioppo et al. 1986), and unlike the sympathetically mediated skin conductance and pupil diameter changes, heightened corrugator EMG activity is specifically found for unpleasant scenes, with relaxation of this muscle below baseline often found for pleasant scenes (Lang et al. 1993).

Figure 5a illustrates the placement of electrodes when measuring facial corrugator EMG activity. Permutation analyses for corrugator EMG (see Fig. 5b) shows that specific scenes reliably elicit corrugator EMG reactions, with an overall mean scene correlation across random cohorts of $0.76 > 0.71$ ($p < 0.05$). Significantly enhanced EMG activity over the corrugator muscle is found for all unpleasant scene contents, with significant decreases in corrugator EMG activity for scenes of adventure, food, and family. Scenes of mutilation prompted more facial muscle

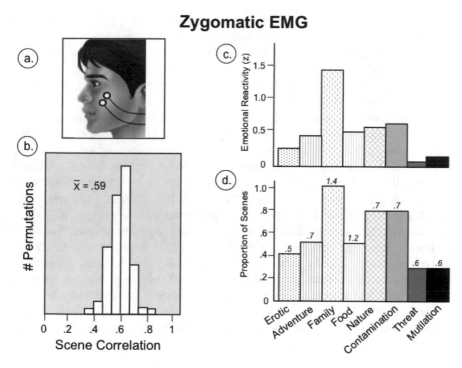

Fig 6 (a) Placement of sensors for measuring zygomatic major EMG activity. (b) The distribution (and mean) of correlations of emotional reactivity (z) scores for scenes resulting from permutation analyses. (c) The mean emotional reactivity (z) score (relative to responses when viewing neutral scenes) averaged over exemplars for each scene content. (d) The proportion of exemplars in each scene content that are among the most reactive (upper half of distribution), and the mean emotional reactivity (z) score for these exemplars (listed above each bar)

activity than all other contents, and scenes of threat and contamination prompted significantly greater corrugator activity than all contents except erotic scenes. When assessing specific exemplars (Fig. 5d), a large proportion of scenes of all unpleasant contents appear among those eliciting the highest corrugator EMG reactions. Although a relatively large proportion of erotic scenes appear among the most reactive scenes, the mean emotional reactivity (z) score for these exemplars is considerably lower (i.e., 0.3) than found for unpleasant scenes.

Figure 6a illustrates the placement of electrodes over the zygomaticus major muscle, which is activated when the cheek is drawn back or tightened such as when smiling (Tassinary et al. 1989). The reliability of specific images in eliciting zygomatic EMG activity is significant, with a mean scene correlation across random cohorts of 0.59 ($p < 0.05$; Fig. 6b). When averaged over exemplars (see Fig. 6c), pleasant scenes of erotic, family, adventure, and nature prompted significantly elevated changes in zygomatic EMG activity, compared to neutral scene viewing ($p < 0.05$), with only family scenes eliciting significantly higher emotional reactivity (z) scores than other pleasant contents. And, although mean zygomatic

(z) reactivity is numerically large for pleasant pictures of food, it does not reach significance ($p = 0.15$), probably because this effect is most pronounced for women (Bradley et al. 2001b). Specific exemplars that were among the most reactive in zygomatic EMG activity (Fig. 6d) include all of the family scenes, which portray babies and children, often smiling, which could implicate a role for facial mimicry in some or all of the zygomatic EMG changes.

On the other hand, a sizable proportion of unpleasant scenes of contamination (~70%) also elicited significant changes (above neutral) in zygomatic EMG activity, which is unexpected if activity over this facial muscle is solely an index of smiling. These data illustrate two important points about facial EMG activity. First, facial muscle activity is not exclusive to a single expression. A grimace communicating disgust, for instance, can involve activity of both the corrugator and zygomatic muscles, leading to co-activation in some affective contexts (Bradley et al. 2001a). In addition to scenes of contamination, erotic scenes also elicited co-activation of corrugator and zygomatic EMG, with some exemplars among the most reactive in both measures. One hypothesis may be that for some subjects (or scenes), pictures of erotica are defensively, rather than appetitively, engaging. On the other hand, facial EMG responses are among the few bodily reactions that are under voluntary control by the individual, and can reflect cultural or political norms that, while communicative in nature, do not necessarily reflect fundamental motivational activation.

5.5 Heart Rate

Early studies of emotional picture perception (e.g., Libby et al. 1973; Klorman et al. 1975; Greenwald et al. 1989) consistently found heart rate slowed (i.e., decelerated) when people view unpleasant scenes. Based on these data, Lacey (1967) hypothesized that cardiac deceleration indexes heightened sensory intake for aversive cues, and, when effects of specific picture content were later assessed, enhanced cardiac deceleration was obtained not only for highly arousing pictures of threat and mutilation, but for all unpleasant contents. When we assessed effects of specific picture content, enhanced cardiac deceleration was obtained not only for highly arousing pictures of threat and mutilation, but also for unpleasant scenes of pollution and loss, which are typically rated lower in arousal (Bradley et al. 2001a; Gomez & Danuser 2010). Cardiac deceleration during aversive picture viewing is reminiscent of a "fear bradycardia" found in animals responding to threat cues (e.g., Campbell et al. 1997) which is vagally mediated and interpreted as reflecting a "stop, look, and listen" stance of heightened sensory intake and orienting (Lacey 1967; Graham 1979). Consistent with a hypothesis of increased sensory intake, later research found that highly arousing pleasant pictures, particularly those involving erotica, also prompt significant initial cardiac deceleration Bradley et al. (2001a) and that all deceleratory cardiac responses are greatly reduced or absent when the same picture is repeatedly presented, attenuating perceptual processing requirements (Bradley et al. 1993; Bradley 2009).

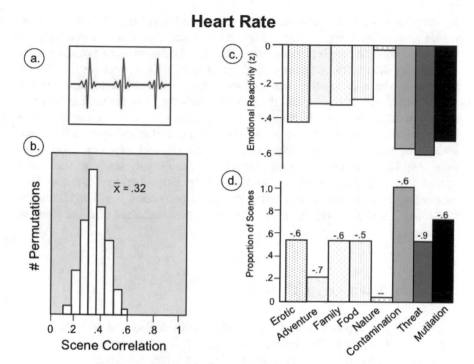

Fig. 7 (**a**) The cardiac waveform illustrating subsequent heart beats. (**b**) The distribution (and mean) of correlations of emotional reactivity (z) scores for scenes resulting from permutation analyses. (**c**) The mean emotional reactivity (z) score (relative to responses when viewing neutral scenes) averaged over exemplars for each scene content. (**d**) The proportion of exemplars in each scene content that are among the most reactive (upper half of distribution), and the mean emotional reactivity (z) score for these exemplars (listed above each bar)

Heart rate is typically measured with the electrocardiogram, producing the well-known cardiac waveform illustrated in Fig. 7a. The length of the time interval between subsequent beats is typically converted offline into the number of beats per minute. Unlike some other physiological measures, the heart is generally busy on a moment-by-moment basis attending to numerous activities linked to its essential role in keeping the body alive, and is strongly coupled to changes in other physiological systems such as respiration and posture, making its sensitivity to emotional or cognitive factors more variable. Thus, the reliability of heart changes for scenes, depicted in Fig. 7b, is somewhat lower than for other physiological measures with a mean scene correlation across random cohorts of 0.32, but nonetheless remains statistically significant ($p < 0.05$).

Figure 7c illustrates emotional reactivity (z) scores for heart rate changes averaged across exemplars in each content category. Significant cardiac deceleration (relative to neutral scene viewing) is found for all scene contents except for nature and family scenes (one tailed $p = 0.06$). Cardiac reactivity (z) scores are equivalent for contamination, threat, and mutilation scenes, and larger than for nature scenes (as are all other contents). Whereas erotic scenes prompt deceleration equivalent to unpleasant contents, unpleasant scenes of threat and contamination prompt greater deceleration than scenes of family, food, or adventure. Consistent with early data suggesting that unpleasant scenes prompt large cardiac deceleration, a sizable proportion of exemplars in each of the unpleasant categories are among the most reactive pictures (see Fig. 7d). None of the nature exemplars were strongly evocative in terms of cardiac deceleration (consistent with the lack of reactivity for this content overall) whereas specific exemplars of erotica, family, and food were among the most reactive, with their emotional reactivity (z) scores comparable to unpleasant scenes. Taken together, cardiac deceleration, perhaps indexing orienting and sensory processing, is significant during emotional scene perception, and heightened for unpleasant, as well as erotic, scenes, and for some exemplars of other pleasant contents.

5.6   Functional Amygdala Activity

Rodent models suggest a role of the amygdala in mediating both defensive (e.g., Davis 1989; LeDoux 1995; Davis & Shi 2000) and appetitive behaviors (Ishikawa et al. 2008), and studies in human and non-human primates support a central role of the amygdala during emotional visual perception through a series of projections to and from the visual cortex (Amaral et al. 1992; Finke et al. 2019; Sabatinelli et al. 2009, 2005; Vuilleumier et al. 2004). The bilateral amygdalae constitute small almond shaped regions deep in the subcortex (Fig. 8a) that are bidirectionally connected with hippocampal (memory), fronto-parietal (attention), insular (autonomic processing), and motor regions, constituting a key hub supporting defensive or appetitive action. Recent studies have consistently found that functional activation of the bilateral amygdala is enhanced when participants view pleasant or unpleasant, compared to neutral scenes (e.g., Chang et al. 2015; Sabatinelli et al. 2009; Sambuco et al. 2020; Wilson et al. 2020).

The reliability of individual scenes in activating the amygdala is not as high as for some measures, but still significant with a mean scene correlation of 0.46 ($p < 0.05$; Fig. 8b). Averaged over scene content (see Fig. 8c), pictures depicting erotica, romance, threat, and mutilation prompt significant functional enhancement in amygdala activity, compared to neutral scene viewing (see Fig. 8c), with scenes of erotica and mutilation showing high reactivity that did not differ. Compared to the least reactive content (adventure), scenes of romance and threat also show enhanced amygdala activation.

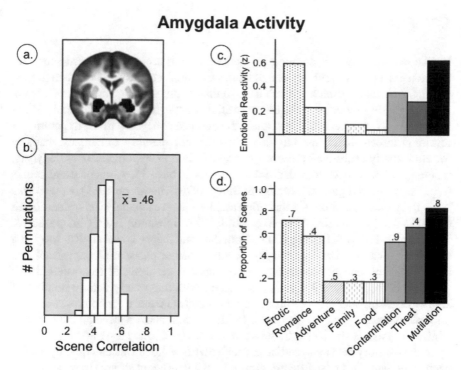

Amygdala Activity

Fig. 8 (a) Illustration of the location of the bilateral amygdalae (solid black regions) in an axial brain slice. (b) The distribution (and mean) of correlations of emotional reactivity (z) scores for scenes resulting from permutation analyses. (c) The mean emotional reactivity (z) score (relative to responses when viewing neutral scenes) averaged over exemplars for each scene content. (d) The proportion of exemplars in each scene content that are among the most reactive (upper half of distribution), and the mean emotional reactivity (z) score for these exemplars (listed above each bar)

On the other hand, amygdala activation for scenes of contamination, which prompts overall high reactivity, was not significantly different from that elicited during neutral scene viewing, suggesting significant variability among exemplars. Consistent with this hypothesis, Fig. 8d indicates that about half of contamination exemplars do appear in the upper half of the distribution (with a relatively high mean emotional reactivity (z) score for these specific scenes. On the other hand, the specific exemplars associated with the most amygdala activation are, for the most part, members of contents that prompt the highest amygdala activation overall, including erotic, threat and mutilation scenes. An exception, perhaps, is that a relatively high proportion of romance exemplars are among the most reactive scenes.

5.7   Free Recall

Unlike evoked 3-system emotional reactions during scene viewing, memory for emotional scenes is a subsequent outcome of initial cognitive and affective processing. Animal research has demonstrated that learning and memory benefit from, and potentially rely on, significant motivational activation, as it is difficult, if not impossible, to study animal cognition in the absence of a motivational imperative—reward or threat—that is used to direct attention and memory. In humans, memory for emotionally evocative events has prompted multiple hypotheses over the years, including a "positivity" bias that holds memory is biased towards pleasant events (e.g., "rosy-colored glasses"; Matlin & Stang 1978; Thompson 1985), as well as a "negativity bias" that proposes that unpleasant events are uniquely well remembered (e.g., "flashbulb memories"; Brown & Kulik 1977; Bohannon 1988; Christianson & Loftus 1987; Harris & Pashler 2005). Both data and theory however, also support a hypothesis that emotionally arousing events, whether pleasant or unpleasant, are associated with enhanced memory performance (e.g., Craik & Blankstein 1975; Eysenck 1976; Walker 1958), and, consistent with these early data, a number of studies assessing memory performance report better memory for both pleasant and unpleasant scenes (e.g., Bradley et al. 1992; Hamann 2001; McGaugh 2004; Steidl et al. 2006) that is similar for both men and women (Bradley et al. 2017a).

In the memory data analyzed here, incidental free recall was obtained by asking each participant (in 1 of 6 different groups viewing different scenes) to write down a word or brief phrase (see Fig. 9a) describing each remembered scene (out of a total possible of 60), providing enough information that another person would be able to identify the exemplar from among the scenes presented. All participants were able to complete free recall within a 5 min allotted time period.

Specific images show very high reliability in terms of free recall, with a mean scene correlation of 0.91 ($p < 0.05$; see Fig. 9b). Figure 9c illustrates emotional memory (z) scores (i.e., recall performance relative to recall of neutral scenes) for specific scene categories, and the pattern is somewhat different from that obtained in many of the physiological measures. Equivalent memory performance is found for scenes of erotic, romance, families, nature, threat, and mutilation, with very poor recall for scenes of adventure, food, and contamination. As illustrated in Fig. 9d, a sizable proportion of the individual exemplars in well-remembered content categories were among the best recalled. These data are consistent with previous data showing better memory for arousing scenes that are either pleasant or unpleasant, together with a small benefit in memory for pleasant scenes that rated in lower arousal (Bradley et al. 2017a), but also suggest that specific scene content is a critical factor mediating free recall performance for emotional scenes.

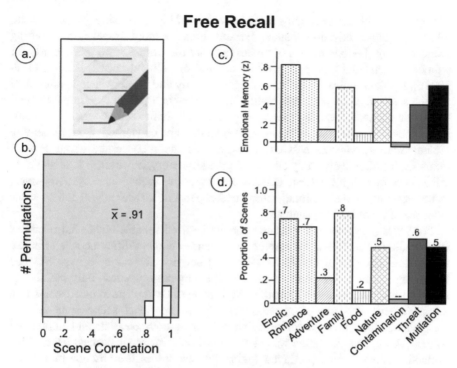

Fig. 9 (**a**) Free recall was measured by writing a brief word or phrase on a sheet of paper. (**b**) The distribution (and mean) of correlations of emotional memory (z) scores for scenes resulting from permutation analyses. (**c**) The mean emotional memory (z) score (relative to responses when viewing neutral scenes) averaged over exemplars for each scene content. (**d**) The proportion of exemplars in each scene content that are among the best recalled (upper half of distribution), and the mean emotional memory (z) score for these exemplars (listed above each bar)

6 Discussion

Specific photographic images are highly reliable elicitors of affective reactions across participants in a variety of 3-systems measures of emotion. The power, to a large degree, is in the picture—scenes that elicited the largest or smallest emotional reactions were quite stable across random cohorts of individuals. Thus, rather than appealing idiosyncratically to different individuals, a specific scene tends to engage enhanced or reduced emotional reactions that is general across participants. Moreover, for a variety of emotional reactions, all or most of the exemplars of a particular scene content were among the most reactive, lending some experimental certainty to selecting stimuli based on scene content.

Among the most reliable (non-evaluative) data measured during affective scene viewing are skin conductance and pupil diameter changes, as well as free recall. For each of these measures, scenes of sex and violence most consistently induced strong emotional reactions (and better recall) in the laboratory, with the majority of exemplars in each content among the most reactive for each measure, consistent with relatively intense activation of appetitive and defensive motivational systems during scene viewing. Despite ratings of modest arousal for erotic scenes (particularly for women, which might be influenced by cultural or political norms, Bradley et al. 2001b), the data indicate that these images strongly and reliably engage emotional reactions. Individual scientists or institutional review boards are sometimes reluctant to use or approve these images in experimental studies. Anecdotally, it seems sometimes that west coast (USA) research tends to be concerned about presenting violent images, whereas east coast research is more concerned about explicit sexuality. To effectively study emotion in the laboratory, however, it is essential to utilize cues that highly activate defensive or appetitive motivational systems, since, in the absence of these stimuli, numerous dependent measures will fail to show evidence of emotional engagement.

For some measures, other scene contents induced reliable emotional reactions (see Bradley et al. 2001a, for further discussion of content differences in affective scene viewing). Corrugator EMG ("frown") activity, for example, was elevated for all unpleasant scene contents (and most exemplars), whereas only pictures of families prompted reliable zygomatic EMG changes. Overall, heart rate deceleration discriminated less than other measures among emotional scene contents, but was, nonetheless, greatest for arousing scenes of both pleasant and unpleasant content. Amgydala activation was elevated not only for erotic scenes, but also for romantic scenes, which portrayed loving interactions in the absence of explicit nudity, suggesting a closer look at this content in other physiological measures. Memory performance was also heightened for scenes of both sex and romance, but also substantially elevated for scenes of families and nature, making it difficult to attribute better recall specifically to intense emotional engagement. Rather, consistent with previous studies demonstrating the effectiveness of specific images in memory performance, additional factors of novelty, distinctiveness, presence of people, etc. (e.g., Bainbridge et al. 2019) may impact emotional scene memory. Taken together, the data identify specific scene contents that are appropriate for inclusion in studies measuring different indices of emotional reactivity.

Although not examined here, some differences exist between men and women in emotional reactivity during scene viewing (e.g., Bradley et al. 2001a; Finke et al. 2017; Sarlo & Buodo 2017). Reports of pleasure and arousal are typically higher for men viewing erotica (and higher for women viewing violence) and both skin conductance changes (Bradley et al. 2001b) and pupil dilation (Finke et al. 2017) are enhanced when men, compared to women, view erotic scenes. Nonetheless, compared to other scene contents, both men and women show enhanced reactivity when viewing erotic scenes, indicating a difference only in degree. Moreover, although specific scenes are reliable elicitors of emotional engagement, of course not all participants are reactive to all scenes. Whereas one experimental impulse may be to select scenes that tend to engage strong affective reactions, another viewpoint argues that including only strong emotional elicitors may reduce the opportunity to observe important individual differences (Lissek et al. 2006), suggesting inclusion of a more comprehensive set that includes scenes that differentially engage emotional reactivity.

Images can be presented in color or grayscale, large or small, for brief or more sustained durations, all of which could affect the size and/or reliability of emotional reactions. Previous studies have determined that evaluative ratings and biological measures of emotional reactivity vary little as function of whether images are presented in color or grayscale (Bradley et al. 2001a, 2003; Codispoti et al. 2001, 2012). Moreover, in the absence of a visual masking stimulus, presentations as brief 25 ms continue to elicit a variety of physiological reactions consistent with emotional engagement (Codispoti et al. 2009). Incredibly, late pupil dilation due to emotional arousal is very similar in magnitude, regardless of whether a scene is presented full screen or repeated as multiple smaller images in a matrix to control local brightness effects (Bradley et al. 2017b). Null effects of these methodological parameters suggest that, to the extent the image is successfully apprehended, motivational activation proceeds. Consistent with this hypothesis, when single images are greatly reduced in size (12.5%; Codispoti & De Cesarei 2007) or spatially blurred (De Cesarei & Codispoti 2010), evaluative ratings and electrodermal responses indicative of emotional engagement disappear.

Image repetition can also have substantial effects on brain and body measures, with repetition suppression—reduced activity for repeated scenes—the most common outcome. In the brain for instance, an extended network that is activated during novel scene processing shows significant reduction with scene repetition, including the amygdala, although differential activation for emotional and neutral scenes is nonetheless retained for at least 4 massed repetitions (Bradley et al. 2015). Similarly, although repetition reduces the size of both skin conductance and pupil diameter changes during scene viewing, differential reactivity for emotional, compared to neutral, scenes remains following modest repetition (Bradley et al. 1993; Bradley & Lang 2015). Heart rate, on the other hand, shows a rather rapid decline of cardiac deceleration that completely disappears with repetition (Bradley et al. 1993; Bradley 2009). Due to differential effects of repetition on 3-system measures, the choice of whether images are repeated or not in an experimental study can be a significant factor in the resulting size and stability of emotional reactions.

A common measure of emotional engagement during scene perception not included in the current analyses are event-related potentials (ERP; measured by sensors placed on the scalp) that can vary in topography, magnitude and/or latency as a function of emotional scene content (e.g., Schupp et al. 2004). ERPs, however, are notoriously noisy on single trials, requiring considerable trial averaging to obtain reasonable estimates of voltage changes. And, because a number of ERP components are particularly sensitive to repetition, reducing in latency and/or amplitude (e.g., Ferrari et al. 2011; Codispoti et al. 2006; Ferrari et al. 2013), a single trial picture analysis such as conducted here is less than optimal for this index of emotional processing.

Taken together, the data confirm that specific scenes reliably elicit affective responses across individuals. On the other hand, the datasets available for the preliminary picture analyses conducted here are missing a number of important controls (e.g. the total number of scenes presented, specific scene contents, the number of exemplars for each content, acquisition of all measures for all participants).

Future research that addresses these paradigmatic differences, and measures 3-system responses in a larger sample of men and women (as well as across lifespan), will provide scientists with an extremely useful database for selecting and balancing images that are most suitable for a specific investigation, as well as allowing more sophisticated multivariate analyses that identifies specific exemplars evidencing cross-system emotional reactivity. Such a database will also be useful in beginning to determine the semantic and/or physical features (e.g. Bainbridge et al. 2019) contributing to the success of specific exemplars. Until such a biological affective picture set is available, however, the data presented here confirm that individual exemplars of specific scene contents reliably engage emotional reactions across participants, and provide initial data-based information for selecting an optimal image set that is suited to the specific goals and measures of the emotional question under investigation.

References

Amaral, D. G., Price, J. L., Pitkanen, A., & Carmichael, S. T. (1992). Anatomical organization of the primate amygdaloid complex. In J. P. Aggleton (Ed.), *The amygdala: Neurobiological aspects of emotion, memory, and mental dysfunction.* (pp.1–66). New York: Wiley.

Bainbridge, W. A., Berron, D., Schütze, H., Cardenas-Blanco, A., Metzger, C., Dobisch, L., …Düzel, E. (2019). Memorability of photographs in subjective cognitive decline and mild cognitive impairment: Implications for cognitive assessment. *Alzheimers Dement (Amst)., 11,* 610–618.

Bohannon, J. N. (1988). Flashbulb memories for the space shuttle disaster: A tale of two theories. *Cognition, 29,* 179–196.

Bradley, M. M. (2009). Natural selective attention: Orienting and emotion. *Journal of Psychophysiology, 46*(1), 1–11. https://doi.org/10.1111/j.1469-8986.2008.00702.x

Bradley, M. M. (2000). Emotion and motivation. In J. T. Cacioppo, L. G. Tassinary, & G. Berntson (Eds.), *Handbook of psychophysiology* (pp. 602–642). New York: Cambridge University Press

Bradley, M. M., Codispoti, M., Cuthbert, B. N., & Lang, P. J. (2001a). Emotion and motivation I: Defensive and appetitive reactions in picture processing. *Emotion, 1*(3), 276–298.

Bradley, M. M., Codispoti, M., Sabatinelli, D., & Lang, P. J. (2001b). Emotion and motivation II: Sex differences in picture processing. *Emotion, 1,* 300–319.

Bradley, M. M., Costa, V. D., Ferrari, V., Codispoti, M., Fitzsimmons, J. R., & Lang, P. J. (2015). Imaging distributed and massed repetitions of natural scenes: Spontaneous retrieval and maintenance. *Human Brain Mapping, 36*(4), 1381–1392. https://doi.org/10.1002/hbm.22708

Bradley, M. M., Greenwald, M. K., Petry, M., & Lang, P. J. (1992). Remembering pictures: Pleasure and arousal in memory. *Journal of Experimental Psychology: Learning, Memory, and Cognition, 18*(2), 379–390. https://doi.org/10.1037//0278-7393.18.2.379

Bradley, M. M., Karlsson, M., & Lang P. J. (2017a). Assessing hedonic bias in emotional scene memory: Implications for clinical science. *Zeitschrift für Psychologie, 225*(3), 223–231. https://doi.org/10.1027/2151-2604/a000306

Bradley, M. M., Sapigao, R., & Lang, P. J. (2017b). Sympathetic ANS modulation of pupil diameter in emotional scene perception: Effects of hedonic content, brightness, and contrast. *Journal of Psychophysiology, 54*(10), 1419–1435. https://doi.org/10.1111/psyp.12890

Bradley, M. M., & Lang, P. J. (1994). Measuring emotion: The Self-Assessment Manikin and the semantic differential. *Journal of Behavior Therapy and Experimental Psychiatry, 25*(1), 49–59. https://doi.org/10.1016/0005-7916(94)90063-9

Bradley, M. M., & Lang, P. J. (2007). The International Affective Picture System (IAPS) in the study of emotion and attention. In J. A. Coan & J. J. B. Allen (Eds.), *Handbook of emotion elicitation and assessment* (pp. 29–46). Oxford University Press.

Bradley, M. M., & Lang, P. J. (2015). Memory, emotion, and pupil diameter: Repetition of natural scenes. *Journal of Psychophysiology, 52*, 1186–1193. https://doi.org/10.1111/psyp.12442

Bradley, M. M., Lang, P. J., & Cuthbert, B. N. (1993). Emotion, novelty, and the startle reflex: Habituation in humans. *Behavioral Neuroscience, 107*, 970–980. https://doi.org/10.1037/0735-7044.107.6.970

Bradley, M. M., Miccoli, L., Escrig, M. A., & Lang, P. J. (2008). The pupil as a measure of emotional arousal and autonomic activation. *Journal of Psychophysiology, 45*(4), 602–607. https://doi.org/10.1111/j.1469-8986.2008.00654.x

Bradley, M. M., Sabatinelli, D., Lang, P. J., Fitzsimmons, J. R., King, W. M., & Desai, P. (2003). Activation of the visual cortex in motivated attention. *Behavioral Neuroscience, 117*(2), 369–380. https://doi.org/10.1037/0735-7044.117.2.369

Brown, R. & Kulik, J. (1977). Flashbulb memories. *Cognition, 5*, 73–99. https://doi.org/10.1016/0010-0277(77)90018-X

Cacioppo, J. T., Petty, R. E., Losch, M. E., & Kim, H. S. (1986). Electromyographic activity over facial muscle regions can differentiate the valence and intensity of affective reactions. *Journal of Personality and Social Psychology, 50*, 260–268. https://doi.org/10.1037//0022-3514.50.2.260

Campbell, B. A., Wood, G., & McBride, T. (1997). Origins of orienting and defensive responses: An evolutionary perspective. In P. J. Lang, R. F. Simons & M. T. Balaban (Eds.), *Attention and orienting: Sensory and motivational processes* (pp. 41–67). Hillsdale, NJ: Lawrence Erlbaum Associates.

Chang, L. J., Gianaros, P. J., Manuck, S. B., Krishnan, A., & Wager, T. D. (2015). A sensitive and specific neural signature for picture-induced negative affect. *PLoS Biology, 13*, e1002180. https://doi.org/10.1371/journal.pbio.1002180

Christianson, S.-Å., & Loftus, E. F. (1987). Memory for traumatic events. *Applied Cognitive Psychology, 1*, 225–239. https://doi.org/10.1002/acp.2350010402

Codispoti, M., Bradley, M. M., Cuthbert, B. N., & Lang, P. J. (2001). Affective reactions to briefly presented pictures. *Journal of Psychophysiology, 38*(3), 474–478. https://doi.org/10.1111/1469-8986.3830474

Codispoti, M., & De Cesarei, A. (2007). Arousal and attention: Picture size and emotional reactions. *Journal of Psychophysiology, 44*, 680–686. https://doi.org/10.1111/j.1469-8986.2007.00545.x

Codispoti, M., De Cesarei, A., & Ferrari, V. (2012). The influence of color on emotional perception of natural scenes. *Journal of Psychophysiology, 49*, 11–16. https://doi.org/10.1111/j.1469-8986.2011.01284.x

Codispoti, M., Ferrari, V. & Bradley, M. M. (2006). Repetitive picture processing: Autonomic and cortical correlates. *Brain Research*, 213–230. https://doi.org/10.1016/j.brainres.2005.11.009

Codispoti, M., Mazzetti, M., & Bradley, M. M. (2009). Unmasking emotion: Exposure duration and emotional engagement. *Journal of Psychophysiology, 46*(4), 731–738. https://doi.org/10.1111/j.1469-8986.2009.00804.x

Craik, F. I. M., & Blankstein, K. R. (1975). Psychophysiology and human memory. In P. H. Venables & M. J. Christie (Eds.), *Res Psychophysiol* (pp. 388–417). London: Wiley.

Davis, M. (1989). The role of the amygdala and its efferent projections in fear and anxiety. In P. Tyrer (Ed.), *Psychopharmacology of anxiety* (pp. 52–79). Oxford: Oxford University Press.

Davis, M., Shi. C.-J. (2000). The amygdala. *Current Biology, 10*. https://doi.org/10.1016/s0960-9822(00)00345-6

De Cesarei, A. D., & Codispoti, M. (2010). Effects of picture size reduction and blurring on emotional engagement. *PLoS ONE, 5*(10), e13399. https://doi.org/10.1371/journal.pone.0013399

Detenber, B. H., & Lang, A. (2010). 16 The influence of form and presentation attributes of media on emotion. In K. Doveling, C. von Scheve, & E.A. Konijn (Eds.), *The Routledge handbook of emotions and mass media*, (pp 275–294). Routledge: London.

de Tommaso, M., Calabrese, R., Vecchio, E., De Vito Francesco, V., Lancioni, G., & Livrea, P. (2009). Effects of affective pictures on pain sensitivity and cortical responses induced by laser stimuli in healthy subjects and migraine patients. *International Journal of Psychophysiology, 74*,139–48. https://doi.org/10.1016/j.ijpsycho.2009.08.004

De Zorzi, L. D., Ranfaing, S., Honoré, J., & Sequeira, H. (2021). Autonomic reactivity to emotion: A marker of subclinical anxiety and depression symptoms? *Journal of Psychophysiology*, e13774. https://doi.org/10.1111/psyp.13774

Dickinson, A., & Dearing, M. F. (1979). Appetitive-aversive interactions and inhibitory processes. In A. Dickinson & R. A. Boakes (Eds.), *Mechanisms of learning and motivation* (pp. 203–231). Hillsdale, NJ: Erlbaum.

Ekman, P. (1971). Universals and cultural differences in facial expressions of emotion. In J. Cole (Ed.), *Nebraska Symposium on Motivation* (Vol. 19, pp. 207–283). Lincoln: University of Nebraska Press.

Eysenck, M. W. (1976). Arousal, learning, and memory. *Psychological Bulletin, 83*, 389–404.

Ferrari, V., Bradley, M. M., Codispoti, M., Karlsson, M., & Lang, P. J. (2013). Repetition and brain potentials when recognizing natural scenes: Task and emotion differences. *Social Cognitive and Affective Neuroscience, 8*(8), 847–854. https://doi.org/10.1093/scan/nss081

Ferrari, V., Bradley, M. M., Codispoti, M., & Lang, P.J. (2011). Repetitive exposure: Brain and reflex measures of emotion and attention. *Journal of Psychophysiology, 48*(4), 515–22. https://doi.org/10.1111/j.1469-8986.2010.01083.x

Ferrari, V. Bruno, N., Chattat, R., & Codispoti, M. (2017). Evaluative ratings and attention across the life span: Emotional arousal and gender. *Cognition & Emotion, 31*, 552–563. https://doi.org/10.1080/02699931.2016.1140020

Finke, J. B., Deuter, C. E., Hengesch, X., & Schächinger, H. (2017). The time course of pupil dilation evoked by visual sexual stimuli: Exploring the underlying ANS mechanisms. *Journal of Psychophysiology, 54*(10), 1444–1458. https://doi.org/10.1111/psyp.12901

Frank, D. W., Costa, V. D., Averbeck, B. B., & Sabatinelli, D. (2019). Directional inter-connectivity of the human amygdala, fusiform gyrus, and orbitofrontal cortex in emotional scene perception. *Journal of Neurophysiology, 122*, 1530–1537. https://doi.org/10.1152/jn.00780.2018

Gomez, P., & Danuser, B. (2010). Cardiovascular patterns associated with appetitive and defensive activation during affective picture viewing. *Journal of Psychophysiology, 47*(3), 540–549. https://doi.org/10.1111/j.1469-8986.2009.00953.x

Graham, F. K. (1979). Distinguishing among orienting, defense, and startle reflexes. In H. D. Kimmel, E. H. van Olst, & J. F. Orlebeke (Eds.), *The Orienting Reflex in Humans. An International Conference Sponsored by the Scientific Affairs Division of the North Atlantic Treaty Organization* (pp. 137–167). Hillsdale, NJ: Lawrence Erlbaum Associates.

Greenwald, M. K., Cook, E. W., & Lang, P. J. (1989). Affective judgment and psychophysiological response: Dimensional covariation in the evaluation of pictorial stimuli. *Journal of Psychophysiology, 3*, 51–64.

Hamann, S. (2001). Cognitive and neural mechanisms of emotional memory. *Trends in Cognitive Sciences, 5*, 394–400. https://doi.org/10.1016/S1364-6613(00)01707-1

Harris, C. R., & Pashler, H. (2005). Enhanced memory for negatively emotionally charged pictures without selective rumination. *Emotion, 5*, 191–199. https://doi.org/10.1037/1528-3542.5.2.191

Henderson, R. R., Bradley, M. M., & Lang, P. J. (2014). Modulation of the initial light reflex during affective picture viewing. *Journal of Psychophysiology, 51*, 815–818. https://doi.org/10.1111/psyp.12236

Hermanns, N., Kubiak, T., & Kulzer, B. (2003). Emotional changes during experimentally induced hypoglycaemia in type 1 diabetes. *Biological Psychology, 63*, 15–44. https://doi.org/10.1016/s0301-0511(03)00027-9

Hess, E. H., & Polt, J. M. (1960). Pupil size as related to interest value of visual stimuli. *Science, 132*, 349–350. https://doi.org/10.1126/science.132.3423.349

Hugdahl, K. (1981). The three system model of fear and emotion: A critical examination. *Biology: Research & Therapy, 19*, 75–85. https://doi.org/10.1016/0005-7967(81)90114-5

Huijbers, M. J., Bergmann, H. C., Rikkert, M. G. M. O, & Kessels, R. P. C. (2011). Memory for emotional pictures in patients with Alzheimer's dementia. *Journal of Aging Research, 2011*, 409364. https://doi.org/10.4061/2011/409364

Ihssen, N., Cox, W. M., Wiggett, A., Fadardi, J. S., & Linden, D. E. (2011). Differentiating heavy from light drinkers by neural responses to visual alcohol cues and other motivational stimuli. *Cerebral Cortex, 21*(6), 1408–1415.

Ishikawa, A., Ambroggi, F., Nicola, S. M., Fields H. L. (2008). Contributions of the amygdala and medial prefrontal cortex to incentive cue responding. *The Journal of Neuroscience, 155*, 573–584

Klorman, R., Weissberg, A. R., & Austin, M. L. (1975). Autonomic responses to affective visual stimuli. *Journal of Psychophysiology, 11*, 15–26.

Konorski, J. (1967). *Integrative activity of the brain: An interdisciplinary approach.* Chicago, IL: University of Chicago Press.

Lacey, J. I. (1967). Somatic response patterning and stress: Some revisions of activation theory. In M. H. Appley & R. Trumbull (Eds.), *Psychological stress: Issues in research* (pp. 14–38). New York: Appleton-Century-Crofts.

Lang, P. J. (1968). Fear reduction and fear behaviour: Problems in treating a construct. In J. M. Shilen (Ed.), *Research in psychotherapy* (Vol. 3) Washington D.C.: American Psychological Association.

Lang, P. J. (1980). Behavioral treatment and bio-behavioral assessment: Computer applications. In J. B. Sidowski, J. H. Johnson, & T A. Williams (Eds.), *Technology in mental health care delivery systems* (pp. 119–137). Norwood, NJ: Ablex Publishing.

Lang, P.J. (2010). Emotion and motivation: Toward consensus definitions and a common research purpose. *Emotion Review, 2*, 229–233. https://doi.org/10.1177/1754073910361984

Lang, P. J., & Bradley, M. M. (2010). Emotion and the motivational brain. *Biological Psychology, 84*(3), 437–450. https://doi.org/10.1016/j.biopsycho.2009.10.007

Lang, P. J., & Bradley, M. M. (2013). Appetitive and defensive motivation: Goal-directed or goal-determined? *Emotion Review, 5*, 230–234.

Lang, P. J. & Bradley, M. M. (2018). What is emotion? A natural science perspective. In R. Davidson, A. Shackman, A. Fox, & R. Lapate (Eds.), *The nature of emotion* (2nd ed., pp. 11–13). Oxford University Press.

Lang, P. J., Bradley, M. M., & Cuthbert, M. M. (1997). Motivated attention: Affect, activation and action. In P. J. Lang, R. F. Simons, & M. T. Balaban (Eds.), *Attention and orienting: Sensory and motivational processes.* Hillsdale, NJ: Lawrence Erlbaum Associates.

Lang, P. J., Bradley, M. M., & Cuthbert, B. N. (2008). *International affective picture system (IAPS): Affective ratings of pictures and instruction manual. Technical Report A-8.* Gainesville, FL: University of Florida.

Lang, P. J., Greenwald, M. K., Bradley, M. M., & Hamm, A. O. (1993). Looking at pictures: Affective, facial, visceral, and behavioral reactions. *Biological Psychology, 30*(3), 261–273.

Lasaitis, C., Ribeiro, R. L., Bueno, O. F. A. (2008). Brazilian norms for the International Affective Picture System (IAPS)—comparison of the affective ratings for new stimuli between Brazilian and North-American subjects. *Jornal Brasileiro de Psiquiatria, 57*, 270–275. https://doi.org/10.1590/S0047-20852008000400008

LeDoux, J.E.(1995). Emotion: Clues from the brain. *Annual Review of Psychology, 46*, 209–235. https://doi.org/10.1146/annurev.ps.46.020195.001233

Libby, W. L., Lacey, B. C., & Lacey, J. I. (1973). Pupillary and cardiac activity during visual attention. *Journal of Psychophysiology, 10*, 270–294.

Lissek, S., Pine, D. S., & Grillon, C. (2006). The strong situation: A potential impediment to studying the psychobiology and pharmacology of anxiety disorders. *Biological Psychology, 72*, 265–270.

Löw, A., Lang, P. J., Smith, J. C., & Bradley, M. M. (2008). Both predator and prey: emotional arousal in threat and reward. *Psychological Science, 19*(9), 865–73. https://doi.org/10.1111/j.1467-9280.2008.02170.x

Matlin, M. W., & Stang, D. J. (1978). *The pollayanna principle: Selectivity in language, memory, and thought.* Cambridge, MA: Schenkman.

McGaugh, J. L. (2004). The amygdala modulates the consolidation of memories of emotionally arousing experiences. *Annual Review of Neuroscience, 27*, 1–28. https://doi.org/10.1146/annurev.neuro.27.070203.144157

Molto, J., Montanes, S., Poy, R., Segarra, P., Pastor, M. C., Tormo, M. P., … Vila, J. (1999). Un Nuevo metodo para el estudio experimental de las emociones: El International Affective Picture System (IAPS). Adaptacion Espanola. *Rev de Psicol. Gral y Aplic, 52*, 55–87.

Plutchik, R. (1980). A general psychoevolutionary theory of emotion. In R. Plutchik & H. Kellerman (Eds.), *Emotion: Theory, research and experience, volume 1: Theories of emotion* (pp. 3–31). New York: Academic Press.

Renfroe, J. B., Bradley, M. M., Okun, M. S., & Bowers, D. (2016). Motivational engagement in Parkinson's disease: Preparation for motivated action. *International Journal of Psychophysiology, 99*, 24–32. https://doi.org/10.1016/j.ijpsycho.2015.11.014

Sabatinelli, D., Bradley, M. M., Fitzsimmons, J. R., & Lang, P. J. (2005). Parallel amygdala and inferotemporal activation reflect emotional intensity and fear relevance. *Neuroimage, 24*, 1265–1270. https://doi.org/10.1016/j.neuroimage.2004.12.015.2005

Sabatinelli, D., Lang, P. J., Bradley, M. M., Costa, V. D., & Keil, A. (2009). The timing of emotional discrimination in human amygdala and ventral visual cortex. *The Journal of Neuroscience, 29*, 14864–14868. https://doi.org/10.1523/JNEUROSCI.3278-09.2009

Sambuco, N., Bradley, M. M., Herring, D. R., & Lang, P. J. (2020). Common circuit or paradigm shift? The functional brain in emotional scene perception and emotional imagery. *Journal of Psychophysiology, 57*(4), e13522. https://doi.org/10.1111/psyp.13522

Sarlo, M., & Buodo, G. (2017). To each its own? Gender differences in affective, autonomic, and behavioral responses to same-sex and opposite-sex visual sexual stimuli. *Physiology & Behavior, 171*, 249–255. https://doi.org/10.1016/j.physbeh.2017.01.017

Schneirla, T. (1959). An evolutionary and developmental theory of biphasic processes underlying approach and withdrawal. In M. Jones (Ed.), *Nebraska Symposium on Motivation* (pp. 1–42). Lincoln: University of Nebraska Press.

Schupp, H. T., Cuthbert, B. N., Bradley, M. M., Hillman, C. H., Hamm, A. O., & Lang, P. J. (2004). Brain processes in emotional perception: Motivated attention. *Cognition and Emotion, 18*, 593–611.

Steidl, S. Mohi-uddin, S., & Anderson, A.K. (2006). Effects of emotional arousal on multiple memory systems: Evidence from declarative and procedural learning. *Learning & Memory, 13*, 650–658. https://doi.org/10.1101/lm.324406

Tassinary, L. G., Cacioppo, J. T., & Geen, T. R. (1989). A psychometric study of surface electrode placements for facial electromyographic recording: I. the brow and cheek muscle regions. *Journal of Psychophysiology, 26*, 1–16. https://doi.org/10.1111/j.1469-8986.1989.tb03125.x

Thompson, C. P. (1985). Memory for unique personal events: Effects of pleasantness. *Motivation and Emotion, 9*, 277–289. https://doi.org/10.1007/BF00991832

Venables P.H., & Mitchell D.A. (1996). The effects of age, sex and time of testing on skin conductance activity. *Biological Psychology, 43*, 87–101.

Verschuere, B., Crombez, G., & Koster, E. (2001). The International Affective Picture System: A Flemish validation study. *Psychologica Belgica, 41*, 205–217.

Vuilleumier, P., Richardson, M. P., Armony, J. L., Driver, J., & Dolan, R. J. (2004). Distant influences of amygdala lesion on visual cortical activation during emotional face processing. *Nature Neuroscience, 7*, 1271–278. https://doi.org/10.1038/nn1341

Walker, E. L. (1958). Action decrement and its relation to learning. *Psychological Review, 65*, 129–142.

Wilson, K. A., James, G. A., Kilts, C. D., & Bush, K. A. (2020). Combining physiological and neuroimaging measures to predict affect processing induced by affectively valent image stimuli. *Scientific Reports, 10*(1), 9298. https://doi.org/10.1038/s41598-020-66109-3

Winton, W. M., Putnam, L. E., & Krauss, R. M. (1984). Facial and autonomic manifestations of the dimensional structure of emotion. *Journal of Experimental Social Psychology, 20*, 195–216.

Computational Emotion Analysis From Images: Recent Advances and Future Directions

Sicheng Zhao, Quanwei Huang, Youbao Tang, Xingxu Yao, Jufeng Yang, Guiguang Ding, and Björn W. Schuller

1 Introduction

With the rapid development and popularity of social networks, such as Twitter[1] and Sina Weibo.[2] people tend to express and share their opinions and emotions online using text, images, and videos. Understanding the information contained in the increasing repository of data is of vital importance to behavior sciences (Pang & Lee 2008), which aim to predict human decision making and enable wide applications, such as mental health evaluation (Guntuku et al. 2019), business recommendation (Pan et al. 2014), opinion mining (Tumasjan et al. 2010), and entertainment assistance (Zhao et al. 2020).

Analyzing media data on an affective (emotional) level belongs to affective computing, which is defined as *"the computing that relates to, arises from, or influences emotions"* (Picard 2000). The importance of emotions has been emphasized for decades since Minsky introduced the relationship between intelligence and emotion (Minsky 1986). One famous claim is *"The question is not whether*

---

[1] https://twitter.com.
[2] http://www.weibo.com.

S. Zhao (✉) · Q. Huang · G. Ding
Tsinghua University, Beijing, China

Y. Tang
PAII Inc., Palo Alto, CA, USA

X. Yao · J. Yang
Nankai University, Tianjin, China

B. W. Schuller
GLAM, Imperial College London, London, UK

intelligent machines can have any emotions, but whether machines can be intelligent without emotions." Based on the types of media data, the research on affective computing can be classified into different categories, such as text (Giachanou & Crestani 2016; Zhang et al. 2018), image (Zhao et al. 2018), speech (Schuller 2018), music (Yang & Chen 2012), facial expression (Li & Deng 2020), video (Wang & Ji 2015; Zhao et al. 2020), physiological signals (Alarcao & Fonseca 2019), and multi-modal data (Soleymani et al. 2017; Poria et al. 2017; Zhao et al. 2019).

The adage *"a picture is worth a thousand words"* indicates that images can convey rich semantics. Therefore, images are used as an important channel to express emotions. Image emotion analysis (IEA) has recently been paid much attention. As compared to analyzing the images' cognitive aspect that is related with objective content (Hanjalic 2006), such as object classification and semantic segmentation, IEA focuses on understanding what emotions can be induced by the images in viewers. The challenges of affective gap and perception subjectivity (Zhao et al. 2018) make IEA a difficult task.

In this chapter, we concentrate on introducing recent advances on IEA— especially our recent efforts from a computational perspective and on suggesting future research directions. First, we briefly introduce some popular emotion representation models from psychology in Sect. 2, define corresponding key computational problems, and provide some representative supervised frameworks in Sect. 3. Second, we introduce the major challenges in IEA in Sect. 4. Third, we present some representative methods on different computational components, such as emotion feature extraction in Sect. 5 and supervised classifier learning as well as domain adaptation in Sect. 6. Then, we introduce some typical datasets for IEA evaluation in Sect. 7 and investigate the performances of different features and classifiers on these datasets in Sect. 8, as emotions can be conveyed by various features, as shown in Fig. 1. Finally, we give a discussion on what questions are still open and provide some suggestions for future research in Sect. 9.

2   Emotion Representation Models from Psychology

Psychologists have proposed different theories to explain the what, how, and why behind human emotions (Plutchik & Kellerman 2013). For example, the James-Lange theory suggests that emotions occur as a result of physiological reactions to events; the Cognitive Appraisal theory claims that the sequence of events first involves a stimulus, followed by thought, which then leads to the simultaneous physiological response and emotion. Some other emotion theories include the Evolutionary theory, the Cannon-Bard theory, the Schachter-Singer Theory, and the Facial-Feedback theory (Plutchik & Kellerman 2013).

Besides emotion, several other concepts (e. g., affect, sentiment, feeling, and mood) are also widely used in psychology. The difference or correlation of these concepts can be found in Munezero et al. (2014). In this chapter, we focus on a computational perspective and do not distinguish them clearly, except sentiment

Fig. 1 The emotions conveyed by different kinds of images are correlated with different features Zhao et al. (2014): (**a**) Aesthetic features (low saturation, cool color, low color difference); (**b**) Attributes (snow, skiing); (**c**) Semantic concepts described by adjective noun pairs (broken car); (**d**) Facial expressions (happiness). (**a**) Fear. (**b**) Excitement. (**c**) Sadness. (**d**) Contentment

for positive/negative/neutral categories and emotion for more fine-grained definitions. Another relevant concept is about expected, induced, or perceived emotion. Expected emotion is the emotion that the image creator intends to make people feel, perceived emotion is what people perceive as being expressed, while induced/felt emotion is the actual emotion that is felt by a viewer. Interested readers can refer to Juslin and Laukka (2004) for more details. Unless otherwise specified, the emotion focused in this chapter is about induced emotion because of the dataset construction process.

To quantitatively measure emotion, psychologists have mainly employed two types of emotion representation models, categorical emotion states (CES) and dimensional emotion space (DES) (Zhao et al. 2018). For CES, a set of preselected categories is used to define emotions. Some popular CES models include binary sentiment (positive and negative, sometimes including neutral), Ekman's six basic emotions (happiness, surprise and *negative* anger, disgust, fear, and sadness) (Ekman 1992), and Mikels's eight emotions (amusement, anger, awe, contentment, disgust, excitement, fear, and sadness) (Mikels et al. 2005). More diverse and fine-grained emotion categories are being increasingly considered. In Plutchik's emotion model (Plutchik 1980), each basic emotion category (anger, anticipation, disgust, fear, joy, sadness, surprise, and trust) is organized into three intensities. For example, the three intensities from low to high for surprise are distraction⟶surprise⟶amazement. Parrott represents emotions with a three-level hierarchy, i.e., primary (positive and negative), secondary (anger, fear, joy, love, sadness, and surprise), and tertiary (25 fine-grained categories) (Parrott 2001). For DES, a 2D, 3D, or higher dimensional Cartesian space is employed to represent emotions, such as valence-arousal-dominance (VAD) (Schlosberg 1954) and activity-temperature-weight (Lee & Park 2011). VAD is the most widely used DES model, where 'V' represents the pleasantness ranging from positive to negative, 'A' represents the intensity of emotion ranging from excited to calm, and 'D' represents the degree of control ranging from controlled to in control.

Intuitively, CES models are easy for users to understand, but limited emotion categories cannot well reflect the complexity and subtlety of emotions. Further, psychologists have not reached a consensus on how many categories should be included. Theoretically, all emotions can be measured as different coordinate points in the continuous Cartesian space. However, such absolute continuous values are difficult for non-experts to understand. Specifically, CES can be transformed to DES but not all Cartesian points can correspond to detailed categories (Alarcão & Fonseca 2018). For example, fear is often related to negative valence, high arousal, and low dominance. In this chapter, the employed CES models mainly include binary sentiment and Mikels's eight emotions, and VAD is employed as the DES model.

3 Key Computational Problems and Supervised Frameworks

Based on different emotion representation models, we can perform different IEA tasks: classification/retrieval based on CES, and regression/retrieval based on DES. Current methods mainly employ supervised methods with the help of available labeled datasets. In this section, we will define the key computational problems and provide representative supervised frameworks.

3.1 Emotion Classification and Regression

Suppose all images in the dataset are grouped into K emotion categories, then emotion prediction can be conceived as a multi-class classification problem. Based on the model trained on given training samples, an emotion category that is most likely evoked in humans is assigned to a test image. Suppose we have N training images $\{(\mathbf{x}_i, y_i)_{i=1}^{N}\}$, where $y_i \in \{1, 2, \cdots, K\}$. Let $g_\mu(\mathbf{x})$ denote the feature extractor of image $\mathbf{x}$, and then our goal is to learn some model $h_\theta(g_\mu(\mathbf{x})) : g_\mu(\mathbf{x}) \to y$ that maps image features $g_\mu(\mathbf{x})$ to emotion labels y, where μ and θ are parameters. Usually, the learning process is transformed to a parameter optimization problem, which can be defined as

$$J(\omega, \theta, \mu) = \sum_{i=1}^{N} f_\omega(h_\theta(g_\mu(\mathbf{x}_i)), y_i),$$

$$[\omega^*, \theta^*, \mu^*] = \arg \min_{\omega, \theta, \mu} J(\omega, \theta, \mu),$$

(1)

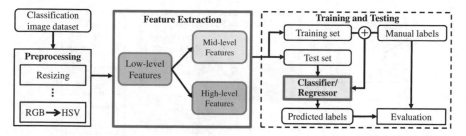

Fig. 2 Commonly used supervised framework of affective image classification and regression. The key components researchers have been studying lie in the solid blue rectangles

where $f_\omega(.,.)$ is a function with parameters ω to compute the loss function $J(\omega, \theta, \mu)$ between the predicted labels and the ground truth, and arg min is the argument of the minimum. Once we work out μ and θ, given a test image $\mathbf{x}_{te}$, we can obtain the prediction label $h_\theta(g_\mu(\mathbf{x}_{te}))$.

Emotion regression assumes that emotions are represented by continuous dimensional values instead of discrete emotion labels, i.e., y is continuous. Except this, the learning process of emotion regression is analogous to emotion classification.

The commonly used supervised framework of affective image classification and regression is shown in Fig. 2. Firstly, some preprocessing is done to 'normalize' the images. Then, different features are extracted for each image, which presents the core of image emotion analysis and will be described in detail. The dataset is split into a training set and a test set. A classifier or regressor is trained using the training set along with the emotion labels based on certain learning models. The images in the test set are then automatically classified by the trained classifier or regressed by the trained regressor. The assigned emotion labels are compared with the ground truth to evaluate the classification or regression performance.

3.2 Emotion Retrieval

Affective image retrieval, firstly named emotional semantic image retrieval (Wang & He 2008), involves searching for images that express similar emotions to the query image. Affective image retrieval can be formalized as a reranking problem to ensure that the top ranked images are the ones emotionally similar to the query image.

Suppose the features and emotion label of a given query image $\mathbf{x}_q$ are $g_\mu(\mathbf{x}_q)$ and y_q, and in the dataset there are N_s emotionally similar images, in which the features and labels of the ith image are $\mathbf{x}_i^s$ and y_i^s, where $y_i^s == y_q, i = 1, 2, \cdots, N_s$, and N_d emotionally different images, in which the features and labels of the jth image are $\mathbf{x}_j^d$ and y_j^d, where $y_j^d \neq y_q, j = 1, 2, \cdots, N_d$. Then, our goal is to minimize

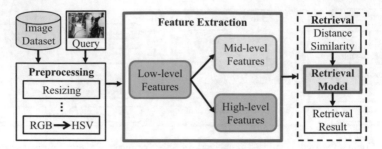

Fig. 3 Commonly used supervised framework of affective image retrieval. The key components researchers have been studying lie in the solid blue rectangles

the distance between the query image and the N_s positive images and maximize the distance between the query image and the N_d negative images:

$$J_s(\theta, \mu) = \sum_{i=1}^{N_s} h_\theta(D(g_\mu(\mathbf{x}_i^s), g_\mu(\mathbf{x}_q))),$$

$$J_d(\theta, \mu) = \sum_{j=1}^{N_d} h_\theta(D(g_\mu(\mathbf{x}_j^d), g_\mu(\mathbf{x}_q))), \qquad (2)$$

$$J(\omega, \theta, \mu) = f_\omega(J_s(\theta, \mu), J_d(\theta, \mu)),$$

$$[\omega^*, \theta^*, \mu^*] = \arg \min_{\omega, \theta, \mu} J(\omega, \theta, \mu),$$

where $D(., .)$ is a distance function to compute the distance between two feature vectors, such as the Minkowski-form distance and the Mahalanobis distance, $h_\theta(.)$ is a function with parameters θ to compute a cost of the query image and the image in the dataset, $f_\omega(., .)$ is a function with parameters ω to compute the total cost $J(\omega, \theta, \mu)$ between the positive cost $J_s(\theta, \mu)$ and the negative cost $J_d(\theta, \mu)$. Once we work out μ and θ, we can get the retrieval results by sorting the cost.

The commonly used supervised framework of affective image retrieval is shown in Fig. 3. The preprocessing and feature extraction parts are similar to the related parts in emotion classification and regression. The distance or similarity is computed between the features of the query image and each image in the dataset. Through some retrieval model, we sort the distance or similarity and obtain the retrieval results, which are compared with the ground truth for evaluation.

4   Major Challenges

Affective Gap The affective gap is one main challenge for IEA, which is defined as the inconsistency between extracted low-level features and induced emotions (Hanjalic 2006; Zhao et al. 2018). As compared to the semantic gap in computer vision,

i. e., the discrepancy between the limited descriptive power of low-level visual features and the richness of user semantics (Smeulders et al. 2020; Liu et al. 2007), the affective gap is even more challenging. Bridging the semantic gap cannot guarantee bridging the affective gap. For example, images containing a barking dog and a loving dog are both about dogs but obviously induce different emotions. To bridge the affective gap, the main efforts have been focusing on designing and extracting discriminative emotion features, ranging from the early hand-crafted features to more recent deep ones. Based on these features, a dominant emotion category (DEC) is assigned to an image by traditional single-label learning-based methods.

Perception Subjectivity Emotion is a highly subjective and complex variable. Different viewers may perceive totally different emotions to the same image, which is influenced by many factors, such as culture, education, personality, and environment (Zhao et al. 2018). For example, for a sudden heavy snow, some may feel excitement to see such rare natural scenes, some may feel sadness because the planned activities have to be cancelled, some may feel amusement since they can build a snowman, etc. For the subjectivity challenge, one direct and intuitive solution is to predict emotions for each viewer via personalized learning models (Zhao et al. 2018). When a large number of viewers are involved, we can assign the image with multiple emotion labels via multi-label learning methods. Since the importance or extent of different labels is actually unequal, predicting the probability distribution of emotions, either discrete (Yang et al. 2017; Zhao et al. 2020) or continuous (Zhao et al. 2017), would make more sense.

Label Noise and Absence Recent deep learning based IEA methods have achieved state-of-the-art performances with the help of large-scale labeled training data. However, in real applications, it is expensive and time-consuming and even impossible to obtain sufficient data with emotion labels to train a deep model. It would be more practical if we can deal with the situation that there are only few or even no emotion labels. We can conduct unsupervised/weakly supervised learning (Wei et al. 2020) and few/zero shot learning (Zhan et al. 2019). One might consider leveraging the large amount of weakly-labeled web images (Wei et al. 2020). Since the associated tags might contain noise that is unrelated to emotion and even to visual semantics, filtering such automatic labels is necessary. Another possible solution is to transfer the well-learned model on one labeled source domain to another unlabeled or sparsely labeled target domain. Direct transfer often results in obvious performance decay, because of the influence of domain shift (Zhao et al. 2021), i. e., the joint distribution of images and emotion labels are different across domains. To bridge the domain shift challenge, we can employ domain adaptation and domain generalization techniques (Zhao et al. 2021).

5 Emotion Features

In this section, we summarize the features that have been widely extracted for IEA, including both hand-crafted and deep features. We first give an brief overview and then introduce some representative ones especially our recent work.

5.1 Hand-Crafted Features

Overview Early efforts on IEA mainly focused on hand-crafting features from different levels. *Low-level features* are used in the earliest IEA methods, which suffer from large affective gap and low interpretability. Some generic features from computer vision, such as Gabor, HOG, and GIST, are directly used in the IEA task (Yanulevskaya et al. 2008). Some specific features derived from elements of art, including color and texture, are implemented (Machajdik & Hanbury 2010). Low-level color features include mean saturation and brightness, vector based mean hue, emotional coordinates (pleasure, arousal and dominance) based on brightness and saturation, colorfulness and color names. Low-level texture features include Tamura texture, Wavelet textures, and gray-level co-occurrence matrix (GLCM) based texture (Machajdik & Hanbury 2010). Low-level shape features, including line segments, angles, continuous lines, and curves, are designed in Lu et al. (2012). As compared to low-level features, *mid-level features* are more interpretable, semantic, and relevant to emotions. Different types of attributes people use to describe scenes, such as materials, surface properties, functions or affordances, spatial envelope attributes, and object presence are modeled (Yuan et al. 2013). Features inspired from principles of art, such as symmetry, emphasis, harmony, and variety, are specially designed (Zhao et al. 2014). *High-level features* describe the detailed content in an image through which viewers can easily understand the semantics and evoked emotions. Some representative high-level features include adjective noun pairs detected by SentiBank Borth et al. (2013) and recognized facial expressions (Yang et al. 2010).

Mid-level Principles-of-art Based Emotion Features The principles of art are defined as the rules, tools, or guidelines of arranging and orchestrating the elements of art in an artwork. They consider various artistic aspects including balance, emphasis, harmony, variety, gradation, movement, rhythm, and proportion (Zhao et al. 2014). The comparison of elements of art and principles of art is shown in Fig. 4. Six principles of art are formulated and implemented systematically in Zhao et al. (2014) based on related art theory and multimedia research. Totally, a 165 dimensional feature can be obtained for each image. For example, emphasis, also known as contrast, is used to stress the difference of certain elements, which can be accomplished by using sudden and abrupt changes in elements. Itten color contrast, which is defined to coordinate colors using the hue's contrasting properties, is implemented (Zhao et al. 2014), including contrast of saturation, contrast of light

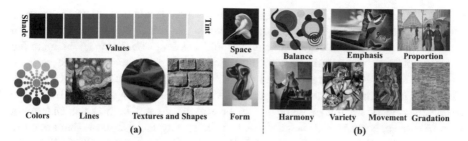

Fig. 4 Illustration of artistic elements and artistic principles, which are designed as low-level and mid-level emotion features. (**a**) Elements of art. (**b**) Principles of art

and dark, contrast of extension, contrast of complements, contrast of hue, contrast of warm and cold, and simultaneous contrast. The results show that principles of art features are more correlated with emotions than elements of art (Zhao et al. 2014). For example, images with high balance and harmony values tend to express positive emotions.

High-Level Adjective Noun Pairs The adjective noun pairs (ANPs) are detected by a large detector library SentiBank (Borth et al. 2013), which is trained using GIST, a 3×256 dimension color histogram, a 53 dimensional LBP descriptor, a Bag-of-Words quantized descriptor using a 1000 word dictionary with a 2-layer spatial pyramid and max pooling, and a 2000 dimensional attribute on about 500k images downloaded from Flickr. Liblinear support vector machine (SVM) (Fan et al. 2008) is used as classifier and early fusion is adopted. The advantages of ANP are that it turns a neutral noun into an ANP with strong emotions and makes the concepts more detectable, as compared to nouns and adjectives, respectively. Finally, a 1200 dimensional double vector representing the probability of the ANPs is obtained.

5.2 Deep Features

Overview With the development of deep learning, especially convolutional neural networks (CNNs), learning-based deep features have been widely employed with superior performances as compared to hand-crafted ones. *Global features* are directly extracted from the whole images. One direct and intuitive method is to employ the output of the last few fully connected (FC) layers as deep features, using either pretrained or finetuned CNN models (Xu et al. 2014; Chen et al. 2015; You et al. 2016). The last few FC layers correspond to high-level semantic features, which might be not enough to represent emotions, especially for abstract images. Therefore, some methods try to extract multi-level deep features (Rao et al. 2020; Zhu et al. 2017; Yang et al. 2018). For example, three parallel networks, namely an Alexnet, an aesthetics CNN, and a texture CNN, are trained with different levels of image patches as input. Deep representations at three levels, i. e., image semantics, image aesthetics, and low-level visual features are extracted. The features from different layers in CNNs are extracted as multi-level representations, which are fed into a bidirectional gated recurrent unit model to exploit the dependency among different levels of features (Zhu et al. 2017). The above methods treat different regions of an image equally. Based on the fact that some regions can determine the emotion of an image while the other regions do not help much and might even reverse, some recent methods focus on extracting *local features* that are more discriminative for IEA (You et al. 2017; She et al. 2020; Zhao et al. 2019; Yao et al. 2020).

Weakly Supervised Coupled Networks (WSCNet) WSCNet contains two branches for joint emotion detection and classification (She et al. 2020). One is the detection branch which is designed to generate region proposals that evoke emotion. A soft sentiment map is generated by a cross-spatial pooling strategy to summarize all the information contained in the feature maps for each category. The regions of interest that are informative for classification are highlighted in the sentiment map. The advantage of such setting is that the network can be trained with image-level emotion labels, without requiring time-consuming region-level annotation. The other is the classification branch designed for the emotion classification task by considering both global and local representations. The global features are extracted from a fully convolutional network (FCN), while the local features are obtained by coupling the generated sentiment map in the detection branch with the global features.

Polarity-Consistent Deep Attention Network (PDANet) The feature maps of PDANet from a FCN are fed into two branches (Zhao et al. 2019), as shown in Fig. 5. Each branch is a multi-layer neural network. One is used to estimate the spatial attention to emphasize the emotional semantic-related regions by two 1×1 convolutional layers and a hyperbolic tangent function. The other is used to estimate the channel-wise attention to consider the interdependency between different channels by one 1×1 convolutional layer and a sigmoid function. The attended semantic vectors that capture the global and local information respectively are concatenated as the final feature representations for IEA tasks.

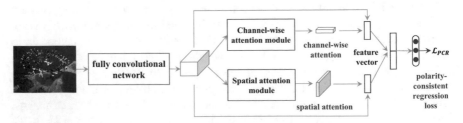

Fig. 5 Overview of the polarity-consistent deep attention network (PDANet) Zhao et al. (2019) to extract attended features for IEA

Attention-Aware Polarity-Sensitive Embedding (APSE) APSE utilizes a hierarchical attention mechanism to learn both polarity and emotion-specific attended representations (Yao et al. 2020). Based on the fact that concrete emotion categories depend on high-level semantic information and that polarity is relevant to low-level features (e. g., color and texture), polarity-specific attention is modeled in lower layers and emotion-specific attention is modeled in higher layers. These two types of attended features are integrated by cross-level bilinear pooling to facilitate the interaction between the information of different levels. After dimensionality reduction and ℓ_2-Normalization, we can obtain the final feature representations.

6   Learning Methods for IEA

In this section, we first summarize the supervised learning methods that have been widely used for emotion classification, regression and retrieval. Then, we introduce some domain adaptation methods.

6.1   Emotion Classification

Shallow Pipeline Based on the modeling process, supervised learning can be classified into generative learning and discriminative learning. Discriminative learning models the conditional distribution of labels y given features $g_\mu(\mathbf{x})$ directly or learns the mappings directly from features $g_\mu(\mathbf{x})$ to labels y. For instance, logistic regression, a binary classification method, models the conditional distribution $p(y|g_\mu(\mathbf{x}); \theta)$ as:

$$h_\theta(g_\mu(\mathbf{x})) = \text{sig}(\theta^T g_\mu(\mathbf{x})), \tag{3}$$

where sig is the sigmoid function $\text{sig}(z) = \dfrac{1}{1 + e^{-z}}$ and θ is the vector of parameters. A generalization of logistic regression to multi-class classification is softmax regression. The perceptron learning algorithm 'forces' the output values of logistic regression to be exactly 0 or 1, based on the threshold function:

$$\text{sig}(z) = \begin{cases} 1, & \text{if } z \geq 0, \\ 0, & \text{if } z < 0. \end{cases} \tag{4}$$

Support vector machines (SVM) try to find a decision boundary that maximizes the geometric margin and can be extended with various non-linear kernels.

Generative learning algorithms try to model class priors $p(y)$ and likelihood $p(g_\mu(\mathbf{x})|y)$, and then, the posterior distribution on $p(y|g_\mu(\mathbf{x}))$ can be derived by Bayes rule:

$$p(y|g_\mu(\mathbf{x})) = \frac{p(g_\mu(\mathbf{x})|y)p(y)}{p(g_\mu(\mathbf{x}))}, \tag{5}$$

where $p(g_\mu(\mathbf{x}))$ can be seen as a normalization factor. Gaussian discriminant analysis assumes that $p(g_\mu(\mathbf{x})|y)$ is distributed according to a multivariate Gaussian distribution, which deals with continuous real-valued features. Naive Bayes, which handles discrete values of $g_\mu(\mathbf{x})$, is based on the assumption that the discrete values are conditionally independent given y. When dealing with multi-class classification, it is often formulated as some extensions of binary classification. The prominent formulations include 'one-versus-all' and 'one-versus-one' classification.

Deep Architecture Recent deep learning based emotion classification methods usually employ several fully-connected (FC) layers to minimize the following cross-entropy loss (She et al. 2020):

$$\mathcal{L}_{CE} = -\frac{1}{N} \sum_{i=1}^{N} \sum_{k=1}^{K} \mathbb{1}_{[k=y_i]} \log p_{i,k}, \tag{6}$$

where K is the number of emotion classes, $\mathbb{1}_{[k=y_i]}$ is a binary indicator, and $p_{i,k}$ is the predicted probability that image i belongs to class k. Directly optimizing the cross-entropy loss might lead some images to be incorrectly classified into categories with opposite polarity. For example, for an image with the emotion "amusement", one model might classify the emotion incorrectly as "sadness" which has an opposite polarity (negative vs. positive). But it is more acceptable if the emotion is classified as "excitement" which has the same polarity (positive). Based on this motivation, a novel polarity-consistent cross-entropy (PCCE) loss is proposed to consider the polarity-emotion hierarchy by increasing the penalty of the predictions that have opposite polarity to the ground truth (Zhao et al. 2020). The PCCE loss is defined as:

$$\mathcal{L}_{PCCE} = -\frac{1}{N} \sum_{i=1}^{N} (1 + \lambda(G(\hat{y}_i, y_i))) \sum_{k=1}^{K} \mathbb{1}_{[k=y_i]} \log p_{i,k}, \tag{7}$$

where λ is a penalty coefficient. Similar to the indicator function, $G(.)$ represents whether to add the penalty or not and is defined as:

$$G(\hat{y}, y) = \begin{cases} 1, & \text{if polarity } (\hat{y}) \neq \text{polarity}(y), \\ 0, & \text{otherwise,} \end{cases} \tag{8}$$

where polarity(.) is a function that maps an emotion category to its polarity (positive or negative).

6.2 Emotion Regression

In the early shallow pipeline, some commonly used regression methods, including linear regression, support vector regression (SVR), and manifold kernel regression, are employed to predict the average dimensional values. For example, SVR is used in (Lu et al. 2012) to predict emotion scores in the VA space.

Similar to emotion classification, deep learning based emotion regression methods also employ several fully-connected (FC) layers to minimize the following mean squared error (MSE):

$$\mathcal{L}_{reg} = \frac{1}{N} \sum_{i=1}^{N} \sum_{j=1}^{N_E} (\hat{y}_i^j - y_i^j)^2, \tag{9}$$

where N_E is the dimension number of the adopted emotion model ($N_E = 3$ for VAD), and y_i^j indicates the emotion label of the j-th dimension for image $\mathbf{x}_i$. Similar to PCCE loss, polarity-consistent regression (PCR) loss is proposed based on the assumption that VAD dimensions can be classified into different polarities (Zhao et al. 2019). The PCR loss is defined as:

$$\mathcal{L}_{PCR} = \frac{1}{N} \sum_{i=1}^{N} \sum_{j=1}^{N_E} (\hat{y}_i^j - y_i^j)^2 (1 + \lambda G(\hat{y}_i^j, y_i^j)). \tag{10}$$

6.3 Emotion Retrieval

We introduced our work on multi-graph learning (MGL) (Zhao et al. 2014) and attention-aware polarity-sensitive embedding (APSE) (Yao et al. 2020) as shallow and deep methods for emotion retrieval. As a (semi-)supervised learning, MGL is widely used for reranking in various domains. For each feature, we can construct a single graph, where the vertices represent image samples and the edges reflect the similarities between sample pairs. By combining the multiple graphs together in a regularization framework, we can learn the optimized weights of each graph to efficiently explore the complementarity of different features (Zhao et al. 2014).

Besides the polarity and emotion-specific attended representations, APSE also consists of a polarity-sensitive emotion-pair (EP) loss to further exploit the polarity-emotion hierarchy (Yao et al. 2020). Suppose K pairs of convolution features constructed from K different categories are formulated as $\{(g_1, g_1^+), \cdots, (g_K, g_K^+)\}$, where g_k and g_k^+ represent the feature representations of anchor point $\mathbf{x}_k$ and positive example $\mathbf{x}_k^+$, respectively, both from the kth category. The EP loss is the combination of inter-polarity loss and intra-polarity loss. Specifically, inter-polarity loss is formulated as:

$$\mathcal{L}_{inter} = \frac{1}{K} \sum_{k=1}^{K} \log(1 + \exp(\frac{1}{N_{\mathcal{Q}_k}} \sum_{j \in \mathcal{Q}_k} g_k^\top g_j^+ - \frac{1}{N_{\mathcal{P}_k}} \sum_{j \in \mathcal{P}_k, j \neq k} g_k^\top g_j^+)), \quad (11)$$

where $\mathcal{P}_k$ and $\mathcal{Q}_k$ represent the sets of emotion categories in the same and opposite polarities to the anchor of the kth category, respectively. $N_{\mathcal{P}_k}$ and $N_{\mathcal{Q}_k}$ are the numbers of corresponding categories. The intra-polarity loss that can differentiate similar categories within the same polarity is defined as:

$$\mathcal{L}_{intra} = \frac{1}{K} \sum_{k=1}^{K} \log(1 + \sum_{j \in \mathcal{P}_k, j \neq k} \exp(g_k^\top g_j^+ - g_k^\top g_k^+)). \quad (12)$$

6.4 Emotion Distribution Learning

Emotion distribution learning is essentially a regression problem. We can directly employ regression methods to predict the probabilities of each emotion category, but the relationship between different emotion categories is ignored. Shared sparse learning (SSL) is employed to learn the probabilities of different emotion categories simultaneously as a distribution (Zhao et al. 2020). SSL is performed based on two assumptions: (1) the images, which are close to one another in the visual feature space, would have similar emotion distributions in the categorical emotion space; (2) the distribution of a test image can be approximately modeled as a linear combination of the distributions of the training images. Specifically, the combination coefficients are learned in the feature space and transferred to the emotion distribution space. The method is also extended to a more general setting, where multiple features are available. The optimal weights for each feature are automatically learned to reflect the importance of different features.

One intuitive method using deep architecture is to replace the cross-entropy loss for classification with some distribution-based losses, such as KL divergence (Yang et al. 2017):

$$\mathcal{L}_{KL} = -\frac{1}{N} \sum_{i=1}^{N} \sum_{k=1}^{K} y_i^j \ln \hat{y}_i^j, \quad (13)$$

where y_i^j and $\hat{y}_i^j$ are the ground truth and predicted probability of the jth emotion category for image $\mathbf{x}_i$. The joint classification and distribution learning (JCDL)

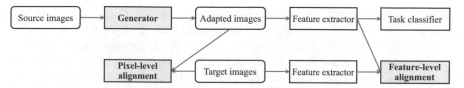

Fig. 6 A generalized domain adaptation framework for IEA with one labeled source domain and one unlabeled target domain. The gray-scale rectangles represent different alignment strategies. Most existing domain adaptation methods can be obtained by employing different component details, enforcing some constraints, or slightly changing the architecture

models both emotion classification and distribution learning simultaneously (Yang et al. 2017).

6.5 Domain Adaptation

Domain adaptation aims to learn a transferable model from a labeled source domain that can perform well on another sparsely labeled or unlabeled target domain (Zhao et al. 2021). Most recent methods focused on the unsupervised setting with a two-stream deep architecture: one stream for training a task model on the labeled source domain, and the other stream for aligning the source and target domains, as shown in Fig. 6. The main difference of existing domain adaptation methods lies in the alignment strategy, which includes discrepancy-based, adversarial discriminative, adversarial generative, and self-supervision-based methods (Zhao et al. 2021).

CycleEmotionGAN++ (CEGAN++) (Zhao et al. 2021) is one state-of-the-art domain adaptation method for IEA. CEGAN++ aligns the source and target domains at both pixel-level and feature-level. First, an adapted domain is generated to perform pixel-level alignment by improving CycleGAN (Zhu et al. 2017) with a multi-scale structured cycle-consistency loss. Dynamic emotional semantic consistency (DESC) is enforced to preserve the emotion labels of the source images during image translation. Second, feature-level alignment is conducted when learning the task classifier. The final objective loss is the combination of task loss, mixed CycleGAN loss, and DESC loss.

7 Released Datasets

In this section, we introduce some datasets that are widely used for performance evaluation of IEA. For clarity, we organize these datasets based on different emotion labels and IEA tasks, i. e., average dimensional values, dominant emotion category, probability distribution, and personalized emotion labels.

Average Dimensional Values *The International Affective Picture System (IAPS)* (Lang et al. 1997) is an emotion evoking image set in psychology with 1182 documentary-style natural color images depicting complex scenes, such as portraits, babies, animals, landscapes, etc. Each image is associated with an empirically derived mean and standard deviation (STD) of VAD ratings in a 9-point rating scale by about 100 college students (predominantly US-American). *The Nencki Affective Picture System (NAPS)* (Marchewka et al. 2014) is composed of 1356 realistic, high-quality photographs with five categories, i. e., people, faces, animals, objects, and landscapes. 204 mostly European participants labeled these images in a 9-point bipolar semantic sliding scale on the VA and approach-avoidance dimensions. *The Emotions in Context Database (EMOTIC)* (Kosti et al. 2017) consists of 18,316 images about people in context in non-controlled environments. There are two kinds of emotion labels: 26 emotion categories and the continuous 10-scale VAD dimensions.

Dominant Emotion Category *IAPSa* (Mikels et al. 2005) is subset of IAPS, which includes 246 images. *Abstract dataset (Abstract)* contains 228 peer rated abstract paintings without contextual content (Machajdik & Hanbury 2010). *ArtPhoto* is an artistic dataset with 806 art photos obtained from a photo sharing site (Machajdik & Hanbury 2010). The *IAPSa*, *Abstract*, and *ArtPhoto* datasets are categorized into eight discrete categories (Mikels et al. 2005): amusement, anger, awe, contentment, disgust, excitement, fear, and sadness. The relationship between emotion categories and dimensional VA values is summarized in Fig. 7a. *The Geneva affective picture database (GAPED)* consists of 520 negative (133 spiders, 158 snakes, 105 human concerns, and 124 animal mistreatment) images, 121 positive (human and animal babies and nature sceneries) images and 89 neutral (inanimate objects) images (Dan-

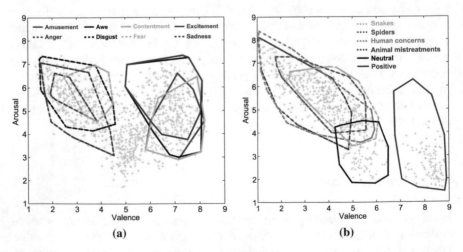

Fig. 7 Representation of the outcome ratings in the valence/arousal space of the (**a**) IAPS and (**b**) GAPED datasets. Polygons represent the surfaces occupied by all the images in a given category

Glauser & Scherer 2011). Besides, these images are also rated with valence and arousal values, ranging from 0 to 100 points. The valence and arousal ratings (changed from [0, 100] to [1, 9]) are shown in Fig. 7b. *Twitter I* (You et al. 2015) consists of 1269 images annotated by 5 Amazon Mechanical Turk (AMT) workers. There are three subsets, i. e., "Five agree" (Twitter I-5), "At least four agree" (Twitter I-4), and "At least three agree" (Twitter I-3). "Five agree" indicates that all the 5 AMT workers labeled the same sentiment label to an image. There are 882 "Five agree" images and all the images receive at least three same votes. *Twitter II* includes 470 positive tweets and 133 negative tweets (Borth et al. 2013) crawled from PeopleBrowsr with 21 hashtags. *EMOd* (Fan et al. 2018) consists of 1019 emotional images with eye-tracking data and different kinds of labels, such as object contour and emotions. *FI* (You et al. 2016) is a large-scale image emotion dataset with 23,308 images labeled using Mikel's emotion categories. The images are obtained by searching from Flickr and Instagram with the eight emotions as keywords and removing noisy data.

Probability Distribution The *Flickr_LDL* and *Twitter_LDL* datasets are constructed to study emotion ambiguity (Yang et al. 2017). There are 10,700 images and 10,045 images in these two datasets, which are labeled by 11 and 8 participants based on Mikel's emotion categories, respectively. Based on the detailed annotations, we can easily obtain the discrete probability distribution of different emotion categories.

Personalized Emotion Labels *Image-Emotion-Social-Net* (*IESN*) (Zhao et al. 2018) is constructed to study personalized emotions. There are more than one million images crawled from Flickr uploaded by 11,347 users. For each image, both the expected emotion from the uploader and actual emotion from each viewer are provided in terms of binary sentiment, Mikel's emotion categories, and continuous VAD values.

8 Experimental Results and Analysis

To give readers a clear understanding of the capabilities of current computational IEA methods, we conduct a series of experiments on different IEA tasks. In this section, we first introduce the evaluation criteria and then report the performance comparison of different representative methods.

8.1 Evaluation Criteria

For emotion classification, the most widely used metric is classification accuracy, which measures the percentage of correctly classified images over all test images (She et al. 2020). For emotion regression, we can use mean squared error, mean absolute error, and the coefficient of determination to evaluate the results (Zhao et al. 2019). For emotion distribution learning, we can either use the sum of squared difference to measure the performance from the aspect of regression (Zhao et al. 2020), or use distance or similarity metrics (e. g., KL divergence, Bhattacharyya coefficient, Chebyshev distance, Clark distance, Canberra metric, cosine coefficient, and intersection similarity) between two distributions to measure whether the predicted distribution and the ground truth is similar (Yang et al. 2017; Zhao et al. 2020). For image retrieval, there are several evaluation metrics: nearest neighbor rate, first tier, second tier, precision-recall curve, F1 score, discounted cumulative gain (DCG), and average normalized modified retrieval rank (ANMRR) (Zhao et al. 2014; Yao et al. 2020).

We employ accuracy for emotion classification, mean squared error (MSE) for emotion regression, ANMRR for retrieval, and KL divergence for distribution learning. For accuracy, the larger the better; while for MSE, ANMRR, and KL divergence, smaller values indicate better results.

8.2   Supervised Learning Results

For emotion classification and regression, we compare the following methods:

- Traditional methods: principles-of-art based emotion features (PAEF) (Zhao et al. 2014), adjective noun pairs (ANP) with SentiBank (Borth et al. 2013), pretrained AlexNet (Krizhevsky et al. 2012), VGG-16 (Simonyan & Zisserman 2015), and ResNet-101 (He 2016). Support vector machine (SVM) or regression (SVR) with a radial basis function (RBF) kernel is used as the learning model.
- Deep methods: fine-tuned (FT) AlexNet, VGG-16, and ResNet-101, Mldr-Net (Rao et al. 2020), SentiNet-A (Song et al. 2018), WSCNet (She et al. 2020), and PDANet (Zhao et al. 2019).

For emotion retrieval, we compare the performance of the following methods: SIFT (Lowe 1999), HOG (Dalal & Triggs 2005), SentiBank (Borth et al. 2013), Multi-graph learning (MGL) (Zhao et al. 2014), JCDL (Yang et al. 2017), and APSE (Yao et al. 2020).

For emotion distribution learning, the compared methods include: Bayes, SVM, kNN, BP, IIS, BFGS, CPNN (Geng et al. 2013), BCPNN, ACPNN (Yang et al. 2017), CNNR (Peng et al. 2015), DLDL (Gao et al. 2017), and JCDL (Yang et al. 2017).

The results of the above compared methods on emotion classification, regression, retrieval, and distribution learning are shown in Fig. 8. From these results, we can conclude that:

1. Traditional hand-crafted low-level features in computer vision, such as SIFT and HOG, do not perform well on IEA tasks. For example, in Fig. 8c, the retrieval performance of SentiBank is much better than SIFT and HOG on the IAPSa dataset.

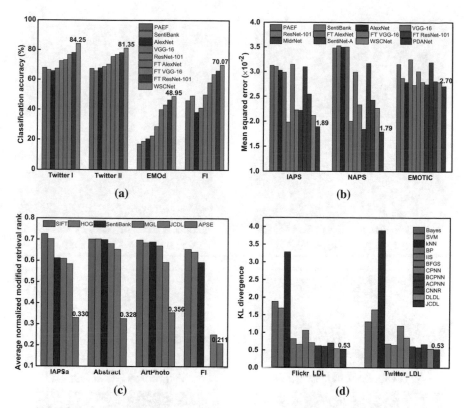

Fig. 8 Performance comparison of supervised learning methods for different IEA tasks, i.e., emotion classification, regression, retrieval, and distribution learning. (**a**) Classification. (**b**) Regression. (**c**) Retrieval. (**d**) Distribution learning

2. Pretraind CNN features, especially the ones extracted from deep models (e.g., ResNet-101), achieve comparable and even better results as compared to hand-crafted specific features, such as PAEF and SentiBank, which demonstrates the generalization ability of deep features to new applications. For example, in Fig. 8a, the pretrained ResNet-101 features achieve 4.63% and 5.92% performance gains on the Twitter I dataset for emotion classification as compared to PAEF and SentiBank.

3. Generally, fine-tuned deep models perform better than pretrained models. This is reasonable, since the pretrained models do not consider the specific characteristics of emotion-related features, while fine-tuned deep models can learn to adapt to the emotion datasets.

4. Deeper models usually perform better, which can be clearly observed when comparing AlexNet and ResNet-101 in Fig. 8a and b.

5. Specially designed models perform the best, such as APSE in Fig. 8c and PDANet in Fig. 8b; by modeling the specific characteristics of emotion, such as polarity-emotion hierarchy and attention mechanisms, these method can better bridge the affective gap.

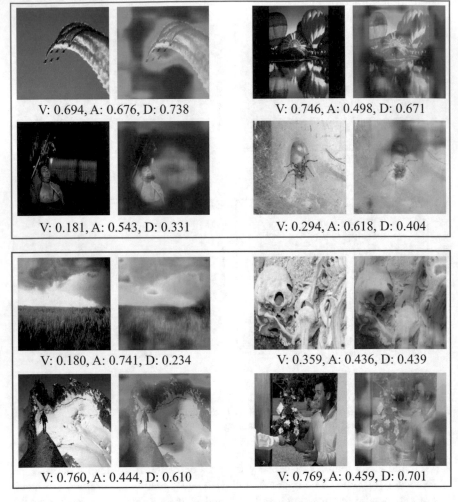

Fig. 9 Visualization of the learned attention maps by PDANet Zhao et al. (2019). From left to right in each image pair are: original image from the test set and the combination of image and heat map. The ground truth VAD values are shown below each pair. Red regions indicate more attention. The attention in the above four examples in the blue rectangle can focus on the salient and discriminative regions, while the below in the red rectangle are failure cases

We visualize the learned attention of PDANet (Zhao et al. 2019) using the heat map generated by the Grad-Cam algorithm (Selvaraju et al. 2017) to show the model's interpretability. The results are shown in Fig. 9. More results on other visualizations can be found in our papers (Yang et al. 2017; Zhao et al. 2019; She et al. 2020; Yao et al. 2020). From the above four examples in the blue rectangle, we can see that PDANet can successfully focus on the salient and discriminative regions that determine the emotion of the whole image. For example, in the top right corner, the attention learned by PDANet focuses on the colorful balloons, which is strongly related to the positive emotion. We also show some failure cases in the red rectangle. As can be seen, for these cases, the background and foreground are difficult to be distinguished or the background is complex.

8.3 Domain Adaptation Results

For unsupervised domain adaptation for IEA, we report the performance comparison between CycleEmotionGAN++ (CEGAN++) with the following baselines:

- Source-only: directly transferring the model trained on the source domain to the target domain;
- Color style transfer methods: *CycleGAN* (Zhu et al. 2017);
- UDA methods: *ADDA* (Tzeng et al. 2017), *SimGAN* (Shrivastava et al. 2017), and *CyCADA* (Hoffman et al. 2018);
- Oracle: training and testing on the target domain, which can be viewed as an upper bound.

The task classifiers use the ResNet-101 (He 2016) architecture pretrained on ImageNet. Please see (Zhao et al. 2021) for more implementation details. The performance comparisons between CEGAN++ and the above-mentioned approaches are shown in Fig. 10. From the results, we can observe that:

1. Because of the influence of domain shift, directly transferring the models trained on the source domain to the target domain does not perform well. For example, when adapting from ArtPhoto to FI, i.e., training on ArtPhoto and directly testing on FI, the classification accuracy is only 23.86%. The model's low

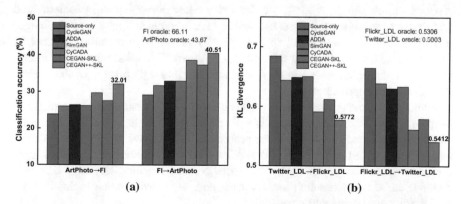

Fig. 10 Domain adaptation results for both emotion classification and distribution learning. For fair comparison and better visualization, the oracle results are shown in detailed numbers in the top right corner. (**a**) Domain adaptation for classification. (**b**) Domain adaptation for distribution learning

transferability from one domain to another motivates the necessity of domain adaptation research.

2. CEGAN++ achieves the best result among all domain adaptation methods for both emotion classification and distribution learning. The superiority of CEGAN++ for adapting image emotions benefits from the following aspects: pixel-level and feature-level alignments to align the source and target domains, dynamic emotional semantic consistency to dynamically preserve the emotion information before and after image translation.

3. There is still an obvious gap between all the domain adaptation methods and the oracle setting that is trained on the target domain. For example, the oracle accuracy on FI is 66.11%, and the best adaptation result is 32.01%. Future efforts are still needed to further bridge the domain shift between different domains.

Figure 11 shows some predicted emotion distributions by different domain adaptation methods on the Twitter-LDL dataset, including one successful example and one failure case. More visualization results can be found in Zhao et al. (2021). From the above example, we can clearly see that the predicted emotion distribution by CEGAN++ is close to the ground truth distribution, which demonstrates its effectiveness for visual emotion adaptation. In the below failure case, we can see that even the oracle does not perform well, which indicates the challenges of IEA, requiring further research efforts.

9   Conclusions and Future Research Directions

We introduced recent advances on image emotion analysis (IEA) from different aspects with the focus on our recent efforts. First, we summarized related psychological studies to understand how emotion is measured. Second, based on the emotion representation models, we defined the key computational problems and widely used supervised frameworks, and then we introduced three major challenges in IEA. Third, we summarized and compared representative methods on emotion feature extraction and learning methods for different IEA tasks. Finally, we briefly described existing datasets and presented an experiment with some of the current state-of-the-art approaches.

Although much research attention has been paid to IEA with promising methods proposed, the overall performance is still not perfect and there is still no solution commonly accepted to address these problems. Many issues in IEA are still open and deserve our further research efforts. We do believe with the progress of multiple disciplines, such as psychology, brain science, and machine learning, IEA will continue to be a hot research topic. At the end, we provide some topics that are well worth considering and investigating.

Context-Aware Image Emotion Analysis Besides extracting discriminative visual features, incorporating available context information can also contribute to the IEA task (Kosti et al. 2020). (1) *Image context*. Similar image content in

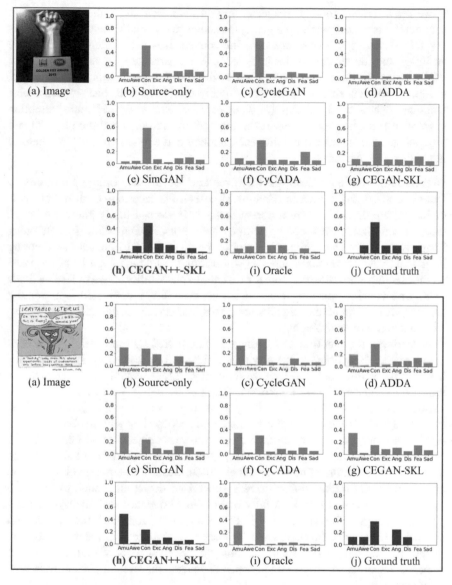

Fig. 11 Visualization of predicted emotion distributions on the Twitter-LDL dataset by CycleEmotionGAN++-SKL (CEGAN++-SKL) Zhao et al. (2021) and several other baselines. In the above example, CEGAN++-SKL can predict similar emotion distribution to the ground truth; while the below example shows a failure case

different contexts might induce totally different emotions, either within an image or across modalities. For example, if we see some soldiers smiling surrounded by flowers, we may feel moved for their contributions to the nation, such as epidemic fighting; but if there is a nearby dead child, we may feel angry for their atrocity.

If we see a famous football player crying on his knees, the audience might feel sad; but if this is after winning a game, the audience especially the team's amateurs my feel excited. (2) *Viewer context*. The context in which a viewer is watching an image and the viewers' prior knowledge (e. g., personality, gender, and culture background) can also contribute a lot to the emotion perception. For example, a viewer's current emotion might be strongly correlated with his/her recent past emotions (Zhao et al. 2018). (3) *Image-viewer interaction*. Humans' emotion perception is a complex process involving both the stimulus and the physical and psychological changes. Combining such implicit and explicit channels are helpful in the final IEA performances.

Determining Intrinsic Emotion Features and Localizing Image Emotions to Image Regions As shown in (Zhao et al. 2014), the emotions of different kinds of images are determined by different features. If we can firstly know the image type, we can select corresponding features that are discriminative for IEA. But what image types should we define for emotion prediction is still unclear. Attempting large scale data-driven approaches is worth trying. Although deep learning based methods achieve promising results for IEA, the explainability on why these methods work, i. e., what features they focus on, has not been fully investigated. Determining the intrinsic features to understand what makes an image amusing, sad or frightening still remains an open problem.

Sometimes, the emotion of an image is determined by the overall appearance of the image. Occasionally, the emotion is reflected by some key image regions. It would be helpful for us to localize these key regions, which can be changed or replaced to change the image emotions (Peng et al. 2014). We can use traditional segmentation methods to segment images into regions and recognize the emotions of each region. Or we can train classifiers to detect the key regions. For example, ANP classifiers are trained hierarchically to localize objects (Chen et al. 2014). More recent emotional region localization methods are based on attention (Zhao et al. 2019) and sentiment maps (She et al. 2020). Besides an emotion classification branch, WSCNet trains another weakly-supervised detection branch to learn the sentiment specific soft map by a fully convolutional network with the cross spatial pooling strategy (She et al. 2020). PDANet jointly considers the spatial and channel-wise attention through which we can obtain the attentive and discriminative regions (Zhao et al. 2019). Jointly combining the advantages of traditional object detection methods and the characteristics of image emotions might motivate new solutions.

Understanding Emotions of 3D Data Most existing works on emotion and sentiment analysis of general images are based on 2D images. But with the wide popularity and public use of somatosensory equipment such as Kinect, more and more 3D data (e. g., 2D images and depth) are created and shared just like personal photos and web videos. Compared with traditional intensity and color images, 3D data contain more information and have several advantages, such as being useful in low light levels and being color and texture invariant (Shotton et al. 2011). Some research efforts have been dedicated to recognizing 3D facial expressions (Sandbach et al. 2012). However, few works on generalized 3D emotion analysis have been published. To the best of our knowledge, no public emotion dataset of general 3D data is released. Building a large scale 3D emotion dataset is an urgent need and of great value. Using social network data may help to reduce the time-consuming and tedious labelling task. With the rapid development of 3D content analysis, understanding the emotions of 3D data will become a hot research topic.

Image Emotion Analysis in the Wild Existing IEA methods are mainly based on specific settings, such as training on small datasets with limited annotators. However, in real-world applications, the IEA problems are much more complex and difficult. For example, the given datasets might contain inaccurate annotations and much noise that is unrelated to emotion; training data is given incrementally and the emotion categories are becoming more fine-grained gradually; the labeled data is unbalanced across different emotion categories; the test set has different styles from the training set; only limited computing resource is available. How to design an effective and efficient IEA model that can still work under these practical settings is still open.

Novel and Real-world Applications Based on IEA Due to the relatively limited progress in the early years, e. g., low performance, emotion has not been widely deployed in real applications. With recent development of deep learning and large-scale datasets, the IEA performance has been and will continue to be significantly boosted. Therefore, we foresee an emotional intelligence era in the near future with many novel and real-world IEA-based applications. For example, we can understand how artists express emotions through their artworks and use the learned principles in painting education. In fashion advertisement, we can design the best matching between clothes and models to attract users' attention and improve user experience, which can lead to increasing sales.

Security, Privacy, and Ethics of IEA As discussed above, viewers' prior knowledge, such as identity, age, and gender, can contribute to the IEA performance. However, this information is confidential, which should not be shared or leaked. Therefore, protecting the security and privacy must be taken into account in real applications. Further, there is no related law regarding the IEA tasks, especially for personalized scenarios. People might not want their emotion to be recognized and used. From the perspective of ethics, it is important to consider such impact, which requires the joint efforts from different communities, such as psychology, cognitive sciences, and computer science.

Acknowledgments This work is supported by the National Natural Science Foundation of China (Nos. 61701273, 61925107, U1936202, 61876094, U1933114), the National Key Research and Development Program of China Grant (No. 2018AAA0100403), the Natural Science Foundation of Tianjin, China (Nos.20JCJQJC00020, 18JCYBJC15400, 18ZXZNGX00110).

References

Alarcão, S. M., & Fonseca, M. J. (2018). Identifying emotions in images from valence and arousal ratings. *Multimedia Tools and Applications, 77*(13), 17413–17435.

Alarcao, S. M., & Fonseca, M. J. (2019). Emotions recognition using EEG signals: A survey. *IEEE Transactions on Affective Computing, 10*(3), 374–393.

Borth, D., Ji, R., Chen, T., Breuel, T., & Chang, S. F. (2013). Large-scale visual sentiment ontology and detectors using adjective noun pairs. In *ACM International Conference on Multimedia* (pp. 223–232).

Chen, M., Zhang, L., & Allebach, J. P. (2015). Learning deep features for image emotion classification. In *IEEE International Conference on Image Processing* (pp. 4491–4495).

Chen, T., Yu, F. X., Chen, J., Cui, Y., Chen, Y. Y., & Chang, S. F. (2014). Object-based visual sentiment concept analysis and application. In *ACM International Conference on Multimedia* (pp. 367–376).

Dalal, N., & Triggs, B. (2005). Histograms of oriented gradients for human detection. In *IEEE Conference on Computer Vision and Pattern Recognition*, (pp. 886–893).

Dan-Glauser, E.S., & Scherer, K. R. (2011). The Geneva affective picture database (GAPED): A new 730-picture database focusing on valence and normative significance. *Behavior Research Methods, 43*(2), 468–477.

Ekman, P. (1992). An argument for basic emotions. *Cognition & Emotion, 6*(3–4), 169–200.

Fan, R. E., Chang, K. W., Hsieh, C. J., Wang, X. R., & Lin, C. J. (2008). Liblinear: A library for large linear classification. *Journal of Machine Learning Research, 9*, 1871–1874 (2008).

Fan, S., Shen, Z., Jiang, M., Koenig, B. L., Xu, J., Kankanhalli, M. S., & Zhao, Q. (2018). Emotional attention: A study of image sentiment and visual attention. In *IEEE Conference on Computer Vision and Pattern Recognition* (pp. 7521–7531).

Gao, B. B., Xing, C., Xie, C. W., Wu, J., & Geng, X. (2017). Deep label distribution learning with label ambiguity. *IEEE Transactions on Image Processing, 26*(6), 2825–2838.

Geng, X., Yin, C., & Zhou, Z. H. (2013). Facial age estimation by learning from label distributions. *IEEE Transactions on Pattern Analysis and Machine Intelligence, 35*(10), 2401–2412.

Giachanou, A., & Crestani, F. (2016). Like it or not: A survey of twitter sentiment analysis methods. *ACM Computing Surveys, 49*(2), 28.

Guntuku, S. C., Preotiuc-Pietro, D., Eichstaedt, J. C., & Ungar, L. H. (2019). What twitter profile and posted images reveal about depression and anxiety. In *AAAI Conference on Artificial Intelligence* (pp. 236–246).

Hanjalic, A. (2006). Extracting moods from pictures and sounds: Towards truly personalized TV. *IEEE Signal Processing Magazine, 23*(2), 90–100.

He, K., Zhang, X., Ren, S., & Sun, J. (2016). Deep residual learning for image recognition. In *IEEE Conference on Computer Vision and Pattern Recognition* (pp. 770–778).

Hoffman, J., Tzeng, E., Park, T., Zhu, J.Y., Isola, P., Saenko, K., Efros, A., & Darrell, T. (2018). Cycada: Cycle-consistent adversarial domain adaptation. In *International Conference on Machine Learning* (pp. 1989–1998).

Juslin, P. N., & Laukka, P. (2004). Expression, perception, and induction of musical emotions: A review and a questionnaire study of everyday listening. *Journal of New Music Research, 33*(3), 217–238.

Kosti, R., Alvarez, J., Recasens, A., & Lapedriza, A. (2020). Context based emotion recognition using emotic dataset. *IEEE Transactions on Pattern Analysis and Machine Intelligence, 42*(11), 2755–2766.

Kosti, R., Alvarez, J.M., Recasens, A., & Lapedriza, A. (2017). Emotion recognition in context. In *IEEE Conference on Computer Vision and Pattern Recognition* (pp. 1667–1675).

Krizhevsky, A., Sutskever, I., & Hinton, G. E. (2012). Imagenet classification with deep convolutional neural networks. In *Advances in neural information processing systems* (pp. 1097–1105).

Lang, P. J., Bradley, M. M., & Cuthbert, B. N. (1997). International affective picture system (IAPS): Technical manual and affective ratings. NIMH Center for the Study of Emotion and Attention (pp. 39–58)

Lee, J., & Park, E. (2011). Fuzzy similarity-based emotional classification of color images. *IEEE Transactions on Multimedia, 13*(5), 1031–1039.

Li, S., & Deng, W. (2020). Deep facial expression recognition: A survey. *IEEE Transactions on Affective Computing* (2020). https://doi.org/10.1109/TAFFC.2020.2981446

Liu, Y., Zhang, D., Lu, G., & Ma, W. Y. (2007). A survey of content-based image retrieval with high-level semantics. *Pattern Recognition, 40*(1), 262–282.

Lowe, D. G. (1999). Object recognition from local scale-invariant features. In *IEEE International Conference on Computer Vision* (pp. 1150–1157).

Lu, X., Suryanarayan, P., Adams Jr., R. B., Li, J., Newman, M. G., & Wang, J. Z. (2012). On shape and the computability of emotions. In *ACM International Conference on Multimedia* (pp. 229–238).

Machajdik, J., & Hanbury, A. (2010). Affective image classification using features inspired by psychology and art theory. In *ACM International Conference on Multimedia* (pp. 83–92).

Marchewka, A., Żurawski, Ł., Jednoróg, K., & Grabowska, A. (2014). The Nencki affective picture system (NAPS): Introduction to a novel, standardized, wide-range, high-quality, realistic picture database. *Behavior Research Methods, 46*(2), 596–610.

Mikels, J. A., Fredrickson, B. L., Larkin, G. R., Lindberg, C. M., Maglio, S. J., & Reuter-Lorenz, P. A. (2005). Emotional category data on images from the international affective picture system. *Behavior Research Methods, 37*(4), 626–630.

Minsky, M. (1986). *The Society of mind*. Simon and Schuster.

Munezero, M. D., Montero, C. S., Sutinen, E., & Pajunen, J. (2014). Are they different? Affect, feeling, emotion, sentiment, and opinion detection in text. *IEEE Transactions on Affective Computing, 5*(2), 101–111.

Pan, S., Lee, J., & Tsai, H. (2014). Travel photos: Motivations, image dimensions, and affective qualities of places. *Tourism Management, 40*, 59–69.

Pang, B., & Lee, L. (2008). Opinion mining and sentiment analysis. *Information Retrieval, 2*(1–2), 1 135.

Parrott, W.G. (2001). *Emotions in social psychology: Essential readings*. Psychology Press.

Peng, K. C., Chen, T., Sadovnik, A., & Gallagher, A. C. (2015). A mixed bag of emotions: Model, predict, and transfer emotion distributions. In *IEEE Conference on Computer Vision and Pattern Recognition* (pp. 860–868).

Peng, K. C., Karlsson, K., Chen, T., Zhang, D. Q., & Yu, H. (2014). A framework of changing image emotion using emotion prediction. In *IEEE International Conference on Image Processing* (pp. 4637–4641).

Picard, R. W. (2000). *Affective computing*. MIT Press.

Plutchik, R. (1980). *Emotion: A psychoevolutionary synthesis*. Harpercollins College Division.

Plutchik, R., & Kellerman, H. (2013). *Theories of emotion* (Vol. 1). Academic Press.

Poria, S., Cambria, E., Bajpai, R., & Hussain, A. (2017). A review of affective computing: From unimodal analysis to multimodal fusion. *Information Fusion, 37*, 98–125.

Rao, T., Xu, M., & Xu, D. (2020). Learning multi-level deep representations for image emotion classification. *Neural Processing Letters, 51*(3), 2043–2061.

Sandbach, G., Zafeiriou, S., Pantic, M., & Rueckert, D. (2012). Recognition of 3d facial expression dynamics. *Image and Vision Computing, 30*(10), 762–773.

Schlosberg, H. (1954). Three dimensions of emotion. *Psychological Review, 61*(2), 81.

Schuller, B. W. (2018). Speech emotion recognition: Two decades in a nutshell, benchmarks, and ongoing trends. *Communications of the ACM, 61*(5), 90–99.

Selvaraju, R. R., Cogswell, M., Das, A., Vedantam, R., Parikh, D., & Batra, D. (2017). Grad-cam: Visual explanations from deep networks via gradient-based localization. In *IEEE International Conference on Computer Vision* (pp. 618–626).

She, D., Yang, J., Cheng, M. M., Lai, Y. K., Rosin, P. L., & Wang, L. (2020). Wscnet: Weakly supervised coupled networks for visual sentiment classification and detection. *IEEE Transactions on Multimedia, 22*(5), 1358–1371.

Shotton, J., Fitzgibbon, A., Cook, M., Sharp, T., Finocchio, M., Moore, R., Kipman, A., & Blake, A. (2011). Real-time human pose recognition in parts from single depth images. In *IEEE Conference on Computer Vision and Pattern Recognition* (pp. 1297–1304).

Shrivastava, A., Pfister, T., Tuzel, O., Susskind, J., Wang, W., & Webb, R. (2017). Learning from simulated and unsupervised images through adversarial training. In *IEEE Conference on Computer Vision and Pattern Recognition* (pp. 2107–2116).

Simonyan, K., & Zisserman, A. (2015). Very deep convolutional networks for large-scale image recognition. In *International Conference on Learning Representations*.

Smeulders, A. W., Worring, M., Santini, S., Gupta, A., & Jain, R. (2020). Content-based image retrieval at the end of the early years. *IEEE Transactions on Pattern Analysis and Machine Intelligence, 22*(12), 1349–1380.

Soleymani, M., Garcia, D., Jou, B., Schuller, B., Chang, S. F., & Pantic, M. (2017). A survey of multimodal sentiment analysis. *Image and Vision Computing, 65*, 3–14.

Song, K., Yao, T., Ling, Q., & Mei, T. (2018). Boosting image sentiment analysis with visual attention. *Neurocomputing, 312*, 218–228.

Tumasjan, A., Sprenger, T. O., Sandner, P. G., & Welpe, I. M. (2010). Predicting elections with twitter: What 140 characters reveal about political sentiment. In *International AAAI Conference on Weblogs and Social Media* (Vol. 10, pp. 178–185).

Tzeng, E., Hoffman, J., Saenko, K., & Darrell, T. (2017). Adversarial discriminative domain adaptation. In *IEEE Conference on Computer Vision and Pattern Recognition* (pp. 7167–7176).

Wang, S., & Ji, Q. (2015). Video affective content analysis: a survey of state-of-the-art methods. *IEEE Transactions on Affective Computing, 6*(4), 410–430.

Wang, W., & He, Q. (2008). A survey on emotional semantic image retrieval. In *IEEE International Conference on Image Processing* (pp. 117–120).

Wei, Z., Zhang, J., Lin, Z., Lee, J. Y., Balasubramanian, N., Hoai, M., & Samaras, D. (2020). Learning visual emotion representations from web data. In *IEEE Conference on Computer Vision and Pattern Recognition* (pp. 13106–13115).

Xu, C., Cetintas, S., Lee, K., & Li, L. (2014). Visual sentiment prediction with deep convolutional neural networks. arXiv:1411.5731.

Yang, J., She, D., Lai, Y., & Yang, M. H. (2018). Retrieving and classifying affective images via deep metric learning. In *AAAI Conference on Artificial Intelligence* (pp. 491–498).

Yang, J., She, D., & Sun, M. (2017). Joint image emotion classification and distribution learning via deep convolutional neural network. In *International Joint Conference on Artificial Intelligence*, (pp. 3266–3272).

Yang, J., Sun, M., & Sun, X. (2017). Learning visual sentiment distributions via augmented conditional probability neural network. In *AAAI Conference on Artificial Intelligence* (pp. 224–230).

Yang, P., Liu, Q., & Metaxas, D. N. (2010). Exploring facial expressions with compositional features. In *IEEE Conference on Computer Vision and Pattern Recognition* (pp. 2638–2644).

Yang, Y. H., & Chen, H. H. (2012). Machine recognition of music emotion: A review. *ACM Transactions on Intelligent Systems and Technology, 3*(3), 40.

Yanulevskaya, V., Van Gemert, J., Roth, K., Herbold, A., Sebe, N., & Geusebroek, J. (2008). Emotional valence categorization using holistic image features. In *IEEE International Conference on Image Processing* (pp. 101–104).

Yao, X., Zhao, S., Lai, Y. K., She, D., Liang, J., & Yang, J. (2020). Apse: Attention-aware polarity-sensitive embedding for emotion-based image retrieval. *IEEE Transactions on Multimedia* (2020). https://doi.org/10.1109/TMM.2020.3042664

You, Q., Jin, H., & Luo, J. (2017). Visual sentiment analysis by attending on local image regions. In *AAAI Conference on Artificial Intelligence* (pp. 231–237).

You, Q., Luo, J., Jin, H., & Yang, J. (2015). Robust image sentiment analysis using progressively trained and domain transferred deep networks. In *AAAI Conference on Artificial Intelligence* (pp. 381–388).

You, Q., Luo, J., Jin, H., & Yang, J. (2016). Building a large scale dataset for image emotion recognition: The fine print and the benchmark. In *AAAI Conference on Artificial Intelligence* (pp. 308–314).

Yuan, J., Mcdonough, S., You, Q., & Luo, J. (2013). Sentribute: Image sentiment analysis from a mid-level perspective. In *International Workshop on Issues of Sentiment Discovery and Opinion Mining* (pp. 1–8).

Zhan, C., She, D., Zhao, S., Cheng, M. M., & Yang, J. (2019). Zero-shot emotion recognition via affective structural embedding. In *IEEE International Conference on Computer Vision* (pp. 1151–1160).

Zhang, L., Wang, S., & Liu, B. (2018). Deep learning for sentiment analysis: A survey. *Wiley Interdisciplinary Reviews: Data Mining and Knowledge Discovery, 8*(4), e1253.

Zhao, S., Chen, X., Yue, X., Lin, C., Xu, P., Krishna, R., Yang, J., Ding, G., Sangiovanni-Vincentelli, A. L., & Keutzer, K. (2021). Emotional semantics-preserved and feature-aligned cyclegan for visual emotion adaptation. *IEEE Transactions on Cybernetics* (2021)

Zhao, S., Ding, G., Gao, Y., Zhao, X., Tang, Y., Han, J., Yao, H., & Huang, Q. (2020). Discrete probability distribution prediction of image emotions with shared sparse learning. *IEEE Transactions on Affective Computing, 11*(4), 574–587.

Zhao, S., Ding, G., Huang, Q., Chua, T. S., Schuller, B. W., & Keutzer, K. (2018). Affective image content analysis: A comprehensive survey. In *International Joint Conferences on Artificial Intelligence* (pp. 5534–5541).

Zhao, S., Gao, Y., Jiang, X., Yao, H., Chua, T. S., & Sun, X. (2014). Exploring principles-of-art features for image emotion recognition. In *ACM International Conference on Multimedia* (pp. 47–56).

Zhao, S., Jia, Z., Chen, H., Li, L., Ding, G., & Keutzer, K. (2019). Pdanet: Polarity-consistent deep attention network for fine-grained visual emotion regression. In *ACM International Conference on Multimedia* (pp. 192–201).

Zhao, S., Li, Y., Yao, X., Nie, W., Xu, P., Yang, J., & Keutzer, K. (2020). Emotion-based end-to-end matching between image and music in valence-arousal space. In *ACM International Conference on Multimedia* (pp. 2945–2954).

Zhao, S., Ma, Y., Gu, Y., Yang, J., Xing, T., Xu, P., Hu, R., Chai, H., & Keutzer, K. (2020). An end-to-end visual-audio attention network for emotion recognition in user-generated videos. In *AAAI Conference on Artificial Intelligence* (pp. 303–311).

Zhao, S., Wang, S., Soleymani, M., Joshi, D., & Ji, Q. (2019). Affective computing for large-scale heterogeneous multimedia data: A survey. *ACM Transactions on Multimedia Computing, Communications, and Applications, 15*(3s), 93.

Zhao, S., Yao, H., Gao, Y., Ding, G., & Chua, T. S. (2018). Predicting personalized image emotion perceptions in social networks. *IEEE Transactions on Affective Computing, 9*(4), 526–540.

Zhao, S., Yao, H., Gao, Y., Ji, R., & Ding, G. (2017). Continuous probability distribution prediction of image emotions via multi-task shared sparse regression. *IEEE Transactions on Multimedia, 19*(3), 632–645 (2017)

Zhao, S., Yao, H., Yang, Y., & Zhang, Y. (2014). Affective image retrieval via multi-graph learning. In *ACM International Conference on Multimedia* (pp. 1025–1028).

Zhao, S., Yue, X., Zhang, S., Li, B., Zhao, H., Wu, B., Krishna, R., Gonzalez, J. E., Sangiovanni-Vincentelli, A. L., Seshia, S. A., & Keutzer, K. (2021). A review of single-source deep unsupervised visual domain adaptation. *IEEE Transactions on Neural Networks and Learning Systems* (2021)

Zhu, J. Y., Park, T., Isola, P., & Efros, A. A. (2017). Unpaired image-to-image translation using cycle-consistent adversarial networks. In *IEEE International Conference on Computer Vision* (pp. 2223–2232).

Zhu, X., Li, L., Zhang, W., Rao, T., Xu, M., Huang, Q., & Xu, D. (2017). Dependency exploitation: a unified cnn-rnn approach for visual emotion recognition. In *International Joint Conference on Artificial Intelligence* (pp. 3595–3601).

The Interplay of Objective and Subjective Factors in Empirical Aesthetics

Rebecca Chamberlain

1 Introduction

The field of empirical aesthetics sets out to understand and predict human aesthetic preferences (Palmer et al., 2013). The origins of modern-day empirical aesthetics reside in the early psychophysical experiments of Gustav Fechner (1876) in his seminal work 'Vorschule der Aesthetik'. Fechner's aesthetics 'from below' positioned objective stimulus properties at the heart of the empirical aesthetic project, providing the foundation for later efforts to establish lawful relationships between stimulus properties and aesthetic preferences (Birkhoff, 1933; Eysenck, 1940) with reference to psychobiological mechanisms of arousal (Berlyne, 1974). Such efforts focused on the predictive value of low-level stimulus properties, such as colour, symmetry, proportion, contrast, contour, and later on collative properties such as order, complexity and ambiguity (Berlyne, 1974). This approach remains common in empirical aesthetics. However, more recent research in the field has placed focus on sensory and cognitive processing dynamics, modelling how observers respond to salient properties of the stimulus (Flavell et al., 2020; Reber et al., 2004), but also incorporating the sensory and cognitive history of the observer (Cutting, 2003; Zajonc, 1968). The latter approach highlights the critical role subjective aspects such as context and exposure play in shaping our aesthetic experiences. Objective and subjective perspectives have been brought together in comprehensive aesthetic models in recent years, bringing both psychological and neuroscientific understanding to the numerous objective and subjective mechanisms identified by researchers in the field (Chatterjee & Vartanian, 2014; Leder et al., 2004; Leder & Nadal, 2014; Pelowski et al., 2017; Tinio, 2013). Finally, contemporary accounts

R. Chamberlain (✉)
Department of Psychology, Goldsmiths, University of London, London, UK
e-mail: r.chamberlain@gold.ac.uk

© The Author(s), under exclusive license to Springer Nature Switzerland AG 2022   115
B. Ionescu et al. (eds.), *Human Perception of Visual Information*,
https://doi.org/10.1007/978-3-030-81465-6_5

focus on the additional role of curiosity and expectation violation in responses to artworks (Muth et al., 2015; Van de Cruys & Wagemans, 2011).

This chapter will seek to address two key questions in the field of empirical aesthetics. The first is to what extent aesthetic preferences are shared or unique. If preferences are found to be completely idiosyncratic this would strongly suggest that attempts to establish lawful relations between stimulus properties and aesthetic preferences are bound to fail. However, if preferences are found to be shared to some degree, this does not necessarily entail that the shared variance among observers is determined by objective stimulus properties, rather than common subjective experiences (Vessel, 2010; Vessel et al., 2018). Therefore, the second question is to what extent objective (characteristics of stimuli) and subjective (characteristics of context) properties are responsible for shaping aesthetic preferences. Having addressed these two critical questions, I will attempt to integrate an individual difference approach with stimulus-based approaches by exploring recent research on aesthetic sensitivity. It is worth noting here that the focus of this chapter is on behavioural empirical studies of preferences for visual stimuli. Much insight can be drawn from neuroscientific perspectives on visual aesthetics (Chatterjee & Vartanian, 2014) and from empirical work in other stimulus domains such as music (Brattico & Pearce, 2013), but such perspectives lie beyond the scope of this chapter.

2 Are Aesthetic Preferences Shared or Unique?

Aesthetic preferences are idiosyncratic (Vessel, 2010; Vessel et al., 2018), but the extent of this idiosyncrasy appears to be strongly dependent on the stimulus category at the focus of research. Vessel and Rubin (2010) and Vessel et al. (2018) investigated the proportions of 'shared' and 'private' taste adult observers displayed across different stimulus categories. Participants were required to make pairwise preference judgments on pictures of real-world scenes and abstract images, and across-observer agreement was computed via pairwise correlations between preference judgments of every pair of participants (Vessel, 2010). Participants showed a high degree of cross-observer agreement for pictures of real-world scenes (46%), while cross-observer agreement for abstract images was significantly lower (20%). In addition, within-observer reliability (correlations in participants' preference estimates between the first and second half of the testing session) was high for both sets of images suggesting that variability in cross-observer agreement could not be attributed to measurement error. In a follow-up study Vessel et al. (2018) measured preferences for a much larger stimulus set including: faces, natural landscapes, interior and exterior architecture, and visual art. Cross-observer agreement was highest for an ethnically diverse sample of faces (66%), and a sample of natural landscapes (29%), lower for architecture (12%), and lower still for visual art (8%). The reasons for variance in cross-observer agreement across these domains could be due to properties of the stimulus; for example averageness, facial symmetry and sexual dimorphism have been shown to be consistent predictors of facial attractiveness (Fink & Penton-Voak, 2002). On the other hand, such variance could be due to shared or unique environmental mechanisms such as mere exposure, which posits that observers develop a preference for stimuli that they have had greater amounts of exposure to (Zajonc, 1968). The following section will explore putative objective predictors of aesthetic preference in more detail.

3 Objective Predictors of Aesthetic Preference

3.1 Symmetry

Symmetry has been described as an 'aesthetic primitive' due to the special status conferred to it by the visual system (Makin et al., 2018). Increased regularity in patterns appears to elicit more fluent visual processing, evidenced by increased accuracy and reduced reaction times in behavioural data (Makin et al., 2016) and by a greater amplitude of the sustained posterior negativity (SPN) in occipital electrodes in event-related potential (ERP) studies (Makin et al., 2016). Correspondingly, increased regularity strongly predicts observers' implicit (Makin et al., 2012) and explicit preferences for random dot patterns (Höfel & Jacobsen, 2003; Jacobsen & Höfel, 2002), an effect that has been replicated in cross-cultural samples (Makin et al., 2018). Preference for symmetry can be conceptualised as a broader preference for perceptual goodness, or Prägnanz in the Gestalt psychological tradition (Palmer & Griscom, 2013). In the context of Makin et al. (2016, 2018) perceptual goodness was mathematically quantified using the Holographic Weight of Evidence Model (Van der Helm & Leeuwenberg, 1996), which is defined as the relationship between the evidence for regularity and the total amount of information in a pattern. These mathematical approaches to stimulus properties overlap with computational approaches to aesthetics which are further elaborated in the section on Global Image Properties below. Beyond the simple dot patterns used in the aforementioned studies (Höfel & Jacobsen, 2003; Jacobsen & Höfel, 2002; Makin et al., 2012, 2016, 2018), symmetry is also a predictor of preference for more complex and ecologically-valid stimuli such as faces, flowers and landscapes (Bertamini et al., 2019; Hůla & Flegr, 2016; Perrett et al., 1999). Two distinct mechanisms may underlie preference for symmetry. The first is perceptual fluency (Reber et al., 2004); more symmetrical stimuli are easier to process by the visual system as evidenced by neuroscientific and behavioural data, and ease of processing gives rise to feelings of pleasure and reward (Makin et al. 2018). On the other hand preference for symmetry may result from sexual selective mechanisms via an association between symmetry and physical fitness, a view that is supported by the fact that symmetry preference is strongest for faces compared with other non-biologically relevant stimuli (Little, 2014).

3.2   Shape and Composition

Rudolf Arnheim (1965) argues compellingly for the significance of perceptual goodness in his seminal work 'Art and Visual Perception', demonstrating its relevance for
higher-order shape and compositional properties of visual stimuli. There has been
much speculation concerning whether the golden ratio (or golden section, denoted
by the symbol ɸ) is a signifier of perceptual goodness in works of art and design,
and the presence of the golden ratio was one of the first objective stimulus properties
to be investigated in empirical aesthetics (Fechner, 1876). However, there is little
evidence to support the existence of a preference for the golden ratio. Rather, in-
depth studies on this topic have revealed preferences converging on prototypical
geometric shapes (McManus, 1980; McManus & Weatherby, 1997) and on compact
triangular shapes (Friedenberg, 2012). In terms of shape contour, a robust preference
for curvature relative to angularity has been found for abstract geometric shapes,
real-life objects and environments (Bar & Neta, 2006; Palumbo et al., 2015, 2020;
Vartanian et al., 2013), a preference which has found to be reliable in cross-cultural
research (Gómez-Puerto et al., 2016). The origin of a preference for curvature
remains a debate in the literature. Some authors suggest it derives from optimal
stimulation of the visual system via Gestalt principles such as good continuation
(Bertamini et al., 2016), while other researchers argue that a preference for curvature
derives from an evolutionary adaptive avoidance of sharp stimuli (Bar & Neta,
2006).

Extending out from preference for proportion and contour of singular forms,
Arnheim (1965) referred to the tension inherent in the configuration of forms,
even in a stimulus as simple as a circle within a frame (Fig. 1). Arnheim posited
that observers prefer specific compositional arrangements that ensure balance and
preserve meaning. This was explored empirically in a series of studies in which
participants rated the goodness of dots placed in different locations in relation to a
surrounding frame (Wickens et al., 2008). The authors discovered a preference for

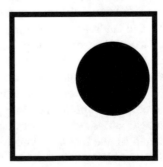

Fig. 1 Arnheim's (1965) example of the tensions inherent in a form within a frame; the disk may
be perceived as being 'drawn toward the contour to the right' (p. 12) and if the distance between
the disk and frame is altered, the effect may be weakened or there may be a contrary repulsion
effect

dots located in the centre and along the medial axes of a rectangular frame, lending support for Arnheim's conjecture. This 'centre-bias' has since been replicated in studies on photographic composition (Abeln et al., 2016) and drives eye movements during free viewing of visual images (Judd et al., 2011; Tseng et al., 2009).

However, the positioning of objects within a frame also interacts with an object's identity, such that objects facing or moving left-to-right are more preferred in the left-hand side of the frame, and vice-versa, a phenomenon termed the inward bias (Wickens et al., 2008). In a similar manner, vertical positioning of objects in a frame interacts with the affordance spaces of those objects, such that a bowl is most preferred in a lower position in a frame, and a light fitting is preferred in a higher position in a frame (Sammartino & Palmer, 2012a). Such interactions make it increasingly difficult to make straightforward predictions concerning which arrangement of forms within a frame will be judged to be the most aesthetically pleasing.

3.3   Colour

Palmer and Schloss (2010) demonstrated that there are robust relationships between colour attributes hue, lightness and saturation and preferences for those attributes. Western observers show relative preferences for hues at the blue end of the spectrum and for relatively more saturated colours. Ou et al. (2004, 2018) theorised that colour preferences are based on semantic associations with particular hues, whilst Hurlbert & Ling (2007) demonstrated that cone-opponent colour processing predicted colour preference curves. However, colour preferences show intriguing hue-lightness interactions, such that observers show a marked dislike for dark yellows and oranges, which are not explained successfully in the aforementioned theories. This pattern of colour preference is accounted for by Ecological Valence Theory (EVT; Palmer & Schloss, 2010) which posits that colour preferences are determined by the emotional valence of objects associated with those colours. Thus, dark yellows and oranges are arguably disliked due to their associations with biological waste, and blues are preferred due to their association with clear skies and water. This theory was empirically supported by amalgamating data from participants on their: object-colour associations, object valence, and object-colour match ratings, creating a weighted affective valence estimate (WAVE). WAVEs predicted participants colour preference data remarkably well (Palmer & Schloss, 2010) and colour preferences could be altered by experimental exposure to objects with negative or positive valence (Strauss et al., 2013). Subsequent studies revealed that colour preferences could also be linked to associations with abstract concepts, such as an observer's university and political affiliation (Schloss et al., 2011; Schloss & Palmer, 2014).

3.4   Order, Complexity and Global Image Properties

In his influential book 'Studies in the new experimental aesthetics: Steps towards an objective psychology of aesthetic appreciation' Daniel Berlyne (1974) posited that stimuli of intermediate complexity generate an optimal level of arousal, and should therefore be most preferred by observers. However, this conjecture has found limited support, with empirical findings obscured by different conceptualisations and manipulations of complexity (Nadal et al., 2010). Recent research has highlighted the complementary role of order or unity in Berlyne's Psychobiological Theory, demonstrating that an optimal balance or combination of order and complexity predicts ratings of soothingness and fascination for images of organised objects (Van Geert & Wagemans, 2019). The interplay of order and complexity was first highlighted by Birkhoff (1933) who developed a mathematical formula for aesthetic preference via a balance of order and complexity (Van Geert & Wagemans, 2020), foreshadowing computational approaches to aesthetics (Brachmann & Redies, 2017).

Image statistical approaches in aesthetics aim to determine Global Image Properties (GIP) of a stimulus that can be automatically computed and related to image preference (Letsch & Hayn-Leichsenring, 2020). Image statistical analysis can produce a number of different measures including: fractality, self-similarity, complexity, and anisotropy (variation in gradient orientations in an image). Statistical analysis of artworks has revealed that they are similar to natural scenes (Graham et al., 2009; Graham & Redies, 2010; Redies et al., 2012) and that different styles and periods of art can be attributed to their underlying image statistics (Hayn-Leichsenring et al., 2017; Mather, 2018). Furthermore, image statistics correlate with verbal descriptions of artworks, suggesting that they capture meaningful aspects of visual stimuli (Letsch & Hayn-Leichsenring, 2020; Lyssenko et al., 2016). Image statistical measures have also been used to study aesthetic responses to artworks, with observers preferring less self-similar (statistical features of the whole image are comparable with smaller parts of the image) paintings of representational still-lifes and landscapes, and less complex portraits (Hayn-Leichsenring et al., 2017). However, research has revealed that image statistics are not robustly predictive of preference for abstract artworks (Letsch & Hayn-Leichsenring, 2020; Mallon et al., 2014). Finally, a reliable preference for fractal images in a specific fractal domain (1.3–1.5) has been found in both artworks and non-artistic images (Graham et al., 2010; Graham & Redies, 2010; Spehar et al., 2003, 2015). Computational approaches constitute a highly objective approach to the study of stimulus-driven aesthetic preference, but as a result can present difficulties in interpretation of experimental findings. This is especially true for images with higher ecological validity which vary not only on these lower-level visual features, but also on mid-level features associated with element grouping and higher-order properties such as semantic associations with both abstract and representational content, and which are not currently captured by these computational methods.

3.5 Do Aesthetic Primitives Exist?

It is easy to mistake the presence of robust relationships between stimulus properties and aesthetic preference as evidence for universal, evolutionarily hard-wired
preferences. However, even the most reliable preferences for particular stimulus
properties can be the result of shared enculturation or exposure. For example, Huang
et al. (2018) found that both adults and 4 year-old children spontaneously attend to
symmetrical patterns, but that preference for symmetrical patterns was evident in
adults but not in children, calling into question the argument that processing fluency
underpins preference for symmetry. Rather, Huang et al. (2018) posit that mere
exposure (Zajonc, 1968) may account for a preference for symmetry in adulthood.
Furthermore, while the story of empirical aesthetics centres around group-level
responses to manipulation of objective stimulus properties, authors consistently
highlight a high level of reliable variance in observers' aesthetic responses to even
very simple stimuli.

Drawing on some of the stimulus properties discussed above, Jacobsen and
Höfel (2002) found evidence of substantial individual differences in preference
for symmetry, while Bertamini et al. (2019) found that individual differences for
symmetry for one stimulus class did not predict preference for symmetry in another
stimulus class, suggesting that a unitary preference for symmetry across stimulus
categories does not exist. Preference for complexity in artworks is determined to
some extent by individual differences in visual working memory capacity (Sherman
et al., 2015) and the soothingness of order is predicted by sub-clinical traits
associated with organising tendencies in obsessive compulsive disorder (Van Geert
& Wagemans, 2019). Cross-cultural research has revealed differences in preferences
for spatial composition, finding that preference for an object's location in a frame
is mediated by the observer's culture's prevailing reading direction (Chokron &
De Agostini, 2000; Ishii et al., 2011; Pérez González, 2012). Furthermore, Schloss
and Palmer (2017) found that Chinese participants' WAVEs were predicted better
by symbolic associations (red=revolution) and US participants' WAVEs by object
associations (red=apple), while Taylor et al. (2013) found that WAVEs did not
predict colour preference in the Himba tribe of Namibia. Finally, McManus et
al. (2010) discovered large and stable individual differences in preferences for
proportioned rectangles, with very simple patterns being ascribed individualised
meanings (McManus & Wu, 2013). This finding lends support to the notion of
the 'Gestalt nightmare', in which even the weakest stimuli elicit complex semantic
associations in the viewer, which presents huge challenges for identifying group-
level preferences (Makin, 2016). Indeed, semantic associations of stimuli often far
outweigh the influence of any lower-level stimulus features on aesthetic preference,
as demonstrated in Martindale's et al. (1990) critical explorations of Daniel
Berlyne's (1974) Psychobiological Theory. The prominent role of individualised
semantic associations casts doubt on the possibility of establishing lawful relations
between stimulus properties and aesthetic preferences.

4   Subjective Determinants of Aesthetic Preference

Having considered stimulus-based properties that influence aesthetic preference, we can now turn to subjective properties. Subjective factors tend be broadly attributed to observer-level (personality, expertise, exposure) and context-level (framing, knowledge about the artist and process) variables. The following section will focus on the latter, and take an individual differences approach to these variables at the conclusion of the section to ascertain the extent to which such contextual factors have predictable effects on aesthetic preference across observers.

4.1   Effect of Context

Context has a large impact on aesthetic preference, particularly for visual works of art. Sammartino and Palmer (2012b) showed that the seemingly robust centre and inward biases for spatial composition could be manipulated by the addition of titles that changed the metaphorical meaning of an image. Complementarily, labelling an artwork with a metaphorically congruent title leads to increased meaning (Cupchik et al., 1994; Leder et al., 2006) and aesthetic appreciation (Leder et al., 2006; Millis, 2001; Russell & Milne, 1997) and providing titles that accentuate particular aspects of the image (e.g. presence of depicted movement) leads to increased sensory awareness of those attributes (Mastandrea & Umiltà, 2016). The presence of an artistic frame around a stimulus can also have an impact on the quality and intensity of aesthetic judgements. Displaying objects in unexpected contexts (e.g. a post-box on a tennis court) induces an aesthetic stance; observers are more likely to respond at the poles of an aesthetic Likert scale for objects in abnormal contexts, and make more neutral aesthetic responses toward objects in semantically congruent contexts (Kirk, 2008). Informing observers that a set of photographs of mouldy food come from an art exhibition in contrast to a health and safety booklet has no impact on reports of disgust but does modulate positive valence toward the photographs (Wagner et al. 2014). Furthermore, perceived beauty and positive affective responses are more tightly linked in artistic contexts (Wagner et al., 2014).

4.2   Effect of Artist and Process

Knowledge about the creative process and the artist herself can also modulate aesthetic responses to artworks. Informing participants that an artwork was made by a professional artist rather than the experimenter leads to increased aesthetic ratings for the same stimuli (Kirk et al., 2009), while labelling an artwork as created by a *famous* artists boosts its aesthetic appraisal further (Mastandrea & Crano, 2019). Contrariwise, attribution of part of the creative process to a computer algorithm leads observers to downgrade their liking of an artwork (Chamberlain et al., 2018) and artworks with an association with criminal activity such as graffiti tags also elicit diminished aesthetic appraisal relative to visually similar artforms such as calligraphy (Chamberlain et al., 2020). These effects likely operate through observers' assumptions about the creative process. The effort heuristic (Kruger et al., 2004) posits that perceived effort is used as proxy for quality in the absence of disambiguating information. In a series of studies, Kruger et al. (2004) showed that participants valued artworks and products more if they were informed that they took longer to create. This effect was most pronounced in situations in which the quality of the object was difficult to determine purely on the basis of sensory information (Kruger et al. 2004). However, the effort heuristic itself is malleable. If observers are required to read a piece of text highlighting the role of talent (in contrast to effort) prior to evaluating objects, experimental effects are reversed and participants rate more quickly created artworks as more valuable (Cho & Schwarz, 2008). Finally, the authenticity of an artwork plays a large role in its aesthetic reception. An artwork's history is important because, being a non-functional item in the practical sense, it is prone to biases around contagion, the notion that it is the end point of a performance, and intuitions about its originality and scarcity (Newman & Bloom, 2012). In support, Newman and Bloom (2012) found that informing observers that an object was a duplication of an existing object led to devaluation of the duplicate, but only in the context of artworks (paintings) not artifacts (cars). Supporting the notion that contagion is also an important factor in the valuation of art, the contact level between creator and object had a much larger impact on perceived value of artworks than artifacts (Newman & Bloom, 2012).

4.3 Stability of Contextual Influences

Whilst categorised as subjective determinants of aesthetic preference, some of the contextual effects described above, such as the effort heuristic or essentialist beliefs associated with duplication, could conceivably account for some of the shared variance in aesthetic attitudes if sufficiently stable within a given cultural setting (Vessel, 2010; Vessel et al., 2018), whilst others are by their nature transient. Effects of authorship on aesthetic preference do not seem to diminish if the responses of expert artists are compared with non-experts (Chamberlain et al. 2018), suggesting that these biases concerning artistic process are not superseded by artistic knowledge. However, individual differences in expertise do determine the magnitude of framing effects where the framing relies on adequate recognition of prestige (Verpooten, 2018; Verpooten & Dewitte, 2017).

Finally, many studies have shown that the personal context of the observer in terms of their demographics and personality affects the kind of artistic stimuli they seek in the first instance. Both expertise and the Big Five personality factor of 'openness to experience' (McCrae, 2007) have been shown to be predictive of preference for abstract and modern art (Batt et al., 2010; Chamorro-Premuzic et al., 2009; Kruger et al., 2004; McManus & Furnham, 2006; van Paasschen et al., 2015). Openness to experience represents a tendency towards intellectual curiosity, aesthetic sensitivity, liberal values, and emotional differentiation (McCrae, 2007) and also predicts preference for the visual arts more generally (Feist & Brady, 2004) and the prevalence of aesthetic 'chills' (Silvia & Nusbaum, 2011). Need for cognitive closure, an aversion toward semantic and sensory ambiguity which can be modulated in a state or trait-like manner, also predicts dislike for abstract art (Ostrofsky & Shobe, 2015) and for ambiguous movie endings (Wiersema et al., 2012). Expertise has a marked influence over how observers inspect and categorise artworks (Augustin & Leder, 2006; Vogt & Magnussen, 2007; Zangemeister et al., 1995) and an observer's willingness to engage with abstract and ambiguous art (Silvia, 2013; van Paasschen et al., 2015). Thus, it can be seen that stable and fluctuating observer-centred and context-centred variables modulate aesthetic preferences in a complex and interacting manner. The next section will attempt to summarise the effects of both objective and subjective predictors of aesthetic preference and introduce an approach that takes into account the action of objective features at the group-level and individual differences at the subject level.

5 Considering the Interplay Between Objective and Subjective Approaches

The previous sections have summarised evidence for both objective and subjective between-groups effects on aesthetic preference. Objective features such as symmetry, proportion, contour, colour and composition show reliable associations with aesthetic preference, particularly for simple stimuli that accentuate the target stimulus property. Similarly, contextual information and inferences about effort and authenticity demonstrate reliable effects on perceived value of visual stimuli. However, a consistent caveat to these group-level effects is the existence of substantial and reliable differences which do not merely represent variance due to error but can instead be attributed to person-level variables. The aetiology of these individual differences can be attributed to multiple sources. Behavioural genetic research implies that variation in genes account for a limited proportion (approximately 30%) of the variance in perceived facial attractiveness (Germine et al., 2015), and a similar proportion of the variance in the intensity of aesthetic appraisal of abstract objects and scenes (Bignardi et al., 2020). The remaining variation likely lies within unique environmental factors, due to individual differences in exposure and enculturation. Individual differences in expertise and personality likely play a strong role in modulating the role of objective predictors, an issue that has been addressed with the revival of the concept of aesthetic sensitivity.

5.1 Aesthetic Sensitivity

A useful way of conceptualising individual differences in empirical aesthetics is through the notion of aesthetic sensitivity. This concept originates in the work of Hans Eysenck, who posited the existence of an individual difference in the ability to detect objective beauty in a stimulus, similar to the notion of a general intelligence factor, g (Eysenck, 1940). It will have become clear that establishing an objective notion of beauty as a property of the stimulus was bound to fail. However, recently researchers have revived the label if not the underlying meaning of Eysenck's aesthetic sensitivity (Corradi et al., 2019, 2020). Under its revised conception, aesthetic sensitivity is the extent to which a particular objective feature (symmetry, contour, complexity) influences an observer's aesthetic valuation. Empirical support for the existence of aesthetic sensitivity was derived from a study which re-examined stimuli from a seminal study on curvature preference (Bar & Neta, 2006) and found both group-level preference for curvature as well as large individual differences, across two different stimulus categories (real objects and abstract designs; Corradi et al. 2019). A follow-up study using a larger range of stimuli again found evidence for high variability in preference for curvature, symmetry, complexity and balance in visual stimuli (Corradi et al. 2020). Furthermore, sensitivity across different stimulus properties was not correlated, although sensitivity was stable over time, echoing existing individual difference research (Bertamini et al., 2019; McManus et al., 2010).

Research exploring the underlying determinants of aesthetic sensitivity is still in its infancy. Individual differences in aesthetic sensitivity for contour and symmetry was found to be weakly predicted by expertise, but not by personality factors such as openness to experience (Corradi et al. 2020). In a similar study, Cotter et al. (2017) found individual differences in preference for curvature could be explained by personality and expertise. It is possible that visual sensitivity, that is the extent to which individuals can visually detect differences in symmetry, contour, balance, may be predictive of aesthetic sensitivity. Research on fractal patterns suggests that observers' preferences for levels of fractality and their visual sensitivity to those particular patterns are tightly linked (Spehar et al., 2015). It would be valuable to investigate whether an observer's ability to detect the curvature of contours, the presence of symmetry and the objective complexity of an image, predicted their aesthetic sensitivity for the same stimulus feature. Whilst the focus of research on aesthetic sensitivity is predominantly focused upon stimulus-based features which influence aesthetic preference, it is reasonable to believe that aesthetic sensitivity could be extended to the realm of subjective factors as well. Some observers may be more or less sensitive to the effect of context, or of factors associated with the artist or artistic process. This is indicated by a study finding that prestige effects (stating that an artwork was located at the Museum of Modern Art in New York rather than a local art gallery) only impact the aesthetic preferences of expert artist observers (Verpooten, 2018; Verpooten & Dewitte, 2017). It is also possible that aesthetic sensitivity functions in a domain-specific manner. Objective and subjective features of natural and man-made objects may influence aesthetic preferences of observers in different ways. It is possible that biologically-relevant stimuli induce sensitivity at the level of stimulus properties, while artworks elicit sensitivity at the level of subjective factors (Vessel & Rubin, 2010, 2018). This domain-specificity may further interact with other individual differences measures (such as expertise) whereby sensitivity to objective and subjective features is determined by the level of artistic knowledge an individual has. The notion of aesthetic sensitivity is a useful tool with which to move beyond group-level principles in empirical aesthetics, and to categorise and predict the individual differences that permeate the data collected in this domain.

6 Conclusion

This chapter has provided an overview of empirical psychological perspectives to aesthetic preferences. It can be seen that contemporary approaches to the investigation of aesthetic preferences are still heavily influenced by early work in the field (Fechner 1876; Berlyne 1974) which strove to identify lawful relationships between objective stimulus properties and aesthetic responses. This approach has to a large extent failed, partly due to the combinatorial influence of objective factors (Makin, 2016) and the myriad subjective influences that often supersede the effects of stimulus properties on aesthetic preference. However, we have seen that there are robust and replicable group-level effects of stimulus features like symmetry and curvature which appear to be culturally invariant (Gómez-Puerto et al., 2016; Makin et al., 2018), suggesting that it is not necessary to abandon all efforts to identify objective determinants of aesthetic preferences. Contextual factors have recently received more attention as researchers pursue more complete models of the aesthetic process. It is clear that information about the artist and the artistic process has a large impact on the strength of aesthetic judgments to artistic stimuli (Chamberlain et al., 2018; Mastandrea & Cruno, 2019; Kirk et al., 2009; Kruger et al., 2004; Newman & Bloom, 2012). Merely framing a sensory experience as being one of viewing an artwork, impacts on the kind of emotional and evaluative response the observer has to the artwork (Wagner et al., 2014; Kirk 2008).

Group-level objective and subjective effects aside, permeating much of this research is the observation that people significantly and reliably differ in their aesthetic responses to stimulus features. The question of why people differ in their aesthetic judgments has been present since the inception of empirical aesthetics, but has gained much more prominence in recent years (Vessel & Rubin, 2010, 2018; Cotter et al., 2017; McManus et al., 2010). Putative mechanisms for individual differences in aesthetic preferences span both genetic and environmental influences. These sources of variance encapsulate differences in exposure via expertise (both practical and intellectual knowledge of the artistic domain) and culture, and trait-level differences due to cognitive ability and personality. While there is a promising line of research exploring the aetiology of individual differences for stimulus features, there is very little research exploring the effect of individual differences in response to contextual manipulations, which is likely to be a fruitful line of research in the future. Furthermore, findings concerning individual differences can be better understood in relation to the notion of aesthetic sensitivity, which posits that individuals' aesthetic responses are driven to a greater or lesser extent by different features of the stimulus and context. By combining what we know about the relatively stable subjective and objective features of an aesthetic experience alongside the sources of variance surrounding them, it seems possible to develop a more complete understanding of the seemingly unpredictable nature of individual aesthetic preferences.

References

Abeln, J., Fresz, L., Amirshahi, S. A., McManus, I. C., Koch, M., Kreysa, H., & Redies, C. (2016). Preference for well-balanced saliency in details cropped from photographs. *Frontiers in Human Neuroscience, 9*. https://doi.org/10.3389/fnhum.2015.00704

Arnheim, R. (1965). *Art and visual perception: A psychology of the creative eye.* Faber & Faber.

Augustin, D., & Leder, H. (2006). Art expertise: A study of concepts and conceptual spaces. *Psychology Science, 48*(2), 135.

Bar, M., & Neta, M. (2006). Humans prefer curved visual objects. *Psychological Science, 17*(8), 645–648. https://doi.org/10.1111/j.1467-9280.2006.01759.x

Batt, R., Palmiero, M., Nakatani, C., & van Leeuwen, C. (2010). Style and spectral power: Processing of abstract and representational art in artists and non-artists. *Perception, 39*(12), 1659–1671. https://doi.org/10.1068/p6747

Berlyne, D. E. (1974). *Studies in the new experimental aesthetics: Steps towards an objective psychology of aesthetic appreciation.* Hemisphere.

Bertamini, M., Palumbo, L., Gheorghes, T. N., & Galatsidas, M. (2016). Do observers like curvature or do they dislike angularity? *British Journal of Psychology, 107*(1), 154–178. https://doi.org/10.1111/bjop.12132

Bertamini, M., Rampone, G., Makin, A. D. J., & Jessop, A. (2019). Symmetry preference in shapes, faces, flowers and landscapes. *PeerJ, 7*, e7078. https://doi.org/10.7717/peerj.7078

Bignardi, G., Ticini, L. F., Smit, D., & Polderman, T. J. (2020). Domain-specific and domain-general genetic and environmental effects on the intensity of visual aesthetic appraisal.. *PsyArXiv.* https://psyarxiv.com/79nbq

Birkhoff, G. D. (1933). *Aesthetic measure.* Harvard University Press.

Brachmann, A., & Redies, C. (2017). Computational and experimental approaches to visual aesthetics. *Frontiers in Computational Neuroscience, 11*, 102. https://doi.org/10.3389/fncom.2017.00102

Brattico, E., & Pearce, M. (2013). The neuroaesthetics of music. *Psychology of Aesthetics, Creativity, and the Arts, 7*(1), 48–61.

Chamberlain, R., Mullin, C., Scheerlinck, B., & Wagemans, J. (2018). Putting the art in artificial: Aesthetic responses to computer-generated art. *Psychology of Aesthetics, Creativity, and the Arts, 12*(2), 177.

Chamberlain, R., Mullin, C., Berio, D., Leymarie, F. F., & Wagemans, J. (2020). Aesthetics of graffiti: Comparison to text-based an pictorial artforms. *Empirical Studies of the Arts.* https://doi.org/10.1177/0276237420951415

Chamorro-Premuzic, T., Reimers, S., Hsu, A., & Ahmetoglu, G. (2009). Who art thou? Personality predictors of artistic preferences in a large UK sample: The importance of openness. *British Journal of Psychology, 100*(3), 501–516. https://doi.org/10.1348/000712608X366867

Chatterjee, A., & Vartanian, O. (2014). Neuroaesthetics. *Trends in Cognitive Sciences, 18*(7), 370–375. https://doi.org/10.1016/j.tics.2014.03.003

Cho, H., & Schwarz, N. (2008). Of great art and untalented artists: Effort information and the flexible construction of judgmental heuristics. *Journal of Consumer Psychology, 18*(3), 205–211. https://doi.org/10.1016/j.jcps.2008.04.009

Chokron, S., & De Agostini, M. (2000). Reading habits influence aesthetic preference. *Cognitive Brain Research, 10*(1–2), 45–49. https://doi.org/10.1016/S0926-6410(00)00021-5

Corradi, G., Belman, M., Currò, T., Chuquichambi, E. G., Rey, C., & Nadal, M. (2019). Aesthetic sensitivity to curvature in real objects and abstract designs. *Acta Psychologica, 197*, 124–130. https://doi.org/10.1016/j.actpsy.2019.05.012

Corradi, G., Chuquichambi, E. G., Barrada, J. R., Clemente, A., & Nadal, M. (2020). A new conception of visual aesthetic sensitivity. *British Journal of Psychology, 111*(4), 630–658. https://doi.org/10.1111/bjop.12427

Cotter, K. N., Silvia, P. J., Bertamini, M., Palumbo, L., & Vartanian, O. (2017). Curve appeal: Exploring individual differences in preference for curved versus angular objects. *I-Perception, 8*(2), 204166951769302. https://doi.org/10.1177/2041669517693023

Cupchik, G. C., Shereck, L., & Spiegel, S. (1994). The Effects of Textual Information on Artistic Communication. *20*(1), 62–78.

Cutting, J. E. (2003). Gustave Caillebotte, French impressionism, and mere exposure. *Psychonomic Bulletin & Review, 10*(2), 319–343. https://doi.org/10.3758/BF03196493

Eysenck, H. (1940). The general factor in aesthetic judgements. *British Journal of Psychology, 31*, 94–102.

Fechner, G. (1876). *Vorschule der aesthetik* (Vol. 1). Brietkopf & Härtel.

Feist, G. J., & Brady, T. R. (2004). Openness to experience, non-conformity, and the preference for abstract art. *Empirical Studies of the Arts, 22*(1), 77–89. https://doi.org/10.2190/Y7CA-TBY6-V7LR-76GK

Fink, B., & Penton-Voak, I. (2002). Evolutionary psychology of facial attractiveness. *Current Directions in Psychological Science, 11*(5), 154–158. https://doi.org/10.1111/1467-8721.00190

Flavell, J. C., Over, H., & Tipper, S. P. (2020). Competing for affection: Perceptual fluency and ambiguity solution. *Journal of Experimental Psychology: Human Perception and Performance, 46*(3), 231–240. https://doi.org/10.1037/xhp0000702

Friedenberg, J. D. (2012). *Aesthetic judgment of triangular shape: Compactness and not the Golden ratio determines perceived attractiveness*. I-Perception.

Germine, L., Russell, R., Bronstad, P. M., Blokland, G. A. M., Smoller, J. W., Kwok, H., Anthony, S. E., Nakayama, K., Rhodes, G., & Wilmer, J. B. (2015). Individual aesthetic preferences for faces are shaped mostly by environments, not genes. *Current Biology, 25*(20), 2684–2689. https://doi.org/10.1016/j.cub.2015.08.048

Gómez-Puerto, G., Munar, E., & Nadal, M. (2016). Preference for curvature: A historical and conceptual framework. *Frontiers in Human Neuroscience, 9*, 712.

Graham, D. J., Friedenberg, J. D., & Rockmore, D. N. (2009). Efficient visual system processing of spatial and luminance statistics in representational and non-representational art. *IS&T/SPIE Electronic Imaging*, 72401N–72401N. http://proceedings.spiedigitallibrary.org/proceeding.aspx?articleid=811744

Graham, D. J., Friedenberg, J. D., Rockmore, D. N., & Field, D. J. (2010). Mapping the similarity space of paintings: Image statistics and visual perception. *Visual Cognition, 18*(4), 559–573. https://doi.org/10.1080/13506280902934454

Graham, D. J., & Redies, C. (2010). Statistical regularities in art: Relations with visual coding and perception. *Vision Research, 50*(16), 1503–1509. https://doi.org/10.1016/j.visres.2010.05.002

Hayn-Leichsenring, G. U., Lehmann, T., & Redies, C. (2017). Subjective ratings of *beauty* and *aesthetics*: Correlations with statistical image properties in Western oil paintings. *I-Perception, 8*(3), 204166951771547. https://doi.org/10.1177/2041669517715474

Höfel, L., & Jacobsen, T. (2003). Temporal stability and consistency of aesthetic judgments of beauty of formal graphic patterns. *Perceptual and Motor Skills, 96*, 30–32.

Huang, Y., Xue, X., Spelke, E., Huang, L., Zheng, W., & Peng, K. (2018). The aesthetic preference for symmetry dissociates from early-emerging attention to symmetry. *Scientific Reports, 8*(1), 6263. https://doi.org/10.1038/s41598-018-24558-x

Hůla, M., & Flegr, J. (2016). What flowers do we like? The influence of shape and color on the rating of flower beauty. *PeerJ, 4*, e2106. https://doi.org/10.7717/peerj.2106

Hurlbert, A. C., & Ling, Y. (2007). Biological components of sex differences in color preference. *Current Biology, 17*(16), R623–R625. https://doi.org/10.1016/j.cub.2007.06.022

Ishii, Y., Okubo, M., Nicholls, M. E. R., & Imai, H. (2011). Lateral biases and reading direction: A dissociation between aesthetic preference and line bisection. *Brain and Cognition, 75*(3), 242–247. https://doi.org/10.1016/j.bandc.2010.12.005

Jacobsen, T., & Höfel, L. (2002). Aesthetic judgments of novel graphic patterns: Analysis of individual judgments. *Perceptual and Motor Skills, 95*, 755–766.

Judd, T., Durand, F., & Torralba, A. (2011). Fixations on low-resolution images. *Journal of Vision, 11*(4), 14–14. https://doi.org/10.1167/11.4.14

Kirk, U. (2008). The neural basis of object-context relationships on aesthetic judgment. *PLoS One, 3*(11), e3754. https://doi.org/10.1371/journal.pone.0003754

Kirk, U., Skov, M., Hulme, O., Christensen, M. S., & Zeki, S. (2009). Modulation of aesthetic value by semantic context: An fMRI study. *NeuroImage, 44*(3), 1125–1132. https://doi.org/10.1016/j.neuroimage.2008.10.009

Kruger, J., Wirtz, D., Van Boven, L., & Altermatt, T. W. (2004). The effort heuristic. *Journal of Experimental Social Psychology, 40*(1), 91–98. https://doi.org/10.1016/S0022-1031(03)00065-9

Leder, H., Belke, B., Oeberst, A., & Augustin, D. (2004). A model of aesthetic appreciation and aesthetic judgments. *British Journal of Psychology, 95*(4), 489–508.

Leder, H., Carbon, C.-C., & Ripsas, A.-L. (2006). Entitling art: Influence of title information on understanding and appreciation of paintings. *Acta Psychologica, 121*(2), 176–198. https://doi.org/10.1016/j.actpsy.2005.08.005

Leder, H., & Nadal, M. (2014). Ten years of a model of aesthetic appreciation and aesthetic judgments: The aesthetic episode - developments and challenges in empirical aesthetics. *British Journal of Psychology, 105*(4), 443–464. https://doi.org/10.1111/bjop.12084

Letsch, P., & Hayn-Leichsenring, G. U. (2020). The composition of abstract images – Differences between artists and laypersons. *Psychology of Aesthetics, Creativity, and the Arts, 14*(2), 186–196. https://doi.org/10.1037/aca0000200

Little, A. (2014). Domain specificity in human symmetry preferences: Symmetry is Most pleasant when looking at human faces. *Symmetry, 6*(2), 222–233. https://doi.org/10.3390/sym6020222

Lyssenko, N., Redies, C., & Hayn-Leichsenring, G. U. (2016). Evaluating abstract art: Relation between term usage, subjective ratings, image properties and personality traits. *Frontiers in psychology, 7*. https://doi.org/10.3389/fpsyg.2016.00973

Makin, A. D. J. (2016). The Gap Between Aesthetic Science and Aesthetic Experience. 30.

Makin, A. D. J., Helmy, M., & Bertamini, M. (2018). Visual cortex activation predicts visual preference: Evidence from Britain and Egypt. *Quarterly Journal of Experimental Psychology, 71*(8), 1771–1780. https://doi.org/10.1080/17470218.2017.1350870

Makin, A. D. J., Pecchinenda, A., & Bertamini, M. (2012). Implicit affective evaluation of visual symmetry. *Emotion, 12*(5), 1021–1030. https://doi.org/10.1037/a0026924

Makin, A. D. J., Wright, D., Rampone, G., Palumbo, L., Guest, M., Sheehan, R., Cleaver, H., & Bertamini, M. (2016). An electrophysiological index of perceptual goodness. *Cerebral Cortex, 26*(12), 4416–4434. https://doi.org/10.1093/cercor/bhw255

Mallon, B., Redies, C., & Hayn-Leichsenring, G. U. (2014). Beauty in abstract paintings: Perceptual contrast and statistical properties. *Frontiers in human neuroscience, 8*. https://doi.org/10.3389/fnhum.2014.00161

Martindale, C., Moore, K., & Borkum, J. (1990). Aesthetic preference: Anomalous findings for Berlyne's psychobiological theory. *The American Journal of Psychology, 103*(1), 53. https://doi.org/10.2307/1423259

Mastandrea, S., & Crano, W. D. (2019). Peripheral factors affecting the evaluation of artworks. *Empirical Studies of the Arts, 37*(1), 82–91. https://doi.org/10.1177/0276237418790916

Mastandrea, S., & Umiltà, M. A. (2016). Futurist art: Motion and aesthetics as a function of title. *Frontiers in Human Neuroscience, 10*. https://doi.org/10.3389/fnhum.2016.00201

Mather, G. (2018). Visual image statistics in the history of Western art. *Art and Perception, 6*(2–3), 97–115. https://doi.org/10.1163/22134913-20181092

McCrae, R. R. (2007). Aesthetic chills as a universal marker of openness to experience. *Motivation and Emotion, 31*(1), 5–11. https://doi.org/10.1007/s11031-007-9053-1

McManus, I. C. (1980). The aesthetics of simple figures. *British Journal of Psychology, 71*(4), 505–524. https://doi.org/10.1111/j.2044-8295.1980.tb01763.x

McManus, I. C., Cook, R., & Hunt, A. (2010). Beyond the Golden section and normative aesthetics: Why do individuals differ so much in their aesthetic preferences for rectangles? *Psychology of Aesthetics, Creativity, and the Arts, 4*(2), 113–126. https://doi.org/10.1037/a0017316

McManus, I. C., & Furnham, A. (2006). Aesthetic activities and aesthetic attitudes: Influences of education, background and personality on interest and involvement in the arts. *British Journal of Psychology, 97*(4), 555–587. https://doi.org/10.1348/000712606X101088

McManus, I. C., & Weatherby, P. (1997). The Golden section and the aesthetics of form and composition: A cognitive model. *Empirical Studies of the Arts, 15*(2), 209–232. https://doi.org/10.2190/WWCR-VWHV-2Y2W-91EE

McManus, I. C., & Wu, W. (2013). "The square is ... bulky, heavy, contented, plain, good-natured, stupid ...": A cross-cultural study of the aesthetics and meanings of rectangles. *Psychology of Aesthetics, Creativity, and the Arts, 7*(2), 130–139. https://doi.org/10.1037/a0030469

Millis, K. (2001). Making meaning brings pleasure: The influence of titles on aesthetic experiences. *Emotion, 1*(3), 320.

Muth, C., Hesslinger, V. M., & Carbon, C.-C. (2015). The appeal of challenge in the perception of art: How ambiguity, solvability of ambiguity, and the opportunity for insight affect appreciation. *Psychology of Aesthetics, Creativity, and the Arts, 9*(3), 206–216. https://doi.org/10.1037/a0038814

Nadal, M., Munar, E., Marty, G., & Cela-Conde, C. J. (2010). Visual complexity and beauty appreciation: Explaining the divergence of results. *Empirical Studies of the Arts, 28*(2), 173–191. https://doi.org/10.2190/EM.28.2.d

Newman, G. E., & Bloom, P. (2012). Art and authenticity: The importance of originals in judgments of value. *Journal of Experimental Psychology: General, 141*(3), 558–569. https://doi.org/10.1037/a0026035

Ostrofsky, J., & Shobe, E. (2015). The relationship between need for cognitive closure and the appreciation, understanding, and viewing times of realistic and nonrealistic figurative paintings. *Empirical Studies of the Arts, 33*(1), 106–113. https://doi.org/10.1177/0276237415570016

Ou, L.-C., Luo, M. R., Woodcock, A., & Wright, A. (2004). A study of colour emotion and colour preference. Part I: Colour emotions for single colours. *Color Research & Application, 29*(3), 232–240. https://doi.org/10.1002/col.20010

Ou, L.-C., Yuan, Y., Sato, T., Lee, W.-Y., Szabó, F., Sueeprasan, S., & Huertas, R. (2018). Universal models of colour emotion and colour harmony. *Color Research & Application, 43*(5), 736–748. https://doi.org/10.1002/col.22243

Palmer, S. E., & Griscom, W. S. (2013). Accounting for taste: Individual differences in preference for harmony. *Psychonomic Bulletin & Review, 20*(3), 453–461. https://doi.org/10.3758/s13423-012-0355-2

Palmer, S. E., & Schloss, K. B. (2010). An ecological valence theory of human color preference. *Proceedings of the National Academy of Sciences, 107*(19), 8877–8882. https://doi.org/10.1073/pnas.0906172107

Palmer, S. E., Schloss, K. B., & Sammartino, J. (2013). Visual aesthetics and human preference. *Annual Review of Psychology, 64*(1), 77–107. https://doi.org/10.1146/annurev-psych-120710-100504

Palumbo, L., Rampone, G., Bertamini, M., Sinico, M., Clarke, E., & Vartanian, O. (2020). Visual preference for abstract curvature and for interior spaces: Beyond undergraduate student samples. *Psychology of Aesthetics, Creativity, and the Arts.*https://doi.org/10.1037/aca0000359

Palumbo, L., Ruta, N., & Bertamini, M. (2015). Comparing angular and curved shapes in terms of implicit associations and approach/avoidance responses. *PLoS One, 10*(10), e0140043. https://doi.org/10.1371/journal.pone.0140043

Pelowski, M., Markey, P. S., Forster, M., Gerger, G., & Leder, H. (2017). Move me, astonish me . . . delight my eyes and brain: The Vienna integrated model of top-down and bottom-up processes in art perception (VIMAP) and corresponding affective, evaluative, and neurophysiological correlates. *Physics of Life Reviews, 21*, 80–125. https://doi.org/10.1016/j.plrev.2017.02.003

Pérez González, C. (2012). Lateral organisation in nineteenth-century studio photographs is influenced by the direction of writing: A comparison of Iranian and Spanish photographs. *Laterality: Asymmetries of Body, Brain and Cognition, 17*(5), 515–532. https://doi.org/10.1080/1357650X.2011.586701

Perrett, D. I., Burt, D. M., Penton-Voak, I. S., Lee, K. J., Rowland, D. A., & Edwards, R. (1999). Symmetry and human facial attractiveness. *Evolution and Human Behavior, 20*(5), 295–307. https://doi.org/10.1016/S1090-5138(99)00014-8

Reber, R., Schwarz, N., & Winkielman, P. (2004). Processing fluency and aesthetic pleasure: Is beauty in the perceiver's processing experience? *Personality and Social Psychology Review, 8*(4), 364–382.

Redies, C., Amirshahi, S. A., Koch, M., & Denzler, J. (2012). PHOG-derived aesthetic measures applied to color photographs of artworks, natural scenes and objects. *European conference on computer vision*, 522–531. http://link.springer.com/chapter/10.1007/978-3-642-33863-2_54

Russell, P. A., & Milne, S. (1997). Meaningfulness and hedonic value of painting: Effects of titles. *Empirical Studies of the Arts, 15*(1), 61–73.

Sammartino, J., & Palmer, S. E. (2012a). Aesthetic issues in spatial composition: Effects of vertical position and perspective on framing single objects. *Journal of Experimental Psychology: Human Perception and Performance, 38*(4), 865–879. https://doi.org/10.1037/a0027736

Sammartino, J., & Palmer, S. E. (2012b). Aesthetic issues in spatial composition: Representational fit and the role of semantic context. *Perception, 41*(12), 1434–1457. https://doi.org/10.1068/p7233

Schloss, K. B., & Palmer, S. E. (2014). The politics of color: Preferences for republican red versus democratic blue. *Psychonomic Bulletin & Review, 21*(6), 1481–1488. https://doi.org/10.3758/s13423-014-0635-0

Schloss, K. B., & Palmer, S. E. (2017). An ecological framework for temporal and individual differences in color preferences. *Vision Research, 141*, 95–108. https://doi.org/10.1016/j.visres.2017.01.010

Schloss, K. B., Poggesi, R. M., & Palmer, S. E. (2011). Effects of university affiliation and "school spirit" on color preferences: Berkeley versus Stanford. *Psychonomic Bulletin & Review, 18*(3), 498–504. https://doi.org/10.3758/s13423-011-0073-1

Sherman, M. T., Seth, A. K., Barrett, A. B., & Kanai, R. (2015). Prior expectations facilitate metacognition for perceptual decision. *Consciousness and Cognition, 35*, 53–65. https://doi.org/10.1016/j.concog.2015.04.015

Silvia, P. J. (2013). Interested experts, confused novices: Art expertise and the knowledge emotions. *Empirical Studies of the Arts, 31*(1), 107–115. https://doi.org/10.2190/EM.31.1.f

Silvia, P. J., & Nusbaum, E. C. (2011). On personality and piloerection: Individual differences in aesthetic chills and other unusual aesthetic experiences. *Psychology of Aesthetics, Creativity, and the Arts, 5*(3), 208–214. https://doi.org/10.1037/a0021914

Spehar, B., Clifford, C. W. G., Newell, B. R., & Taylor, R. P. (2003). Universal aesthetic of fractals. *Computers & Graphics, 27*(5), 813–820. https://doi.org/10.1016/S0097-8493(03)00154-7

Spehar, B., Wong, S., van de Klundert, S., Lui, J., Clifford, C. W. G., & Taylor, R. P. (2015). Beauty and the beholder: The role of visual sensitivity in visual preference. *Frontiers in Human Neuroscience, 9*. https://doi.org/10.3389/fnhum.2015.00514

Strauss, E. D., Schloss, K. B., & Palmer, S. E. (2013). Color preferences change after experience with liked/disliked colored objects. *Psychonomic Bulletin & Review, 20*(5), 935–943. https://doi.org/10.3758/s13423-013-0423-2

Taylor, C., Clifford, A., & Franklin, A. (2013). Color preferences are not universal. *Journal of Experimental Psychology: General, 142*(4), 1015–1027. https://doi.org/10.1037/a0030273

Tinio, P. P. L. (2013). From artistic creation to aesthetic reception: The mirror model of art. *Psychology of Aesthetics, Creativity, and the Arts, 7*(3), 265–275. https://doi.org/10.1037/a0030872

Tseng, P. H., Carmi, R., Cameron, I. G. M., Munoz, D. P., & Itti, L. (2009). Quantifying center bias of observers in free viewing of dynamic natural scenes. *Journal of Vision, 9*(7), 4–4. https://doi.org/10.1167/9.7.4

Van de Cruys, S., & Wagemans, J. (2011). Putting reward in art: A tentative prediction error account of visual art. *I-Perception, 2*(9), 1035–1062. https://doi.org/10.1068/i0466aap

Van der Helm, P., & Leeuwenberg, E. (1996). Goodness of visual regularities: A nontransformational approach. *Psychological Review, 103*(3), 429–456.

Van Geert, E., & Wagemans, J. (2019). Order, complexity, and aesthetic preferences for neatly organized compositions. *Psychology of Aesthetics, Creativity, and the Arts.*https://doi.org/10.1037/aca0000276

Van Geert, E., & Wagemans, J. (2020). Order, complexity, and aesthetic appreciation. *Psychology of Aesthetics, Creativity, and the Arts, 14*(2), 135–154. https://doi.org/10.1037/aca0000224

van Paasschen, J., Bacci, F., & Melcher, D. P. (2015). The influence of art expertise and training on emotion and preference ratings for representational and abstract artworks. *PLoS One, 10*(8), e0134241. https://doi.org/10.1371/journal.pone.0134241

Vartanian, O., Navarrete, G., Chatterjee, A., Fich, L. B., Leder, H., Modrono, C., Nadal, M., Rostrup, N., & Skov, M. (2013). Impact of contour on aesthetic judgments and approach-avoidance decisions in architecture. *Proceedings of the National Academy of Sciences, 110*(Supplement_2), 10446–10453. https://doi.org/10.1073/pnas.1301227110.

Verpooten, J. (2018). Expertise affects aesthetic evolution in the domain of art: Evidence from artistic fieldwork and psychological experiments. In Z. Kapoula, E. Volle, J. Renoult, & M. Andreatta (Eds.), *Exploring Transdisciplinarity in art and sciences (pp. 303–326).* Springer International Publishing. https://doi.org/10.1007/978-3-319-76054-4_16

Verpooten, J., & Dewitte, S. (2017). The conundrum of modern art: Prestige-driven Coevolutionary aesthetics trumps evolutionary aesthetics among art experts. *Human Nature, 28*(1), 16–38. https://doi.org/10.1007/s12110-016-9274-7

Vessel, E. A. (2010). Beauty and the beholder: Highly individual taste for abstract, but not real-world images. *Journal of Vision, 10*(2), 1–14. https://doi.org/10.1167/10.2.18

Vessel, E. A., & Rubin, N. (2010). Beauty and the beholder: Highly individual taste for abstract, but not real-world images. *Journal of vision, 10*(2), 18–18.

Vessel, E. A., Maurer, N., Denker, A. H., & Starr, G. G. (2018). Stronger shared taste for natural aesthetic domains than for artifacts of human culture. *Cognition, 179*, 121–131. https://doi.org/10.1016/j.cognition.2018.06.009

Vogt, S., & Magnussen, S. (2007). Expertise in pictorial perception: Eye-movement patterns and visual memory in artists and laymen. *Perception, 36*(1), 91–100. https://doi.org/10.1068/p5262

Wagner, V., Menninghaus, W., Hanich, J., & Jacobsen, T. (2014). Art schema effects on affective experience: The case of disgusting images. *Psychology of Aesthetics, Creativity, and the Arts, 8*(2), 120–129. https://doi.org/10.1037/a0036126

Wickens, T., Palmer, S. E., & Gardner, J. (2008). Aesthetic issues in spatial composition: Effects of position and direction on framing single objects. *Spatial Vision, 21*, 421–449.

Wiersema, D. V., van der Schalk, J., & van Kleef, G. A. (2012). Who's afraid of red, yellow, and blue? Need for cognitive closure predicts aesthetic preferences. *Psychology of Aesthetics, Creativity, and the Arts, 6*(2), 168–174. https://doi.org/10.1037/a0025878

Zajonc, R. B. (1968). Attitudinal effects of mere exposure. *Journal of Personality and Social Psychology, 9*, 1–27.

Zangemeister, W. H., Sherman, K., & Stark, L. (1995). Evidence for a global scanpath strategy in viewing abstract compared with realistic images. *Neuropsychologia, 33*(8), 1009–1025.

Advances and Challenges in Computational Image Aesthetics

Giuseppe Valenzise, Chen Kang, and Frédéric Dufaux

1 Introduction

Decades of advancements in image/video acquisition, coding, and communication have made it possible to capture high-quality pictures and videos using devices within everyone's reach. As a result, a sheer amount of visual data is continuously produced and uploaded to social platforms, e.g., 350 million photos are posted every day on Facebook,[1] and 500 hours of new videos are uploaded on YouTube every minute (as of January 2021).[2] Visual media catalyze and attract people's attention and time, with relevant effects from a social perspective. In particular, they represent an immense ecosystem for marketing, in which the "likes" are the primary source of value (John et al. 2017). In this context, it becomes more and more important to predict in an automatized fashion what a human observer would like to watch, using a computer algorithm. The impact and economic value of such prediction are evident in applications like advertising and communication, personal photo triage, image-based content retrieval, etc. Besides, predicting and understanding what makes up image preference is critical in image enhancement and image recommendation, and, overall, it would contribute to a better understanding of human perception.

---

[1] https://www.socialreport.com/insights/article/360000094166-The-Latest-Facebook-Statistics-2018.

[2] https://blog.youtube/press/.

G. Valenzise (✉) · C. Kang · F. Dufaux
Université Paris-Saclay, CNRS, CentraleSupélec, Laboratoire des Signaux et Systèmes, Gif-sur-Yvette, France
e-mail: giuseppe.valenzise@l2s.centralesupelec.fr; chen.kang@l2s.centralesupelec.fr; frederic.dufaux@l2s.centralesupelec.fr

The mechanisms underpinning image preference are complex and variegated. In computer science and multimedia, these mechanisms have been studied from different angles including, among others, *interestingness*, *surprise/amazement* and *beauty*. These concepts are often mixed and confused with each other, even if they are clearly associated to different preference processes. Interestingness Gygli et al. (2013) is the ability to attract our attention due to the familiarity of what we know and like. It is produced by either universal factors (popularity of the subject of the image, relevance at a certain historical moment, etc.) or personal factors (link to individuals' life experiences, work, family, tastes, etc.). On the other hand, the *surprise/amazement* mechanism is related to how much the picture content departs from our expectations. Interestingness and amazement are important dimensions to define image *memorability* (Isola et al. 2011), which is the ability to remember the content of the image. Finally, the *beauty* of a picture is the quality or aggregate of qualities that give pleasure to the senses, or pleasurably exalt the mind or spirit (definition from the Merriam-Webster dictionary), and is the matter of study of *aesthetics*. While in the rest of this chapter we will focus on this last mechanism, we stress that all the mentioned processes interact with each other, e.g., image beauty can help predict memorability (Constantin et al. 2019), etc. As a result, it is difficult, if not impossible, to disentangle aesthetic judgments from the other concurrent dimensions. This may introduce significant biases in collecting subjectively annotated datasets targeting one of these specific mechanisms, and represents a considerable challenge in the study of image aesthetics.

In this chapter, we deal with *computational aesthetics* as defined by F. Hoenig, i.e., "the research of computational methods that can make applicable aesthetic decisions in a similar fashion as humans can" (Hoenig 2005). This definition puts the emphasis on both *computability*, i.e., the fact that computational aesthetics should provide measurable output (e.g., a classification as beautiful or not, or a rating on a scale of beauty), and *applicability*, i.e., it should be functional in practical applications. The link between computational and empirical aesthetics lies in the way the human judgments are elicited and collected (which we will discuss further in this chapter when talking about aesthetic datasets). According to Hoenig, computational aesthetics should be restricted to the *form*, and not the content, to make aesthetic computation as objective as possible. However, it is not clear to which extent this separation between content and form can be made in practice, and certainly this difference is not considered in most of the existing aesthetic datasets (which are the essential fuel for modern computational aesthetic techniques).

1.1   What Makes a Picture Beautiful?

Before analyzing computational methods for aesthetic prediction, a natural question that arises is then: *what makes a picture beautiful?* This question has indeed been a matter of philosophical debates for over twenty centuries, and has been closely linked for a long time to the concept of art (at least, for the case of classical Western arts[3] (Maître 2018). In ancient Greece and Rome, and in different forms through the Middle Ages and until the Renaissance, aesthetics is dominated by *objectivism*. Beauty is seen as an intrinsic property of an object, which is independent from who looks at it. Classical art implements these universal canons of beauty, which have been coded into well-established rules of proportions, composition, etc. These canons continue to largely inspire art and photography nowadays (e.g., through compositional rules such as the rule of thirds, etc.). This objectivist interpretation provides the foundation to most computational aesthetics methods. On the other hand, *subjectivist* approaches consider beauty as the result of an individual, personal visual experience, summarized by the well-known phrase "beauty is in the eye of the beholder".[4] Subjectivism becomes predominant in the sixteenth century, continuing in romantic and modern art. Among the numerous interpretations of aesthetics, Kant's vision is probably one of the most relevant for computational aesthetics, as it tries to reconcile the subjectivist and objectivist points of view (Zuckert 2007). The universality of beauty is given by "common sense": an object is beautiful not only because it is beautiful for the observer, but also because it is deemed to be beautiful for everybody else. Modern data-driven approaches to aesthetics, which we will discuss later in this chapter, rely somehow on this Kantian interpretation of objectivism, in that they assume aesthetic judgments provided by a pool of human observers approximate the true aesthetic value of a picture.

Modern views on aesthetics tend to agree that objects considered to be "beautiful" have some intrinsic properties recognized by all observers. However, the final decision about whether the object is beautiful or not is purely individual. Neuroscience and experimental psychology seem to support this *interactionist* interpretation: while objective visual cues convey beauty, the resulting aesthetic appraisal is subjective and depends on how the visual cues are processed by higher-level cognitive areas in the brain (Reber et al. 2004). Factors that can affect this processing include cultural background, education, age, mood of the observers, etc. The interactionist viewpoint sets the motivation for a personalized image aesthetics prediction (Park et al. 2017; Ren et al. 2017), where the goal is to adapt a generic aesthetics model for an individual user's preference. We will briefly overview some personalized aesthetic models at the end of this chapter.

Despite the relatively young existence of photography compared to other visual arts, the assessment criteria of pictures have evolved significantly since the first photographic plates in the 1830s. In the early days, photography focused on accurately recording objects, people and scenes (Rosenblum 2008). In the late 1800s, when photography was recognized as an art, photos were assessed using the same criteria as classical paintings. In the twentieth century, several photographic

---

[3]Notice that this relation has become looser in modern and contemporary art, where producing beautiful depictions is often not the primary purpose of the artwork.

[4]This sentence is attributed to the nineteenth-century Irish novelist Margaret Hungerford. However, the expression has a much older origin, e.g., see Shakespeare's *Love's Labour Lost* (1588): "Beauty is bought by judgment of the eye".

movements started to develop. The realism of photos, which was the most relevant criterion till the beginning of 1900s, was questioned by surrealist photographic movements that developed along with artistic *avant-gardes* of that time. Starting from the 1960s, photography was highly influenced by the development of mass media, advertisement, and pop art, and more recently by digital post-processing, which is nowadays accepted as a part of photographic content creation. As for other forms of art, therefore, the aesthetic assessment of photography is a complex, multi-factorial task, where the influence of the cultural, demographic, and historical contexts plays a crucial role. Thus, it is of paramount importance to specify the scope and objectives of computational aesthetics, which we will discuss in the next section.

This chapter presents an overview of computational aesthetics, including the principal dimensions of analysis, the available sources of annotated data, the algorithmic approaches to predict aesthetic judgments and their performance, as well as the open challenges in the field. We target readers with general knowledge in image processing and machine learning, intending to provide an entry point to this domain through a summary of state of the art, valuable references, and general hints for practitioners and researchers willing to work in this field.

The chapter is organized as follows. We present the main dimensions in computational aesthetics in Sect. 2: this will help us to restrict our attention to general aesthetics, which is the mainstream approach followed nowadays. In Sect. 3, we present some aesthetic datasets proposed in the literature, and we discuss the main aspects to consider when creating or choosing an aesthetic dataset. Section 4 is the core of the chapter and provides a (non-exhaustive) overview of the most popular approaches to predict aesthetics proposed so far, using either hand-crafted or learning-based representations. In Sect. 5, we discuss what we believe are the most urgent challenges in the field of computational aesthetics: dealing with subjectivity, and explaining aesthetic predictions.

2 Dimensions in Computational Aesthetics

There are several dimensions that contribute to creating a taxonomy of image aesthetic quality assessment methodologies, as illustrated in Fig. 1 and discussed below.

2.1 Input Type

Depending on the assumptions made on the type and variety of input images, aesthetic assessment methodologies can be categorized into *general* or *task-specific* methods. The former category aims at predicting the aesthetic value of a picture without making specific assumptions on the content of the image, which can span a broad spectrum of objects and scenes (natural, man-made, portraits, animals, etc.).

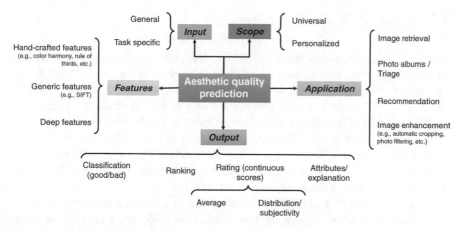

Fig. 1 The different dimensions that compose the aesthetic quality assessment problem

While an a priori knowledge of the semantic content of the picture can greatly aid aesthetic prediction, assuming a closed-set classification setting for image aesthetics would be limiting in some practical applications. Many computational methods proposed in the literature thus do not make this assumption. However, they might internally rely on some form of content classification to improve performance (Luo et al. 2011; Sun et al. 2017). The purpose of a picture can also affect significantly its aesthetic value. For instance, Tifentale and Manovich divide images into several classes (e.g., competitive photography, vernacular, amateur, etc.) and suggest that different evaluation criteria are appropriate for each of them (Tifentale & Manovich 2018). However, most of the existing large-scale aesthetic datasets do not make this distinction. As an example, the AVA dataset (Murray et al. 2012), which is one of the largest reference datasets used in aesthetics, is collected based on photographic challenges but includes as well a large number of amateur-level photographs.

On the other hand, task-specific methods analyze aesthetics for specific kinds of pictures, e.g., aesthetics of faces (Bianco et al. 2018b; Xu et al. 2018), buildings (He et al. 2019), food (Sheng et al. 2018a) or of synthetic images such as video games (Ling et al. 2020). In some particular cases, computational aesthetic approaches can be designed to target non photographic content and artworks, such as paintings (Amirshahi et al. 2013; Hayn-Leichsenring et al. 2017). The general aesthetic problem is more challenging than specific aesthetic tasks, due to the wide variety of content on which minimal or no assumptions can be made beforehand. In the rest of the chapter, we will address the general aesthetic prediction problem, pointing when needed to works addressing specific aesthetic tasks.

2.2 Scope of the Aesthetic Problem

The predictions of a computational aesthetic algorithm can either target a *universal*, "average" observer (or a population of observers), or rather a specific user. In this chapter we mainly discuss the first viewpoint, which is also the most explored in the literature. It is evident that the validity of a universal aesthetic approach is conditioned on the consensus that human observers would achieve in judging the aesthetic value of a picture. Recent methods take into consideration the intrinsic variability in aesthetic assessment across different observers, e.g., they predict a distribution of aesthetic scores or some subjectivity measure (Kang et al. 2019). We discuss the important role of subjectivity in Sect. 5.1.

In contrast with this setting, *personalized* image aesthetics aims to predict the personal preference of a given observer, based on a set of previously annotated pictures or contextual information that enable one to restrict the space of possible aesthetic scores for that person. In this respect, personalized image aesthetics relies substantially on the subjectivist and interactionist foundations of aesthetics. We will briefly discuss personalized aesthetics in Sect. 5.1.3.

2.3 Aesthetic Features

An essential component of any image aesthetic prediction pipeline consists of extracting meaningful features from a picture. The first aesthetic features to be considered were *hand-crafted*, and mainly inspired by guidelines commonly used in photography, such as the rule of thirds, the use of negative space, the color harmony, etc. (see, e.g., Datta et al. (2006), Ke et al. (2006), Luo and Tang (2008), Aydın et al. (2014)), or by mathematical principles, as the classical work of Birkhoff (1933). An advantage of using hand-crafted features is the interpretability of aesthetic predictions. However, the purely objectivist interpretation assumed by these approaches does not take into account the subjective nature of aesthetic judgments, and thus often fails to provide accurate results for a broad range of contents and situations as encountered in real-world applications. We discuss in greater detail hand-crafted methods in Sect. 4.2.

More recently, the availability of large-scale datasets with human annotations (Murray et al. 2012; Kong et al. 2016) has promoted the adoption of data-driven methods, which rely on features extracted from images without a direct association to specific aesthetic attributes or rules. We can broadly consider two classes of features in this category: on one hand, generic features that could be used for other tasks not related to aesthetics (e.g., SIFT (Marchesotti et al. 2011)), and *deep* features learned directly from data. Differently from hand-crafted features, methods based on data-driven features do not look for the presence of specific attributes in the picture, but rather try to infer a relation between image pixels and aesthetic judgments given by humans, which provide the ground-truth for the evaluation. In this respect, they are less dependent on the initial hypotheses made on the definition of beauty; however, they incur the risk of overfitting the specific conditions in which the features have been learned (e.g., context and methodology of the subjective evaluation, type of content, or hidden patterns in the data). This constitutes a significant challenge toward understanding the factors explaining the predicted aesthetic scores. We present and analyze some relevant deep-learning-based aesthetics approaches in Sect. 4.4.

2.4 Output Prediction

Computational aesthetic methods can predict *classes* (typically binary such as "good/bad" quality, or "amateur/professional", etc.), *ratings* or *rankings* among images. In addition, an algorithm can also predict specific attributes or additional information that can help explain the subjective score (e.g., Aydın et al. (2014)). The first two output types require a single image as input, while the ranking by definition applies to a set of at least two or more images, with the goal to sort them in order of beauty (Kong et al. 2016; Park et al. 2017). The choice between classification and rating is mainly driven by the dataset used, i.e., whether subjective scores have been collected using a binary or any rating scale (discrete or continuous). In some cases, scores originally obtained on a rating scale are converted into binary classes to employ systems trained for classification, e.g., images with average scores less/higher than 5 on a 10 level scale are tagged as bad/good quality. In general, rating scales can provide a better reliability and discrimination of aesthetic scores compared to binary evaluations (Siahaan et al. 2016).

Since ground-truth aesthetic scores are typically obtained by a pool of voters, they represent samples from a distribution of votes. Traditionally, data-driven methods have been concentrating on predicting point estimates such as the average aesthetic score (Deng et al. 2017; Kao et al. 2015). However, recent work tends to estimate directly distributions of scores (Jin et al. 2016a; Talebi & Milanfar 2018; Jin et al. 2018) or measures of subjectivity (Kang et al. 2019), to explicitly model the variability of aesthetic judgments. We discuss in more detail subjectivity prediction in Sect. 5.1.

2.5 Applications

A dimension of analysis of aesthetic quality prediction includes the target applications. These can be varied and range from recommendation to retrieval and enhancement. Some examples of applications that use automatic aesthetic prediction include automatic image cropping (Guo et al. 2018), color (Deng et al. 2018) and composition enhancement (Zhang et al. 2013), photo filter recommendation (Sun et al. 2017), photo triage and album creation (Chang et al. 2016; Kuzovkin et al.

2017), etc. In the rest of the chapter we do not focus on any specific application scenario, but rather on the prediction methodologies.

3 Visual Aesthetics Datasets

Image datasets with aesthetic quality annotations are fundamental to developing computational methods to predict aesthetic appreciation. With the development of computational aesthetics in the mid 2000s, a number of aesthetic datasets were proposed, with different features and label types, to facilitate the training of classifiers based on hand-crafted features. In the 2010s, the creation of large-scale aesthetic datasets such as AVA has enabled researchers to apply deep-learning approaches to this problem, substantially pushing forward the accuracy of aesthetic prediction. In this section we present a review of some popular aesthetic datasets (see Table 1). Our goal is to offer a critical view of some of the main design criteria and trends in constructing aesthetic datasets. To this end, we organize the presentation by discussing some relevant characteristics that are likely to affect the choice of the most appropriate dataset in a given application scenario and the design of new ones.

3.1 Number of Images and Number of Votes per Image

One of the main features of a dataset is its *size*, i.e., the total number of images. Conventional quality assessment datasets collected in lab environments have a limited size of a few tens or hundreds of stimuli due to the costs and time requirements to perform the subjective test campaigns. Datasets obtained through crowdsourcing, instead, can reach a few thousands of stimuli. Finally, crawling annotations from existing websites allows one to obtain hundreds of thousands or millions of annotated images automatically, at the cost of higher noise and possible data bias. For example, the AVA dataset was obtained by crawling over 250k images from DPChallenge (see Sect. 3.2), with an average of 210 votes per image, enabling the use of deep-learning-based methods and becoming a reference dataset in computational aesthetics. We report some statistics of the AVA dataset in Fig. 2.

Often, the total number of votes that can be collected is limited due to time or budget constraints. This is also the case, e.g., of crowdsourcing or lab experiments. In these scenarios, there is a trade-off between the dataset size and the *number of votes per image*. A larger number of images enables better coverage of the vast spectrum of content variety encountered in practical situations. On the other hand, having more votes per image generally yields a better estimation of the picture's aesthetic value, as it reduces the confidence intervals of the estimated scores or score distributions. In technical quality assessment, it is generally recommended

Table 1 Overview of some popular aesthetic datasets according to several characteristics. ACR: Absolute Category Rating; AFC: Alternative Forced Choice pairwise comparison; MOS: Mean Opinion Score

Dataset	Year	Number of images	Votes/image	Image source	Labels	Voting scale	Collection method	Additional labels/attributes
Photo.net (Datta et al. 2006; Datta & Wang 2010)	2006/2008	~20k	≥10	Photo.net	binary (high/low quality);rating (1-100)	Discrete 1–7	Crawling	"originality", number of views and ratings
CUHK (Ke et al. 2006)	2006	~12k	≥100	DPChallenge	Binary (high/low quality)	Discrete 1–10	Crawling	N.A.
CUHKPQ (Tang et al. 2013)	2013	17,673	10	Professional photography websites	Binary (high/low quality)	Ternary (low, high, uncertain)	Crawling	7 semantic classes
Hidden Beauty (Schifanella et al. 2015)	2015	~15k	≥5	Flickr	5-levels discrete ACR	5-levels discrete ACR	crowdsourcing (crowdflower)	4 semantic classes
AVA (Murray et al. 2012)	2012	~255k	Between 78 and 549 (avg. 210)	DPChallenge	Discrete 1–10	Discrete 1–10	Crawling	Challenge information, semantic and style labels (for some images)
IAD (Lu et al. 2015b)	2015	1.5M	N.A.	DPChallenge, Photo.net	Binary	Discrete 1–10 and 1–7	Crawling	Camera parameters for some images
AVA-PD (Kairanbay et al. 2019)	2019	~119k	..........Same as AVA..........					AVA + age, gender, location attributes

(continued)

Table 1 (continued)

Dataset	Year	Number of images	Votes/image	Image source	Labels	Voting scale	Collection method	Additional labels/attributes
AVA-reviews (Wang et al. 2019)	2019	40k	....	.... Same as AVA	.... Same as AVA	....		AVA + text comments (6 per image)
AVA-Captions (Ghosal et al. 2019)	2020	∼ 230k	....			....		AVA + filtered text comments (∼ 5.58 per image)
FACD (Sun et al. 2017)	2017	1280 reference, 28,160 filtered (22 filters per image)	3 comparisons for each filtered image	AVA (8 most popular categories)	Preferences, scores, top preferred filters for each reference	3 AFC	crowdsourcing (AMT)	Semantic classes, filters
Princeton Adobe Photo Triage (Chang et al. 2016)	2016	15,545 (in 5,953 series)	≥ 10 per image pair	User-generated (from personal albums)	Raw preferences, ranking, Bradley-Terry scores	2 AFC + comments	crowdsourcing	Positive/negative comments. categories
AROD (Schwarz et al. 2018)	2018	380k	6,868 on average	Flickr (2k spatial resolution images)	Continuous in [0, 1]	Indirect ("faves")	Crawling	N.A.
PCCD (Chang et al. 2017)	2017	4235	N.A.	gurushots.com	Text comments, normalized rating	Rating scale 1–10, text comments	Crawling	7 aesthetic attributes
AADB (Kong et al. 2016)	2016	10k	5	Flickr	Score distribution, attributes	5-levels discrete, positive/negative attributes	crowdsourcing (AMT)	11 attributes, individual rater IDs

IAE (Yu et al. 2019)	2019	22k	10	Flickr and Instagram	Ratings, binary classes	4-level ACR	lab (aesthetics), crowdsourcing (emotions)	Emotion categories
Waterloo IAA (Liu & Wang 2017)	2017	1k	26	Photo.net	MOS	Single stimulus continuous	lab (ITU rec.)	5 semantic classes
FLICKR-AES (Ren et al. 2017)	2017	40k	5	Flickr	Ratings	5-level discrete ACR	crowdsourcing (AMT)	rater ID
REAL-CUR (Ren et al. 2017)	2017	~2870	1 (with repetitions)	Personal albums	....	N.A.		Rater ID
EVA (Kang et al. 2020)	2020	4070	≥ 30	AVA (medium-high quality)	Aesthetic scores, attribute scores, attribute importance	11-levels ACR (global score), 4-level Likert scale (attributes), binary (attribute importance)	crowdsourcing (custom website)	raters ID, voting time, voting difficulty, 6 semantic classes

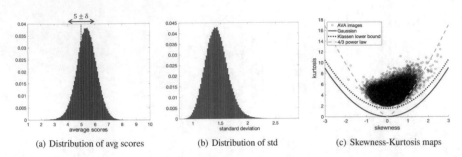

(a) Distribution of avg scores (b) Distribution of std (c) Skewness-Kurtosis maps

Fig. 2 Some statistics of the AVA dataset (Murray et al. 2012), perhaps the most popular dataset used in computational aesthetics. (**a**) Normalized distribution of the average scores of each image. The distribution can be modeled by as a Gaussian, with an average of 5.38, which is slightly lower than the mid-point of the rating scale (i.e., 5.5). Many computational aesthetics methods obtain binary labels from these scores, by labeling as *high-quality* those images with scores larger than $5 + \delta$, and as *low-quality* those images with scores lower than $5 - \delta$. The images with average scores in the interval $5 \pm \delta$ are often discarded as they are considered aesthetically ambiguous. Notice that this interval is *not* symmetric around the mean score of the dataset. (**b**) Normalized distribution of the standard deviations of the image scores. It has a longer tail (images with high std) compared to a Gaussian. (**c**) Skewness-Kurtosis maps (Park & Zhang 2015) can be used to visualize the consensus in the scores, and can be matched against theoretical bounds (here, the bound for a truncated Gaussian distribution; the Klassen lower bound for unimodal distributions; and a power law). See Sect. 5.1 for further details on the interpretation of these maps

that stimuli are voted by at least 15 observers (ITU-R 2012), with the underlying assumption that the distribution of votes is unimodal and approximately normal. This is not often the case for aesthetic quality assessment, where score distributions could be multimodal or strongly skewed, and thus a higher number of samples might be necessary. Furthermore, in lab experiments, all the stimuli are generally voted by the same set of raters (allowing one to apply some inter-rater agreement reliability analysis (Siahaan et al. 2016)), which is rarely the case for large-size datasets.

The trade-off between dataset size and score precision on video quality prediction using a deep neural network has been investigated in Götz-Hahn et al. (2019). Interestingly, the authors find that, when the total budget of votes is sufficiently high (larger than 1000 votes), the quality prediction performance appears relatively stable. For example, for a total budget of 100k votes, training prediction models based on deep neural networks using 1000 images with 100 votes per image, or 100,000 images with only one vote per image, produces quality score predictions with similar accuracy. Conversely, for smaller budgets (of 1000 images or less), intermediate budget allocations (e.g., five votes for 200 different images) provide higher performance. Notice that the quality evaluation task in Götz-Hahn et al. (2019) targeted technical video quality as intended in a video streaming setting rather than aesthetics. An extension of these observations to aesthetic quality is still missing.

3.2   Image Source

Depending on their source website or device, the images in a dataset might have very different technical and aesthetic qualities. Similarly, their annotations could vary significantly across data sources, e.g., they can be given by people with little background or knowledge in photography, groups of knowledgeable practitioners, or even professional photographers. A typical source of annotated images is photo amateurs and professional websites, such as Flickr, Photo.net, DPChallenge, etc., and social media platforms such as Instagram.

Flickr is probably the largest public source of photos online, with several hundreds of billions pictures hosted by the website. The uploaded pictures come with a number of metadata, including photographic attributes such as exposure time, aperture, camera model, and in some cases geolocalization. In addition, for each image it is possible to get the number of views and the "faves", i.e., the number of times an image has been liked by users. This information is used in some works as a proxy to aesthetic scores (Schwarz et al. 2018).

Photo.net is one of the oldest photo repositories used to produce aesthetic datasets. It hosts almost 5 million high-quality pictures taken by photographers with different experience from hobbyists to professionals. Datta et al. (2006), Datta and Wang (2010) collected one of the first aesthetic datasets based on Photo.net, which has been thereafter referred to with the same name as the website. Images from Photo.net have two kinds of annotations: aesthetics and originality, both rated on a discrete scale with 7 levels. Later versions of the website fused the two attributes in a single value, based on the observation that the two quantities are highly correlated.

DPChallenge is another website for photography amateurs and enthusiasts, which collects over 650k images organized in more than 3000 weekly thematic contests (challenges). The challenges are a fundamental component of the website to motivate users to submit their pictures, which span a broad range of qualities. Each photo can be voted on a discrete scale with 10 levels. The distribution of the average image scores is well modeled as a normal distribution with an average slightly higher than 5, while the standard deviation of the scores is slightly positively skewed with a longer tail. The number of votes per image can be significant (in the order of several hundreds). However, the aesthetic scores can be highly influenced by the thematic context of the challenge. The same holds for the subjectivity of the collected scores (Kang et al. 2019). The popular AVA dataset (Murray et al. 2012) has been created from DPChallenge, and is itself often used as a source to build other aesthetic datasets (Kairanbay et al. 2019; Kang et al. 2020). DPChallenge has inspired more recently other websites such as *Gurushots.com* and *500px*, which also employ similar concepts as the challenges, and collect user comments with the goal to offer personalized advice and improvement tips to photographers.

Finally, some datasets do not rely on online resources to collected voted images (e.g., to avoid copyright issues), and rather employ personal pictures or photo albums (Chang et al. 2016).

3.3   Voting Methodology and Aesthetic Labels

Existing datasets have been collected with different methodologies and experimental procedures, which makes it difficult in general to compare aesthetic scores across databases. Siahaan et al. (2016) have studied the impact of the voting scale on the reliability and repeatability of subjective aesthetic scores. They find that a 5-level absolute category rating (ACR) scale provides mean opinion scores (MOS) with better *reliability* (which can be measured, e.g., by inter-observer agreement) and *repeatability* across different datasets. Other rating scales, and in particular categorical binary scales (e.g., "high/low quality") tend to produce noisier aesthetic labels and thus are not recommended. Unfortunately, a large part of the datasets available in the literature seems not to respect these recommendations.

The choice of the questions and adjectives in the voting scale is critical in aesthetics. Differently from conventional technical quality assessment (ITU-R 2012), only few datasets employ some form of training of the raters to ensure that the task is clear and to provide examples of the stimuli used in the test (Kang et al. 2020; Schifanella et al. 2015; Liu & Wang 2017). Pairwise comparisons approaches can partially solve this issue, as they require choosing the preferred stimulus between two alternatives (two-alternative forced choice, or three-alternative forced choise in case a tie option is given). Pairwise comparisons involve a smaller cognitive load, and eliminate the need for training. However, the number of pairs to compare grows quadratically with the number of stimuli, which requires in practice the use of some form of approximate design (Li et al. 2013) or active sampling (e.g., Ye et al. (2014)). The collected preferences can be transformed into relative quality scores by applying some heuristics (e.g., vote counts) or psychometric scaling (Chang et al. 2016), such as the Thurstone or the Bradley-Terry-Luce (BTL) models. Fusing rating scales and pairwise preferences, e.g., to merge or align subjective datasets, is an active research topic (Zerman et al. 2018; Perez-Ortiz et al. 2019), which is still unexplored for aesthetics.

The labels made available in aesthetic datasets may include the simple raw data, or some form of processed data. In the CUHK dataset (Ke et al. 2006), for instance, the average rating scores are filtered to remove images with uncertain quality (those lying in the middle of the rating distribution), and only the top/bottom 10% of the pictures are retained and classified as high/low quality. A similar strategy is typically followed to create binary labels for classification on the AVA dataset (Murray et al. 2012), by discarding images with an average score between $5 - \delta$ and $5 + \delta$ (with $\delta = 0$ corresponding to using the whole dataset, see Fig. 2a). Typical values of δ range between 0 and 2.5.

In some cases, the raw scores are collected in an *indirect* way, by retrieving different but presumably related information, and require further processing to be converted into aesthetic labels. For example, the authors of Suchecki and Trzciski (2017) collect 1.7 million photos from Flickr, and assign them an aesthetic score which is a function of the average number of daily views of the picture. The AROD dataset (Schwarz et al. 2018) also crawls images from Flickr but considers the number of "faves" in the equation. While this data is largely available and cheap to collect, "faves" or "likes" are only loosely connected to aesthetics, and might be rather related to other preference mechanisms (interestingness, amazement), as discussed in Sect. 1.

3.4   Collection Method

There are essentially three approaches to collect aesthetic annotations. In *laboratory* experiments, the pictures are voted by a pool of observers in a particular test room, typically illuminated and equipped according to quality assessment recommendations such as the ITU-R BT.500 (ITU-R 2012) to provide controlled and reproducible testing conditions. Lab experiments generally include a subject screening for visual acuity/color perception, and a training phase, which depends on the methodology, to present the rating scale, the nature of the quality attribute to evaluate, and the use of the voting interface. Subjective quality campaigns performed in the labs are generally the best option to obtain precise and reliable subjective scores. However, they entail a significant cost in terms of data collection time—the use of a special test environment makes it impossible to massively parallelize the test.

Crowdsourcing resolves the limitations of lab experiments, in that they enable massive parallel voting, at the cost of reliability and repeatability. These are inevitably degraded due to the lack of effective controls of the engagement of raters, as well as the huge variety in the display devices, internet connection quality and viewing conditions. To partially alleviate this problem, it is highly advisable to include quality checks (such as "gold standards" test questions) in such a way to enable later the detection and filtering of potential unreliable votes or raters. Examples of quality checks for aesthetic crowsourcing are available, e.g., in Schifanella et al. (2015), Siahaan et al. (2016), Chang et al. (2016). Crowdsourcing has become one of the most popular approaches to collecting subjective scores (see, e.g., Ribeiro et al. (2011)), and has been employed in many aesthetic datasets.

Finally, a common approach that has been used to build aesthetic datasets consists of *crawling* aesthetic annotations (ratings, comments, preferences) directly from existing online sources, as described in Sect. 3.2.

3.5   Additional Labels and Attributes

In addition to aesthetic scores, datasets can offer additional labels to enable multi-task applications (Kao et al. 2017b), or provide contextual information for aesthetic prediction. Typical additional labels include the semantic class of the picture, generally categorized based on the content, e.g., nature, portraits, buildings, etc. In some cases, the aesthetic data is complemented by textual annotations and comments crawled from the web or collected during the experiments. The text information has been used to provide aesthetic explanations, leveraging natural language processing architectures (Wang et al. 2019). Perceptual attributes directly contribute to aesthetic judgments, and some datasets focus on measuring them, although not in an aesthetic context. It is the case, for example, for colorfulness (Zerman et al. 2019) or dynamic range (Hulusic et al. 2016). Other datasets provide additional attributes such as the emotional response, which are not directly related to aesthetics, but can participate in image preference formation (Yu et al. 2019). Finally, aesthetic scores can be augmented with unique identifiers of voters, to facilitate personalized aesthetics applications.

4 Approaches to Computational Aesthetics

In the following, we review the main approaches to computational aesthetics proposed in the literature. Two general families of methods can be distinguished: those based on hand-crafted or generic features, and those that try to deduce the aesthetic quality of a picture directly from data, in an end-to-end fashion. Before presenting in more details these two paradigms, we briefly describe some preliminary work aimed at defining a mathematical model of aesthetics. All the methods introduced here build on an objectivist interpretation of aesthetics. Readers interested in computational aesthetics can also refer to the experimental survey of Deng et al. (2017).

4.1 Mathematical Approaches

Although it does not explicitly provide an algorithm to compute aesthetics on a computer (in fact, computers had not yet been invented at that time), the mathematical theory proposed by the mathematician and statistician George D. Birkhoff in 1933 (Birkhoff 1933) is generally considered as the predecessor of all quantitative models of aesthetics. Formalizing the artistic principle of "unit in variety", Birkhoff suggested the measurement of aesthetics as a ratio:

$$M = \frac{\text{Order}}{\text{Complexity}}. \tag{1}$$

The aesthetic measure can then be interpreted as the reward that the observer gets in terms of perceiving a pleasing harmony (order) when putting in an effort to focus and integrate a scene (complexity).

Despite his efforts to prove the validity of his conjecture in different fields of arts, Birkhoff was not able to bring convincing empirical evidence to his theory, also due to the lack of modern mathematical and signal processing tools to analyze pictures. Nevertheless, Birkhoff's ideas have been rediscovered and utilized in later work, with the aid of more modern mathematical tools, e.g., the Kolmogorov complexity is employed in Machado and Cardoso (1998) and Rigau et al. (2008) to compute the complexity of the image (a JPEG or fractal compression of the picture are used to approximate the Kolmogorov complexity, which is not computable), together with more sophisticated image processing tools such as image segmentation. Recently, a mathematical formulation of aesthetics based on thermodynamics that partially extends the principles of Birkhoff has been proposed in Lakhal et al. (2020).

4.2 Hand-Crafted Features

Modern approaches to computational aesthetics have abandoned the search for a holistic mathematical formulation of beauty in favor of a more pragmatical data-driven vision of the problem. The hypothesis is that aesthetics resides in a set of attributes and features of an image, and the relation between these features and aesthetic judgment can be deduced by observing a large number of pictures annotated by humans. The general pipeline of this data-driven approach consists therefore of three steps: (1) choose or collect a photographic dataset with aesthetic annotations; (2) extract a set of relevant image features from each photo in the dataset; (3) train a classifier (typically, a support vector machine—SVM) or a regressor to predict aesthetic scores based on the extracted features of unseen images (Kuzovkin 2019). By relevant features, we intend features that can be related to specific aesthetic attributes (color, composition, etc., see Fig. 3 for some examples). These features provide valuable information to the classifier or regressor, which learns how to combine them to produce a synthetic overall aesthetic score. Since we already discussed the collection of aesthetics datasets in Sect. 3, we will focus on the feature extraction and the prediction scheme in the following section.

4.2.1 Initial Works

Two seminal works in modern computational aesthetics were proposed by Datta et al. (2006) and Ke et al. (2006) in 2006. In addition to collecting the first aesthetics datasets, they introduce a set of aesthetic features and a general prediction framework based on classification (e.g., using a support vector machine—SVM) to determine if a picture has a high or low aesthetic level. Many later works follow a similar approach and use similar features.

Datta et al. (2006) collected the Photo.net dataset, containing approximately 3800 pictures (see Table 1). They consider 56 features, including:

- *low-level and color* features such as the average pixel intensity to characterize the use of light (exposure); a colorfulness measure computed as a distance between

(a) Rule of thirds   (b) Positive and negative space

(c) Depth of field   (d) Color harmony

Fig. 3 Some photographic rules and concepts that serve as models to design aesthetic features. (**a**) The rule of thirds is a well-known composition rule suggesting that salient objects in the picture should be positioned along or at the intersections ("powerpoints") of the horizontal/vertical lines dividing the height and length of the image into 3 equal parts. (**b**) Negative space is the area surrounding the main subject in the photo (positive space), which should be left unoccupied to facilitate the focus of the observer on the region of interest. A disregard for negative space may produce cluttered and unclear pictures. (**c**) The depth of field is the distance between the closest and farthest objects in a photo that appear sharp. Using a low depth of field (an effect sometimes referred to as *bokeh*) is a powerful way to concentrate the attention on the subject of the picture (by emphasizing the negative space through blur), and is considered aesthetically appealing. (**d**) Similar to harmony in music, colors in photography can produce more or less harmonic combinations. The rules of color harmony are numerous (see, e.g., Moon and Spencer (1944)). They are based on the principle of avoiding colors that are too close on the color wheel (shown in the right part of the image), which would create ambiguity (similar to dissonance in music). Instead, an aesthetically pleasing combination should include complementary colors or combinations of colors lying on simple geometric shapes on the color wheel (e.g., in this example, the three main colors can be imagined to be at the vertices of a triangle). Figure best viewed in color

the distribution of color (in the LUV color space) of the image and a reference distribution with uniform color probabilities; the average saturation and hue;

- *composition*-related features, which are inspired by photographic rules. These include a measure of the *rule of thirds*, computed as the average intensities in the center portion of the image, in the HSV color space; an indicator of the *depth of field* based on a wavelet decomposition of the image; aspect ratio; a region composition indicator based on color segmentation;

- *familiarity*, intended as the average distance of an image to other images in the dataset in terms of color, texture and shape;
- *texture* features based on a wavelet decomposition in the HSV space to quantify the graininess or smoothness of the textures;
- *shape convexity* features, which compute the portion of the image containing convex objects, and are related to the assumption made by authors that convex and regular shapes produce a positive aesthetic response.

An SVM classifier trained with a selected subset of these features obtains an accuracy ranging between 62 and 70%, depending on the margin left between the ground-truth binary classes. This system has been later extended in Datta and Wang (2010) and has been put online with the name ACQUINE (aesthetic quality inference engine), which computes an aesthetic rating for a given input image.

The work of Ke et al. (2006) has a similar approach. The goal is to classify whether an image is a professional or amateur picture. To this end, the authors crawled 60,000 photos from DPChallenge, choosing the ones voted by at least one hundred viewers. The two aesthetic classes are obtained by taking the highest and lowest 10% average rates. The features proposed in this work try to capture mainly high-level photographic concepts by using image processing and computer vision tools, and include:

- two *simplicity* measures. One is computed from edge maps in the picture: in professional pictures the edges are concentrated round the middle of the image, reducing the quantity of distracting structure in the background (similar to the concept of negative space in photography, see Fig. 3); the other is the hue count, another way to gauge the cluttering of a photo;
- *color palette*, computed as the histogram of a version of the image with quantized color levels. The number of professional/amateur photos that are the nearest neighbors to the current image in this histogram space determine the class of the picture;
- *low-level features*, including a measure of blur, and intensity features such as contrast and exposure.

These features are then used into a naive Bayes classifier to discriminate between professional and amateur photos. The reported classification accuracy peaks at 72% when professional/amateur photos correspond to the 10% highest/lowest average scores. Later work show that for less favorable class splits, the accuracy is lower and generally ranging between 60 and 70%.

4.2.2   Considering the Salient Object of the Picture

The two methods discussed above obtained encouraging performances, although the accuracy is still relatively limited. Later work has further improved classification accuracy by extending the feature set and/or the classification strategy. A class of methods takes in consideration explicitly the role of the *subject* of the picture. For example, Luo and Tang (2008) employ a similar approach as Ke et al. (2006), but they compute different criteria depending on whether an image region belongs to the subject or to the background. The distinction subject/background is done based on a simple blur-based heuristic. Mai et al. (2011, 2012) analyze the salient regions of an image using a saliency map predictor, to determine whether the composition of the photo respects the rule of thirds and the principle of simplicity (e.g., by using the negative space or a low depth of field, see Fig. 3). Zhang et al. (2014) adopt a more sophisticated approach inspired by human perception, where aesthetics is evaluated along *visual scan paths* (represented as graphlets), to mimic human visual attention mechanisms. The idea to embed visual attention mechanisms in computational aesthetics has been further explored with deep-learning-based methods (see Sect. 4.4).

4.2.3   Including Semantic Information

Another strategy to augment aesthetic features consists in taking into account the semantics of the picture, and in particular high-level features related to the *image content*. For instance, Dhar et al. (2011) employ a complex set of features, including both low-level ones (as in the works described above) and high-level features describing composition (depth of field, salient object, etc.), content (faces, presence of animals, indoor-outdoor, etc.) and sky illumination. The high-level descriptors are obtained by several classification subsystems (SVM classifiers), a scheme that scales poorly with the number of possible objects to recognize. As we will see next, this limitation is partially solved by using deep learning models, which can easily represent and predict a vast ensemble of object classes. Image content significantly affects which visual features are relevant to predict aesthetics (e.g., the way to perceive beauty of a landscape is forcibly different from the aesthetics of portraits) (Simond et al. 2015). In this respect, Luo et al. (2011) mix the subject detection strategy with image categorization and propose a different subject/background segmentation and extract visual features differently depending on the class of the picture.

4.2.4   Multi-Dimensional Approaches

Some methods based on hand-crafted features do not simply aim at predicting a global aesthetic class or score, but rather treat aesthetics as a *multi-dimensional* problem, where the overall evaluation is obtained as the composition of several aesthetic attributes. This viewpoint has the advantage to provide a better interpretability of *why* an image is aesthetically pleasing or not. Lo et al. (2012) propose a visual interface with a sort of "radar" plot (see Fig. 4) where the magnitude of five attributes (saturation, color, composition, contrast and richness) is displayed. The

(a) original   (b) edited   (c) aesthetic attributes

Fig. 4 The multi-dimensional representation of aesthetics proposed in Aydın et al. (2014). For each image, five photographic attributes are evaluated. The overall aesthetic score is given by a combination of the attribute scores. Decomposing the aesthetic scores into multiple components enables one to explain why a photo is aesthetically pleasing, and can be used to guide an enhancement process. In this example, an original image (**a**) with low dynamic range (tone) and drab colors is edited to increase colorfulness and contrast, while also putting more emphasis on the subject (**b**). The attributes scores for the two images can be intuitively displayed in a radar plot (**c**). The area enclosed by the polygon in the plot gives an indication of the overall aesthetic score. Figure best viewed in color

surface of the polygon connecting the different attribute scores give an indication of the overall aesthetic quality. A similar approach is proposed in Aydın et al. (2014), where the attributes are linked to photographic concepts and are calibrated by an original experimental procedure. On the opposite of these multi-dimensional approaches are methods that consider aesthetics from the perspective of a single attribute, e.g., by considering only color harmony (Lu et al. 2015a, 2016).

4.2.5   Leveraging Users' Comments

In addition to visual features, some datasets report also text comments from users (see Sect. 3). This data can provide valuable information to predict aesthetics. For example, the authors of San Pedro et al. (2012) employed hidden Markov models to analyze text comments crawled from DPChallenge. They compared the features associated to text with image-based features (combined using a support vector regression to predict aesthetic scores), and found that, interestingly, the text-based features perform substantially better than image-based ones on a regression task. The fusion of text and image features provide only a marginal advantage. It must be noted, though, that the feature extraction mechanism for text comments is likely to generalize poorly to comments using expressions not contained in the dataset. We will see next that the idea of employing text comments has been further exploited in the context of deep-learning-based methods, where comments are also generated by the prediction algorithm to endow the aesthetic judgments with partial explainability.

To conclude this overview on hand-crafted approaches, it is worth mentioning works targeting task-specific input (and not general aesthetics as for the methods described above), such as images of people. In those cases, features describe specific aspects related to faces, such as the pose, the expressions and lighting (Li et al. 2010; Redi et al. 2015).

4.3   Generic Features

So far we have discussed methods that try to encode explicitly the best practices of photography. The advantage of these methods is that, in many cases, it is possible to identify the factors that lead to a certain aesthetic score. However, the performance of hand-crafted features rest limited due to several reasons, e.g., the features are not exhaustive (they cannot cover all the possible photographic principles), and they are based on simple heuristics, i.e., they try to encode complex rules by simple, low-level processing. As a result, these methods have a low ability to generalize to similar cases, resulting in a generally large variance of the prediction performance.

Marchesotti et al. (2011) proposed a very different approach. Instead of using specific aesthetic features, they argue that the aesthetic information is implicitly embedded into *generic* image features, which encode the distribution of local image statistics. The motivation behind this approach is that, at the time this work was proposed, generic image features such as the Bag of Visual Words (BOVW, Csurka et al. (2004)) and Fisher Vectors (FV, Jaakkola et al. (1999)) displayed excellent capabilities to deal with complex semantic tasks, which suggests that they could also lead to good performance for aesthetics. The hypothesis is that generic local features can reveal information about the local sharpness or color distribution that, when aggregated from patch level to image level, is sufficiently rich to summarize the global characteristics of images (mix of sharp and blur edges, color harmony, etc.). In this respect, hand-crafted features capture specific instances of these global characteristics. To test this hypothesis, the authors extract SIFT (Scale-invariant feature transform) features from the image. The SIFT features describe the local gradient orientations at keypoints detected by a scale-space blob detector (Lowe 1999). In addition to SIFT, some color descriptors are also considered. The features are aggregated at the image level, using either a discrete histogram (BOVW), or a more sophisticated modeling of the second-order statistics (FV) using a high-dimensional Gaussian mixture model, which yields continuous features. The two features are inputted to an SVM classifier to predict the aesthetic class (high/low quality). The results obtained by the authors on the Photo.net and the CUHPK datasets (see Sect. 3) show significant gains (from 5 to 10%) in terms of accuracy compared to hand-crafted approaches such as Datta et al. (2006) and Ke et al. (2006).

The results of Marchesotti et al. (2011) are particularly relevant in the field of computational aesthetics, since they demonstrated for the first time that generic, aesthetic-agnostic features could outperform a carefully hand-crafted feature design based on well-established photographic rules. Later, the same authors extended their work to add some form of explainability, by including text comments from AVA and mining them to discover relevant aesthetic attributes (Marchesotti 2013). These works prelude a trend that has become the main approach in computer vision and multimedia nowadays, i.e., learning generic features directly from data using deep neural networks.

4.4 Deep Learning Approaches

The method based on generic features presented above is still employing a hand-crafted design of low-level features (SIFT or color descriptors). In other words, the design of the features is *independent* of the data, and the task of making an efficient use of them to predict aesthetic scores is left to the classifier. The advent of deep neural networks changed significantly the paradigm of feature extraction, making it *data driven*: a high-dimensional (often, in the order of 10^6 parameters) neural network model is learned in an end-to-end fashion, by optimizing a differentiable loss function using directly the images and the corresponding labels as input, without the need to pre-compute any handcrafted features. A class of deep neural networks of particular interest for image processing is convolutional neural networks (CNN). The interested reader can refer to Goodfellow et al. (2016) for an introduction to deep learning. We review in the following some of the main approaches and challenges to employ deep convolutional neural networks for computational aesthetics.

4.4.1 Preserving Global and Local Information

As mentioned above, deep neural networks typically contain millions of parameters to learn (called also weights), e.g., the VGG-16 architecture (Simonyan & Zisserman 2014) used in many aesthetic works has 134 millions of parameters. This makes their use very demanding both in terms of computational time and memory consumption (Bianco et al. 2018a). In practice, to keep the problem tractable with the available graphical processing units (GPUs), especially at the beginning of the deep learning era input images were resized to a lower resolution (e.g., 224 × 224 pixels) in order to be used on pre-trained models, which were then fine-tuned for a specific application. Nevertheless, resizing images to small, square thumbnails in the case of aesthetic evaluation can seriously alter both the composition of the image and the presence of small but relevant details, compromising aesthetic assessment. Initial works applying CNN architectures to computational aesthetics addressed this issue.

The first deep-learning-based system for aesthetic classification was proposed by Lu et al. (2014) under the name of **RAPID** (Rating pictorial aesthetics using deep learning). To deal with the resizing and aspect ratio problems, RAPID employs a *two-column* network (see Fig. 5a): two identical networks (in this case, AlexNet is used (Krizhevsky et al. 2012)) with independent weights are fed with different inputs, and their features are then merged into one or more shared layers (typically

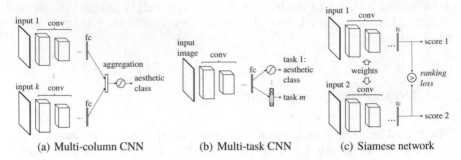

(a) Multi-column CNN   (b) Multi-task CNN   (c) Siamese network

Fig. 5 Some deep neural network architectures used in computational aesthetics. (**a**) Multi-column CNNs are a way to handle different inputs (images, attributes, patches, etc.). These are processed by parallel networks, which could have or not the same architecture and shared weights. The output of the columns is then merged in an aggregation layer to obtain an aesthetic class or rating. (**b**) Multi-task networks are designed instead to perform different tasks which are correlated. The input image is processed by a single network, and the tasks are differentiated at the last layers. The difficulty with these networks is to find a good balance between tasks in the training. (**c**) Siamese networks are composed by two identical networks (with shared weights), which are trained simultaneously by minimizing a *ranking loss*

fully connected). The two networks are trained jointly. The first column in RAPID takes as input the whole picture, warped (resized and padded) to 224 × 224 spatial resolution. In the second column, the input is a patch (again of 224 × 224 pixels) randomly extracted from the image at the original resolution. The evaluation of the two columns is repeated 50 times to average the results across different random patches. In this way, the network learns to evaluate global and local information, both necessary to predict the aesthetic class of an image. RAPID achieves 73% classification accuracy on the AVA dataset, which is higher than any other previously proposed hand-crafted features on this dataset. The performance is slightly improved (74%) when adding an extra column to the network with style information (available for some images in AVA).

This approach is later extended in Lu et al. (2015c), which proposes a deep multi-patch aggregative network (**DMA-Net**) with five columns. In this case, the input to each column is an original-resolution patch extracted ramdomly from the image, and the five branches are sharing weights to speed-up training. The features from the columns are merged using either an order-independent pooling operator (e.g., average or max pooling), or using a fully connected network with a sorting layer. The reported classification accuracy with the best configuration is 75.4%. A different strategy is considered by Mai et al. (2016) in the multi-net adaptive spatial pooling CNN (**MNA-CNN**). They add an adaptive spatial pooling layer upon the regular convolution and pooling layers to handle a limitation of the conventional CNN design, where the presence of fully-connected layers assumes a fixed-size feature vector. The idea is to perform max pooling over local image regions, but fixing the output size instead of the receptive field's size. This strategy is repeated for different adaptive spatial pooling sizes to obtain a multi-scale representation. MNA-CNN achieves a classification accuracy of 77.1% on AVA.

The multi-column principle introduced by DMA-Net has proved to be very effective in preserving local and global information, and has been employed by many deep-learning-based approaches later on. Ma et al. (2017) improved the selection of patches in their adaptive a layout-aware multi-patch (**A-Lamp**) CNN. Differently from DMA-Net, A-Lamp selects patches adaptively based on the content of the image, using a pre-trained saliency model. An attribute-graph representation of salient patches is then assembled using the areas of the patches, as well as their reciprocal orientation and distance. This information is processed by layout-aware sub-network to capture the topology and layout of the picture. The selected patches follow then a multi-patch sub-network with an aggregation layer at the end, similar to DMA-Net. Finally, the two subnets are merged through a learned aggregation layer. The A-Lamp approach reaches a classification accuracy of 82.5% on AVA, showing that a saliency-driven choice of patches can bring substantial advantages over a random or fixed patch selection strategy. Sheng et al. (2018b) propose a multi-patch (**MP**) network with an attention mechanism (Stollenga et al. 2014): instead of using a pre-trained saliency model as in A-Lamp, the selection of salient patches in MP is learned directly from aesthetic labels, by assigning different weights to different image patches. Among the different weight assignment schemes considered, an adaptive one (MP_{ada}) obtains 83.03% classification accuracy on AVA. The state-of-the-art aesthetic classification methods in 2020 employ a combination of multi-patch networks, attention mechanisms and global features (Liu et al. 2020; Xu et al. 2020), achieving a classification accuracy of 83.59% on the standard AVA test set.

4.4.2 Content-Adaptive CNNs

As discussed in Sect. 4.2.3, considering the semantic content of a picture can help in assessing aesthetics. Compared to hand-crafted approaches, deep-learning-based methods can capture semantic information much better, and indeed many CNN architectures for aesthetic prediction employ the availability of additional content labels whenever possible (e.g., AVA provides additional information related to content and style, see Sect. 3).

The common way used in the literature to employ semantic information is to add a scene classifier in the deep model. A typical categorization used in aesthetics is based on 7 classes: *human, plant, architecture, landscape, static, animal* and *night*. These categories were initially proposed by Tang et al. (2013) and have been later used in many deep aesthetic models. The MNA-CNN network (Mai et al. 2016) discussed above includes a scene-categorization CNN fine-tuned on these 7 categories. Wang et al. (2016) build a multi-scene deep learning model (**MSDLM**) by cascading four convolutional layers of AlexNet (Krizhevsky et al. 2012), which is supposed to recognize the kind of scene, with a scene convolutional layer composed of 7 parallel convolutional blocks corresponding to 7 possible scene categories. The scene group layers are pre-trained on images of a specific category to improve the classification performance. This work achieves an accuracy of 76.95% on AVA.

Another way to leverage semantic information of the scene consists of *multi-task* learning, in which a main task (aesthetics) is learned together with other additional tasks—in this case, a predictor of the image category (see Fig. 5b). Since both tasks are optimized concurrently in the network, the relative importance of the two task losses is a critical factor for a successful multi-task learning. Kao et al. (2017b) propose two possible solutions to determine the task weights. In their basic multi-task CNN architecture (**MT-CNN**), the relative importance of the aesthetic and semantic tasks is fixed to be $2/M$, where M is the number of categories ($M = 29$ semantic tags from AVA is used here). This network achieves an accuracy of 78.56% on AVA. The relative weights of the tasks can also be discovered directly from data, based on a Bayesian interpretation of multi-task learning. In particular, the relationship between tasks is embedded in the loss function under the form of a covariance matrix between the task-specific network parameters (corresponding to layers where parameters are not shared between tasks). The training procedure then consists of alternating steps of gradient descent and covariance matrix update. This network is called multi-task relationship learning CNN (**MTRL-CNN**). The classification accuracy with learned task weights rises to 79.08%. Despite the elegant mathematical formulation behind MTRL-CNN, the simultaneous calibration of the tasks remains challenging in practice, and later work has shown that training the network in two stages (by fine-tuning a semantic predictor) can lead to better aesthetics classification (Murray & Gordo 2017).

4.4.3 Aesthetic Regression

Providing a two-class aesthetic prediction may be insufficient in many applications where a finer-granularity assessment is desirable (e.g., for image enhancement). In those cases, it is more appropriate to estimate an *aesthetic rating* through a regression network. In particular, existing methods have focused on predicting the *average* score for an image, as given by human raters, e.g., a value between 1 and 10 for the AVA dataset. It is relatively straightforward to modify the architectures presented above to predict a continuous aesthetic score rather than a binary value. For instance, in Kao et al. (2015) the last layer of the network, which is a two-way softmax in aesthetic classification, is replaced by a single neuron to produce a scalar value. The loss used is the mean squared error. The performance criteria in the case of regression is no longer the accuracy, but rather measures such as mean squared error (MSE), root-mean-square error (RMSE), mean residual sum of squared errors (MRSSE), Pearson or Spearman rank-order correlation coefficients (PCC or SROCC, respectively). Nevertheless, it is typical to also provide classification results by thresholding the predicted scores, e.g., to the cut value of $5 \pm \delta$ in AVA (see Sect. 3.3), to benchmark the proposed methods with the state of the art. Current deep-learning-based methods for predicting the aesthetic mean score reach a correlation with ground-truth slightly in excess of 0.7, which is significantly lower than the performance of no-reference technical quality assessment metrics, where the correlations are generally well higher than 0.8. This fact confirms the challenging nature of aesthetic quality assessment, but also raises some questions regarding the subjectivity of ground-truth scores (see Sect. 5.1).

To partially take into account the intrinsic subjectivity of aesthetics, a particular class of aesthetic regression networks aims at predicting the *distribution* of scores, rather than their mean. These systems include the popular neural image assessment (**NIMA**, Talebi and Milanfar (2018)), the aesthetic prediction model (**APM**, Murray and Gordo (2017)) and others (Jin et al. 2016a, 2018). We will discuss these techniques in more detail in Sect. 5.1.

4.4.4 Fusing Hand-Crafted and Deep Features

As discussed at the beginning of this section, an advantage of hand-crafted features over deep-learning-based methods is the intrepretability of aesthetic predictions. Some computational aesthetics approaches try to integrate the benefits of pure deep models and hand-crafted attributes by proposing mixed solutions fusing expert knowledge with data-driven features.

For example, Kucer et al. (2018) consider a mix of 331 hand-crafted features, obtained by some of the methods discussed in Sect. 4.2, and of deep features extracted by deep CNN such as VGG or ResNet. Using a tree-based learner, the authors show that, even if individually these feature sets are dominated in performance by current neural networks solutions, the (early or late) fusion of the features can provide competitive performance. In addition, the use of the tree-based learning approach allows one to deduce the importance of each feature in the aesthetic decision, and to significantly reduce the size of the feature set to less than 15% of the original size. The accuracy of this method on AVA is 81.95%, which is competitive with respect to more recent methods based on deep learning only. Notice that the explainability, i.e., which attributes are more relevant to the aesthetic decision, is achieved only in an average sense here, but not per picture.

A very different approach is that of Wang et al. (2017), who propose a deep network based on the Chatterjee's visual neuroscience model (Deep Chatterjee's machine, **DCM**) (Chatterjee 2003). The Chatterjee's model provides some insights on how humans perceive aesthetic quality: the human brain works as a multi-level system, in which the visual sensory input first processes a number of relevant features through a set of parallel pathways. Afterwards, the output of these pathways are associated and synthesized at a higher level into an aesthetic decision. Inspired by this framework, DCM computes several aesthetic attributes in parallel, using either hand-crafted features (in this case, simply the hue, saturation and value color representation), or CNNs which are trained in a supervised manner to predict one of the 14 AVA style labels (*complementary colors, duotones, vanishing point,* etc.). In a second step, a high-level synthesis network is used to fuse the attributes, and the overall network is trained to learn the distribution of votes (using the Kullback-Leibler divergence as metric). The authors also provide an interesting study on the sensitivity of aesthetic prediction on the transformation of the input image (e.g., reflection, rotation, noise, etc.), which provides useful hints to perform data augmentation for aesthetics. The reported classification accuracy on AVA is 78.08%.

4.4.5 Learning an Aesthetic Ranking

The works that we have reviewed so far cast aesthetic prediction as either a classification or regression problem. In practice, often an aesthetic decision involves the comparison of two or more pictures, e.g., to decide which photo to keep in a personal album. It is clear that aesthetic classification is not sufficient in this case, and even a continuous rating might be imprecise when assessing the preference between two images. As an alternative, some works propose learning a ranking relationship directly from data, using a *ranking loss*.

Kong et al. (2016), who also proposed the AADB dataset (see Sect. 3), employ a Siamese network (Chopra et al. 2005) that takes as input a pair of images and directly predicts their relative ranking and aesthetic scores (see Fig. 5c). The network is constituted by two identical branches with shared weights, and is trained by minimizing the following *contrastive* loss term:

$$\mathcal{L}_{\text{contrast}} = \sum_{i,j} \max \left(0, \alpha - \eta(y_i \geq y_j)(\hat{y}_i - \hat{y}_j)\right), \tag{2}$$

where y_i and $\hat{y}_i$ are the ground-truth and predicted average rating for image i, $\eta(y_i \geq y_j) = 1$ if $y_i \geq y_j$ and $\eta(y_i \geq y_j) = -1$ otherwise, and α is a margin parameter. The contrastive loss penalizes predictions that invert the original aesthetic ranking of images more than predictions that preserve this ranking. In this second case, predictions that provide the correct ranking and estimate scores spaced out by at least the margin α are less penalized to focus the learning process on the difficult pairs with similar ratings. In addition to the contrastive loss, a regression term (e.g., MSE) is also added to anchor the predicted scores to the original rating scale. This basic Siamese architecture is integrated into an attribute and content-adaptive network, and experiments show an overall SROCC of approximately 0.56, and a classification accuracy of 77.33% on AVA. Performance on AADB is higher (correlation in excess of 0.67). Interestingly, the authors also provide a cross-dataset train/test evaluation, showing that a network trained on AADB has very poor performance (SROCC $\approx$ 0.15) on AVA, and vice-versa. This opens up a number of questions regarding the generalization capabilities of deep-learning-based aesthetic predictors.

A different ranking loss is employed in Schwarz et al. (2018), which uses a *triplet network* architecture to learn an aesthetic distance in the feature space (Hoffer & Ailon 2015). Compared to the Siamese architecture, the triplet network has three columns with shared weights, which receive three inputs: an anchor image a, an aesthetically similar image p and an aesthetically dissimilar image n. The network is trained by minimizing a triplet loss:

$$\mathcal{L}_{\text{triplet}} = \sum_{a,p,n} \max\left(0, \alpha + \|\Phi_a - \Phi_p\|_2^2 - \|\Phi_a - \Phi_n\|_2^2\right), \qquad (3)$$

where Φ_a, Φ_p and Φ_n are embeddings (i.e., deep CNN features in this case) for a, p and n, respectively, and α is a margin parameter. Intuitively, the triplet loss pushes images that have similar aesthetic level to be close in the feature space, and images which have very different aesthetic values to have very different embeddings, thus enforcing a ranking among images. The reported results of the fine-tuned network on AVA do not show significant improvement over the Siamese architecture described above (accuracy of 75.83%), although the two networks are not comparable as Schwarz et al. (2018) does not include attribute and semantic information.

To conclude this section, we report in Fig. 6 the classification accuracy on the AVA dataset of some of the deep-learning-based methods discussed above. We can clearly see a performance improvement (over 10% gain) in accuracy in the past six years. Also, we observe that performance have been saturating in the last years to slightly less than 84% when $\delta = 0$ is used to label the aesthetic classes in AVA. It seems difficult nowadays to go far beyond this value using the AVA dataset. This limit raises questions regarding the nature of aesthetic data used as ground-

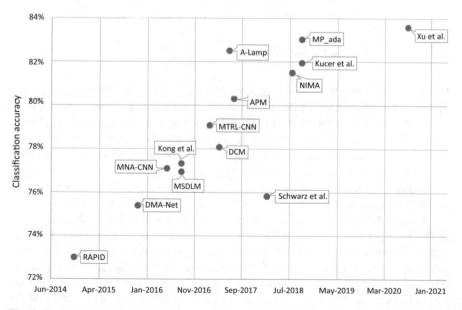

Fig. 6 Evolution of binary classification accuracy on the AVA dataset for some relevant deep-learning-based methods

truth: as discussed in Sect. 3, the aesthetic scores crawled from DPChallenge can be significantly influenced by the semantic context (challenge, content, etc.), which makes the ground-truth scores irremediably noisy and affected by other factors than aesthetics, such as interestingness. How to collect large aesthetic datasets with clean labels is still an open question, and only little work has been devoted to it in the multimedia community, compared to the more traditional technical quality assessment problem, for which guidelines and recommendations have been available for several decades (e.g., ITU-R (2012)).

5 Challenges in Computational Aesthetics: Subjectivity and Explainability

The overview of computational aesthetic methods presented in the previous section demonstrates that substantial progress has been made in this field in the last 15 years. However, it also points out some limitations and weaknesses of the current state of the art in computational aesthetics. In addition to the still limited accuracy of aesthetic prediction approaches, we have already mentioned some open challenges in the field of computational aesthetics, including the reliability of the ground-truth scores, the capability to explain the aesthetic judgments, and the subjective nature of aesthetic decisions. In this section we discuss these challenges, and in particular the dimensions of *subjectivity* and *explainability* in computational aesthetics.

5.1 Dealing with Subjectivity

In Sect. 1 we have introduced the classical subjectivist/objectivist debate in aesthetics. As we have mentioned there, the vast majority of existing computational aesthetics methods embrace an objectivist hypothesis on the aesthetic quality of photos. Specifically, they assume beauty is a property of the picture, produced by a combination of its attributes, which is essentially belonging to the object rather than the observer, thus being *universal*. This hypothesis legitimates the identification of an aesthetic score as a pooling operation over a set of opinions (e.g., average, or majority vote, etc.), which is taken as the ground truth of aesthetic prediction.

In practice, while opinions of multiple observers might follow a common trend, individual opinions are inherently subjective. The causes of this *subjectivity* are varied. They can be imputed to the inner state of the viewer and his/her contingent feelings, mood, sensations, etc. In photography, subjectivity can occur due to different evaluation criteria followed by photographers (Barrett 2020), which are also influenced by the historical epoch, cultural context and demographics of the observer (Kairanbay et al. 2019; Redi et al. 2016). The level of expertise of the viewers can also impact the perception of aesthetics (Lebreton et al. 2016), e.g.,

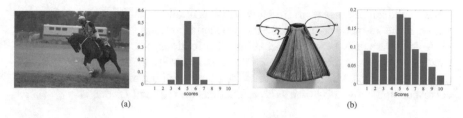

Fig. 7 Subjectivity in image aesthetics. The two photos (taken from the AVA dataset) have exactly the same average aesthetic score. However, their normalized score distribution (displayed on the right panels) reveals a very different degree of consensus of human raters. (**a**) A photo with low subjectivity. (**b**) A photo with high subjectivity

functional magnetic resonance imaging (fMRI) scans have revealed significant differences in the neural activities between architects and non-architects when evaluating photos of buildings (Kirk et al. 2009). A study carried out using magnetoencephalography has discovered significant differences in brain activity when assessing the beauty of photos and paintings in male and female participants (Cela-Conde et al. 2009).

Due to subjectivity, the opinions of individual viewers may be in disagreement with each other. We define the aesthetic subjectivity of a picture as the *degree of consensus* about its aesthetic value when this is judged by a panel of human observers (Kang et al. 2019). Figure 7 illustrates this definition with two example images from the AVA dataset. Compared to the traditional technical quality assessment, where inter-viewer agreement is generally high, in aesthetics the human judgments tend to be more dispersed. In the following, we discuss some attempts to include the subjectivity dimension in computational aesthetics.

5.1.1 Predicting Score Distributions

A popular way to consider aesthetic subjectivity is to predict the *distribution* of the image aesthetic scores. This is represented as a vector of probabilities over a set of ordinal values instead of a single one-dimensional estimate (e.g., average score or the aesthetic class). Predicting score distributions requires adapting computational aesthetics techniques to process categorical probability distributions as labels. In particular, while conventional loss functions may be used (e.g., the Huber loss is used to reduce the impact of outliers by Murray and Gordo in the APM network (Murray & Gordo 2017)), algorithms to predict score distributions employ different loss terms for training. More specifically, employing a simple vector distance such as the L2 norm between histogram vectors is in general sub-optimal, as it does not consider the ordinal nature of the aesthetic ratings. For example, given a reference score distribution on a 5-level discrete scale $p_1 = (1, 0, 0, 0, 0)$, the two following score distributions $p_2 = (0, 1, 0, 0, 0)$ and $p_3 = (0, 0, 0, 0, 1)$ have the same Euclidean distance from p_1. However, it is intuitive that p_2 is closer to p_1 than p_3, since the aesthetic scores where the probability mass is concentrated are closer.

Among distances between probability distributions, one that has been widely used in aesthetics is the *Earth mover's distance* (EMD). For two discrete distributions p and q, the EMD is computed as the L2 norm of the difference between their corresponding cumulative distribution functions (cdf) P and Q, that is:

$$\text{EMD}(p, q) = \left[\sum_{i=1}^{K} P(i) - Q(i) \right]^{\frac{1}{2}}, \quad (4)$$

where K is the number of score levels (e.g., $K = 10$ for AVA). By employing the cumulative distributions, the EMD is sensitive to the order of the probability masses. The use of EMD to predict aesthetic score distributions was first proposed by Wu, Hu and Gao in 2011 (Wu et al. 2011). They introduce a modified support vector regression algorithm called support vector distribution regression (SVDR), trained with a squared EMD. In addition, they also proposed a weighting mechanism to penalize more errors on images which have a reliable ground-truth score distribution, called reliability-sensitive learning (RSL). The reliability is measured as the number of votes received by the image: the higher the number of votes, the closer the sample histogram is to the true population distribution. The EMD has been later used by other aesthetic prediction methods, including the popular NIMA system (Talebi & Milanfar 2018). Similar ideas to Wu et al. (2011), in particular the reliability term, have been employed by others afterwards, e.g., it has been integrated in a label distribution learning framework in Cui et al. (2017) (however, a hinge loss is used there).

Other distances between probability distributions can be considered. For instance, Jin et al. (2016a) predict aesthetic histograms via a modified VGG-16 network trained with the χ^2 (Chi-square) distance, defined as:

$$\chi^2(p, q) = \frac{1}{2} \sum_{i=1}^{K} \frac{(p_i - q_i)^2}{p_i + q_i}. \quad (5)$$

This distance gives less importance to the difference between large bins, and was successfully used for texture and object classification, local descriptor matching, etc. (Pele & Werman 2010).

Another family of methods to predict aesthetic distributions employs distances (or, more precisely, pseudo-distances) borrowed from information theory. We already mentioned the Deep Chatterjee's Machine (DCM, Wang et al. (2017)) in Sect. 4.4.4. It approximates the underlying aesthetic distributions as Gaussians, and measures their distance with the *Kullback-Leibler* (KL) divergence, which in this case has a simple closed-form expression:

$$\text{KL}(p, q) = \log \frac{\sigma_q}{\sigma_p} + \frac{\sigma_p^2 + (\mu_p - \mu_q)^2}{2\mu_q^2} - \frac{1}{2}, \quad (6)$$

where $\mu_p, \mu_q, \sigma_p, \sigma_q$ are the means and standard deviations of p and q, respectively. The Gaussian approximation of p and q does not just allow simplification the computation of the KL divergence, but also solves the issue of defining the KL for values with zero probability mass. However, the hypothesis of normality of the distributions seems somewhat too strong, at least for the AVA dataset: although in Murray et al. (2012) it is found that most images in the dataset have an approximately Gaussian distribution of scores, later studies (Park & Zhang 2015) have shown that the distributions are better approximated as power laws. Indeed, this is even more evident for the images with extreme scores, which have skewed distributions. Another drawback of Eq. (6) is that the KL divergence is *asymmetric* $(KL(p, q) \neq KL(q, p))$. To overcome this limitation, the KL divergence is often symmetrized as $KL_{sym} = \frac{1}{2}(KL(p, q) + KL(q, p))$.

To consider the ordinal nature of the ratings and solve the asymmetry of the KL divergence, Jin et al. (2018) employ a cumulative Jensen-Shannon divergence (CJS) loss. The Jensen-Shannon divergence is a symmetrized KL divergence of the two distributions p and q with respect to their average $m = \frac{1}{2}(p + q)$. In CJS, the Jensen-Shannon divergence is computed on the cumulative distributions P and Q:

$$\text{CJS}(p, q) = \frac{1}{2}\left[\sum_{i=1}^{K} P \log \frac{P(i)}{M(i)} + \sum_{i=1}^{K} Q \log \frac{Q(i)}{M(i)}\right], \qquad (7)$$

where M is the cdf of m. In addition to the plain CJS loss, the authors also include a reliability weight inspired by Wu et al. (2011), with the difference that they use the *kurtosis* of the ratings distribution instead of the number of voters. The use of kurtosis as a measure of subjectivity was proposed also in Park and Zhang (2015) before (see next section).

Although predicting score distributions can provide complete information about aesthetic consensus, the predicted distributions are in practice difficult to interpret. Since evaluating the prediction of histograms requires choosing a distance metric between distributions, comparing the results of different methods may not be conclusive. In fact, to validate the proposed approach, these works often resort to extracting simpler aesthetic measures such as the average or aesthetic class from the estimated distributions, in order to compare to the state of the art. In addition, the ratings in large aesthetic datasets such as AVA tend to concentrate around the middle quality (see Fig. 2a). As a result, most of the training samples have a distribution that is approximately Gaussian and centered around the middle score. This over-representation of images with mediocre quality leads to a sort of "center bias" in the prediction: the estimated distributions tend to resemble the average score distribution of the dataset, entailing poor prediction performance for images with very high or low quality. This phenomenon occurs as well for mean score regression, and a traditional solution in aesthetics consists of excluding images with average ratings close to the middle of the rating scale from training (Datta et al. 2006; Ke et al. 2006; Lu et al. 2014). Another option to mitigate the score imbalance consists of using resampling or a weighting scheme to balance the loss during training. For example, in Jin et al. (2016a) the weights are computed as the inverse of the (binned) distribution of the average aesthetic score over the AVA dataset. In this way, less frequent scores are assigner larger weights and are penalized more during training, thus effectively driving the network to focus on rare samples.

5.1.2 Measures of Subjectivity

While predicting the distribution of aesthetic ratings gives an idea of the consensus of human observers on the quality of a picture, in many cases it is desirable to extract a single, scalar measure of subjectivity, e.g., to be used as a quality metric or a penalty term in an optimization or learning process. A few works have addressed this problem, by computing some significant statistic based on the rating distributions (e.g., the variance or higher-order moments), and evaluating its prediction through machine learning approaches.

Kim et al. (2020) study the objectivity and subjectivity in aesthetic quality assessment. The "objectivity" is identified with the task of predicting the mean aesthetic score or an aesthetic class, which corresponds to the classical setup in computational aesthetics and to the perspective we have taken in the previous part of this chapter. The term subjectivity, instead, is quantified as the *standard deviation* (std) of the scores. Based on these definitions, the authors propose a prediction scheme for the two terms. They first crawl a new database from DPChallenge containing more than 300k pictures posted over a time interval of 12 years. This long time horizon allows the authors to make some interesting observations regarding the evolution of objectivity and subjectivity: e.g., due to the increase of the photographic device quality, the average aesthetic scores in DPChallenge have increased with time, while the average subjectivity has decreased. Afterwards, the authors extract 295 features from each image, which are combined through an SVM to predict either the mean or the std of the scores. Through a feature selection process, it is also possible to understand which are the most significant features in each of the two tasks. Notice that both objectivity and subjectivity here are *quantized to two classes*, i.e., the prediction is a binary classification problem. The separation into two classes discards images with medium std values (similar to what is typically done on mean scores with the parameter δ). Under these assumptions, the classification accuracy for the mean score prediction is 71.6%. For std, it lowers down to around 67%, with larger inter-category variations (e.g., for landscape images the std prediction accuracy exceeds 77%, while for architecture it is around 61%). While overall std prediction seems more difficult, the results are encouraging, showing that predicting subjectivity is feasible. The authors also investigate the sources of subjectivity through an analysis of text comments associated to the images (downloaded from DPChallenge). The "unusualness" and the coexistence of both aesthetic merits and defects explains the high levels of subjectivity.

The conclusion that subjectivity can be predicted with reasonable accuracy is somehow contradicted by the work of Kang et al. (2019), although the results cannot be directly compared as the evaluation schemes are different (regression in this case). The correlation coefficient between the predicted std and the ground-truth is only ≈ 0.3, compared to correlations in excess of 0.7 obtained by state-of-the-art methods to predict the mean aesthetic score. We hypothesize that the higher performance in Kim et al. (2020) is significantly influenced by the removal of samples with medium std values, which are the most significant portion of the data (see Fig. 2b). The authors of Kang et al. (2019) also propose other subjectivity measures in addition to std, including two novel measures based on information theory. These measures compute the distance of the ratings distribution of an image to an ideal distribution having maximum entropy (and thus, minimum consensus). Even if these new measures can be predicted slightly better than std on the AVA dataset (which may imply they are more robust to noise), the overall prediction performance remains poor, most probably due to the complex, contextual factors leading to little aesthetic consensus.

Park and Zhang (2015) present an original and very interesting analysis of the consensus in aesthetics (in particular, for the AVA dataset). Instead of using the variance of the scores, which is seriously distorted by highly skewed and bounded data, they consider the fourth moment of the distribution, i.e., *kurtosis*, as an indicator of subjectivity. Kurtosis measures how long are the tails of a distribution. The kurtosis of a distribution is linked to its skewness by the relation: kurtosis $\geq$ (skewness)$^2 + 1$. Therefore, to characterize subjectivity, Park and Zhang study the distributions of images in the skewness-kurtosis plane—a representation they call *SK maps* (see Fig. 2c), which has been used in physics and finance to study the deviations from Gaussianity. The SK maps provide insightful information about the subjectivity of images in AVA. First, it is observed that there is a strong non-Gaussianity in the scores of the AVA images. In particular, images with average scores around 5 tend to have a wide range of kurtosis, which implies they follow very different (and non Gaussian) distributions. In addition, images with low aesthetic scores (i.e., with positive skewness) tend to have higher kurtosis, i.e., there is more aesthetic consensus in judging aesthetically unpleasing pictures than high-quality ones. Finally, the SK maps differ significantly based on the content category, which is coherent with the content-dependent subjectivity observed in other works afterwards.

Based on the SK map representation, Park and Zhang also present a mathematical *dynamic model* to explain subjectivity in aesthetic perception. The approach is based on the classical drift-diffusion model, previously used by psychologists to explain behavioral data in emotion analysis tasks. The drift-diffusion model assumes that, in the absence of any external stimulus, the human mind performs an internal random walk. When a decision between two or more options is to be made, the brain accumulates evidence favoring each of the alternatives over time. The combination of these "clues" (attractors) with the noise component (random walk) can be depicted as a particle drifting and diffusing between two boundaries, until it reaches one of them. Similarly, when the aesthetic judgment converges to one state (e.g., good or bad aesthetic quality), the aesthetic decision is taken. This simple drift-diffusion model allows the explanation of most of the behaviors observed in the SK maps, and provides a foundation for results obtained by later studies (Kim et al. 2020). In particular, when multiple, balanced attractors are present (i.e., both positive and negative aesthetic attributes), the judgment tends to converge towards a mediocre aesthetic score. Moreover, the convergence time is longer, i.e., humans employ a longer time to evaluate images with larger subjectivity. This conclusion is supported by a user study in which the authors recorded the voting time. Even more interestingly, the drift-diffusion model suggests that it is the mixture of positive and negative attractors in a training sample that misguide most machine learning methods, making the subjectivity prediction performance poor. Instead, since subjectivity is the result of a dynamic system, a proper learning scheme should embed this dynamic aspect, e.g., using an active learning approach. Unfortunately, this original perspective, which might open new directions in the understanding of aesthetic subjectivity, has not been further investigated in follow-up work on computational aesthetics.

5.1.3   Personalized Aesthetics

A different approach to subjectivity in computational aesthetics departs substantially from the methods that we have analyzed so far in this chapter. Instead of focusing on the *universal* scope of aesthetics (see Fig. 1), we briefly describe in the following some methods that aim at predicted *personalized* aesthetics for a particular person. As we mentioned in Sect. 1, personalized computational aesthetics assumes an interactionist interpretation of aesthetics, where the individual perception is the result of the interaction between some objective, intrinsic features of a photo, with a subjective processing/interpretation.

Personalized aesthetics algorithms aim to adapt a generic aesthetic predictor to the individual tastes of a person, based on the availability of a small set of annotations from that user. To this end, they employ tools often used in image recommendation and user profiling, such as active learning, collaborative filtering or residual learning. Park et al. (2017) propose a joint regression and ranking algorithm to score and rank a set of user-specific images $\mathcal{T}$. The system first extracts a subset S of training images from a general aesthetics dataset (e.g., AVA). The images to extract are selected as the nearest neighbors to the images in $\mathcal{T}$. In a second phase, the user ranks a small subset of images in $\mathcal{T}$. Finally, combining these two sources of information, the system learns to predict all the scores and ranks in the remaining images of $\mathcal{T}$. The authors use a max-margin learning algorithm, in particular, an SVR (inputted with a feature vector of 4096 elements, extracted from the second last layer of AlexNet (Krizhevsky et al. 2012)) for learning the universal aesthetic part, and a ranking SVM (R-SVM) to learn a ranking model given the partial orders on the training data. The two losses are combined to jointly learn a *ranking support vector regression* (R-SVR). The results, validated by a user study, are promising and show that the proposed approach can produce cleaner ranking predictions compared to a general aesthetic model alone.

Ren et al. (2017) make similar hypotheses, in particular, that only a small number of annotated examples from a user is available. To be able to still learn significant personalized aesthetic scores in this setting, they adopt a residual-based model adaptation scheme to *learn a scalar offset* to the generic aesthetic score predicted by a universal aesthetic predictor. The authors start by collecting two datasets: one is FLICKR-AES, containing 40k Flickr images rated by 210 unique AMT annotators; the other is REAL-CUR (Real Album Curation Dataset) which contains 14 real users' photo albums with aesthetic scores provided by the album owners. Afterwards, they estimate aesthetic attributes (with a network fine-tuned on the AADB dataset attributes) and the image category (content class) for each image in FLICKR-AES. An analysis on these results and the ground-truth user preferences reveals strong correlations between personal preferences and attributes/content of an image. This observation is key for the proposed approach: in fact, predicting a score offset using an end-to-end optimization would be unfeasible, given the very small percentage of images annotated with individual preference. Instead, the predicted attributes and classes, represented as 10-dimensional categorical distributions (obtained by the last softmax layer in the attribute and content prediction networks) are used as input features for an SVR to predict an offset for a given image. This system is also extended to an active learning scenario, where the model is updated while the users evaluates new images; in this case, the choice of the images to score can be optimized according to heuristic criteria.

In some circumstances, collecting extra labels for specific users to perform personalization is impractical or time consuming. A simpler alternative consists in sensing user-specific aesthetic preferences from the user's personal favoring behavior on social media platforms. Cui et al. (2020) leverage this idea and collect personalized preferences from a set of 50k professional photos downloaded from Flickr. Photos are considered "professional" if they have been posted by one of the top 200 photographers in the ranking of the website. Analyses on this image set show that users tend to prefer images which have some common aesthetic features. However, learning personal preference on this dataset is difficult as, on average, users favor only a very small portion of the total number of images. Therefore, similar to the works discussed above, the authors learn first a universal aesthetic model to extract meaningful aesthetic features. Afterwards, they use a *collaborative filtering* approach to minimize a twofold objective: on one side, a pairwise loss term to guarantee that the user-specific ranking on favored vs. non-favored is respected (under the hypothesis that a favored picture is aesthetically better for the user); on the other hand, a regularization term to smooth out the predicted scores in such a way that they are not too distant from the average ratings. As the authors also point out, the major pitfall of this approach is in the assumption that "faves" approximate somehow the aesthetic value of a picture. Nevertheless, as we have discussed throughout this chapter, this assumption is often made in computational aesthetics to collect data at low cost, even though it can lead to noisy prediction and hardly interpretable results.

5.2 Explaining Aesthetic Scores

While the mainstream aesthetic research has focused on improving the prediction
of aesthetic scores or classes, relatively little has been done to understand *why* an
image is aesthetically pleasing or not. This question is particularly challenging for
deep-learning-based methods, due to the very high dimensionality of the employed
models that make them significantly hard to interpret. Nonetheless, some works
have tried to analyze the predictions of neural networks in aesthetics, or to justify the
aesthetic scores by producing explaining text comments. Moreover, some datasets
have been collected with the specific purpose of providing extra ground-truth labels
to facilitate aesthetic explainability.

5.2.1 Visualization Techniques

An approach to explain aesthetic scores obtained by a convolutional neural network
consists in analyzing the filters and the features learned by the network. This
category of methods has been quite popular in computer vision in the early stages
of development of deep CNN to visualize what the network was learning (Zeiler &
Fergus 2014). For instance, analyzing the filters at different layers of a classification
network shows that initial layers perform low-level filtering (e.g., gradients, Gabor
filters, etc.), while deeper layers are optimized to capture higher-level structures and
parts of objects. This kind of visualization has been also applied to networks that
predict aesthetics (Kao et al. 2016; Jin et al. 2016b). However, the conclusions from
this inspection are in general very limited, as the learned patterns reflect the same
kind of behavior observed in non-aesthetic networks, making them difficult to be
interpreted.

Another technique to analyze the features learned by a CNN is to study *class
activation maps* (CAM) (Zhou et al. 2016). In the simplest setting, CAMs can be
obtained for classification networks satisfying a particular structure, i.e., having a
global averaging pooling layer followed by a single fully connected layer before
the output layer. In this case, for a given input image and a certain class, the
score of the class is mapped back to the previous convolutional layer to generate
a corresponding class activation map. CAMs can be visualized as low-resolution
images, which highlight the class-specific discriminative regions. Later work (e.g.,
Grad-CAM (Selvaraju et al. 2017)) extends this visualization technique to a much
wider variety of networks, by propagating back the gradient of a target class to
a convolutional layer of the net. Class activation maps have been employed also
in the case of computational aesthetics. Kairanbay et al. (2017) build on the CAM
visualization to provide a justification of high vs. low aesthetic quality. They observe
that aesthetically pleasing images tend to have activation maps with energy well
concentrated around salient objects of the picture. Conversely, photos belonging to
the low-quality class have activations that are spread around the picture and on non-
interesting regions. The authors speculate that this behavior reflects basic rules of

photography, such as the importance of focusing on the subject and the concept of negative space (see Fig. 3). However, such observations are verified qualitatively only on a few images, and it seems difficult to generalize this conclusion to more complex scenes or photos where the subject is not clearly identified. Zhang et al. (2018) extends this analysis by visualizing activations at different levels of a multi-task network that predicts simultaneously an aesthetic class and one of the 66 AVA semantic tags. Thus, in addition to activation maps for aesthetic attributes, they also study CAMs for attributes. Jointly predicting the activation maps for the two tasks has the potential to not only localize aesthetically salient areas in the picture, but also to explain why they are important (by intersecting the two maps). However, the conclusions remain still vague and difficult to justify when considering a wide variety of content. An interesting application of computing activation maps for aesthetics consists of automatically cropping a picture by keeping the most aesthetically relevant regions (Kao et al. 2017a; Zhang et al. 2018).

Murray and Gordo (2017), whose APM model we have introduced earlier, employ a different visualization technique compared to CAM. They leverage the concept of *adversarial examples* (Goodfellow et al. 2014), i.e., input samples that are imperceptibly modified to completely alter the prediction of a network, while looking essentially the same to a human observer. Based on this concept, they change the score distributions of test images to be slightly better or worse than the original sample. Then, they modify the image by gradient descent in such a way to obtain a new image that matches the altered distribution. Visualizing which pixels have been modified in the original test image in order to improve or reduce aesthetic scores provides an indication of the regions of the picture that are used by the model to make predictions. Compared to CAM representations, this technique allows one to obtain higher-resolution visualizations. The authors notice that most changes are localized in salient regions of the pictures, confirming observations from previous work. However, an inspection of the error images leaves still many open questions about the interpretability of these maps. In addition, the adversarial examples demonstrate that even imperceptible modifications in the original pixels can yield significant changes in the image scores. This fact indicates that aesthetic networks are also prone to adversarial attacks as other computer vision applications such as object classification, and raises some fundamental questions about how much neural-network-based computational aesthetic predictors are reliable.

5.2.2 Generating Text Explanations

As we have discussed above, aesthetic explanation approaches based on network activation maps or other visualization techniques alone have not been able so far to provide convincing evidence of why a given picture is beautiful or not. A more explicit approach to generate plausible explanations consists of producing a text comment about the qualities and defects of a photo.

We have already discussed in Sect. 4 a few seminal works linking aesthetic quality not only to pixel-based characteristics, but also on associated textual comments from users (San Pedro et al. 2012; Marchesotti 2013). The considerable progress that deep learning techniques have brought to natural language processing (NLP) has enabled the use of advanced image captioning techniques in computational aesthetics. One of the first works in this direction is the one of Chang et al. (2017). They propose a *multi-aspect* aesthetic captioning system, where more than one aspect of an image can be commented, e.g., composition, color arrangement or subject contrast. This approach has a very reasonable foundation: in fact, it mimics some earlier studies in computational aesthetics that tried to decompose the global quality as a combination of some basic attributes (Aydın et al. 2014). The authors propose two architectures, both based on CNN-LSTM (long short term memory units) to produce a set of captions for a given image. It has to be noted as well that the authors also offer a new dataset with aesthetic captions crawled from a professional photographers website (https://gurushots.com/), called the photo critique captioning dataset (PCCD), see Table 1.

Wang et al. (2019) combine aesthetic classification and captioning into a multi-task network called *neural aesthetic image reviewer* (NAIR). This work leverages a dataset of 40k images extracted from AVA (AVA-reviews, see Table 1), that the authors collect based on images with text comments in AVA. To select images, they remove aesthetically ambiguous pictures ($\delta = 0.5$). The proposed network includes a part for image aesthetic classification based on a single-column CNN, and a part for vision-to-language generation that generates natural-language comments using a sequence of LSTM units.

Recently, Ghosal et al. (2019) have proposed a new dataset with 230k images and 1.5M captions for aesthetic image captioning called AVA-Captions. The dataset is obtained by cleaning the raw comments in AVA to retain the most discriminative n-grams, which are then used to train a CNN-LSTM network in a weakly-supervised way. The labels for training are obtained by processing the filtered captions, in such a way to extract terms corresponding to different attributes. However, instead of using fixed attributes as in Chang et al. (2017), here the attributes are discovered from data using *latent Dirichlet allocation* (LDA), a generative probabilistic model used in text modeling and retrieval. LDA clusters semantically similar terms, which correspond to classes of images (e.g., faces, landscapes, etc.). The discovered attributes go beyond the typical aesthetic attributes (color, contrast, composition, etc.) and include some semantic labels (e.g., "sky", "sport","action shot"), but also opinions and judgments on the content (e.g., "cute expression", "great action"). The generated captions display more diversity than those obtained on the noisy (original) captions from AVA, which tend to be monotonous and repetitive. The captioning is evaluated through a subjective experiment, showing a relatively good agreement with human opinions about the quality of a caption, which is mainly intended here as the informativeness and naturalness of the generated comment. Unfortunately, the produced text explanations depend significantly on the quality of the original captions, and judging their aesthetic relevance remains still an open problem.

5.2.3   Datasets with Aesthetic Attributes

The techniques to explain aesthetics based on data visualization or captioning described above can provide hints on the relevant regions or aspects of a photo. However, several drawbacks are related to these methods, particularly the difficulty of assessing their performance and their significant dependence on the input training data (especially for generated comments). These observations bring us back to a fundamental challenge in computational aesthetics, which we have mentioned many times throughout this chapter: collecting large-scale datasets with reliable, clean, and rich labels. At the time of this writing, there is still no aesthetic dataset able to provide, at the same time, a large number of annotated images *and* reliable, high-quality aesthetic scores. We have already discussed the features and limitations of some popular aesthetic datasets in Sect. 3. To study aesthetic explainability, aesthetic datasets should be complemented with additional information, e.g., aesthetic attributes to explain why an image is aesthetically pleasing or not.

Few datasets in the literature have explicitly elicited aesthetic attributes information from human raters. A notable example is AADB (Kong et al. 2016), where images are annotated with 11 aesthetic attributes. These attributes were defined based on expert knowledge: professional photographers were consulted to define a set of attributes that span the main dimensions of photography (color, light, composition, focus) and that can provide a natural vocabulary for practical applications from photo editing to retrieval. The set of selected attributes include: "interesting content", "object emphasis", "good lighting", "color harmony", "vivid color", "shallow depth of field", "motion blur", "rule of thirds", "balancing element", "repetition", and "symmetry". These attributes are assigned binary labels by each user. While the AADB attributes have an aesthetic valence, it is not clear whether they are sufficient to capture the wide range of factors that concur to form an aesthetic judgment. In addition, images in AADB are rated by only 5 users, which makes it difficult in practice to compute significant mean attribute values.

Recently, Kang et al. (2020) have proposed an Explainable Visual Aesthetics (EVA) dataset, which aims at partially solving the issues of AADB and other similar datasets. An example of the voting interface is illustrated in Fig. 8. In EVA, attributes are simplified to four general categories: "light and color", "composition and depth", "quality" (intended as technical quality), and "semantics". The attributes span different levels of factors affecting image aesthetics, from perceptual (light and color, technical quality), to photographic technique (composition, depth) and interpretation of the scene (semantics). Compared to AADB, the attributes are less detailed, and thus the information about why an image is beautiful is more generic. However, they are more inclusive and general, which might be beneficial to describe factors which are outside the vocabulary pre-defined by the experimenters. In addition, EVA attributes have two measurements: one to gauge the attribute magnitude (on a Likert scale) for a given image; the other to assess the attribute relevance (on a binary scale) in producing the overall aesthetic score. In addition to image aesthetic scores and attributes, EVA collects also the "difficulty" encountered by the user to rate an image, which is somehow related to the personal aesthetic

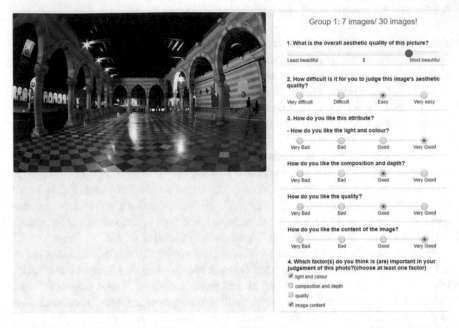

Fig. 8 Voting interface in the EVA dataset. In addition to aesthetic scores (discrete 11-levels scale), additional aesthetic attributes are collected (using 4-levels Likert scales), as well as their relevance (on a binary scale) to forming the overall aesthetic quality

uncertainty and might have interesting links to the study of subjectivity discussed earlier in this section. Furthermore, differently from previous datasets, the data collection in EVA includes a detailed training phase, in which raters are instructed about the meaning of attributes (with visual examples) and on how to use the rating scales, following common guidelines widely adopted in technical quality assessment (ITU-R 2012). EVA includes 4070 images, which is less than half of the images of AADB; however, each image has at least 30 votes. Despite the limited number of images, and the possible noise in the labels due to the crowdsourcing acquisition, the EVA dataset represents in our opinion a good starting point for further work on collecting better ground-truth labels for computational aesthetics.

6 Concluding Remarks

Computational aesthetics is a challenging and rapidly evolving field, at the intersection of multimedia quality, human perception and machine learning. In this chapter, we have given a general overview of this domain, from the philosophical debates around the interpretations of aesthetics, to the modern techniques to predict human aesthetic judgments. After the initial attempts to formulate aesthetics as a mathematical object by Birkhoff in the 1930s, computational aesthetics has undergone an incredible development, in particular with the rise of data-driven methods in the past 15 years. We have discussed the fundamental role that datasets play in understanding aesthetic evaluation, and the different dimensions that should be taken into account when approaching computational aesthetics (focusing in particular on general aesthetics).

Computational methods to predict aesthetic classes based on deep neural networks can nowadays achieve a binary prediction accuracy higher than 83% on the benchmark AVA dataset (Murray et al. 2012). The classification performance on this dataset has now reached a plateau, in which it seems difficult to substantially improve predictions by just changing the architectures of the networks used. We have argued that this limit is somehow related to the noise in the aesthetic scores collected by crawling amateur or professional photography websites, as well as the intrinsic *uncertainty* of aesthetic evaluation, which is subjective in nature. We have thus pointed to some fundamental challenges in modern computational aesthetics: dealing with the subjectivity of the aesthetic scores; explaining aesthetic decisions; and building clean and reliabile large-scale datasets.

We conclude the chapter by mentioning that, in addition to the topics covered here, there are several other aspects related to aesthetics that could be further considered. In particular, in addition to numerous applications of image aesthetics to enhancement, recommendation, etc., mentioned throughout the chapter, we need to mention video aesthetics (Yeh et al. 2013; Bhattacharya et al. 2013) and related applications (e.g., thumbnailing (Song et al. 2016)), and finally recent studies linking brain-computer interfaces to the generation of aesthetically pleasing pictures (Spape et al. 2021), which appear to be a promising avenue to understand and predict aesthetic judgment mechanisms.

References

Amirshahi, S. A., Denzler, J., & Redies, C. (2013). Jenaesthetics—a public dataset of paintings for aesthetic research. In *Poster workshop at the european conference on computer vision*.

Aydın, T. O., Smolic, A., & Gross, M. (2014). Automated aesthetic analysis of photographic images. *IEEE Transactions on Visualization and Computer Graphics, 21*(1), 31–42.

Barrett, T. (2020). *Criticizing photographs: An introduction to understanding images*. Routledge.

Bhattacharya, S., Nojavanasghari, B., Chen, T., Liu, D., Chang, S. F., & Shah, M. (2013). Towards a comprehensive computational model for aesthetic assessment of videos. In *Proceedings of the 21st ACM international conference on Multimedia* (pp. 361–364).

Bianco, S., Cadene, R., Celona, L., & Napoletano, P. (2018a). Benchmark analysis of representative deep neural network architectures. *IEEE Access, 6*, 64270–64277.

Bianco, S., Celona, L., & Schettini, R. (2018b). Aesthetics assessment of images containing faces. In *2018 25th IEEE international conference on image processing (ICIP)* (pp. 2820–2824). IEEE.

Birkhoff, G. D. (1933). *Aesthetic measure*. Cambridge, MA: Harvard University Press.

Cela-Conde, C. J., Ayala, F. J., Munar, E., Maestú, F., Nadal, M., Capó, M. A., del Río, D., López-Ibor, J. J., Ortiz, T., Mirasso, C., et al. (2009). Sex-related similarities and differences in the neural correlates of beauty. *Proceedings of the National Academy of Sciences, 106*(10), 3847–3852.

Chang, H., Yu, F., Wang, J., Ashley, D., & Finkelstein, A. (2016). Automatic triage for a photo series. *ACM Transactions on Graphics (TOG), 35*(4), 1–10.

Chang, K. Y., Lu, K. H., & Chen, C. S. (2017). Aesthetic critiques generation for photos. In *Proceedings of the IEEE international conference on computer vision* (pp. 3514–3523).

Chatterjee, A. (2003). Prospects for a cognitive neuroscience of visual aesthetics. *Bulletin of Psychology and the Arts, 4*, 55–60. https://doi.org/10.1037/e514602010-003

Chopra, S., Hadsell, R., & LeCun, Y. (2005). Learning a similarity metric discriminatively, with application to face verification. In *2005 IEEE computer society conference on computer vision and pattern recognition (CVPR'05)* (vol. 1, pp. 539–546). https://doi.org/10.1109/CVPR.2005.202

Constantin, M. G., Kang, C., Dinu, G., Dufaux, F., Valenzise, G., & Ionescu, B. (2019). Using aesthetics and action recognition-based networks for the prediction of media memorability. In *MediaEval 2019 workshop*. France: Sophia Antipolis. https://hal.archives-ouvertes.fr/hal-02368920.

Csurka, G., Dance, C., Fan, L., Willamowski, J., & Bray, C. (2004). Visual categorization with bags of keypoints. In *Workshop on statistical learning in computer vision, ECCV* (vol. 1, pp. 1–2). Prague.

Cui, C., Fang, H., Deng, X., Nie, X., Dai, H., & Yin, Y. (2017). Distribution-oriented aesthetics assessment for image search. In *Proceedings of the 40th international ACM SIGIR conference on research and development in information retrieval* (pp. 1013–1016).

Cui, C., Yang, W., Shi, C., Wang, M., Nie, X., & Yin, Y. (2020). Personalized image quality assessment with social-sensed aesthetic preference. *Information Sciences, 512*, 780–794.

Datta, R., Joshi, D., Li, J., & Wang, J. Z. (2006). Studying aesthetics in photographic images using a computational approach. In *European conference on computer vision* (pp. 288–301). Springer.

Datta, R., & Wang, J. Z. (2010). ACQUINE: aesthetic quality inference engine-real-time automatic rating of photo aesthetics. In *Proceedings of the international conference on multimedia information retrieval* (pp. 421–424).

Deng, Y., Loy, C.C., & Tang, X. (2017). Image aesthetic assessment: An experimental survey. *IEEE Signal Processing Magazine, 34*(4), 80–106.

Deng, Y., Loy, C. C., & Tang, X. (2018). Aesthetic-driven image enhancement by adversarial learning. In *2018 ACM multimedia conference on multimedia conference* (pp. 870–878). ACM.

Dhar, S., Ordonez, V., & Berg, T. L. (2011). High level describable attributes for predicting aesthetics and interestingness. In *CVPR 2011* (pp. 1657–1664). IEEE.

Ghosal, K., Rana, A., & Smolic., A. (2019). Aesthetic image captioning from weakly-labelled photographs. In *ICCV 2019 workshop on cross-modal learning in real world*.

Goodfellow, I. J., Shlens, J., & Szegedy, C. (2014). Explaining and harnessing adversarial examples. Preprint. arXiv:1412.6572.

Goodfellow, I., Bengio, Y., & Courville, A. (2016). *Deep learning*. MIT press.

Götz-Hahn, F., Hosu, V., Lin, H., & Saupe, D. (2019). No-reference video quality assessment using multi-level spatially pooled features. Preprint. arXiv:1912.07966.

Guo, G., Wang, H., Shen, C., Yan, Y., & Liao, H. Y. M. (2018). Automatic image cropping for visual aesthetic enhancement using deep neural networks and cascaded regression. *IEEE Transactions on Multimedia, 20*(8), 2073–2085.

Gygli, M., Grabner, H., Riemenschneider, H., Nater, F., & Van Gool, L. (2013). The interestingness of images. In *Proceedings of the IEEE international conference on computer vision* (pp. 1633–1640).

Hayn-Leichsenring, G. U., Lehmann, T., & Redies, C. (2017). Subjective ratings of beauty and aesthetics: correlations with statistical image properties in western oil paintings. *i-Perception, 8*(3), 2041669517715474.

He, J., Wang, L., Zhou, W., Zhang, H., Cui, X., & Guo, Y. (2019). Viewpoint assessment and recommendation for photographing architectures. *IEEE Transactions on Visualization and Computer Graphics*, 25(8), 2636–2649. https://doi.org/10.1109/TVCG.2018.2853751.

Hoenig, F. (2005). Defining computational aesthetics. In *Proceedings of the first eurographics conference on computational aesthetics in graphics, visualization and imaging* (pp. 13–18).

Hoffer, E., & Ailon, N. (2015). Deep metric learning using triplet network. In *International workshop on similarity-based pattern recognition* (pp. 84–92). Springer.

Hulusic, V., Valenzise, G., Provenzi, E., Debattista, K., & Dufaux, F. (2016). Perceived dynamic range of HDR images. In *IEEE int. conference on quality of multimedia experience* (pp. 1–6).

Isola, P., Xiao, J., Torralba, A., & Oliva, A. (2011). What makes an image memorable? In *CVPR 2011* (pp. 145–152). IEEE.

ITU-R. (2012). Methodology for the subjective assessment of the quality of television pictures. ITU-R Recommendation BT.500-13.

Jaakkola, T. S., Haussler, D., et al. (1999). Exploiting generative models in discriminative classifiers. *Advances in Neural Information Processing Systems*, 487–493.

Jin, B., Segovia, M. V. O., & Süsstrunk, S. (2016a). Image aesthetic predictors based on weighted CNNs. In *IEEE international conference on image processing* (pp. 2291–2295). Phoenix, AZ, USA: IEEE.

Jin, X., Chi, J., Peng, S., Tian, Y., Ye, C., & Li, X. (2016b). Deep image aesthetics classification using inception modules and fine-tuning connected layer. In *2016 8th international conference on wireless communications & signal processing (WCSP)*, (pp. 1–6). IEEE.

Jin, X., Wu, L., Li, X., Chen, S., Peng, S., Chi, J., Ge, S., Song, C., & Zhao, G. (2018). Predicting aesthetic score distribution through cumulative Jensen-Shannon divergence. In *Thirty-second AAAI conference on artificial intelligence*.

John, L. K., Mochon, D., Emrich, O., & Schwartz, J. (2017). What's the value of a like. *Harvard Business Review*, 95(2), 108–115.

Kairanbay, M., See, J., Wong, L. K., & Hii, Y. L. (2017). Filling the gaps: Reducing the complexity of networks for multi-attribute image aesthetic prediction. In *Proceedings of the IEEE international conference on image processing* (pp. 3051–3055). IEEE.

Kairanbay, M., See, J., & Wong, L. K. (2019). Beauty is in the eye of the beholder: Demographically oriented analysis of aesthetics in photographs. *ACM Transactions on Multimedia Computing, Communications, and Applications*, 15(2s), 1–21. https://doi.org/10.1145/3328993.

Kang, C., Valenzise, G., & Dufaux, F. (2019). Predicting Subjectivity in Image Aesthetics Assessment. In: 21st international workshop on multimedia signal processing (MMSP'2019), Kuala Lumpur, Malaysia. https://hal.archives-ouvertes.fr/hal-02191142.

Kang, C., Valenzise, G., & Dufaux, F. (2020). EVA: An Explainable Visual Aesthetics Dataset. In: *Joint workshop on aesthetic and technical quality assessment of multimedia and media analytics for societal trends (ATQAM/MAST'20)*. Seattle, USA: ACM Multimedia. https://hal.archives-ouvertes.fr/hal-02934292.

Kao, Y., Wang, C., & Huang, K. (2015). Visual aesthetic quality assessment with a regression model. In *IEEE international conference on image processing (ICIP)* (pp. 1583–1587). IEEE.

Kao, Y., Huang, K., & Maybank, S. (2016). Hierarchical aesthetic quality assessment using deep convolutional neural networks. *Signal Processing: Image Communication*, 47, 500–510.

Kao, Y., He, R., & Huang, K. (2017a). Automatic image cropping with aesthetic map and gradient energy map. In *2017 IEEE international conference on acoustics, speech and signal processing (ICASSP)* (pp. 1982–1986). IEEE.

Kao, Y., He, R., & Huang, K. (2017b). Deep aesthetic quality assessment with semantic information. *IEEE Transactions on Image Processing*, 26(3), 1482–1495.

Ke, Y., Tang, X., & Jing, F. (2006). The design of high-level features for photo quality assessment. In *IEEE int. conference on computer vision and pattern recognition (CVPR)* (vol. 1, pp. 419–426). IEEE.

Kim, W. H., Choi, J. H., & Lee, J. S. (2020). Objectivity and subjectivity in aesthetic quality assessment of digital photographs. *IEEE Transactions on Affective Computing, 11*(3), 493–506. https://doi.org/10.1109/TAFFC.2018.2809752.

Kirk, U., Skov, M., Christensen, M. S., & Nygaard, N. (2009). Brain correlates of aesthetic expertise: a parametric fMRI study. *Brain and Cognition, 69*(2), 306–315.

Kong, S., Shen, X., Lin, Z., Mech, R., & Fowlkes, C. (2016). Photo aesthetics ranking network with attributes and content adaptation. In *European conference on computer vision* (pp. 662–679). Springer.

Krizhevsky, A., Sutskever, I., & Hinton, G. E. (2012). Imagenet classification with deep convolutional neural networks. *Advances in Neural Information Processing Systems, 25*, 1097–1105.

Kucer, M., Loui, A. C., & Messinger, D. W. (2018). Leveraging expert feature knowledge for predicting image aesthetics. *IEEE Transactions on Image Processing, 27*(10), 5100–5112.

Kuzovkin, D. (2019). Assessment of photos in albums based on aesthetics and context. Theses, Université Rennes 1. https://hal.inria.fr/tel-02345620.

Kuzovkin, D., Pouli, T., Cozot, R., Meur, O. L., Kervec, J., & Bouatouch, K. (2017). Context-aware clustering and assessment of photo collections. In *Proceedings of the symposium on computational aesthetics* (pp. 1–10)

Lakhal, S., Darmon, A., Bouchaud, J. P., & Benzaquen, M. (2020). Beauty and structural complexity. *Physical Review Research, 2*(2), 022058.

Lebreton, P., Raake, A., & Barkowsky, M. (2016). Evaluation of aesthetic appeal with regard of user's knowledge. *Electronic Imaging, 2016*(16), 1–6.

Li, C., Loui, A. C., & Chen, T. (2010). Towards aesthetics: A photo quality assessment and photo selection system. In *Proceedings of the 18th ACM international conference on Multimedia* (pp. 827–830).

Li, J., Barkowsky, M., & Le Callet, P. (2013). Boosting paired comparison methodology in measuring visual discomfort of 3dtv: performances of three different designs. In *Stereoscopic displays and applications XXIV* (vol. 8648, p. 86481V). International Society for Optics and Photonics.

Ling, S., Wang, J., Huang, W., Guo, Y., Zhang, L., Jing, Y., & Le Callet, P. (2020). A subjective study of multi-dimensional aesthetic assessment for mobile game image. In *Proceedings of the 1st workshop on quality of experience (QoE) in visual multimedia applications* (pp. 47–53).

Liu, W., & Wang, Z. (2017). A database for perceptual evaluation of image aesthetics. In *2017 IEEE international conference on image processing (ICIP)* (pp. 1317–1321). https://doi.org/10.1109/ICIP.2017.8296495.

Liu, D., Puri, R., Kamath, N., & Bhattacharya, S. (2020). Composition-aware image aesthetics assessment. In *Proceedings of the IEEE/CVF winter conference on applications of computer vision (WACV)*.

Lo, K. Y., Liu, K. H., & Chen, C. S. (2012). Intelligent photographing interface with on-device aesthetic quality assessment. In *Asian conference on computer vision* (pp. 533–544). Springer.

Lowe, D. G.: Object recognition from local scale-invariant features. In *Proceedings of the seventh IEEE international conference on computer vision* (vol. 2, pp. 1150–1157). IEEE (1999)

Lu, X., Lin, Z., Jin, H., Yang, J., & Wang, J. Z. (2014). RAPID: Rating pictorial aesthetics using deep learning. In *Proceedings of the 22nd ACM international conference on Multimedia* (pp. 457–466). ACM.

Lu, P., Peng, X., Li, R., & Wang, X. (2015a). Towards aesthetics of image: a bayesian framework for color harmony modeling. *Signal Processing: Image Communication, 39*, 487–498.

Lu, X., Lin, Z., Jin, H., Yang, J., & Wang, J. Z. (2015b). Rating image aesthetics using deep learning. *IEEE Transactions on Multimedia, 17*(11), 2021–2034. https://doi.org/10.1109/TMM.2015.2477040.

Lu, X., Lin, Z., Shen, X., Mech, R., & Wang, J. Z. (2015c). Deep multi-patch aggregation network for image style, aesthetics, and quality estimation. In *Proceedings of the IEEE international conference on computer vision* (pp. 990–998)

Lu, P., Peng, X., Zhu, X., & Li, R. (2016). An EL-LDA based general color harmony model for photo aesthetics assessment. *Signal Processing, 120*, 731–745.

Luo, Y., & Tang, X. (2008). Photo and video quality evaluation: Focusing on the subject. In *European conference on computer vision* (pp. 386–399). Springer.

Luo, W., Wang, X., & Tang, X. (2011). Content-based photo quality assessment. In *2011 international conference on computer vision* (pp. 2206–2213). IEEE.

Ma, S., Liu, J., & Wen Chen, C. (2017). A-lamp: Adaptive layout-aware multi-patch deep convolutional neural network for photo aesthetic assessment. In *Proceedings of the IEEE conference on computer vision and pattern recognition* (pp. 4535–4544).

Machado, P., & Cardoso, A. (1998). Computing aesthetics. In *Brazilian symposium on artificial intelligence* (pp. 219–228). Springer.

Mai, L., Le, H., Niu, Y., & Liu, F. (2011). Rule of thirds detection from photograph. In *2011 IEEE international symposium on Multimedia* (pp. 91–96).

Mai, L., Le, H., Niu, Y., Lai, Y. C., & Liu, F. (2012). Detecting rule of simplicity from photos. In *Proceedings of the 20th ACM international conference on Multimedia* (pp. 1149–1152)

Mai, L., Jin, H., & Liu, F. (2016). Composition-preserving deep photo aesthetics assessment. In *Proceedings of the IEEE conference on computer vision and pattern recognition* (pp. 497–506).

Maître, H. (2018). Qu'est-ce qu'une belle photo? Essai sur l'esthétique en photographie numérique. https://hal.archives-ouvertes.fr/hal-01864135/.

Marchesotti, L., Perronnin, F., & Meylan, F. (2013). Learning beautiful (and ugly) attributes. In *BMVC* (vol. 7, pp. 1–11).

Marchesotti, L., Perronnin, F., Larlus, D., & Csurka, G. (2011). Assessing the aesthetic quality of photographs using generic image descriptors. In *IEEE international conference on computer vision* (pp. 1784–1791). IEEE.

Moon, P., & Spencer, D. (1944). Geometric formulation of classical color harmony. *Journal of the Optical Society of America (1917-1983), 34*(1), 46.

Murray, N., & Gordo, A. (2017). A deep architecture for unified aesthetic prediction. Preprint. arXiv:1708.04890.

Murray, N., Marchesotti, L., & Perronnin, F. (2012). AVA: a large-scale database for aesthetic visual analysis. In *2012 IEEE conference on computer vision and pattern recognition*, (pp. 2408–2415). IEEE.

Park, T. S., & Zhang, B. T. (2015). Consensus analysis and modeling of visual aesthetic perception. *IEEE Transactions on Affective Computing, 6*(3), 272–285.

Park, K., Hong, S., Baek, M., & Han, B. (2017). Personalized image aesthetic quality assessment by joint regression and ranking. In *2017 IEEE winter conference on applications of computer vision (WACV)* (pp. 1206–1214). IEEE.

Pele, O., & Werman, M. (2010). The quadratic-chi histogram distance family. In *European conference on computer vision* (pp. 749–762). Springer.

Perez-Ortiz, M., Mikhailiuk, A., Zerman, E., Hulusic, V., Valenzise, G., & Mantiuk, R. (2019). From pairwise comparisons and rating to a unified quality scale. *IEEE Transactions on Image Processing, 29*, 1139–1151. https://doi.org/10.1109/TIP.2019.2936103. https://hal.archives-ouvertes.fr/hal-02400863.

Reber, R., Schwarz, N., & Winkielman, P. (2004). Processing fluency and aesthetic pleasure: Is beauty in the perceiver's processing experience? *Personality and Social Psychology Review, 8*(4), 364–382.

Redi, M., Rasiwasia, N., Aggarwal, G., & Jaimes, A. (2015). The beauty of capturing faces: Rating the quality of digital portraits. In *2015 11th IEEE international conference and workshops on automatic face and gesture recognition* (vol. 1, pp. 1–8). IEEE.

Redi, M., Crockett, D., Manovich, L., & Osindero, S. (2016). What makes photo cultures different? In *Proceedings of the 24th ACM international conference on Multimedia* (pp. 287–291).

Ren, J., Shen, X., Lin, Z., Mech, R., & Foran, D. J. (2017). Personalized image aesthetics. In *Proceedings of the IEEE international conference on computer vision* (pp. 638–647).

Ribeiro, F., Florêncio, D., Zhang, C., & Seltzer, M. (2011). Crowdmos: An approach for crowdsourcing mean opinion score studies. In *IEEE international conference on acoustics, speech and signal processing* (pp. 2416–2419). IEEE.

Rigau, J., Feixas, M., & Sbert, M. (2008). Informational aesthetics measures. *IEEE Computer Graphics and Applications, 28*(2), 24–34.

Rosenblum, N. (2008). *A world history of photography.* New York, USA: Abbeville Press.

San Pedro, J., Yeh, T., & Oliver, N. (2012). Leveraging user comments for aesthetic aware image search reranking. In *Proceedings of the 21st international conference on World Wide Web* (pp. 439–448).

Schifanella, R., Redi, M., & Aiello, L. M. (2015). An image is worth more than a thousand favorites: Surfacing the hidden beauty of flickr pictures. In *ICWSM'15: Proceedings of the 9th AAAI international conference on weblogs and social media.* AAAI.

Schwarz, K., Wieschollek, P., & Lensch, H. P. A. (2018). Will people like your image? learning the aesthetic space. In *2018 IEEE winter conference on applications of computer vision (WACV)* (pp. 2048–2057). https://doi.org/10.1109/WACV.2018.00226.

Selvaraju, R., Cogswell, M., Das, A., Vedantam, R., Parikh, D., & Batra, D. (2017). Grad-CAM: Visual explanations from deep networks via gradient-based localization. In *Proceedings of the IEEE international conference on computer vision* (pp. 618–626).

Sheng, K., Dong, W., Huang, H., Ma, C., & Hu, B. G. (2018a). Gourmet photography dataset for aesthetic assessment of food images. In *SIGGRAPH Asia 2018 technical briefs* (pp. 1–4).

Sheng, K., Dong, W., Ma, C., Mei, X., Huang, F., & Hu, B. G. (2018b). Attention-based multi-patch aggregation for image aesthetic assessment. In *Proceedings of the 26th ACM international conference on Multimedia* (pp. 879–886).

Siahaan, E., Hanjalic, A., & Redi, J. (2016). A reliable methodology to collect ground truth data of image aesthetic appeal. *IEEE Transactions on Multimedia, 18*(7), 1338–1350. https://doi.org/10.1109/TMM.2016.2559942.

Simond, F., Arvanitopoulos, N., & Süsstrunk, S. (2015). Image aesthetics depends on context. In *IEEE international conference on image processing (ICIP)* (pp. 3788–3792). IEEE.

Simonyan, K., & Zisserman, A. (2014). Very deep convolutional networks for large-scale image recognition. Preprint. arXiv:1409.1556.

Song, Y., Redi, M., Vallmitjana, J., & Jaimes, A. (2016). To click or not to click: Automatic selection of beautiful thumbnails from videos. In *Proceedings of the 25th ACM international on conference on information and knowledge management* (pp. 659–668).

Spape, M., Davis, K., Kangassalo, L., Ravaja, N., Sovijarvi-Spape, Z., & Ruotsalo, T. (2021). Brain-computer interface for generating personally attractive images. *IEEE Transactions on Affective Computing.* https://doi.org/10.1109/TAFFC.2021.3059043.

Stollenga, M. F., Masci, J., Gomez, F., & Schmidhuber, J. (2014). Deep networks with internal selective attention through feedback connections. In *Proceedings of the 27th international conference on neural information processing systems* (vol. 2, pp. 3545–3553).

Suchecki, M., & Trzciski, T. (2017). Understanding aesthetics in photography using deep convolutional neural networks. In *2017 Signal processing: Algorithms, architectures, arrangements, and applications (SPA)* (pp. 149–153). https://doi.org/10.23919/SPA.2017.8166855.

Sun, W., Chao, T., Kuo, Y., & Hsu, W. H. (2017). Photo filter recommendation by category-aware aesthetic learning. *IEEE Transactions on Multimedia, 19*(8), 1870–1880. https://doi.org/10.1109/TMM.2017.2688929.

Talebi, H., & Milanfar, P. (2018). NIMA: Neural image assessment. *IEEE Transactions on Image Processing, 27*(8), 3998–4011.

Tang, X., Luo, W., & Wang, X. (2013). Content-based photo quality assessment. *IEEE Transactions on Multimedia, 15*(8), 1930–1943.

Tifentale, A., & Manovich, L. (2018). Competitive photography and the presentation of the self. In *Exploring the selfie* (pp. 167–187). Springer.

Wang, W., Zhao, M., Wang, L., Huang, J., Cai, C., & Xu, X. (2016). A multi-scene deep learning model for image aesthetic evaluation. *Signal Processing: Image Communication, 47*, 511–518.

Wang, Z., Liu, D., Chang, S., Dolcos, F., Beck, D., & Huang, T. (2017). Image aesthetics assessment using Deep Chatterjee's machine. In *International joint conference on neural networks (IJCNN)* (pp. 941–948). https://doi.org/10.1109/IJCNN.2017.7965953.

Wang, W., Yang, S., Zhang, W., & Zhang, J. (2019). Neural aesthetic image reviewer. *IET Computer Vision, 13*(8), 749–758.

Wu, O., Hu, W., & Gao, J. (2011). Learning to predict the perceived visual quality of photos. In *International conference on computer vision* (pp. 225–232). https://doi.org/10.1109/ICCV.2011.6126246.

Xu, M., Chen, F., Li, L., Shen, C., Lv, P., Zhou, B., & Ji, R. (2018). Bio-inspired deep attribute learning towards facial aesthetic prediction. *IEEE Transactions on Affective Computing*, 227–238.

Xu, Y., Zhang, N., Wei, P., Sang, G., Li, L., & Yuan, F. (2020). Deep neural framework with visual attention and global context for predicting image aesthetics. *IEEE Access*, 1–1. https://doi.org/10.1109/ACCESS.2020.3015060.

Ye, P., & Doermann, D. (2014). Active sampling for subjective image quality assessment. In *Proceedings of the IEEE conference on computer vision and pattern recognition* (pp. 4249–4256).

Yeh, H. H., Yang, C. Y., Lee, M. S., & Chen, C. S. (2013). Video aesthetic quality assessment by temporal integration of photo-and motion-based features. *IEEE Transactions on Multimedia, 15*(8), 1944–1957.

Yu, J., Cui, C., Geng, L., Ma, Y., & Yin, Y. (2019). Towards unified aesthetics and emotion prediction in images. In *2019 IEEE international conference on image processing (ICIP)* (pp. 2526–2530). https://doi.org/10.1109/ICIP.2019.8803388.

Zeiler, M. D., & Fergus, R. (2014). Visualizing and understanding convolutional networks. In *European conference on computer vision* (pp. 818–833). Springer.

Zerman, E., Hulusic, V., Valenzise, G., Mantiuk, R., & Dufaux, F. (2018). The relation between MOS and pairwise comparisons and the importance of cross-content comparisons. In *Human vision and electronic imaging conference, IS&T international symposium on electronic imaging*, Burlingame, USA. https://hal.archives-ouvertes.fr/hal-01654133.

Zerman, E., Rana, A., & Smolic, A. (2019). Colornet-estimating colorfulness in natural images. In *IEEE international conference on image processing* (pp. 3791–3795). IEEE.

Zhang, F., Wang, M., & Hu, S. (2013). Aesthetic image enhancement by dependence-aware object recomposition. *IEEE Transactions on Multimedia, 15*(7), 1480–1490. https://doi.org/10.1109/TMM.2013.2268051.

Zhang, L., Gao, Y., Zhang, C., Zhang, H., Tian, Q., & Zimmermann, R. (2014). Perception-guided multimodal feature fusion for photo aesthetics assessment. In *Proceedings of the 22nd ACM international conference on Multimedia* (pp. 237–246).

Zhang, C., Zhu, C., Xu, X., Liu, Y., Xiao, J., & Tillo, T. (2018). Visual aesthetic understanding: Sample-specific aesthetic classification and deep activation map visualization. *Signal Processing: Image Communication, 67*, 12–21.

Zhou, B., Khosla, A., Lapedriza, A., Oliva, A., & Torralba, A. (2016). Learning deep features for discriminative localization. In *Proceedings of the IEEE conference on computer vision and pattern recognition* (pp. 2921–2929).

Zuckert, R. (2007). *Kant on Beauty and Biology: An Interpretation of the 'Critique of Judgment'*. Cambridge University Press.

Shared Memories Driven by the Intrinsic Memorability of Items

Wilma A. Bainbridge

1 Introduction

At all waking moments, we are experiencing a continuous, never-ending flow of sensory information. Even during a normal morning routine, you may be watching the news on TV, scrolling through social media, eating breakfast, and conversing with your family, all simultaneously. While our memories are rich and detailed (Brady et al., 2008; Bainbridge et al., 2019), we usually cannot remember everything (Cowan, 2010). When asked about that morning the following week, some details might be preserved in your memory (e.g., what you wore that day), while others may be completely gone from memory (e.g., what you ate for breakfast). While various cognitive processes will influence what you remember from that day—your emotional state, what you are actively paying attention to, your level of fatigue— the events themselves will also have a large influence over what you remember. For example, a particularly distinctive news headline may be captured in your memory, even if you are groggy or distracted. The intrinsic power of the stimulus to influence our memories—the intrinsic *memorability* of an event—has become a hot topic in the fields of human perception and memory. A growing body of work aims to understand what factors drive the memorability of certain items over others, and what consistencies in memory across people may imply about the underlying mechanisms of perception and memory.

This chapter will discuss our current understanding of stimulus memorability as it relates to human perception. It will begin in Sect. 2 with an overview of the concept of memorability, and a how-to guide on how memorability can be quantified behaviorally for any type of stimulus. Next, Section 3 will discuss our

W. A. Bainbridge (✉)
Department of Psychology, University of Chicago, Chicago, IL, USA
e-mail: wilma@uchicago.edu

© The Author(s), under exclusive license to Springer Nature Switzerland AG 2022
B. Ionescu et al. (eds.), *Human Perception of Visual Information*,
https://doi.org/10.1007/978-3-030-81465-6_7

current psychological understanding of memorability and how it relates to other perceptual and semantic properties of a stimulus. Finally, Section 4 will present the latest neuroscientific understanding of memorability, with results suggesting that memorability reflects a *prioritization signal* of a perceptual input. Throughout, we will discuss what these findings may imply for the computational exploration of memorability.

2 Memorability for Visual Events

While many would agree that intuitively some images are more memorable to us than others, it is not a given that memorability would be a quantifiable attribute for a given image. It has long been known that memories are highly malleable, idiosyncratic, and dependent on our own personal experiences. Distinct cognitive processes and behaviors have been identified for viewing familiar (i.e., previously experienced) faces, like those of celebrities, versus completely novel faces (Rossion et al., 2003; Eger et al., 2005). For example, our ability to recognize a face from a different viewpoint improves when we are highly familiar with that face (Klatzky & Forrest, 1984; Megreya & Burton, 2006; Jenkins et al., 2011). Relatively low consistency has been observed across observers for many other attributes of an image; for example, participants do not agree on which faces are the most typical, interesting, kind, or even which they think will be most memorable (Bainbridge, 2017). Thus, initially one might expect that memory performance for a given image is almost entirely observer-dependent, and that the stimulus itself may contribute relatively low predictive power.

However, the first studies on memorability revealed a remarkable consistency in the images that people remembered and forgot (Isola et al., 2011; Bainbridge et al., 2013). In spite of our unique individual experiences, in a large and diverse sample of participants tested across the United States, there were some face and scene images that most people remembered, and some that most people forgot (see Fig. 1). Importantly, the image itself as a factor contributed to more than half of the variance in memory performance (Bainbridge et al., 2013), implying that the images we view are just as important as our own state and prior experiences in determining what we ultimately remember and forget. Further, these results suggested that we can conceptualize *memorability* as an intrinsic, quantifiable property of an image; an image can be 80% memorable or 20% memorable, and one can use a "memorability score" to predict memory performance for a new set of observers.

Since these first findings of consistent memory performance in face and scene images, memorability consistency has been observed across a diverse range of stimulus types (Fig. 1). Consistent memorability has been observed in highly dynamic, rich visual stimuli such as videos (Cohendet et al., 2019; Newman et al., 2020), movie scenes (Cohendet et al., 2018), and faces across transformations of viewpoint and expression (Bainbridge, 2017). Consistent memorability has also been observed in highly human-constructed types of visual content, such as

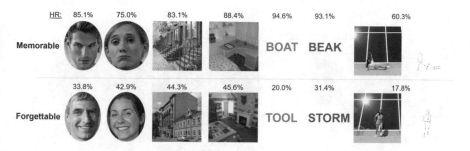

Fig. 1 Example memorable and forgettable items. Shown here are example stimuli at the opposite ends of memorability (indicated here as hit rate), in the domains of faces (Bainbridge et al., 2013), scenes (Isola et al., 2011), words (Xie et al., 2020), and dance moves even with visual information about the dancer removed (Ongchoco et al., 2021)

visualizations and infographics (Borkin et al., 2013). Conversely, memorability has been observed for stimulus types with relatively low visual information such as words (Xie et al., 2020) and actions across visual formats (Ongchoco et al., 2021). While the current chapter will largely focus on the memorability of images, current evidence suggests that we would find similar patterns across other types of stimuli.

2.1 How Do We Capture and Operationalize Memorability for a Stimulus?

It is relatively straightforward to gather the "ground truth" memorability scores for a set of stimuli. Memorability has been most commonly tested (and quantified) using a *continuous recognition* task (Fig. 2a), where participants view a stream of images (or videos), and press a button whenever they spot a repeat from earlier in the sequence (Isola et al., 2011). This task is used most commonly because it is relatively time efficient and engaging for the participant—participants are making judgments as each image is presented, and so we can quantify engagement and memory performance in real-time. However, the specific task used is flexible, as memorability scores from a continuous recognition task have also been shown to replicate in paradigms using separate study and test phases (Goetschalckx et al., 2017) and in perceptual tasks that surprise participants with a memory test at the end (e.g., incidental memory paradigms: Bainbridge et al., 2017; Goetschalckx et al., 2019b; Bainbridge, 2020).

In conducting a continuous recognition task, there are many important considerations when designing the experiment to collect memorability scores (Fig. 2):

1. The parameters should be determined for the memory test.

Memorability effects have been shown to be robust across very different experimental parameters. Even if an image is shown for only 13ms (Broers et al., 2018), or up to 10s (Borkin et al., 2015), its memorability is likely to influence

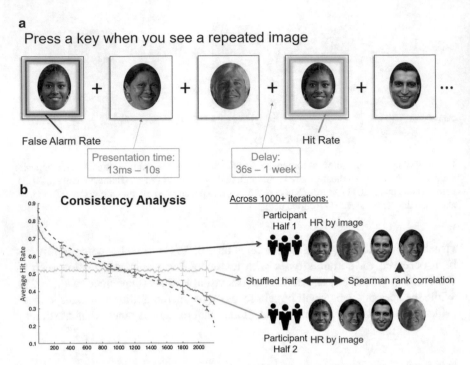

Fig. 2 The key methods for conducting a memorability experiment. (**a**) The general methods for a memorability experiment: Participants see a stream of images and press a key when they see a repeat. From these key presses, each image receives a false alarm rate and a hit rate, which both serve as memorability scores. The experimenter has flexibility in their choices in terms of image type, presentation time, and delay between image repeats. (**b**) The split-half consistency analysis to determine how consistent memory performance is across people. Across 1000+ iterations, participants are split into two random halves and their memorability scores are correlated (Spearman's rank correlation) and compared to a shuffled image order. The graph plots ranked memorability score for participant half 1 (blue dotted line), participant half 2 (solid green line), and the shuffled distribution (gray line)

human memory performance. Similarly, gaps between image repeats for as little as 36s (Isola et al., 2013), or as long as a week (Goetschalckx et al., 2017) still result in the same items emerging as memorable or forgettable. One important consideration is that with a continuous recognition task, target images (those for which you are collecting memorability scores) must be separated by filler images in between target repeats. These filler images often consist of "vigilance repeats", repetitions of filler images at the range of 1-5 images apart, to serve as exclusion criteria for participants who are inattentive and not noticing image repeats even at short delays. Generally, a ratio of ¼ targets to ¾ filler is most common, and filler images should not be distinguishable from target images (in terms of visual, semantic, or categorical properties), to prevent participants from acting differently for targets versus fillers. If memorability scores are desired for all items, then the target images should counterbalanced across participants, so that each item serves as a target for a large number of participants.

Another consideration is how to incentivize high performance in participants. Past studies have incentivized participants to provide as much data as possible, by paying participants based on number of images viewed in the stream (e.g., Isola et al., 2011). Other studies have paid participants a consistent payment amount and only refused payments to participants who did not respond on the task (e.g., Bainbridge et al., 2013). Some studies require participants to perform well on the vigilance task in order to continue with the task (including a requirement to maintain low false alarms; Isola et al., 2011), while others have not required performance minimums (e.g., Bainbridge, 2020). One important note to keep in mind is that the tasks can be rather difficult (e.g., Bainbridge, 2017), and those with poor memory should not necessarily be punished. Introducing a reward for high memory performance could also alter memory performance, although reward has shown no interaction with stimulus memorability or memory performance (Bainbridge, 2020). Thus far, data quality and across-participant consistency has been relatively high, even without the introduction of high rewards or punishments (e.g., Bainbridge, 2020).

For researchers wanting to create their own memorability experiments, I have created a publicly available online tool[1] that can generate the entirety of the code for a memorability experiment, given a few inputs from the researcher on these parameters of the study.

2. The experiment should be run with a large and diverse sample of participants online.

Memorability experiments have been largely run online (on platforms such as Amazon Mechanical Turk,[2] AMT), because of the rapid access to large numbers of diverse participants. Running these experiments in a smaller convenience sample (e.g., with local college students) may hamper the generalizability of the results; it would be impossible to know whether consistencies in memory performance exist regardless of diverse and broad experiences across people, or due to commonalities in that narrow participant sample (e.g., a face that looks like a university's dean may be highly memorable to that university's students, but not to people outside that university). It is also important to collect a large number of memory responses per stimulus, in order to quantify consistencies across people in memory performance. At the minimum, there should be at least 40 participants making a memory rating on any given item, although around 80 participants has been shown to result in the most stable memorability scores (Isola et al., 2013). That being said, smaller, targeted studies could be useful (or necessary) when examining memorability patterns in special populations, such as those with Alzheimer's Disease (Bainbridge et al., 2019).

---

[1]The Memorability Experiment Maker: http://wilmabainbridge.com/makeexperiments.html (Bainbridge, 2017).

[2]Amazon Mechanical Turk: https://www.mturk.com/

Another important consideration is whether your stimulus set matches your participant pool—e.g., if you are testing participants within the United States for face memorability, are the face stimuli representative of the diverse demographics of the US (Bainbridge et al., 2013)? This question not only applies for faces, but also for other stimulus types—does it make sense to test participants in Iceland for memory of scene images representing American urban city-scapes?; Does it make sense to test memorability for words in a non-native language? One important note is that all of the research presented in this chapter is tested with participants, laboratories, and stimuli based in the United States. It is still a fascinating and open question how memorability effects may generalize in separate cultural contexts (e.g., is face memorability consistent across countries?). Finally, researchers may want to determine a recruitment sample size with room for error, as they may wish to exclude participants who fail on too many vigilance trials, or who make too many false alarms—both indicators of low attention or random button pressing.

3. Memorability scores can be calculated for each stimulus based on memory performance.

Any measure of memory performance can be used as a "memorability score". Both hit rates (HR; proportion of participants who successfully recognized an image repeat) and false alarm rates (FA; proportion of participants who falsely remembered an item on its first presentation) have been shown to be consistent across observers (Isola et al., 2011; Bainbridge et al., 2013). Different factors can contribute to high HRs or high FAs; for example, an item with high HRs could be one that is highly memorable, or one that tends to cause a lot of responses (both high HRs and high FAs). Images can thus be conceptualized as falling into one of four categories:

- **High HR, High FA:** "trigger happy" images that evoke a lot of responses, of both accurate memory as well as false alarms.
- **High HR, Low FA:** memorable images—those where people can accurately recognize an image and have few false alarms.
- **Low HR, Low FA:** forgettable images—where people do not make false memories, and also do not remember seeing them when they have.
- **Low HR, High FA:** false memory images—people do not have accurate memories for these images, but somehow make many false memories for them.

All four categories have been shown to be highly consistent; if an image is "trigger happy" for one set of participants, it will likely be "trigger happy" for another set (Bainbridge et al., 2012). While some questions may want to target the study of HR or FA specifically, the two measures can also be combined, with measures such as d' (d-prime, measured by Z-scored HR minus Z-scored FA) and corrected recognition (CR = HR − FA). These measures also show high consistencies across participants (Bainbridge et al., 2013; Bainbridge & Rissman, 2018). Thus, we as experimenters are relatively flexible in what value we decide to take as the "memorability score" for a given image—HR, FA, d', or CR.

4. Significant memorability score consistency should be validated.

To ensure memorability scores are meaningful for this set of stimuli (and because it is always important to replicate research findings), researchers should conduct a *consistency analysis* (Fig. 2b) on their set of results (Isola et al., 2011a). Generally, this has been performed by randomly splitting the participant pool into two halves and re-calculating memorability scores within each participant half for each stimulus. Then, a Spearman's rank correlation is calculated between the two halves, to answer the question: Do these two groups of participants remember and forget the same items as each other? These split-halves are conducted across a large number of iterations (usually 1,000-10,000) and the mean Spearman rank correlation is taken as the consistency score. This is compared to a permuted chance level across many iterations, where two participant split-halves are correlated after shuffling their image order. If memory scores are consistent across participants, the split-half consistency should be significantly higher than this permuted null distribution of consistency.

After these steps, these consistent human-based memorability scores can then be used to answer a myriad of research questions (some of which we outline below).

There have also been in-roads in the realms of computer vision and machine learning to provide automatic quantification of the memorability of an image (Khosla et al., 2013; Khosla et al., 2015) or video (Shekhar et al., 2017; Cohendet et al., 2018). However, using computer-estimated memorability scores in place of ground-truth human ratings should be applied with caution. Some work suggests that current deep learning networks for memorability prediction cannot successfully generalize to image sets with more fine-grained category structure or other types of images like faces and visualizations (Squalli-Houssaini et al., 2018), suggesting that these networks may be sensitive to a specific subset of the factors that drive the memorability of an image. For example, deep neural networks trained to predict the memorability for a diverse set of photographs could instead be predicting visual categories of the image that may correlate with memorability but not predict memorability when controlled for (e.g., toy stores may be more memorable than mountain scenes, but can it still find the most memorable mountain?). These algorithms also have been shown to have limited ability to predict memory performance for special populations, such as those with early stages of Alzheimer's Disease (Bainbridge et al., 2019). However, these limitations could also relate to the training sets of these neural networks; broader and more representative stimulus training sets and more flexible architectures could bridge this gap between human and computer performance (Needell & Bainbridge, 2021).

Instead of using computer-predicted memorability as a replacement for human-measured memorability, the two methods can complement each other in their uses. When studying the psychological and neuroscientific mechanisms that underlie memorability in the human brain, it is essential that ground-truth human scores serve as the main sources of exploration. As it is still unclear what precise information computational models are leveraging to make their predictions, we do not want to create mechanistic claims that could be driven merely by low-level visual or categorical differences. However, computational memorability may also be incredibly helpful for stimulus selection—one could quickly measure the predicted memorability of a stimulus sets to ensure they are roughly controlled for memorability. One could also use these networks to generate images meant to drive strong memory behavior (Goetschalckx et al., 2019a). Finally, computational networks assessed against human memory performance could guide development of systems intended to model the human perception and memory systems (Cichy & Kaiser, 2019).

2.2   Why Should We Consider Memorability?

Now that we have collected memorability scores for a stimulus, what can we do with them? Most straightforwardly, memorability scores are incredibly powerful because they allow for informed predictions about what people will remember or forget. Because stimulus memorability accounts for as much variance in memory performance as all other factors (Bainbridge et al., 2013), this means that incredibly memorable or forgettable stimuli can be selected to drive memory, regardless of the state of the observer. I have shown that memorable images are remembered better than forgettable images no matter how deeply you are attending to and engaging in the images (Bainbridge, 2020). Even if you are just judging whether a fixation cross (+) is black or white, you will remember the irrelevant face behind it if it is memorable. Similarly, even if you are performing a task as deep as judging the honesty of a face, you will still forget it if it is forgettable. I have also shown that reward does nothing to flip these effects—even if you are incentivized with a monetary reward to remember a forgettable image or forget a memorable image, you cannot do either (Bainbridge, 2020). You will still remember the memorable image you were paid to forget over the forgettable image you were paid to remember. Researchers have also found that these memorability scores translate seamlessly across tasks—even if tested with other surrounding image contexts (Bylinskii et al., 2015; Bainbridge et al., 2017), in tasks with a delay (Goetschalckx et al., 2017), or with tasks that only surprise you with a memory test after you study the images (Bainbridge et al., 2017; Goetschalckx et al., 2019b; Bainbridge, 2020), the same images emerge as memorable and forgettable. This means that one can design a task with intentionality—to strongly drive memory, have images at both extremes (both memorable and forgettable), or approximate the natural spread of memorability (a Gaussian distribution).

The striking consistency and resilience of this effect has important implications both for the real world and the scientific. In the real world, we can actively design our lives to be more memorable or quantify the memorability of things around us. In a positive sense, we can design educational material to be more memorable to students, or we can design museums to leave a lasting memory on the visitor. In fact, we have found that some dance movements within the diverse genres of ballet and Korean pop are more memorable than others, and one could envision designing a particularly memorable hit music video, or a memorable sequence for a competition

(Ongchoco et al., 2021). It is also important to be aware of potentially negative ways in which memorability could be utilized in the real world—for example, one could make advertisements, slogans, or characters that are unforgettable; and indeed, that is often the original aim of many marketing campaigns (e.g., to make an advertising jingle you cannot get out of your head). It is important that researchers be cautious in how they apply these new principles. We personally vet downloads of our own data to limit access to only educational and non-profit research purposes.

Beyond these real-world applications, memorability has important uses for the scientific community. As outlined earlier, it is incredibly easy to get memorability scores for any given set of stimuli. In fact, we have previously used these steps to collect the memorability scores from a decade-old functional magnetic resonance imaging (fMRI) face memory experiment (Rissman et al., 2010), to uncover new decodable patterns of memorability from those data. These results also highlight the fact that memorability exists everywhere, and thus could influence prior findings that did not control for memorability. In the most extreme case, experiments that contrast memory for different stimulus images may be revealing effects entirely driven by the memorability of the images and not the manipulation at hand. For a (yet untested) example, studies contrasting memory performance or brain patterns for familiar celebrity faces versus novel non-celebrities may be eliciting patterns driven by the memorability of the images rather than familiarity—celebrities may generally tend to have more memorable faces (that drive them to become more famous), and so memorable celebrity faces may trigger a separate set of processes from the mixed bag of memorability for the faces of ordinary people. To avoid such concerns about memorability confounding with manipulations of interest, it would be prudent to test the memorability of stimuli in advance when designing an experiment. Many databases with thousands of quantified memorability scores already exist for faces (*10k US Adult Faces Database*: Bainbridge et al., 2013), scene images (Isola et al., 2011; *FIGRIM Dataset*: Bylinskii et al., 2015), objects (*MemCat Dataset*: Goetschalckx et al., 2019), and abstract visualizations (*MASSVIS Dataset*: Borkin et al., 2013), from which new experimental stimuli could be selected. Taking memorability into account also gives the experimenter power in what sorts of effects they want to see in their study. If they want to eliminate any concerns about memorability acting as a confound with effects of interest, experiments could select stimuli of all medium memorability, or normally or uniformly distributed across the range of memorability scores. Alternatively, if an experimenter wants to drive particularly strong memory effects, they could intentionally select the most memorable, forgettable, and/or false-alarm-able stimuli for their experiments. This can be used to create high-powered experiments, in contrast with traditional memory experiments where it can be difficult to have enough trials that are forgotten or falsely remembered.

Reanalyzing prior data with memorability in mind could also provide fundamental insights into perception and memory that echo beyond this idea of stimulus properties. These insights can come at a very reasonable price, as they do not require the design and collection of new in-lab experimental data. Instead, the stimuli used in a prior experiment on perception, memory, attention, decision making, emotion, social psychology (et cetera) can be put online in a rapid memorability experiment (using the steps outlined previously), and data can be reanalyzed with memorability as an added factor. For example, we have analyzed image-level performance on a previously collected memory test for 394 participants with different levels of dementia (ranging from healthy elderly controls, to cognitive impairments, to Alzheimer's Disease), and found that certain images are more diagnostic than others (Bainbridge et al., 2019; Bai et al., 2021). Specifically, images that were highly memorable to healthy controls but highly forgettable to those developing dementia were able to better diagnose a held-out set of participants than other image sets of the same size. With these results, one could envision designing highly efficient and brief diagnostic tests for dementia that only use the most diagnostic images. In a therapeutic sense, one could imagine using tools to reinforce memory or provide assistance for particularly forgettable items, or create environments that are intrinsically memorable. As the wealth of open access and Big Data increases with new initiatives in the field and resources like the Open Science Framework[3] and the Human Connectome Project,[4] it becomes easier to unearth memorability effects from a wide range of experiments. Looking at a diversity of participants, tasks, stimuli, and analytic methods promises to reveal key insights into the underlying mechanisms for memory, and provide a large pool of low-hanging, meaningful, open questions that can be answered without collecting new data.

In fact, research on memorability has already delivered new insights into the human perceptual and mnemonic systems. In exploring the underlying causes of the consistent memorability across people, we can learn more about the factors that drive memory, the processes at the intersection of perception and memory, as well as the mechanisms underlying how the brain stores information in memory. Section 3 discusses our current understanding of what memorability means, and how it relates to a larger psychological framework of human cognition.

3   What Does It Mean for Memorability to Be an Intrinsic Image Property?

We have demonstrated that memorability is highly consistent across observers, and thus can be conceptualized as a specific property for an image that reliably translates across tasks and observers. This property serves as a measure of memory likelihood—we can use this measure to make predictions about what others will remember or forget. However, it is still unclear what underlying features define an image's memorability, and how it relates to other properties of an image. Is memorability a proxy for another singular image property that is easily image computable (e.g., brightness)? Or, is it some sort of linear combination of several

---

[3]The Open Science Framework: http://osf.io
[4]The Human Connectome Project: http://www.humanconnectomeproject.org/

properties of an image? Or, might it represent some more complex interaction of the characteristics of an image? Sections 3.1–3.3 explore these three different possibilities for what memorability may represent and how it may be calculated from an image.

3.1 Memorability as a Singular Attribute

When we quantify images, we can think of their properties roughly falling into two different groups: low-level features and high-level features. Low-level features encompass characteristics that can be directly computed from an image without semantic or experiential knowledge, for example, color, brightness, contrast, spatial frequency, and other edge information (e.g., Bainbridge & Oliva, 2015). Conversely, high-level features relate to semantic information such as image category (e.g., "beach") and categorical descriptors (e.g., "natural scene", "outdoor scene"). High-level features also encompass subjective ratings of an image, like aesthetics or emotionality. For the purposes of this chapter, "mid-level" computer vision features (e.g., individual objects) can be conceptually grouped with these high-level features. One early question in the study of memorability was whether it was a low-level or high-level attribute of an image, and whether it merely reflected another already-known stimulus property.

Current evidence shows that memorability is not synonymous with other low-level properties. Image color is not highly predictive of image memorability (Isola et al., 2011), nor is spatial frequency (Bainbridge et al., 2017). Other features that can be extracted from an image, such as its visual saliency, or its gist, have also showed limited explanatory power for memorability (Isola et al., 2011). Additionally, while faces are often quantified by measuring the distances across features, faces with higher differences from the average face are not necessarily more memorable (Bainbridge, 2019). In fact, one can create two sets of images where their average image is indistinguishable, but their images exist at opposite ends of the memorability spectrum (Bainbridge et al., 2017; Bainbridge, 2019).

Memorability also does not serve as a proxy for an alternate high-level property, such as aethetics. In fact, in spite of an intuition that we may be motivated to remember images we find beautiful, memorability shows relatively low (and negative) correlations with image aesthetics as well as ratings of interestingness (Isola et al., 2013). Similarly, for dance movements, more aesthetic, emotional, or difficult movements are not necessarily more memorable (Ongchoco et al., 2021). In the realm of faces, several face attributes show a correlation with memorability: trustworthiness, kindness, emotionality, atypicality, unfamiliarity, and others (Bainbridge et al., 2013). However, no singular attribute fully captures memorability, and one can have a highly memorable face without having any of these other features. Further, while memorability is highly consistent to a face identity even across viewpoint and expression changes (in other words, a *person* has an intrinsic memorability, not just a singular image of their face), these other attributes do not show significant consistency within an identity (Bainbridge, 2017). Perhaps even more surprising is that for images in general, observers are very poor at predicting what they will remember and forget; there is a non-significant negative correlation between what people think they will remember, and what they actually do remember (Isola et al., 2013). These results highlight the elusive nature of memorability, and how many of our intuitions of what causes these consistencies across people may in fact be false. These results also show that memorability is not reducible down to a single low- or high-level image attribute as far as we know.

3.2 Memorability as a Combination of Attributes

It thus seems clear that memorability is not capturing a low-level or high-level property already used to quantify images. However, perhaps a combination of these properties can be used to successfully predict memorability, just as other high-level attributes of an image can be broken down into a combination of several properties. For example, although it is often considered and rated as a single dimension, facial attractiveness can be quantified as a combination of symmetry, skin quality, youthfulness, and cultural templates of attractiveness (e.g., Perrett et al., 1999; Schmid et al., 2008). Is memorability similarly distillable into a series of properties that can be used to quantify an image? In the realm of faces, a LASSO regularized regression including twenty attributes to quantify faces (e.g., attractiveness, trustworthiness, dominance, intelligence) and memories (e.g., typicality, commonality, subjective ratings of memorability) was only able to explain less than half of the variance in memorability scores (Bainbridge et al., 2013). For more complex stimuli like dance movements, a set of ten attributes including beauty, emotionality, complexity of movement, speed, difficulty, atypicality, and subjective memorability only captured 6.40% of the variance in memorability scores (Ongchoco et al., 2021). And, for more semantically-based stimuli like words, attributes commonly used in linguistics like the concreteness or frequency of a word did not explain unique variance for the memorability of a word (Xie et al., 2020). These combinations of attributes are able to better predict memorability than a singular attribute alone, and the relative weighting on each property can reveal what types of information have more impact on what people ultimately remember. However, the fact that none of these combined models can explain much of the variance in memorability suggests that memorability may exist as something beyond a linear combination of various features.

3.3 Memorability as an Arrangement of Attributes

Rather than representing a linear combination of specific properties, memorability could instead represent an arrangement across properties. For example, rather than it being that more attractive faces are more memorable, instead it could be that more *extreme* faces (highly attractive *and* highly unattractive) are more memorable. Images can be conceptualized along a multi-dimensional space, where each dimension represents an attribute and a single image can be represented as a point, located by the vector made up of its score on each of these attribute dimensions. A highly atypical or distinctive image with extreme values on its attributes would be on the outskirts of this distribution, while a more typical or common image with attributes near the mean or prototype would exist near the center of this distribution. The clustering structure of items in a set could also be predictive of memorability, where items with representations similar to others may be more forgettable, where items with more distinctive representations may be more memorable. Prior work has suggested that atypical or distinctive faces tend to be the most memorable (Light et al., 1979; Winograd, 1981; Bartlett et al., 1984; Vokey & Read, 1992), and perhaps these same intuitions apply more generally across memorability for images.

Indeed, there is some converging evidence that memorability may represent the location of a stimulus in such an attribute-based distribution. In the realm of images, images that are located in sparser areas of the attribute space (as defined by features extracted from convolutional neural networks) tend to be more memorable (Lukavský & Děchtěrenko, 2017). However, it is still an open question what attributes constitute such a space, whether they contribute in equal weight, and whether there are separate influences from low-level visual features, versus high-level semantic information. Some work specifically looking at scene images proposes that high-level similarities (i.e., being of the same scene category) but low-level dissimilarities (i.e., having large color differences) may be most correlated with memorability (Koch et al., 2020). However, memorability effects still occur for stimulus categories that are relatively matched for low-level visual information and contain the same level of semantic information, like faces (Bainbridge et al., 2013). Conversely, memorability effects also still occur for semantically rich and diverse stimuli with relatively low visual information, like concrete nouns (Xie et al., 2020). So it is still unclear if these principles of similarity drive memorability similarly across stimulus types.

Perhaps the most convincing evidence for memorability as a reflection of a representational space comes from the realm of words and computational linguistics. The Global Vectors for Word Representation (GloVe) model (Pennington et al., 2014) is a model that creates a vector for a given word representing its relationship to other words. GloVe characterizes words by their co-occurrences in real-world text, with the idea that words that tend to co-occur in a sentence tend to be more semantically related. For example, the word "foot" may frequently co-occur in a sentence with many words, like "shoe", "hand", or "ball"; in contrast, a word like "dime" may co-occur with fewer words (e.g., "coin"), and thus have fewer semantic connections as well. If this GloVe model for semantic relatedness captures how we represent words in memory, then the network structure could show some relationship to memorability. For example, it could be that these highly interconnected words (or "roots" of the network) are the most memorable items, while the most sparsely connected words (or "leaves") are the most forgettable items. In fact, this is what we observe if we make predictions of memorability based on this network structure (Xie et al., 2020); in our dataset of 300 concrete nouns, "foot" was the most memorable (96.3% of online observers successfully recalled it), while "dime" was the most forgettable (only 16.2% successfully recalled it). In a multiple regression model, the GloVe score for a given word explained significant, unique variance in memorability for that word, while other linguistic attributes such as concreteness (Brysbaert et al., 2014) and word frequency (Davies & Gardner, 2013) explained no additional unique variance. Memory behavior also matched many of the predictions one would make if the roots of the network are more memorable than the leaves. First, one would predict that during the retrieval process, you would visit the roots first and then traverse the network to reach the outer leaves; indeed, we observe that retrieval speed is faster for memorable items than forgettable ones. When failing to retrieve an item, one would also predict that intrusions (falsely recalled items) would most commonly be these roots first visited in the retrieval process. Indeed, intrusions had significantly higher memorability than the median memorability of the set.

The combination of these findings suggests that memorability reflects the position of an item in our mental network of knowledge and prior experiences. Rather than being driven by any one attribute or combinations of attributes, it is instead an item's location in a larger network of items arranged by similarity across these attributes that determines an item's memorability. I will discuss what this might mean about the brain in Sect. 4.

However, there is some initial evidence that the relationship between the stimulus space and memorability may not be uniform across all stimuli (Kramer et al., 2021). For example, initial evidence suggests that within some object categories, highly atypical items that are dissimilar from other within-category items are memorable (e.g., an atypical kitchen appliance, like a hearth, is more memorable than a stove), while for other object categories, highly typical items that are similar to other within-category items are memorable (e.g., a typical weapon, like a pistol, is more memorable than a tank). In fact, while studies on images have suggested that visually distinctive and sparsely distributed items are more memorable (Lukavský & Děchtěrenko, 2017; Koch et al., 2020), studies on words have suggested that semantically connected items are more memorable (Xie et al., 2020). There is also evidence that the predictions of memorability for real-world scene images derived from a deep learning neural network correlate with memory patterns in the rhesus macaque (Jaegle et al., 2019), even though these monkeys have not experienced a wide range of scenes that would allow them to construct these mental networks of similarity. Thus, while the idea that memorability reflects a network-like arrangement of mental representations is an attractive one, there are still many open questions about what exact measure memorability reflects, and how it can be predicted regardless of stimulus category (faces, scenes, words) or granularity of that category (scenes versus kitchens).

With this working hypothesis that memorability is defined by an image's relationship to other images, we can now delve into the brain and explore whether we find supporting evidence. Moreover, we can look under the hood to see how processing of memorability may relate to other neural processes, like vision, attention, and memory encoding.

4 The Brain Mechanisms Underlying Memorability

Thus far, we have discussed memorability as a property of a stimulus—stimuli are intrinsically memorable or forgettable, and this influences the likelihood for an observer to remember that image. However, memorability is also tied to a pair of cognitive processes triggered by the image: the process of perception, and the process of memory encoding. Thus, when we see a memorable (or forgettable) item, what patterns may we observe in the brain?

There are four main hypotheses that would predict how memorability should influence processing in the brain. First and most uninterestingly, we may see nothing in the brain when looking for a "signature of memorability" (neural differences between memorable and forgettable images; Sect. 4.1). Memorability appears to be a complex property, irreducible to a simple set of other measures. Many high-level image properties do show patterns in the brain, such as whether a scene image is natural or manmade or open or closed (Kravitz et al., 2011; Park et al., 2011), and whether the objects in it are big or small (Konkle & Oliva, 2012). However, not all properties we respond to behaviorally show a strong signal in the brain, as the ability to detect a signal usually requires high, consistent signal across a localized set of neurons, replicable across participants. These signals must also be prolonged enough and in cortical areas accessible enough to be detectable by a method like fMRI, which has low temporal resolution and high but imperfect spatial resolution (one unit of a MRI brain image—a voxel—still can reflect the average of the firing of 100,000 neurons). However, if we do observe differences between memorable and forgettable images in the brain, a second hypothesis would be that that memorability effects could be reflected in visual processing (Sect. 4.2). Since memorability is an intrinsic property to a specific image, regardless of the observer, it seems that it could reflect a perceptual calculation that would be reflected during early vision, or heightened attention to a visual feature (Sect. 4.3). A third hypothesis is that we would see memorability effects during memory encoding (Sect. 4.4). As memorability scores are operationalized by successful memory encoding and retrieval, we may see effects much like those observed during other memory encoding tasks at the individual subject level. Finally, a fourth hypothesis is that we uncover a new pattern in the brain related to memorability, as some sort of intermediate step between perception and memory (Sect. 4.5).

4.1 Can We Find Memorability in the Brain?

The first investigation of memorability in the brain tested whether there were any differences between viewing memorable images and forgettable images in the first place (Bainbridge et al., 2017). Sixteen participants in an MRI scanner viewed a stream of images and performed a relatively simple but fast-paced perceptual task— when they saw a face, they had to quickly categorize its gender (male/female), and when they saw a scene, they had to quickly categorize its location (indoor/outdoor). Unbeknownst to these participants, half of the faces and scenes were highly memorable, while the other half were highly forgettable—determined in advance from online memorability studies (Isola et al., 2011; Bainbridge et al., 2013). Furthermore, these stimuli were controlled for a range of potential attributes that could be confounded with memorability. The memorable and forgettable faces were matched on low-level properties like spatial frequency and color, high-level properties like ratings of their emotionality, attractiveness, friendliness, and confidence, and demographics like their gender, race, and age. The memorable and forgettable scenes were matched on low-level properties like spatial frequency, color, number of objects, and size of objects, and on high-level properties like whether they were indoor or outdoor, natural or manmade, and had no people or animals in them. Thus only the memorability of these items differed between conditions. Participants were not aware of any memory-related nature of the task and so would not utilize any honed mnemonic strategies. Instead, they were given a surprise memory test only after getting outside the scanner.

We discovered that when contrasting memorable versus forgettable images, there was in fact a significant, strong, bilateral swath of heightened signal for memorable images, bridging from late visual areas to subcortical mnemonic areas (Fig. 3). It

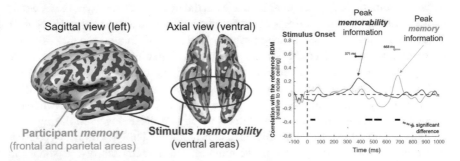

Fig. 3 Neuroscience findings of memorability. Utilizing fMRI (left and center), we have replicated across multiple experiments a bilateral swath of memorability patterns along the ventral visual stream extending into the medial temporal lobe (Bainbridge et al., 2017; Bainbridge & Rissman, 2018). In contrast, patterns related to an individual's memory have been identified in frontal and parietal areas. Utilizing magnetoencephalography (right), we have also identified a temporal separation of these processes, where memorability-based information is discriminable after early vision, but before memory encoding processes (Khaligh-Razavi et al., 2016)

appeared that memorability effects do exist in the brain. And, these effects were not driven by other properties (because we controlled for all other properties known to correlate with memory), nor by intentional mnemonic strategies (as participants believed this was a purely visual task). The next question was how these effects related to those of other cognitive processes.

4.2 Memorability and the Visual System

In the brain during perception, incoming visual information generally traverses a path (the "ventral visual stream") that begins at areas for processing low-level visual information like edge eccentricity and orientation (i.e., early visual cortex, EVC), and then high-level information like stimulus category is parsed in downstream regions along the inferotemporal cortex (Kravitz et al., 2013). Just as one key psychological question is how memorability relates to low-level and high-level properties for an image, a similar neuroscientific question is how this sensitivity to memorability in the brain relates to early and late visual regions.

In our studies of memorability, we have consistently failed to observe effects of memorability in early visual cortex (Bainbridge et al., 2017; Bainbridge & Rissman, 2018), suggesting that these effects are not driven by low-level visual features. In contrast, several pieces of evidence seem to suggest that memorability may relate to higher order visual processes. Memorability effects for images have been repeatedly observed in late visual areas along the inferotemporal cortex, both during memory encoding (Bainbridge et al., 2017) as well as during retrieval (Bainbridge & Rissman, 2018). For a cued word recall task examining memorability in the absence of visual input, memorability signals were instead present in semantic areas such as the anterior temporal lobe, rather than perceptual areas (Xie et al., 2020). In the temporal domain, the timing of memorability decoding occurs around the same time as other late perceptual processes, at around 150–400 ms after stimulus onset (Khaligh-Razavi et al., 2016; Mohsenzadeh et al., 2019), and after early visual processes at around 100ms. These results suggest that the brain shows sensitivity to the memorability of a stimulus during late perceptual processes.

4.3 Memorability and Attention

However, some counterintuitive findings have also emerged from these late visual areas. For example, the fusiform face area (FFA) is a localized region that shows high sensitivity to face images but not scenes, while the parahippocampal place area (PPA) conversely shows high sensitivity to scenes but not faces. Bainbridge et al. (2017) observed that both regions showed sensitivity to the memorability for both the preferred and un-preferred category; for example, one could detect scene memorability from the FFA. These results could suggest that increased brain activation related to stimulus memorability is partially due to attention-driven boosts in signal. For example, heightened attention to memorable stimuli may result in increased activation across visual areas in comparison to forgettable stimuli, resulting in these effects even across category-selective areas.

While the interaction of attentional state and memorability is still an open question, various evidence suggests that memorability effects cannot be solely explained by heightened attention. A series of behavioral studies found that memorable items do not necessarily capture attention (i.e., bottom-up attention); your eyes (and your spotlight of attention) are not automatically drawn to memorable items when searching for a target (Bainbridge, 2020). Similarly, intentional efforts to control attention (i.e., top-down attention) also do not affect memorability; even with highly attentive tasks or rewards to drive your attention, you will always remember memorable items better than forgettable ones (Bainbridge, 2020). In recent work directly contrasting attentional state and memorability, we have observed no correlation between both factors, and they contribute unique variance to predictions of ultimate memory behavior (Wakeland-Hart et al., 2021). Differences in activity for memorable versus forgettable images has also not been identified in areas typically associated with attention, such as regions within the frontal and parietal cortices (Culham et al., 2001). However, future work will need to investigate further the links between attention and memorability during the memory encoding process.

4.4 Memorability and the Memory System

Patterns for memory in the brain have been frequently defined using a method looking at "subsequent memory", in which trials during encoding are sorted post-hoc based on whether they were subsequently remembered or not (Brewer et al., 1998; Wagner et al., 1998). This contrast theoretically reveals which brain regions show activity based on an item's memory fate (i.e., whether it will be successfully encoded and maintained in memory), and has often identified areas in the frontal and parietal lobes (Rissman et al., 2010; Kim, 2011). Memorability could potentially serve as another way to access this subsequent memory signal—since memorable items tend to be subsequently remembered, perhaps the contrast of memorable vs. forgettable will be identical to that for remembered vs. forgotten. However, surprisingly, we find a dissociation between these two effects; regardless of whether an item is remembered or forgotten by a participant, their brain still shows sensitivity to its memorability (Bainbridge et al., 2017). And, patterns for these two contrasts of information suggest distinct cortical areas, with memorability sensitivity in ventral areas, and subsequent memory in frontal and parietal areas (Bainbridge & Rissman, 2018). These results suggest distinct processes related to *stimulus* memorability versus *subject* memory. Indeed, temporally resolved methods show that memory encoding (identified by differentiable signal for subsequently remembered versus forgotten items) occurs after patterns of memorability; early vision occurs early around 100 ms, then sensitivity to memorability at 150–400 ms, and then memory encoding at 600–800 ms (Khaligh-Razavi et al., 2016). Thus, this sensitivity to memorability in the brain is not due to the process of memory encoding, but some sort of signal that occurs *before* encoding.

4.5   Memorability as a Prioritization Signal

It thus seems clear that the brain is sensitive to the memorability of an item, and not because memorable items are visually distinct, nor because they elicit heightened attention, nor because of a difference in successful encoding. Instead, this sensitivity to memorability comes online during an intermediate time point between early vision and memory encoding (Khaligh-Razavi et al., 2016). Sensitivity to memorability has also been identified in memory-related areas in the medial temporal lobe, like the hippocampus and perirhinal cortex (PRC). The PRC has been considered by some researchers to act as a novelty detector (Desimone, 1996; Brown & Aggleton, 2001; Daselaar et al., 2006), but perhaps it may be sensitive to subtler statistical differences across items, like their memorability. In the word domain, temporal lobe structures (specifically, the anterior temporal lobe) also show a sensitivity to memorability in the absence of a perceptual experience of that item (Xie et al., 2020). Thus, memory-related temporal areas may be the seat where this memorability signal originates, even if the signal differs from those of memory encoding.

Why would memorability be "computed" by any particular region of the brain? Our current hypothesis is that memorability represents a *priority signal* for a stimulus. We cannot remember everything we perceive—our memories are limited from moment to moment. Thus, our brains must rapidly and efficiently sort information for memory encoding. Perhaps these findings on memorability have detected this sorting signal, where high priority items are those with certain statistical characteristics that recommend they be encoded into memory, while low priority items are safe to be forgotten. This interpretation is highly suggested by the connection between semantic networks and word memorability, where high-priority and highly memorable items are those items where we start our memory searches, with the highest semantic connections (Xie et al., 2020). However, this pattern is not only found in the domain of words; for images as well, we see a distinctive concentric pattern of memorability in late visual and memory areas. Specifically, memorable images are neurally similar to each other, while forgettable items are more dispersed. These patterns suggest that memorable items do not just trigger higher signal in the brain, but a patterned signal, with memorable items at the roots of a larger structure (Fig. 4).

This hypothesis is still new but largely testable. We can design tasks to manipulate the priority of an item and see how this influences memory, by examining how patterns of memorability emerge for novel stimulus categories with designed statistical relationships. We can also see how memorability relates to other

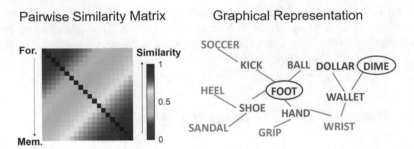

Fig. 4 Depiction of memorability as a priority signal. The left depicts the pairwise representational similarity matrix that has been repeatedly observed in the brain (the areas shown in Fig. 3). If the correlations of brain patterns are calculated between each pair of stimuli, then memorable items show high similarity, while forgettable items show low similarity to each other and other items. This suggests a mental representation like the one on the right, where memorable items are more centralized and forgettable items are more dispersed. This shape is also suggested by the GloVe model and the findings of Xie et al. (2020), where more memorable items (e.g., "foot") have a larger number of semantic connections and are located at the roots of a network, in contrast with more forgettable items (e.g., "dime") which have fewer connections and are located at the leaves of the network

concepts like processing fluency or information density. These findings promise to guide meaningful exploration in the domains of computer science as well; can memorability of an item be used as a guiding principle for designing user interfaces, or human-computer interactions, whereby computer systems sort information or behaviors by their need to be remembered?

5 Conclusion

The study of image memorability is a nascent but promising topic, with important implications for the fields of human perception and human memory, as well as implications for computational models of these processes. In Sect. 2, I motivated the necessity to consider memorability in both the scientific and the real worlds, and presented practical tips and tools so the reader can dive into their own studies of memorability (even just using their own pre-existing data). In Sect. 3, I discussed memorability's role as an image property, and its relationship to other low- and high-level image attributes. Finally, in Sect. 4, I delved into the neural mechanisms underlying memorability effects, and how they could reflect memorability's role as a prioritization signal.

We currently know more about what memorability *isn't* than what it is. We know it is not just a stand-in for another already known image attribute, or a combination of other pre-existing attributes. We know memorability signals in the brain are not mere reactions to visual differences, or signals of heightened attention, or patterns of memory encoding. In terms of what we do know, we see evidence that sensitivity to memorability occurs somewhere between perception and memory, and we take this as preliminary evidence that it might reflect how we sort (or prioritize) perceptual information for memory encoding. A key future direction will be the creation of generative models of memorability, whether developed through psychophysics, neuroscience, or computational models. The ability to create honed predictions about stimulus memorability will in turn allow for precise predictions of individuals' memories, which will have resounding impacts in both the psychological and applied realms.

There are many exciting future directions from which we can continue the study of memorability. All of the work I have discussed has been in the visual domain, with a large focus on static images. Future work will need to elaborate the memorability of stimuli across dynamic episodes (e.g., interactions, conversations), modalities (e.g., olfaction, audition), and across items (e.g., across associations and contexts). These findings also highlight the importance of considering the many factors that influence a behavior; while the system performing the behavior (the human) is important to consider, so are the inputs to that system as well (e.g., Bainbridge & Baker, 2020). Beyond memorability, a deeper look into stimulus properties, their consistencies (or differences) across people, and their related behavioral phenomena may spur many valuable directions of inquiry. One related and equally intriguing stimulus property we are now beginning to investigate is the propensity for an image to trigger false memories—certain images cause the same visual false memories across people even when these false versions have never been visually experienced (dubbed the *Visual Mandela Effect*; Prasad and Bainbridge, 2021). More broadly, these stimulus-centric investigations have high potential for providing new insights into the mechanisms of human cognition, by understanding how specific inputs trigger different behavioral outputs.

In sum, memorability promises to revolutionize our understanding of visual memory. It has started to reveal the intricate processes occurring in the brain between the perception and encoding of an item. It also presents a way to measure and control memories through the items we are remembering. It is with these explorations into the items we see that we may hope to take agency over our memories.

References

Bai, Y., Schütze, H., Jessen, F., Spottke, A., Nestor, P., Bürger, K., Schneider, A., Peters, O., Priller, J., Wiltfang, J., Laske, C., Teipel, S. J., Düzel, E., & Bainbridge, W. A. (2021). Memorability analysis for diagnostic photographs in cognitive assessment: Linking behavioral performance with biomarker status. *Alzheimer's association international conference*, Online.

Bainbridge, W. A. (2017). The memorability of people: Intrinsic memorability across transformations of a person's face. *Journal of Experimental Psychology: Learning, Memory, and Cognition, 43*, 706–716.

Bainbridge, W. A. (2019). Memorability: How what we see influences what we remember. In K. Federmeier & D. Beck (Eds.), *Psychology of learning and motivation* (Vol. 70, pp. 1–27).

Bainbridge, W. A. (2020). The resiliency of image memorability: A predictor of memory separate from attention and priming. *Neuropsychologia, 141*, 107408.

Bainbridge, W. A., & Baker, C. I. (2020). Boundaries extend and contract in scene memory depending on image properties. *Current Biology, 30*, 537–543.

Bainbridge, W. A., Berron, D., Schütze, H., Cardenas-Blanco, A., Metzger, C., Dobisch, L., et al. (2019). Memorability of photographs in subjective cognitive decline and mild cognitive impairment for cognitive assessment. *Alzheimer's & Dementia: Diagnosis, Assessment & Disease Monitoring, 11*, 610–618.

Bainbridge, W. A., Dilks, D. D., & Oliva, A. (2017). Memorability: A stimulus-driven perceptual neural signature distinctive from memory. *NeuroImage, 149*, 141–152.

Bainbridge, W. A., Isola, P., Blank, I., & Oliva, A. (2012). Establishing a database for studying human face photograph memory. *Proceedings of the 34th Annual conference of the cognitive science society*.

Bainbridge, W. A., Isola, P., & Oliva, A. (2013). The intrinsic memorability of face photographs. *Journal of Experimental Psychology: General, 142*, 1323–1334.

Bainbridge, W. A., & Oliva, A. (2015). A toolbox and sample object perception data for equalization of natural images. *Data in Brief, 5*, 846–851.

Bainbridge, W. A., & Rissman, J. (2018). Dissociating neural markers of stimulus memorability and subjective recognition during episodic retrieval. *Scientific Reports, 8*, 8679.

Bartlett, J. C., Hurry, S., & Thorley, W. (1984). Typicality and familiarity of faces. *Memory & Cognition, 12*, 219–228.

Borkin, M. A., Bylinskii, Z., Kim, N. W., Bainbridge, C. M., Yen, C. S., Borkin, D., Pfister, H., & Oliva, A. (2015). Beyond memorability: Visualization recognition and recall. *IEEE Transactions on Visualization and Computer Graphics, 22*, 519–528.

Borkin, M. A., Vo, A. A., Bylinskii, Z., Isola, P., Sunkavailli, S., Oliva, A., et al. (2013). What makes a visualization memorable? *IEEE Transactions on Visualization and Computer Graphics, 19*, 2306–2315.

Brady, T. F., Konkle, T., Alvarez, G. A., & Oliva, A. (2008). Visual long-term memory has a massive storage capacity for object details. *Proceedings of the National Academy of Sciences, 105*, 14325–14329.

Brewer, J. B., Zhao, Z., Desmond, J. E., Glover, G. H., & Gabrieli, J. D. E. (1998). Making memories: Brain activity that predicts how well visual experience will be remembered. *Science, 281*, 1185–1187.

Broers, N., Potter, M. C., & Nieuwenstein, M. R. (2018). Enhanced recognition of memorable pictures in ultra-fast RSVP. *Psychonomic Bulletin & Review, 25*, 1080–1086.

Brown, M. W., & Aggleton, J. P. (2001). Recognition memory: What are the roles of the perirhinal cortex and hippocampus? *Nature Reviews Neuroscience, 2*, 51–61.

Brysbaert, M., Warriner, A. B., & Kuperman, V. (2014). Concreteness ratings for 40 thousand generally known English word lemmas. *Behavioral Research Methods, 46*, 904–911.

Bylinskii, Z., Isola, P., Bainbridge, C., Torralba, A., & Oliva, A. (2015). Intrinsic and extrinsic effects on image memorability. *Vision Research, 116*, 165–178.

Cichy, R. M., & Kaiser, D. (2019). Deep neural networks as scientific models. *Trents in Cognitive Sciences, 23*, 305–317.

Cohendet, R., Demarty, C.-H., Duong, N. Q. K., & Engilberge, M. (2019). VideoMem: Constructing, analyzing, predicting short-term and long-term video memorability. In *IEEE/CVF international conference on computer vision (ICCV)* (pp. 2531–2540).

Cohendet, R., Yadati, K., Duong, N. Q. K., & Demarty, C.-H. (2018). Annotating, understanding, and predicting long-term video memorability. In *Proceedings of the 2018 ACM on international conference on multimedia retrieval (ICMR)* (pp. 178–186).

Cowan, N. (2010). The magical mystery four: How is working memory capacity limited, and why? *Current Directions in Psychological Science, 19*, 51–57.

Culham, J. C., Cavanagh, P., & Kanwisher, N. G. (2001). Attention response functions: Characterizing brain areas using fMRI activation during parametric variations of attentional load. *Neuron, 32*, 737–745.

Daselaar, S. M., Fleck, M. S., & Cabeza, R. (2006). Triple dissociation in the medial temporal lobes: Recollection, familiarity, and novelty. *Journal of Neurophysiology, 96*, 1902–1911.

Davies, M., & Gardner, D. A. (2013). *A frequency dictionary of contemporary American English: Word sketches*. Routledge.

Desimone, R. (1996). Neural mechanisms for visual memory and their role in attention. *Proceedings of the National Academy of Sciences of the USA, 93*, 13494–13499.

Eger, E., Schweinberg, S. R., Dolan, R. J., & Henson, R. N. (2005). Familiarity enhances invariance of face representations in human ventral visual cortex: fMRI evidence. *NeuroImage, 26*, 1128–1139.

Goetschalckx, L., Andonian, A., Oliva, A., & Isola, P. (2019a). Ganalyze: Towards visual definitions of cognitive image properties. In *Proceedings of the IEEE international conference on computer vision* (pp. 5744–5753).

Goetschalckx, L., Moors, P., & Wagemans, J. (2019b). Incidental image memorability. *Memory, 27*, 1273–1282.

Goetschalckx, L., & Wagemans, J. (2019). MemCat: A new category-based image set quantified on memorability. *PeerJ, 7*, e8169.

Goetschalckx, L., Moors, P., & Wagemans, J. (2017). Image memorability across longer time intervals. *Memory, 26*, 581–588.

Isola, P., Xiao, J., Parikh, D., Torralba, A., & Oliva, A. (2013). What makes a photograph memorable? *IEEE Transactions on Pattern Analysis and Machine Learning, 36*, 1469–1482.

Isola, P., Xiao, J. X., Torralba, A., & Oliva, A. (2011). What makes an image memorable? *24th IEEE conference on computer vision and pattern recognition (CVPR), 145*–152.

Jaegle, A., Mehrpour, V., Mohsenzadeh, Y., Meyer, T., Oliva, A., & Rust, N. (2019). Population response magnitude variation in inferotemporal cortex predicts image memorability. *eLife, 8*, e47596.

Jenkins, R., White, D., Montfort, X. V., & Burton, A. M. (2011). Variability in photos of the same face. *Cognition, 121*, 313–323.

Khaligh-Razavi, S.-M., Bainbridge, W.A., Pantazis, D., & Oliva, A. (2016). From what we perceive to what we remember: Characterizing representational dynamics of visual memorability. *bioRxiv*, https://doi.org/10.1101/049700.

Khosla, A., Bainbridge, W. A., Torralba, A., & Oliva, A. (2013). Modifying the memorability of face photographs. *Proceedings of the international conference on computer vision (ICCV)*.

Khosla, A., Raji, A. S., Torralba, A., & Oliva, A. (2015). Understanding and predicting image memorability at a large scale. In *International conference on computer vision (ICCV)* (pp. 2390–2398).

Kim, H. (2011). Neural activity that predicts subsequent memory and forgetting: A meta-analysis of 74 fMRI studies. *NeuroImage, 54*, 2446–2461.

Klatzky, R. L., & Forrest, F. H. (1984). Recognizing familiar and unfamiliar faces. *Memory & Cognition, 12*, 60–70.

Koch, G. H., Akpan, E., & Coutanche, M. N. (2020). Image memorability is predicted by discriminability and similarity in different stages of a convolutional neural network. *Learning & Memory, 27*, 503–509.

Konkle, T., & Oliva, A. (2012). A real-world size organization of object responses in occipitotemporal cortex. *Neuron, 74*, 1114–1124.

Kramer, M. A., Hebart, M. N., Baker, C. I., & Bainbridge, W. A. (2021). Revealing the relative contributions of conceptual and perceptual information to visual memorability. *Annual Meeting of the Vision Sciences Society, 2021*.

Kravitz, D. J., Peng, C. S., & Baker, C. I. (2011). Real-world scene representations in high-level visual cortex: It's the spaces more than the places. *Journal of Neuroscience, 31*, 7322–7333.

Kravitz, D. J., Saleem, K. S., Baker, C. I., Ungerleider, L. G., & Mishkin, M. (2013). The ventral visual pathway: An expanded neural framework for the processing of object quality. *Trends in Cognitive Science, 17*, 26–49.

Light, L., Kayra-Stuart, F., & Hollander, S. (1979). Recognition memory for typical and unusual faces. *Journal of Experimental Psychology: Human Learning and Memory, 5*, 212–228.

Lukavský, J., & Děchtěrenko, F. (2017). Visual properties and memorizing scenes: Effects of image-space sparseness and uniformity. *Attention, Perception, & Psychophysics, 79*, 2044–2054.

Megreya, A. M., & Burton, A. M. (2006). Unfamiliar faces are not faces: Evidence from a matching task. *Memory & Cognition, 34*, 865–876.

Mohsenzadeh, Y., Mullin, C., Oliva, A., & Pantazis, D. (2019). The perceptual neural trace of memorable unseen scenes. *Scientific Reports, 9*, 1–10.

Needell, C., & Bainbridge, W. A. (2021). Embracing new techniques in deep learning for estimating image memorability. arXiv, 2105.10598.

Newman, A., Fosco, C., Casser, V., Lee, A., McNamara, B., & Oliva, A. (2020). Multimodal memorability: Modeling effects of semantics and decay on video memorability. *European Conference on Computer Vision (ECCV)*, arXiv:2009.02568.

Ongchoco, J. D. K., Chun, M., & Bainbridge, W. A. (2021). What moves us? The intrinsic memorability of dance. The Open Science Framework. https://osf.io/e3h2z/

Park, S., Brady, T. F., Greene, M. R., & Oliva, A. (2011). Disentangling scene content from spatial boundary: Complementary roles for the parahippocampal place are and lateral occipital complex in representing real-world scenes. *Journal of Neuroscience, 31*, 1333–1340.

Pennington, J., Socher, R., & Manning, C. D. (2014). GloVe: Global vectors for word representation. In *Proceedings of the 2014 conference on empirical methods in natural language processing (EMNLP)* (pp. 1532–1543).

Perrett, D. I., Burt, D. M., Penton-Voak, I. S., Lee, K. J., Rowland, D. A., & Edwards, R. (1999). Symmetry and human facial attractiveness. *Evolution and Human Behavior, 20*, 295–307.

Prasad, D., & Bainbridge, W. A. (2021). The Visual Mandela Effect as evidence for shared and specific false memories across people. PsyArXiv, 10.31234/osf.io/nzh3s.

Rissman, J., Greely, H. T., & Wagner, A. D. (2010). Detecting individual memories through the neural decoding of memory states and past experience. *Proceedings of the National Academy of Sciences, USA, 107*, 9849–9854.

Rossion, B., Schiltz, C., & Crommelinck, M. (2003). The functionally defined right occipital and fusiform "face areas" discriminate novel from visually familiar faces. *NeuroImage, 19*, 877–883.

Schmid, K., Marx, D., & Samal, A. (2008). Computation of a face attractiveness index based on neoclassical canons, symmetry, and golden ratios. *Pattern Recognition, 41*, 2710–2717.

Shekhar, S., Singal, D., Singh, H., Kedia, M., & Shetty, A. (2017). Show and recall: Learning what makes videos memorable. In *Proceedings of the IEEE international conference on computer vision (ICCV)* (pp. 2730–2739).

Squalli-Houssaini, H., Duong, N. Q. K., Gwenaelle, M., & Demarty, C.-H. (2018). Deep learning for predicting image memorability. In *2018 IEEE international conference on acoustics, speech and signal processing (ICASSP)* (pp. 2371–2375).

Vokey, J. R., & Read, J. D. (1992). Familiarity, memorability, and the effect of typicality on the recognition of faces. *Memory & Cognition, 20*, 291–302.

Wagner, A. D., Schacter, D. L., Rotte, M., Koutstaal, W., Maril, A., & Dale, et al. (1998). Building memories: Remembering and forgetting of verbal experiences as predicted by brain activity. *Science, 281*, 1188–1191.

Wakeland-Hart, C. D., deBettencourt, M. T., Bainbridge, W. A., & Rosenberg, M. D. (2021). Predicting visual memory across images and within individuals. PsyArXiv, 10.31234/osf.io/zbu3k.

Winograd, E. (1981). Elaboration an distinctiveness in memory for faces. *Journal of Experimental Psychology: Human Learning and Memory, 7*, 181–190.

Xie, W., Bainbridge, W. A., Inati, S. K., Baker, C. I., & Zaghloul, K. (2020). Memorability of words in arbitrary verbal associations modulates memory retrieval in the anterior temporal lobe. *Nature Human Behaviour, 4*, 937–948.

Memorability: An Image-Computable Measure of Information Utility

Zoya Bylinskii, Lore Goetschalckx, Anelise Newman, and Aude Oliva

1 Introduction

People are remarkably good at remembering images and their details, even when those images do not hold personal significance or contain recognizable places (Brady et al. 2008; Konkle et al. 2010a,b; Standing 1973). Foundational memory studies and the follow-up computational work (Isola et al. 2011a,b, 2014) proved that images have intrinsic traits that make some of them memorable and others forgettable. The earliest computational studies quickly ruled out low-level features like color and contrast and showed that neither aesthetics nor preference explain memorability (Isola et al. 2011a,b, 2014; Khosla et al. 2015). And, interestingly, despite people being remarkably consistent in what they remembered and forgot, their subjective judgements about what was memorable versus forgettable were inaccurate (Isola et al. 2014). Thus, memorability was found to be intrinsic to the images studied, largely independent of the observers and their

Z. Bylinskii (✉)
Adobe Research, San Jose, CA, USA
e-mail: bylinski@adobe.com

L. Goetschalckx
Department of Cognitive Linguistic and Psychological Sciences, Carney Institute for Brain Science, Brown University, Providence, RI, USA
e-mail: lore_goetschalckx@brown.edu

A. Newman
Stanford University, Stanford, CA, USA
e-mail: anelise@stanford.edu

A. Oliva
Massachusetts Institute of Technology, Cambridge, MA, USA
e-mail: oliva@mit.edu

© The Author(s), under exclusive license to Springer Nature Switzerland AG 2022   207
B. Ionescu et al. (eds.), *Human Perception of Visual Information*,
https://doi.org/10.1007/978-3-030-81465-6_8

opinions, and yet not easily described by previously-studied high- or low-level features (Rust & Mehrpour 2020).

These discoveries sparked a line of research dedicated to building computational models to understand and predict image memorability. The memorability games first introduced by Isola et al. (2011b) became the gold standard for collecting objective measurements of human memorability (Bainbridge et al. 2013; Borkin et al. 2013; Bylinskii et al. 2015; Khosla et al. 2015) and the basis for memorability datasets that fueled further work on memorability prediction. Driven by the promise of automatic applications for memory manipulation, assistive devices, and more effective visuals, computational models of memorability became more complex and extended to cover many types of stimuli.

This chapter will provide an overview of these computational efforts. In Sect. 2, we start our discussion with the datasets that power the computational models of memorability. We mention considerations for data curation and provide a list and descriptions of the image memorability datasets available to date, how they were sourced, and which additional properties they contain. Section 3 provides an overview of different model designs, from support vector machines to different types of neural networks (including CNNs, RNNs, and GANs). We discuss model design considerations, including interpretability, and provide a curated list of the top-performing published models. In Sect. 4, we cover our current understanding about which features of images and videos make them more or less memorable, from low-level pixel features to semantic and contextual features, including objects, saliency, motion, and emotion. We wrap up with a discussion of applications in Sect. 5, future directions for research in Sect. 6, and our proposed unifying explanation for the "magic sauce" of memorability in Sect. 7.

2   Datasets: From Visual Content to Scores

Data is at the heart of most computational models. A good dataset can make a simple model shine; a poor dataset will undercut even the most apt modeling decisions. We begin this chapter with a discussion of the factors that are important for collecting a memorability dataset, followed by a brief overview of existing datasets. Memorability scores for the stimuli in all these datasets were collected using a variation on the memory game protocol from the seminal memorability paper by Isola et al. (2011b). This section will focus on the stimuli used for the memorability games.

Designing datasets for memorability studies requires careful data curation, so that neither the insights obtained from the analyses nor the models trained on this data are biased due to confounding variables. The following properties should be considered:

- **Diversity**. Collecting stimuli with good variability along the relevant feature axes will facilitate spread in the human memorability scores and allow models to learn a more robust signal from the data (Khosla et al. 2015). Even within a single scene category, images can vary in terms of the objects contained, the viewing angle, the amount of light, etc. (Bylinskii et al. 2015; Goetschalckx and Wagemans 2019).

- **Quantity**. Having a large number of stimuli will have two benefits: (i) the effects of confounding variables have a larger chance of being washed out, and (ii) larger, more powerful models can be trained when more data is available. The best performing models today are particularly data-hungry neural networks (Fajtl et al. 2018; Khosla et al. 2015; Perera et al. 2019). Having a sufficient number of participant responses per stimuli is also important, as having too few participants can produce an artificially low split-half consistency value. The Spearman-Brown formula (Spearman 1910; Brown 1910; Goetschalckx et al. 2018) can be used to calculate an appropriate number of responses to collect in order to reach a stable value for split-half consistency.
- **Balance**. It is important to decide up front whether to explicitly balance the data by having similar numbers of exemplars per category (Bylinskii et al. 2015; Goetschalckx & Wagemans 2019) or to sample according to some natural distribution (e.g., sampling photos of faces according to names from the U.S. census (Bainbridge et al. 2012)). If a dataset has cluttered indoor scenes, one can consider the addition of cluttered and uncluttered outdoor as well as uncluttered indoor scenes (Bylinskii et al. 2015). For specialized datasets like faces, consider genders and races (Bainbridge et al. 2012); for graphic designs, figures, or visualizations, consider publication sources and design categories (Borkin et al. 2013). Building off prior work can help balance for visual features and semantic content that has been previously found to drive memorability (e.g., the presence of faces, emotional content, zoomed-in objects, etc.; see Sect. 4).

Further, there are a number of considerations at play when assembling the stimuli for use in memorability studies. They are outlined below.

Permissions and Appropriateness Stimuli used in memorability datasets are often drawn from previously-curated open-source datasets used in computer vision, including the SUN scenes dataset (Isola et al. 2011a; Xiao et al. 2010), Aesthetic Visual Analysis (AVA) (Khosla et al. 2015; Murray et al. 2012), Abnormal Objects (Khosla et al. 2015; Saleh et al. 2013), or Moments in Time (Monfort et al. 2019; Newman et al. 2020). As with any image or video dataset, it is important to take care that you have permission to use and share the stimuli before publishing your data and to filter for quality and appropriateness.

Filtering to Avoid Confounds Once sourced, some preprocessing of the data may be required, in particular to guarantee that irrelevant factors (e.g., the size, aspect ratio, image quality, or speed—in the case of videos) are held constant, to avoid confounding the results. Some of the processing, including cropping image size (Bylinskii et al. 2015; Isola et al. 2011b) can be done automatically, while the rest may require manual curation. This type of curation can be amenable to crowdsourcing tasks (e.g., removing stimuli with undesirable properties like watermarks, special effects, etc. (Newman et al. 2020)).

Controlling for Familiarity Finally, the memorability studies described in this work assume that participants are seeing the stimuli for the first time. To avoid confounding familiarity effects, it may be necessary to filter the dataset ahead of time to remove landmarks, faces, artwork, and other potentially recognizable content.

2.1 Consistency Across Participants

Many studies have confirmed that the memorability of visual stimuli—be they natural scenes, portraits, visualizations, objects, or actions—is remarkably consistent across viewers (Fig. 1). This level of consistency between participants is itself roughly consistent across studies with different participant groups and stimulus sets, as shown in Table 1. Consistency is measured as the Spearman rank correlation between memorability rankings produced by different groups of participants, and falls in the range 0.68–0.83 for image datasets and 0.57–0.73 for video datasets. Note that split-half consistency tends to increase with number of participants and levels off with sufficient data points. Early studies (Isola et al. 2011a, 2014, 2011b) showed that indoor images with people are consistently more memorable than natural scene images, but this observation did not fully account for inter-observer consistency. Later, studies run within-category, where only indoor images of a single scene category were shown (e.g., kitchens), continued to exhibit similarly

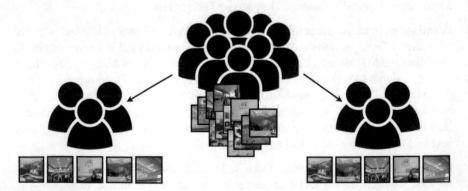

Fig. 1 Consistency is evaluated by randomly splitting the participants in a memorability experiment in half, computing memorability scores based on the data from each set of participants separately, and ranking the dataset images according to those scores. The correlation between the sets of rankings is reported. This procedure is repeated for multiple splits, and the results are averaged to produce the final consistency score (ρ)

Table 1 Image and video memorability datasets

Dataset	Num. Stimuli	ρ[a]	Type of stimuli
SUN (Isola et al. 2011b)	2,222	0.75	Mixed photographs
Face Mem. (Bainbridge et al. 2013)	2,222	0.68	US adult faces
MASSVIS (Borkin et al. 2013)	393	0.83	Data visualizations and infographics
FIGRIM (Bylinskii et al. 2015)	1,754	0.74	Scenes from 21 indoor and outdoor categories
Object Mem. (Dubey et al. 2015)	850	0.76	Scenes with object segmentations
LaMem (Khosla et al. 2015)	60,000	0.68	Diverse images from other computer vision datasets
MemCat (Goetschalckx & Wagemans 2019)	10,000	0.78	5 broad image categories (with sub-categories)
VISCHEMA (Akagunduz et al. 2019)	800	–	Subset of FIGRIM with additional annotations
LNSIM (Lu et al. 2020)	2,632	0.78	Natural outdoor scenes without salient objects
Movie Mem. (Cohendet et al. 2018)	660	0.57	Video clips from previously-seen films
VideoMem (Cohendet et al. 2019)	10,000	0.62	Seven-second video clips
Memento10k (Newman et al. 2020)	10,000	0.73	Three-second, dynamic video clips

[a]Consistency refers to inter-observer split-half consistency in the hit rates (HR), measured with Spearman correlation, and reported as $-1 \leq \rho \leq 1$. The number of stimuli listed in the table above corresponds to those with memorability scores (on which consistency scores could be calculated). Many of the datasets above also contain a larger number of curated stimuli without memorability scores, used as fillers in the memorability games. Other studies (Khosla et al. 2015; Newman et al. 2020) used the same stimuli as targets and fillers for different participants, thereby not requiring separate sets of stimuli

high inter-observer consistency scores (Bylinskii et al. 2015). Analogous levels of consistency were observed once scene and object classes were more carefully controlled for (Dubey et al. 2015; Goetschalckx & Wagemans 2019; Lu et al. 2020). Specialized image sets including face images (Bainbridge et al. 2013) and information visualizations (Borkin et al. 2013), as well as video datasets (Cohendet et al. 2019; Newman et al. 2020), maintained high inter-observer consistency, once again validating the intrinsic nature of memorability.

High inter-observer consistency means that memorability scores are eligible for automatic prediction. The rest of this section will go into greater detail about how the stimuli for these memorability studies were collected and the additional annotations that they contain, which will be useful for the computational analyses and models in the following sections.

2.2   Natural Scenes

The original memorability dataset by Isola et al. (2011b) contains a random sampling of scene categories from the SUN dataset (Xiao et al. 2010), of which 2222 images have memorability scores. The images were resized and cropped to the same size, so that neither size nor aspect ratio acted as confounding variables. They also come with human-annotated object segmentation labels (Russell et al. 2008), which were originally used to correlate memorability with various object classes. A follow-up work by Isola et al. (2014) also collected aesthetic and interestingness judgements for each of these images, as well as subjective judgements as to whether humans consider them memorable.

The FIGRIM dataset (Bylinskii et al. 2015) sampled scene categories in a more targeted way. It represents 21 indoor and outdoor SUN scene categories, each of which has at least 300 exemplars at sufficient resolution (at least 700×700 pixels; as above, images were preprocessed to a consistent size before the experiment). Memorability scores were collected for 1754 target images. An additional 7674 filler images are available.

LNSIM (Lu et al. 2020) was a dataset intended to capture the memorability of scenes without the confounding effects of salient and memorable objects. Towards this goal, the authors collected images from MIR Flickr (Huiskes & Lew 2008), AVA (Murray et al. 2012), affective images (Machajdik & Hanbury 2010), the image saliency datasets MIT1003 (Judd et al. 2009) and NUSEF (Ramanathan et al. 2010), and SUN (Xiao et al. 2010). They further filtered the images to "only be composed of outdoor natural scenes not having any human, animal and man-made object". Memorability scores for 2632 images were measured based on an average of 80 observers per image and calculated using the same procedure as the LaMem dataset (Khosla et al. 2015). The images come hand-tagged with scene category labels from 71 scene categories obtained from WordNet (Miller 1995).

2.3   Diverse Photographs

LaMem (Khosla et al. 2015) is the largest and most varied image memorability dataset collected to date (Fig. 2). Its size—60k images with memorability scores— makes it particularly effective for training machine learning models. Its images come from MIR Flickr (Huiskes & Lew 2008), AVA (Murray et al. 2012), affective images (Machajdik & Hanbury 2010), the image saliency datasets MIT1003 (Judd et al. 2009) and NUSEF (Ramanathan et al. 2010), SUN (Xiao et al. 2010), an image popularity dataset (Khosla et al. 2014), the Abnormal Objects dataset (Saleh et al. 2013), and PASCAL (Farhadi et al. 2009). Thus, these images contain a variety of object and scene types and vary in aesthetic and affective value. Since subsets of the LaMem images contain additional labels, Khosla et al. (2015) were able to analyze how a variety of factors correlated with memorability, including popularity

Fig. 2 LaMem (Khosla et al. 2015) contains 60k images sampled from different computer vision datasets varying in the types of scenes and objects portrayed, as well as in aesthetic and affective value. All images are provided with collected memorability scores

scores (Khosla et al. 2014), eye fixations (Judd et al. 2009), emotions (Machajdik & Hanbury 2010), and aesthetic scores (Murray et al. 2012).

The MemCat image set has a category-based structure, with images belonging to five broad semantic categories (animal, food, landscape, sports, and vehicle), each with at least 20 sub-categories (e.g., animal: bear, duck; food: burrito, salad; landscape: desert, lake; sports: baseball, surfing; vehicle: airplane, train). While the broad category labels explained roughly 40% of the variance in the MemCat scores, images of the same category still differed consistently in memorability. With 2K images per category, one of MemCat's intended uses is to promote further research into within-category memorability variance. Images were taken from ImageNet (Deng et al. 2009), COCO (Lin et al. 2014), SUN (Xiao et al. 2010), and the Open Images Dataset (Kuznetsova et al. 2018). The source data sets offer additional annotations such as bounding boxes or segmentation maps. Finally, the authors took care to account for potentially confounding influences including the presence of people in non-people categories, large readable text, oddities, etc.

Dubey et al. (2015) sampled images from the PASCAL-S dataset (Li et al. 2014), a fully segmented subset of PASCAL VOC 2010 (Everingham et al. 2011), and cleaned up the segmentations to only contain clearly-visible, complete, and nameable objects. The resulting dataset contains 850 images with a total of 3412 segmented objects (~4 objects per image). Rather than capturing the memorability of whole images using the set-up from prior work (Isola et al. 2011b), whereby images presented for encoding and recognition are interspersed, Dubey et al. first showed participants whole images in an encoding stage, followed by individual objects (extracted from images) in a recognition stage to capture the memorability of individual objects (Dubey et al. 2015). As shown in Goetschalckx et al. (2018), memorability rankings collected with an interspersed paradigm versus a paradigm with separate stages are highly correlated.

2.4 Specialized Image Collections

The original studies on scene memorability (Isola et al. 2011a,b) sparked research on specialized stimuli collections, including faces and information visualizations. The 10k US Adult Faces Database (Bainbridge et al. 2012, 2013) contains 10,168 face photographs obtained by sampling the US Census for first and last names and downloading color face photographs available via Google Image Search, manually filtered to exclude celebrities, children, and low-quality or unusual images. The resulting database follows the gender, age, and race distributions of the adult US population. For 2222 face photographs, memorability scores were collected, along with another 20 facial and personality traits (using a crowdsourcing survey). Bainbridge et al. (2013) then reported which of these traits were correlated with face memorability.

Borkin et al. (2013) collected a total of 2070 data visualizations and infographics from different publication sources, which were then hand-tagged with taxonomic category (bar graph, table, diagram, map, etc.). Memorability scores were collected using the standard study setup for 393 of these visualizations, which were also hand-tagged with multiple attributes (clutter, colorfulness, etc.). Follow-up work (Borkin et al. 2015) segmented the visualizations into components (using LabelMe (Russell et al. 2008)), and obtained eye movements as well as captions about the visualizations from memory. Additional memorability scores were collected using a modified study setup and longer viewing durations (10 s/image), to account for the increased information content in visualizations compared to natural images.

2.5 Videos

Large-scale video memorability datasets have emerged to spur research into memorability of dynamic stimuli. The currently available datasets have focused on short video clips (<10 s) that are treated as discrete stimuli without audio for the purposes of continuous-recognition memorability experiments.

VideoMem (Cohendet et al. 2019) consists of 10,000 seven-second video clips taken from raw footage intended for reprocessing into advertisements or television shows. As such, the videos consist primarily of staged, professionally-shot scenes. VideoMem features a variety of content including people, animals, inanimate objects, and nature scenes. It contains memorability scores at two different delays: a short delay (a few minutes after viewing) and a longer delay (a couple days after viewing) to enable study into how memorability rankings may or may not reorder over time.

Memento10k (Newman et al. 2020) contains three-second "in-the-wild" video clips. These videos were originally posted to media sharing sites like YouTube and Flickr. They were then manually filtered to remove objectionable content or artificial artifacts like captions, cartoons or post-processing. Like VideoMem, Memento10k contains varied semantic content, encompassing people, animals, objects, and landscapes; however, because the videos were shot by laypeople, Memento10k encompasses more variability in levels of motion and video quality. For each Memento video, five human-written captions were collected describing the contents of the clip.

Earlier work on computational video memorability attempted to identify the features that contributed to memorability, but often relied on smaller datasets and paradigms that were more challenging to scale than the popular continuous-recognition experiments. Cohendet et al. (2018) collected the Movie Memorability Dataset, which measures long-term memorability over weeks or years using clips from popular movies. Their experimental setup differs somewhat from the traditional memory game experiment in that the first viewing of the stimuli took place before the start of the experiment, and viewing delay was estimated by asking participants when they had watched the movie in question. The authors found that semantic features derived from video captions were most correlated with the memorability scores of these clips. Han et al. (2015) leveraged fMRI data obtained from participants viewing videos in order to produce a computational model that aligns audiovisual features with brain data. Shekhar et al. (2017) derived memorability ratings for 100 videos using response time on a verbal recall task, and explored the contribution of deep, semantic, saliency, spatio-temporal, and color features to predict these scores.

3   Models: From Pixels to Features

In the last section we discussed that memorability can be treated as an image-computable measure, largely independent of the observer. In this section we review the range of computational models that have been applied to predicting image and video memorability, from the more traditional machine learning models to state-of-the-art deep neural networks. In all cases, these models have been trained on memorability datasets and evaluated on either a held-out portion of the same dataset or on a separate memorability dataset altogether. A summary of the different image memorability models is provided in Table 2, with the reported prediction scores taken directly out of the published papers (whenever available). Similarly, Table 3 contains the prediction scores of video memorability models.

Table 2 Model performance on image memorability prediction, as reported in past papers. This is the Spearman correlation between the predicted and measured memorability scores, with human upper bound defined as inter-observer consistency

| | Dataset | | |
Model	LaMem (Khosla et al. 2015)	SUN (Isola et al. 2011b)	Figrim (Bylinskii et al. 2015)
Human (upper bound)	0.68	0.75	0.74
MemBoost (Perera et al. 2019)	0.67	0.66	0.57
AMNet (Fajtl et al. 2018)	0.68	0.65	–
MemNet (Khosla et al. 2015)	0.64	0.63	–
CNN-MTLES (Jing et al. 2016)	0.50	–	–
MemoNet (Baveye et al. 2016)	–	0.64	–
Hybrid-CNN+SVR (Zarezadeh et al. 2017)	–	0.62	–
Mancas & Le Meur (Mancas et al. 2013)	–	0.48	–
Isola (Isola et al. 2011b)	–	0.46	–

Table 3 Model performance on video memorability prediction

| | Dataset | |
Model	VideoMem (val) (Cohendet et al. 2019)	Memento10k (test) (Newman et al. 2020)
Human (upper bound)	0.616	0.730
SemanticMemNet (Newman et al. 2020)	0.556	0.663
VideoMem-Semantic (Cohendet et al. 2019)	0.503	0.552
MemNet (frames baseline) (Khosla et al. 2015)	0.425	0.485

3.1 Support Vector Machines

Before neural networks became the tool of choice for many computer vision prediction tasks, a common machine learning approach was to extract low-level feature descriptors like GIST (Oliva & Torralba 2001), HOG (Dalal & Triggs 2005) or SIFT (Lowe 2004) from images, often at multiple spatial scales (Lazebnik et al. 2006), and then to train a Support Vector Machine (SVM) to map from the assembled feature vectors to the target labels. For problems with real-valued labels (like memorability scores), Support Vector Regression (SVR) was used instead (Drucker et al. 1996; Fan et al. 2008). In the case of memorability, it was found that HOG2x2 (Khosla et al. 2012b; Wang et al. 2010) was one of the most predictive automatic image features when used with a linear SVR machine (Isola et al. 2014; Khosla et al. 2013, 2012b).

Differential Weighting of Features Instead of extracting image features from the image as a whole, another approach is to differentially weight features obtained from different regions of an image, if there is good reason to suppose that certain image regions should contribute more to the prediction. For instance, multiple studies have reported that not all image regions are remembered equally well (Akagunduz et al. 2019; Khosla et al. 2012a). Akagunduz et al. (2019) explicitly ask participants in a memory task to indicate which regions made them recognize an image. Pooling this information across participants results in consistent ground truth maps which the authors call Visual Memory Schemas (VMS). They report that spatially pooling and weighting image features (e.g., GIST, SIFT, HOG) by the VMS not only yields better SVR predictions than without doing spatial pooling, but also outperforms spatial pooling and weighting with eye-fixation maps or saliency maps. In later work, the authors also propose a way to predict the VMS of an image itself (Kyle-Davidson et al. 2019, 2020). Inspired by the observation that visual attention is highly related to memory (Hollingworth & Henderson 2002; Hollingworth & Williams 2001; Wolfe et al. 2007), some work has also looked at spatially pooling visual features based on computational saliency maps (Celikkale et al. 2015).

What Is SVM and SVR?
A Support Vector Machine (SVM) is a machine learning model that classifies data points by finding a hyperplane in feature space that separates the training data into different categories. At training time, the SVM takes in labeled training points and finds a decision boundary that correctly separates the data with the biggest possible margin, or distance between the data and the correct side of the boundary. At test time, prediction involves determining which side of the decision boundary the test points are on in order to assign them a label. Support Vector Regression (SVR) extends the formulation of SVMs to regression problems with real-valued labels, instead of class labels, by finding the hyperplane that best fits the greatest number of training points. At test time, prediction involves finding the point on the hyperplane corresponding to the test data point.

3.2 Convolutional Neural Networks

Deep Features Deep representations learned by convolutional neural networks (CNNs) have proven to be the most successful computational features at approximating human memorability (Dubey et al. 2015; Khosla et al. 2015; Shekhar et al. 2017). These features are extracted from a layer (most commonly the penultimate one) of a pre-trained neural network, which has often been trained for the task of ImageNet (Russakovsky et al. 2015) classification. Later layers of neural networks are known to capture image semantics, in the form of distributions of objects over the image (Bylinskii et al. 2015; Sharif Razavian et al. 2014). For instance, Dubey et al. (2015) used features extracted from the AlexNet CNN (Krizhevsky et al. 2012) trained on ImageNet to predict object memorability.

Apart from using CNNs for prediction, there is a second way in which CNNs can provide insight into memorability: as a model for the way memorability emerges from neural processing in the brain (Rust & Mehrpour 2020; Jaegle et al. 2019). In particular, Jaegle et al. (2019) found that in the later layers of a CNN trained for image classification, the response magnitude of nodes in the network correlate with memorability. This is consistent with the authors' observation that population response magnitude in the IT cortex of the (monkey) brain predicts memorability.

Transfer Learning Transfer learning is a common strategy that can increase model performance when the target task—in our case, memorability prediction—has a relatively small dataset. The simplest form of transfer learning involves pre-training a network on a task for which a large dataset is available and then fine-tuning some subset of the network's layers on the target task with the target dataset. MemNet (Khosla et al. 2015), for example, is based on the AlexNet architecture (Jia et al. 2014; Krizhevsky et al. 2012) that was pre-trained for a classification task on a 3.6-million image dataset consisting of a combination of ImageNet (Russakovsky et al. 2015) and Places (Zhou et al. 2014). Only then was it fine-tuned on the 60k-image LaMem dataset to predict real-valued memorability scores (Khosla et al. 2015). Similarly, MemoNet (Baveye et al. 2016) is a fine-tuned GoogleNet model (Szegedy et al. 2015). AMNet (Fajtl et al. 2018) includes as a backbone a fine-tuned ResNet model (He et al. 2016). Perera et al. (2019) found that fine-tuning the last (regression) layer performed better than fine-tuning or retraining the whole network, because this approach was less likely to suffer from over-fitting to the training set. Video models have turned to even more complex pre-training regimes. SemanticMemNet (Newman et al. 2020), which predicts video memorability, contains an image-based stream that was pre-trained on ImageNet and LaMem, as well as video and optical flow streams pre-trained on ImageNet and Kinetics (Carreira & Zisserman 2017). The semantic embedding model from (Cohendet et al. 2019) used as its base a video captioning model (Engilberge et al. 2019) that was also pre-trained on LaMem.

Size Matters Perera et al. (2019) experimentally confirmed that the more powerful classification networks performed better on memorability prediction (i.e., AlexNet (Krizhevsky et al. 2012) performing worst, and ResNet152 (He et al. 2016) best). As CNN architectures continue to improve, we may find that more powerful backbones contribute to improved performance on memorability prediction, particularly in the relatively new domain of video prediction. However, the amount of data available is an important factor as well. As a case in point, Khosla et al. (2015) found that when fine-tuning on the larger LaMem dataset, the resulting network performed better on both LaMem and SUN datasets, even compared to a network trained and tested on the SUN dataset. This is because having too little data with which to train or fine-tune can result in model over-fitting, which reduces the generalization ability of the network on held-out data, regardless of which dataset it comes from.

What Is a CNN?

A Convolutional Neural Network (CNN) is a machine learning model that learns a very complex function to map an input—often an image or video—to a desired output, given a large dataset. It works by applying a sequence of linear and non-linear operations to the input. In a CNN, the linear operations are most frequently convolutions, thus giving the model its name. Each operation is defined by a set of parameters or weights, which must be learned from the training data. The learning process involves optimizing the output of the network in order to minimize some loss function (for example, a classification or regression loss) using gradient descent. Once trained, the sequence of operations with learned parameters can be applied to a new input to produce the final prediction. The sheer number of degrees of freedom in these models (due to the number of operations and parameters), as well as the sophisticated optimization algorithms used for training them, make for powerful models that are popular for a large range of tasks.

3.3 Recurrent Neural Networks

Rather than processing an image all at once as in a standard CNN architecture, Recurrent Neural Networks (RNNs) allow the model to parse an image in pieces, aggregating evidence before making a prediction. Fajtl et al. (2018) showed gains in performance from using an RNN-based architecture with soft attention in order to make three passes over an image, each time focusing on a different set of image regions, before predicting the final memorability score. Using a larger and more complex model than the CNN-based MemNet (Khosla et al. 2015) gives this model greater predictive power. Another advantage of this model is that the soft attention can be visualized as heatmaps over the image regions attended to at each of the three passes. This is useful for determining what evidence the model uses for its predictions, and which parts of the image are most informative for determining the memorability score.

Newman et al. (2020) also explored using RNNs to improve memorability prediction on videos. LSTMs (Hochreiter & Schmidhuber 1997) are a type of RNN that are frequently used for processing or generating natural language. SemanticMemNet uses an LSTM (Hochreiter & Schmidhuber 1997) to predict verbal captions for a video. It uses the additional supervision provided by the language descriptions in Memento10k (Newman et al. 2018) to encourage learning a feature space that explicitly encodes semantic features. The authors also experimented with using an RNN to predict raw hit rates at different viewing delays.

What Is An RNN?

Recurrent Neural Networks (RNNs) are neural networks with "loops" in them, where the prior state of the network is fed as input to future states, allowing previously gathered information to persist. They are popular for sequential tasks, most commonly language-related tasks like translation and image captioning. However, they are also used in cases where processing an input in pieces makes sense. For instance, when combined with soft attention, they can process an image not all at once, but in a sequence of "glimpses", where each "glimpse" focuses the network on a particular region of an image. One of the most common types of RNNs is an LSTM (Long short-term memory, Hochreiter and Schmidhuber 1997), popular for its ability to capture long-term dependencies via a set of computational control gates specifically designed to let some information flow through unchanged, and other information to be attenuated.

3.4 Generative Adversarial Networks

Another technique for understanding image memorability, beyond predicting memorability scores, is to directly visualize the qualities that make an image memorable. Goetschalckx et al. (2019a), for instance, re-purposed a Generative Adversarial Network (GAN) (Goodfellow et al. 2014) to explore image perturbations that either increase or decrease the memorability of images (Fig. 3). They found directions in latent space that best correlated with changes in image memorability, as measured by the MemNet model (Khosla et al. 2015). By automatically visualizing increasingly memorable images, they could observe how the GAN modifies the composition of the image and the objects within.

Rather than using a pre-trained GAN, related work (Kyle-Davidson et al. 2020) trained a GAN from scratch and had it accept an additional input value (M) representing a desired memorability score for the output image. The memorability of the output was measured by an auxiliary model based on the aforementioned Visual Memory Schemas (Akagunduz et al. 2019). By varying M while keeping the latent vector (i.e., the standard GAN input) constant, this framework also produces visualizations of images gradually increasing in memorability.

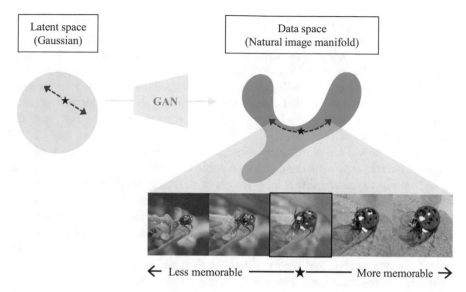

Fig. 3 A GAN can be used to transform samples drawn from some latent space (for instance, samples of Gaussian noise) into samples lying in the data space that the model has been trained on—e.g., approximating natural images. Moving along various latent directions, the model can generate novel outputs, that have not otherwise been previously seen (starting with the seed image, marked with a star). See Jahanian et al. (2020) for a discussion about the steerability of GAN models

What Is a GAN?
Generative Adversarial Networks (GANs) (Goodfellow et al. 2014) are most commonly used to synthesize fake images that look realistic. They work by generating convincing, novel samples from a very complex, high-dimensional data distribution—in this case, the distribution of natural images. They are trained by playing off two models against each other. The Generator learns to generate samples from the target distribution by taking a random vector as input (the GAN's "inspiration") and transforming it into a valid image. The Discriminator is then tasked with distinguishing the fake, generated samples from real samples (i.e., natural images) from the training set. As the Discriminator gets better at separating real from fake images, the Generator is forced to generate increasingly more realistic samples, and vice versa.

3.5 Visualizations and Model Interpretability

Knowing that a particular image is memorable does not necessarily tell you *which* information is retained. Reasoning that not all image regions contribute equally to overall memorability, Khosla et al. (2012b) proposed a probabilistic model that assigns different weights to different regions based on six locally computed image features (gradient, saliency, color, texture, shape, semantics). This can be done automatically without the need for additional human annotations. Not only did accounting for local information in addition to global features improve the prediction of overall memorability scores, it also allowed for visualizing the weights as interpretable heat maps. These heat maps often emphasized regions depicting people as contributing most to the overall memorability, and plain backgrounds contributing the least.

As CNN models are particularly effective at predicting memorability, working out their internal representations yields valuable insights into which features result in high and low memorability scores. Khosla et al. (2015) adopt different strategies to achieve this with MemNet. One is to sort the units within a layer of the network based on their correlation with the predicted memorability score, compute an average across the images that maximally activate the unit, and compare those averages. Another strategy, based on network dissection (Bau et al. 2017), is to identify image patches that highly activate individual units and then compare the activated patches from units that are positively versus negatively correlated with memorability. Finally, one can generate memorability heat maps by running the model on multiple, overlapping sub-regions of the image. Each pixel in the heat map represents the average memorability prediction across the sub-regions that contain it (Fig. 4). Together, these strategies revealed that MemNet tends to predict high memorability for images containing people or animals, busy images, and images with text. Open and natural scenes, landscapes and textured surfaces tend to result in lower memorability.

Another approach that facilitates model interpretation is visualizing what changes in an image when its model-predicted memorability increases or decreases, as in the GANalyze framework (Goetschalckx et al. 2019a). For example, this framework showed that MemNet cares about the relative size of the main object

Score: 0.407 (Low)

Fig. 4 MemNet prediction and memorability heat map for an example image. Left: Input image of Katholieke Universiteit Leuven ©Rob Stevens. Right: MemNet is a convolutional neural network fine-tuned to predict memorability scores (Khosla et al. 2015). The heat map is created by running the network over multiple, overlapping sub-regions and assigning each pixel a color based on the average predicted memorability of the regions that contain it. Here, it highlights the bell tower and bug sculpture as memorable regions in the image, with higher memorability predictions assigned to a more "zoomed in" image. While other techniques mostly revealed semantic features, GANalyze discovered important dimensions that are orthogonal to object class.

4 Memorability: From Low-Level to High-Level Features

Since the original memorability experiments of Isola et al. (2011b), follow-up work has added further evidence to the observation that memorability is a robust property of images that is not amenable to simple explanation, but instead appears multifaceted (see Rust and Mehrpour (2020) for a review). It is correlated with scene category, but remains predictable when scene category is controlled for (Bylinskii et al. 2015; Goetschalckx and Wagemans 2019). It is correlated with the presence of certain elements—most notably, faces and people (Baveye et al. 2016; Bylinskii et al. 2015; Dubey et al. 2015; Fajtl et al. 2018; Khosla et al. 2015)—but remains predictable when those objects are not present (Lu et al. 2018, 2020). It cannot be explained away by image aesthetics, popularity, or affective value either (Cohendet et al. 2018; Goetschalckx et al. 2019a; Isola et al. 2014). Moreover, human observers are bad at predicting what is memorable or forgettable (Isola et al. 2014). So while no simple explanation for memorability has been proposed, in this section we will discuss some of the factors that contribute to image and video memorability, by applying the analysis tools and computational models from the previous section. In the concluding discussion (Sect. 7), we hypothesize a unifying explanation to these results.

4.1 Low-Level Pixel Features

Dubey et al. (2015) have found a weak positive correlation between memorability and the brightness and high contrast of objects. Using a GAN trained for memorability, Goetschalckx et al. (2019a) confirmed that brighter and more colorful images tend to be produced when optimizing for more memorable images. For instance, redder hues are produced when they are realistic (e.g., for ripe fruit). Lu et al. (2018) found that some HSV-based features could be used to predict the memorability of natural scene images without objects, though this predictive power is low ($\rho < 0.30$).

For generic photographs, however, low level features (in the form of simple pixel statistics like color and contrast) are commonly either weakly correlated or uncorrelated with memorability (Dubey et al. 2015; Isola et al. 2011a, 2014, 2011b; Lu et al. 2020). In general, perceptual features are not retained in long term visual memory (Brady et al. 2011; Konkle et al. 2010a).

4.2 Mid-Level Semantic Features

Objects Multiple studies have commented on the increased intrinsic memorability of images and videos containing people, faces, and body parts (Bylinskii et al. 2015; Dubey et al. 2015; Khosla et al. 2015; Baveye et al. 2016; Fajtl et al. 2018; Newman et al. 2020) and low memorability for landscapes (Bylinskii et al. 2015; Goetschalckx & Wagemans 2019; Isola et al. 2011b; Khosla et al. 2015; Newman et al. 2020). By using images with available semantic segmentations (Li et al. 2014), i.e., images in which all or most of the objects have been delineated and annotated, Dubey et al. (2015) showed that the memorability of an image is "greatly affected by the memorability of its most memorable object" ($\rho = 0.40$). For instance, animal, person, and vehicle were found to be the most memorable object classes, and images containing these objects were more likely to be memorable overall. These objects tend to dominate the focus and foreground of photographs, and are not commonly occluded (Dubey et al. 2015). In contrast, furniture was found to be the least memorable object category. The attention-based model of Fajtl et al. (2018) was used to visualize regions of an image contributing most to memorability, and confirmed that these regions frequently contained people and human faces.

Objects are also important in video memorability prediction. The importance of semantic features, including objects, actors, and the actions that involve them, has increasingly led to their inclusion in video memorability models (Newman et al. 2020; Cohendet et al. 2019, 2018). The semantic embedding model from VideoMem (Cohendet et al. 2019) was based on a video captioning model, and SemanticMemNet (Newman et al. 2020) includes a branch to explicitly generate video captions to encourage features that encode semantic information.

Object Interactions Object interactions are key to the memorability of individual objects as well as the memorability of the image containing them. In particular, objects that are out of context with respect to the other items in a scene make for particularly memorable images (Bylinskii et al. 2015; Standing 1973). Also, as the pure number of objects in an image increases, competition for attention decreases the memorability of even the most memorable object classes, like animals and vehicles (Dubey et al. 2015). Interestingly, the memorability of people in images is least sensitive, compared to other object classes, to the presence of other objects in an image (Dubey et al. 2015).

Saliency and Eye Fixations Multiple studies have explored the connection between image memorability and saliency (Dubey et al. 2015; Khosla et al. 2015; Mancas et al. 2013; Lu et al. 2020; Shekhar et al. 2017; Lu et al. 2018; Celikkale et al. 2015; Akagunduz et al. 2019). Mancas et al. (2013) ran computational saliency models on images and found that the most memorable images have localized regions of high saliency, while the least memorable images do not. Khosla et al. (2015) reported that more memorable images tend to have more consistent human eye fixations. Dubey et al. (2015) similarly found a large positive correlation ($\rho = 0.71$) between fixation count on an object in an image and that object's memorability.

Part of this trend is driven by the fact that objects that are not fixated at all are not remembered. The other aspect is that images that contain more close-ups or larger objects will tend to have more consistent fixations clustered on those objects (also see *image composition* below). As the number of objects in an image increases, it becomes significantly harder to predict the memorability of objects using fixation counts alone. While computational saliency is intended to simulate human attention and serve as an approximation of eye fixation patterns, they are not the same thing. Computational saliency can be used as a replacement to other low-level features in predicting memorability (Mancas et al. 2013). Lu et al. (2020) found that the performance of a saliency model on saliency tasks is not correlated with its performance on memorability prediction, affirming that computational saliency in this regard should be viewed as a pre-computed combination of other low-level features rather than an independent high-level semantic feature. Alternatively, rather than being used directly as an input feature, saliency maps can also be used to spatially pool other low-level input feature and improve memorability predictions (Celikkale et al. 2015).

Image Composition More memorable images tend to focus on a key object or image region, and to center it in the photograph while maintaining a homogeneous background. For instance, a photograph of a puppy is more memorable when it is a close-up and the puppy occupies a larger portion of the photograph (Goetschalckx et al. 2019a). This is similar to Dubey et al. (2015) finding that if fewer objects compete for attention, then a single object becomes quite memorable, and the image as a whole becomes memorable by extension. Kim et al. (2013) showed that features computed based on the relative sizes of objects, their centeredness, and the unusualness of their size given the overall semantic class are strong predictors of memorability. When GANalyze (Goetschalckx et al. 2019a) modifies a seed image to become more memorable, it typically makes the main object larger and more centered, simplifies the image, and reduces clutter. The authors furthermore note that "more memorable images have more interpretable semantics". In an additional experiment, they show that when GANalyze is trained to modify object size directly, the image variants with the larger object size are indeed more likely to be remembered by participants in a memory task. However, the effect is not as strong as when memorability was targeted as a whole, indicating that memorability is more than object size alone. Simpler, more orderly shapes are more memorable than a disarray or lack of structure. Fajtl et al. (2018) visualizations confirm that images with higher memorability display more concentrated peaks of memorable content, whereas lower memorability images tend to have memorability more distributed across the image. Finally, Mancas et al. (2013) proposed a feature to capture the presence of strong contrasted structures in an image, as opposed to small details and cluttered backgrounds, and found that it positively predicted memorability.

Motion and Action Features Using videos as stimuli has facilitated the analysis of the effects of motion on memory. Newman et al. (2020) evaluated the effectiveness of different feature extractors that did or did not explicitly encode motion for predicting video memorability. They found that a simple image-based extractor that

Fig. 5 High and low memorability videos from the Memento dataset (Newman et al. 2020). Like images, memorable videos tend to contain people, faces, and body parts, while forgettable videos are more likely to be of natural and otherwise static scenes

operated only on static frames performed as well as a video-based extractor, but that combining information from static frames, video, and optical flow produced the best results. They also observed that low-memorability videos are often static compared to high-memorability videos (Fig. 5).

4.3 High-Level and Contextual Features

Aesthetics Aesthetics are distinct from memorability, with little to no correlation in the LaMem dataset (Khosla et al. 2015; Jing et al. 2016) and a weak, but negative correlation in the SUN dataset (Isola et al. 2014). Participants tend to rate images depicting nature as most aesthetic (e.g., coast and lake scenes), yet natural landscapes typically score low on memorability. Modifying an image to increase its aesthetics (while keeping semantic class constant) does have a positive effect on memorability, albeit a rather small one (Goetschalckx et al. 2019a). Goetschalckx et al. (2019a) furthermore confirmed that optimizing images for memorability and optimizing images for aesthetics leads to different image manipulations.

Emotions Emotionally salient objects are memorable (Bradley et al. 1992; Buchanan et al. 2002; Cahill & McGaugh 1995). Hence, different studies have considered the role of emotional features in predicting image memorability. In the LaMem dataset, images evoking negative emotions (e.g., disgust, anger, fear) were overall more memorable than those evoking positive emotions (e.g., awe, contentment), with amusement being a memorable exception (Khosla et al. 2015). Isola et al. (2011a) found that images described as peaceful are typically not well remembered. Having a subject in a photo with more pronounced and expressive eyes, on the other hand, seems to increase the memorability of a portrait (Goetschalckx et al. 2019a). In Jing et al. (2016), a sentiment attribute inspired by eight basic emotions was the best memorability predictor among other high-level attributes (e.g., aesthetics). Other work that included emotional features combined with other high-level features (e.g., object categories) also demonstrated a predictive ability for these features (Isola et al. 2011a; Celikkale et al. 2015). Finally, Baveye et al. (2016) recommend that memorability datasets should have the appropriate emotional feature distribution (i.e., be balanced), based on the observation that emotionally negative images have more predictable memorability than neutral or positive ones.

Popularity and Interestingness Intuitively, one might expect memorable images to be popular or interesting. However, studies show that memorability does not reduce to either of those attributes. The top 25% most memorable LaMem images indeed are more popular, as determined by their log-normalized view count on Flickr. This is likely because they stand out in some way. However, there is little difference between all other images (Khosla et al. 2015). When asking participants to judge the interestingness of an image in the SUN dataset, those judgments correlate negatively with memorability, but only weakly (Isola et al. 2014; Gygli et al. 2013).

Scene Category Perera et al. (2019) empirically showed that a network originally trained on scene classification transfers more appropriate features for memorability prediction than a network trained on object classification, although a network trained on both performs best (Zhou et al. 2014; Khosla et al. 2015; Zhou et al. 2017). This seems to indicate that scene category drives a lot of the predictive power in image memorability. Indeed, Isola et al.'s original paper (Isola et al. 2011b) reports that scene category alone is highly predictive of memorability ($\rho = 0.37$). Lu et al. (2020) obtain a similar result ($\rho = 0.38$) across their dataset of natural outdoor scene images, LNSIM. Their images do not contain any salient objects (people, animals, man-made structures, etc.) and yet they still demonstrate high inter-observer consistency ($\rho = 0.78$). Finally, 43% of the variance in the MemCat dataset was captured by which of five broad categories an image belonged to (Goetschalckx and Wagemans 2019). However, scene category is far from the whole story. Memorability scores in the MemCat dataset were still consistent across observers within each of the five categories separately (Goetschalckx & Wagemans 2019). This still holds in cases where the scene category is even more strictly controlled for, and in this case, objects and their distributions help to drive memorability (Bylinskii et al. 2015). Finally, GANalyze (Goetschalckx et al. 2019a) is able to increase image memorability while keeping the scene category constant.

Despite all the work showing that memorability has a strong intrinsic component, features extracted automatically from image pixels account for only about half the total variance observed in the memorability scores. The rest may be due to individual or context factors, which we can refer to as the extrinsic factors (Bylinskii et al. 2015) and discuss below.

Observer Attention Unlike saliency, which approximates the attention patterns of a population in aggregate, Bylinskii et al. (2015) considered whether an individual's pattern of eye movements could predict whether that individual would remember an image. The model was an SVM trained to separate eye fixation patterns on a target image from eye fixation patterns on other images. This model achieved approximately 60% accuracy at predicting if a given image would be remembered by an individual based on their eye fixation patterns alone. Using this person-specific information was more accurate than the population-level predictor (average memorability scores), especially for the images in the mid-memorability range.

Contextual Features Images that stand out from their image context (i.e., other images presented in the memory task) or differ from our expectations based on an internal model of the world, are more likely to be remembered. Bylinskii et al. (2015) were able to show this by operationalizing contextual distinctiveness in terms of how unlikely an image's features are in the feature distribution defined by the image context. Similarly, Lukavský et al. (2017) found that people remember images better if they are far away from their nearest neighbors in a conceptual representational space. Goetschalckx et al. (2019b) compared these two automatic distinctiveness measures with a perceived distinctiveness measure based on participants' ratings, as well as a measure of an image's atypicality for its abstract scene category. All four variables were significantly intercorrelated. Perceived distinctiveness predicted memorability scores best.

Furthermore, of the 60k images in the LaMem dataset, those originally sampled from the Abnormal Objects dataset (Saleh et al. 2013) are extremely memorable (Khosla et al. 2012a). Landscape images in Lu et al.'s dataset (Lu et al. 2020) belonging to unusual categories (as indicated by the category name having a low word frequency in language) tended to be more memorable. Finally, Kim et al. (2013) report that accounting for how unusual object sizes are given their class can improve memorability predictions.

Lastly, another way in which context matters is through effects of image sequences and presentation order, as demonstrated by Perera et al. (2019). This confirmed earlier results from Bylinskii et al. (2015).

5 Applications: From Summarization to Creation

As computational models have recently approached human-level performance at predicting what people will find memorable, the doors have opened to applications that could benefit from an estimate of human memorability. In this section, we provide a taste of some of these applications. Making more of them a reality depends on additional progress to be made along the future research directions proposed in the following section.

Filtering Visual Streams With a growing stream of information and an increase in low-cost, low-power image/video capture devices (phones, GoPros, internet of things, etc.), filtering through content to find the nuggets worth saving becomes increasingly tedious and time-consuming. Such a task could be outsourced to computational agents armed with an appropriate filtering criteria. Here, memorability can play a significant role, as a high-level image property that bundles together low-level, semantic, and contextual features. Which of the dozens of nearly-identical photos should be saved for later? Which frames or snapshots can represent the contents of a video in summary form? Current computational models of memorability could be used for ranking and effectively filtering visual content.

Assistive Goggles Imagine an automated tutor that reminds the wearer of the identities of the most forgettable objects and people, and either coaches the user's memory or presents the labels in an augmented reality layer. Augmented Reality (AR) is a technology that integrates digital graphics and virtual objects into a display of the real world. It is already being used for training and education scenarios in medicine (Barsom et al. 2016), construction (Li et al. 2018), driving (Gabbard et al. 2014), and K-12 education (Holstein et al. 2018). As a potential tool for augmenting the human memory of the average person, it holds big promises for the future.

Photography Aide Consumer cameras are increasingly being upgraded with machine-learning based functionalities for guiding the user towards capturing better-quality shots. These include new tools to help users automatically select a better portrait angle or orientation for a photograph (Fried et al. 2020; Ma et al. 2019). A more sophisticated aide could guide the photographer to select a more memorable shot during real-time capture, or to re-position, adjust, and remove elements either before or after a picture is taken, by optimizing for memorability.

Effective Communication Key players in the education space (e.g., educational content producers, intelligent tutoring systems, etc.) could benefit students by presenting content in a more memorable way. For instance, prior work has looked at data visualizations and their ability to effectively communicate information via memorable presentations of data and title wording (Newman et al. 2018; Borkin et al. 2015; Xiong et al. 2019; Kong et al. 2018, 2019). Armed with similar insights, a marketing or advertising effort could make use of predictions of how to arrange the objects in a scene to make the target product or message stand out in a memorable way. Along the same lines, a tourist agency could design more memorable experiences and increase re-visitations (Hung et al. 2016; Kleinlein et al. 2019).

Manipulating Memorability What if an app could make your holiday pictures extra memorable or the picture on your resume more likely to be remembered by a recruiter? Our growing ability to predict and understand memorability has led researchers to think about the possibility of automatically manipulating an image's memorability. For example, Khosla et al. (2012a) speculated that their probabilistic model of the memorability of images and their sub-regions (Khosla et al. 2012b) could offer a starting point for memorability manipulation work. Deep style transfer has also been put forward as a way to boost an image's memorability score (Siarohin et al. 2017, 2019). By transferring the style of a seed image onto the original image, the modified version also tends to have a more abstract, artistic flavor to it. Furthermore, the memorability of a face image can be manipulated successfully using warping techniques, all while maintaining the identity of the face (Khosla et al. 2013). More recent work has turned to GANs for this purpose (Goetschalckx et al. 2019a; Sidorov 2019). While Goetschalckx et al.'s (2019a) GAN framework

Fig. 6 More or less memorable images generated by the GANalyze framework (Goetschalckx et al. 2019a) with computed memorability scores as insets. More memorable images tend to focus on a large, central key object while reducing background clutter

successfully increased and decreased the memorability of images (Fig. 6), this was only possible by using seed images that were GAN-generated to begin with—i.e., within the latent space of the GAN. However, recent success in GAN inversion (i.e., projecting a real image into a GAN's latent space (Zhu et al. 2020; Abdal et al. 2019; Bau et al. 2019; Anirudh et al. 2020; Creswell and Bharath 2019)) suggests that it might be possible to extend these results to real, user-supplied imagery. While automatically boosting an image's memorability is an exciting possible direction, similar to automatically beautifying portraits, one must consider the potential concerns about image authenticity that it raises.

6   Future Directions

Convolutional neural networks can now closely predict the average memorability score of an image. Perera et al. (2019) present a model that is able to reach human-level performance on the LaMem dataset (Khosla et al. 2015), the largest memorability dataset to date. They pose the question: is memorability prediction solved?

Despite the success of computational models of image memorability, there are still aspects of memorability prediction and utilization that merit further work. We discuss some of these directions below.

Customized Predictions Producing the average memorability score of an image overlooks possible variability in the population (Bylinskii et al. 2015; Perera et al. 2019). Variability may exist among subpopulations or specialists, people from different cultures and environments (i.e., LaMem uses US crowdworkers on Amazon's Mechanical Turk platform), and among individuals. Drilling down to the individual level for customized applications of memorability is an exciting prospect. Can we predict whether a particular image will be memorable to a particular

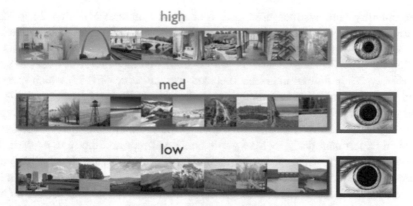

med

low

Fig. 7 Pupillometry analysis shows that at recall, images with the lowest memorability cause a dilation in pupil size relative to images with the highest memorability, on an individual basis (Võ et al. 2017)

individual? While Bylinskii et al. (2015) and Võ et al. (2017) showed that eye movements and pupillometry (Fig. 7), respectively, could be used for individualized memorability predictions, predictions are not yet accurate nor robust enough to be deployed in applications and devices. Deep learning based face and eye tracking technology (Krafka et al. 2016; Zhang et al. 2015; Park et al. 2020) and other automatically-collected physiological measurements (Papoutsaki et al. 2016; Qian et al. 2018) may provide a way forward.

Retention over Different Time Intervals The memorability games used to create most of the available datasets (Table 1) typically measure memorability over intervals of a couple of minutes. By varying the number of images presented between a target image and its repeat (i.e., the "lag"), past work has explored to what extent image memorability is stable over shorter and longer intervals (Isola et al. 2011b; Võ et al. 2017). Goetschalckx et al. (2018) used a more traditional long-term memory task with a separate study and test phase that allowed them to study intervals as long as a week. In addition, different mathematical formulations have been proposed to compute memorability scores based on responses collected at varying lags (Khosla et al. 2015; Newman et al. 2020).

An image's memorability score naturally decays over time, but even after a few seconds, some images are already consistently more likely to be forgotten (Isola et al. 2011b; Võ et al. 2017). The decay is best described by a log-linear function (Isola et al. 2011b; Goetschalckx et al. 2018) and is slower for more memorable images (Võ et al. 2017; Goetschalckx et al. 2018). Despite changes in raw scores over time, memorability ranks are largely conserved (Isola et al. 2011b; Goetschalckx et al. 2018), though more substantial differences might appear when comparing intervals significantly differing in length (Goetschalckx et al. 2018).

Video memorability studies have likewise compared different intervals. Cohendet et al. (2019) report a significant, albeit moderate, correlation between video memorability rankings measured after a couple of minutes and after 24 to 72 h. The correlation was likely attenuated by the low number of responses collected per video, however. Cohendet et al. (2018) examined even longer durations by asking study participants about well-known films that they had seen weeks to years previously. They find an inter-observer consistency score of 0.57, which is lower than the values of most memorability studies but still significant (see Table 1). The lower consistency could be due to the long delay between initial and repeat viewing, the relatively low number of participant annotations per video, or the atypical experiment design where participants self-reported the time of their first viewing. Similar to images, the Memento10k videos (Newman et al. 2020) also showed slower decay if they had higher memorability scores to begin with. Unlike with images, the decay was best described by a linear function. Because the authors examined relatively short delays (up to ten minutes between viewings), it is possible that at longer delays, a log-linear trend may be more appropriate. The authors proposed a computational model to simultaneously capture a video's memorability and decay rate. Models that attempt to predict memorability as a function of time interval (how memorable will this image be in a day? a week? a year?) or by directly predicting the decay rate for an image or video (Newman et al. 2020) are rare. These questions deserve more attention.

Alternative Media Much of the work in computational memorability thus far has focused on images. Compared to the number of computational models that have been proposed to predict memorability scores for images, those available for videos are much fewer (Cohendet et al. 2018, 2019; Newman et al. 2020) and they do not yet reach human-level performance (see Table 3). As such, perfecting the nuances of video memorability prediction is an important future direction.

Furthermore, the prior work discussed in this chapter has investigated purely visual media (images and videos without sound). Future work can explore the influence of auditory features (voices, sound effects, music, etc.) on memorability, independently of, or in combination with, visual features. Some work has additionally been done in the space of word memorability (Mahowald et al. 2018; Madan 2020), with findings that reinforce those in visual domains, in that distinct, easily-visualizable, non-ambiguous words are the most memorable (Mahowald et al. 2018). Mahowald found that animacy was most correlated with word memorability, and further that words that were rated as related to 'danger' and 'usefulness' were more memorable (Mahowald et al. 2018). The memorability of combinations of words, in the form of descriptions or titles, has yet to be studied, especially in the context of conveying information, and making messages or data "stickier" (Newman et al. 2018; Borkin et al. 2015; Xiong et al. 2019; Kong et al. 2018, 2019).

7 Concluding Discussion

Putting it all together, what is the "magic sauce" of memorability? What is the common thread that ties the findings from past memorability studies together, across photographs, visualizations, videos, and words?

We propose that content is memorable if it has a high *utility of information*. We remember that which surprises us, that which contradicts our current model of the world and of events, or that which is likely to be relevant or useful in the future. Remembering a surprising (or dangerous, untrustworthy, etc.) event or person will prepare us better for future encounters, and for adjusting our world view accordingly. This is why stimuli that are distinct, relative to their contexts, are memorable.

The benefit of large, diverse memorability datasets with many observers is that they capture the robustly memorable and forgettable content. These studies tell us something about the human condition: What has the highest utility of information to any observer? Universal trends include emotional/affective stimuli, unexpected actions, social aspects, animate objects (human faces, gestures, interactions, etc.), and tangible (small, manipulable) objects. Memorability is not about aesthetics or low-level visual features like color or contrast. Rather, memorability captures the higher-level properties of semantics (objects and actions) and composition (layout and clutter) in an image or video.

As a demonstrated image-computable attribute, memorability has the capability of being used as a powerful image descriptor or feature representation for downstream tasks that depend on image understanding and selection. Cognitively-inspired computation is still in its relative infancy. Memorability paints a promising path into the A.I. future.

Acknowledgments We thank the Vannevar Bush Faculty Fellowship Program of the ONR (N00014-16-1-3116 to A.O.). Thank you also to Wilma A. Bainbridge for her insightful comments on prior versions of this chapter, as well as to the other editors of this collection.

References

Abdal, R., Qin, Y., & Wonka, P. (2019). Image2StyleGAN: How to embed images into the StyleGAN latent space? In *2019 IEEE/CVF international conference on computer vision (ICCV)* (pp. 4431–4440). https://doi.org/10.1109/ICCV.2019.00453.

Akagunduz, E., Bors, A., & Evans, K. (2019). Defining image memorability using the visual memory schema. *IEEE Transactions on Pattern Analysis and Machine Intelligence, 42*(9), 2165–2178.

Anirudh, R., Thiagarajan, J. J., Kailkhura, B., & Bremer, P. T. (2020). MimicGAN: Robust projection onto image manifolds with corruption mimicking. *International Journal of Computer Vision, 128*(10), 2459–2477. https://doi.org/10.1007/s11263-020-01310-5.

Bainbridge, W., Isola, P., Blank, I., & Oliva, A. (2012). Establishing a database for studying human face photograph memory. In *Proceedings of the annual meeting of the cognitive science society* (vol. 34).

Bainbridge, W. A., Isola, P., & Oliva, A. (2013). The intrinsic memorability of face photographs. *Journal of Experimental Psychology: General, 142*(4), 1323.

Barsom, E. Z., Graafland, M., & Schijven, M. P. (2016). Systematic review on the effectiveness of augmented reality applications in medical training. *Surgical Endoscopy, 30*(10), 4174–4183.

Bau, D., Zhou, B., Khosla, A., Oliva, A., & Torralba, A. (2017). Network dissection: Quantifying interpretability of deep visual representations. In *Proceedings of the IEEE conference on computer vision and pattern recognition* (pp. 6541–6549).

Bau, D., Strobelt, H., Peebles, W., Wulff, J., Zhou, B., Zhu, J. Y., & Torralba, A. (2019). Semantic photo manipulation with a generative image prior. *ACM Transactions on Graphics (Proceedings of ACM SIGGRAPH), 38*(4), 1–11. https://doi.org/10.1145/3306346.3323023.

Baveye, Y., Cohendet, R., Perreira Da Silva, M., & Le Callet, P. (2016). Deep learning for image memorability prediction: The emotional bias. In *Proceedings of the 24th ACM international conference on Multimedia* (pp. 491–495).

Borkin, M. A., Vo, A. A., Bylinskii, Z., Isola, P., Sunkavalli, S., Oliva, A., & Pfister, H. (2013). What makes a visualization memorable? *IEEE Transactions on Visualization and Computer Graphics, 19*(12), 2306–2315.

Borkin, M. A., Bylinskii, Z., Kim, N. W., Bainbridge, C. M., Yeh, C. S., Borkin, D., Pfister, H., & Oliva, A. (2015). Beyond memorability: Visualization recognition and recall. *IEEE Transactions on Visualization and Computer Graphics, 22*(1), 519–528.

Bradley, M. M., Greenwald, M. K., Petry, M. C., & Lang, P. J. (1992). Remembering pictures: pleasure and arousal in memory. *Journal of Experimental Psychology: Learning, Memory, and Cognition, 18*(2), 379.

Brady, T. F., Konkle, T., Alvarez, G. A., & Oliva, A. (2008). Visual long-term memory has a massive storage capacity for object details. *Proceedings of the National Academy of Sciences, 105*(38), 14325–14329.

Brady, T., Konkle, T., Alvarez, G., & Oliva, A. (2011). Are real-world objects represented as bound units? independent decay of object details from short-term to long-term memory. *Journal of Vision, 11*(11), 1289–1289.

Brown, W. (1910). Some experimental results in the correlation of mental abilities. *British Journal of Psychology, 1904–1920, 3*(3), 296–322. https://doi.org/10.1111/j.2044-8295.1910.tb00207.x.

Buchanan, T. W., & Adolphs, R. (2002). The role of the human amygdala in emotional modulation of long-term declarative memory. *Advances in Consciousness Research, 44*, 9–34.

Bylinskii, Z., Isola, P., Bainbridge, C., Torralba, A., & Oliva, A. (2015). Intrinsic and extrinsic effects on image memorability. *Vision Research, 116*, 165–178.

Cahill, L., & McGaugh, J. L. (1995). A novel demonstration of enhanced memory associated with emotional arousal. *Consciousness and Cognition, 4*(4), 410–421.

Carreira, J., & Zisserman, A. (2017). Quo vadis, action recognition? A new model and the kinetics dataset. In: *2017 IEEE Conference on computer vision and pattern recognition, CVPR 2017*, Honolulu, HI, USA, July 21–26, 2017 (pp. 4724–4733). https://doi.org/10.1109/CVPR.2017.502.

Celikkale, B., Erdem, A., & Erdem, E. (2015). Predicting memorability of images using attention-driven spatial pooling and image semantics. *Image and Vision Computing, 42*, 35–46.

Cohendet, R., Yadati, K., Duong, N. Q., & Demarty, C. H. (2018). Annotating, understanding, and predicting long-term video memorability. In: Proceedings of the 2018 ACM on international conference on multimedia retrieval (pp. 178–186). ACM.

Cohendet, R., Demarty, C., Duong, N. Q. K., & Martin, E. (2019). VideoMem: Constructing, analyzing, predicting short-term and long-term video memorability. In *Proceedings of the IEEE international conference on computer vision* (pp. 2531–2540).

Creswell, A., & Bharath, A. A. (2019). Inverting the generator of a generative adversarial network. *IEEE Transactions on Neural Networks and Learning Systems, 30*(7), 1967–1974. https://doi.org/10.1109/TNNLS.2018.2875194.

Dalal, N., & Triggs, B. (2005). Histograms of oriented gradients for human detection. In *2005 IEEE computer society conference on computer vision and pattern recognition (CVPR'05)* (vol. 1, pp. 886–893). IEEE.

Deng, J., Dong, W., Socher, R., Li, L.-J., Li, K., & Fei-Fei, L. (2009). Imagenet: A large-scale hierarchical image database. In *2009 IEEE conference on computer vision and pattern recognition* (pp. 248–255). https://doi.org/10.1109/CVPR.2009.5206848.

Drucker, H., Burges, C. J., Kaufman, L., Smola, A., & Vapnik, V. (1996). Support vector regression machines. *Advances in Neural Information Processing Systems, 9*, 155–161.

Dubey, R., Peterson, J., Khosla, A., Yang, M. H., & Ghanem, B. (2015). What makes an object memorable? In *Proceedings of the ieee international conference on computer vision* (pp. 1089–1097).

Fried, O., Lu, J., Zhang, J., Měch, R., Echevarria, J., Hanrahan, P., & Landay, J. A. (2020). Adaptive photographic composition guidance. In *Proceedings of the 2020 CHI conference on human factors in computing systems, CHI '20* (pp. 1–13). ACM. https://doi.org/10.1145/3313831.3376635. https://dl.acm.org/doi/10.1145/3313831.3376635.

Engilberge, M., Chevallier, L., Perez, P., & Cord, M. (2019). Sodeep: A sorting deep net to learn ranking loss surrogates. In *Proceedings of the IEEE/CVF conference on computer vision and pattern recognition (CVPR)*.

Everingham, M., & Winn, J. (2011). The pascal visual object classes challenge 2012 (voc2012) development kit. *Pattern Analysis, Statistical Modelling and Computational Learning*, Tech. Rep, vol. 8.

Fajtl, J., Argyriou, V., Monekosso, D., & Remagnino, P. (2018). Amnet: Memorability estimation with attention. In *Proceedings of the IEEE conference on computer vision and pattern recognition* (pp. 6363–6372).

Fan, R. E., Chang, K. W., Hsieh, C. J., Wang, X. R., & Lin, C. J. (2008). Liblinear: A library for large linear classification. *Journal of Machine Learning Research, 9*(Aug), 1871–1874.

Farhadi, A., Endres, I., Hoiem, D., & Forsyth, D. (2009). Describing objects by their attributes. In *2009 IEEE conference on computer vision and pattern recognition* (pp. 1778–1785). IEEE.

Gabbard, J. L., Fitch, G. M., & Kim, H. (2014). Behind the glass: Driver challenges and opportunities for ar automotive applications. *Proceedings of the IEEE, 102*(2), 124–136.

Goetschalckx, L., & Wagemans, J. (2019). MemCat: A new category-based image set quantified on memorability. *PeerJ, 7*, e8169. https://doi.org/10.7717/peerj.8169. https://peerj.com/articles/8169.

Goetschalckx, L., Moors, P., & Wagemans, J. (2018). Image memorability across longer time intervals. *Memory, 26*(5), 581–588. https://doi.org/10.1080/09658211.2017.1383435. https://doi.org/10.1080%2F09658211.2017.1383435.

Goetschalckx, L., Andonian, A., Oliva, A., & Isola, P. (2019a). Ganalyze: Toward visual definitions of cognitive image properties. In *Proceedings of the IEEE international conference on computer vision* (pp. 5744–5753).

Goetschalckx, L., Moors, P., Vanmarcke, S., & Wagemans, J. (2019b). Get the picture? Goodness of image organization contributes to image memorability. *Journal of Cognition, 2*(1), 22.

Goodfellow, I., Pouget-Abadie, J., Mirza, M., Xu, B., Warde-Farley, D., Ozair, S., Courville, A., & Bengio, Y. (2014). Generative adversarial nets. In Z. Ghahramani, M. Welling, C. Cortes, N. D. Lawrence, K. Q. Weinberger (Eds.) *Advances in neural information processing systems (NIPS)* (vol. 27, pp. 2672–2680). Red Hook, NY: Curran Associates.

Gygli, M., Grabner, H., Riemenschneider, H., Nater, F., & Van Gool, L. (2013). The interestingness of images. In *2013 IEEE international conference on computer vision (ICCV)*. Red Hook, NY: IEEE. https://doi.org/10.1109/iccv.2013.205.

Han, J., Chen, C., Shao, L., Xintao, H., Jungong, H., & Tianming, L. (2015). Learning computational models of video memorability from fMRI brain imaging. *IEEE Transactions on Cybernetics, 45*(8), 1692–1703.

He, K., Zhang, X., Ren, S., & Sun, J. (2016). Deep residual learning for image recognition. In *Proceedings of the IEEE conference on computer vision and pattern recognition* (pp. 770–778).

Hochreiter, S., & Schmidhuber, J. (1997). Long short-term memory. *Neural Computation, 9*, 1735–80. https://doi.org/10.1162/neco.1997.9.8.1735.

Hollingworth, A., & Henderson, J. M. (2002). Accurate visual memory for previously attended objects in natural scenes. *Journal of Experimental Psychology: Human Perception and Performance, 28*(1), 113.

Hollingworth, A., Williams, C. C., & Henderson, J. M. (2001). To see and remember: Visually specific information is retained in memory from previously attended objects in natural scenes. *Psychonomic Bulletin & Review, 8*(4), 761–768.

Holstein, K., Hong, G., Tegene, M., McLaren, B. M., & Aleven, V. (2018). The classroom as a dashboard: Co-designing wearable cognitive augmentation for k-12 teachers. In *Proceedings of the 8th international conference on learning analytics and knowledge, LAK '18* (pp. 79–88). New York, NY, USA: Association for Computing Machinery. https://doi.org/10.1145/3170358.3170377.

Huiskes, M. J., & Lew, M. S. (2008). The mir flickr retrieval evaluation. In *Proceedings of the 1st ACM international conference on Multimedia information retrieval* (pp. 39–43).

Hung, W. L., Lee, Y. J., & Huang, P. H. (2016). Creative experiences, memorability and revisit intention in creative tourism. *Current Issues in Tourism, 19*(8), 763–770. https://doi.org/10.1080/13683500.2013.877422.

Isola, P., Parikh, D., Torralba, A., & Oliva, A. (2011a). Understanding the intrinsic memorability of images. In *Advances in neural information processing systems* (pp. 2429–2437).

Isola, P., Xiao, J., Torralba, A., & Oliva, A. (2011b). What makes an image memorable? In *CVPR 2011* (pp. 145–152). IEEE.

Isola, P., Xiao, J., Parikh, D., Torralba, A., & Oliva, A. (2014). What makes a photograph memorable? *IEEE Transactions on Pattern Analysis and Machine Intelligence, 36*(7), 1469–1482. https://doi.org/10.1109/tpami.2013.200. https://doi.org/10.1109%2Ftpami.2013.200.

Jaegle, A., Mehrpour, V., Mohsenzadeh, Y., Meyer, T., Oliva, A., & Rust, N. (2019). Population response magnitude variation in inferotemporal cortex predicts image memorability. *eLife, 8*. https://doi.org/10.7554/elife.47596.

Jahanian, A., Chai, L., & Isola, P. (2020). On the "steerability" of generative adversarial networks. In *International conference on learning representations*.

Jia, Y., Shelhamer, E., Donahue, J., Karayev, S., Long, J., Girshick, R., Guadarrama, S., & Darrell, T. (2014). Caffe: Convolutional architecture for fast feature embedding. In *Proceedings of the 22nd ACM international conference on Multimedia* (pp. 675–678).

Jing, P., Su, Y., Nie, L., & Gu, H. (2016). Predicting image memorability through adaptive transfer learning from external sources. *IEEE Transactions on Multimedia, 19*(5), 1050–1062.

Judd, T., Ehinger, K., Durand, F., & Torralba, A. (2009). Learning to predict where humans look. In *2009 IEEE 12th international conference on computer vision* (pp. 2106–2113). IEEE.

Khosla, A., Xiao, J., Isola, P., Torralba, A., & Oliva, A. (2012a). Image memorability and visual inception. In *SIGGRAPH Asia 2012 technical briefs* (pp. 1–4).

Khosla, A., Xiao, J., Torralba, A., & Oliva, A. (2012b). Memorability of image regions. In *Advances in neural information processing systems* (pp. 296–304).

Khosla, A., Bainbridge, W. A., Torralba, A., & Oliva, A. (2013). Modifying the memorability of face photographs. In *Proceedings of the IEEE international conference on computer vision* (pp. 3200–3207).

Khosla, A., Das Sarma, A., & Hamid, R. (2014). What makes an image popular? In *Proceedings of the 23rd international conference on World wide web* (pp. 867–876).

Khosla, A., Raju, A. S., Torralba, A., & Oliva, A. (2015). Understanding and predicting image memorability at a large scale. In *Proceedings of the IEEE international conference on computer vision* (pp. 2390–2398).

Kim, J., Yoon, S., & Pavlovic, V. (2013). Relative spatial features for image memorability. In *Proceedings of the 21st ACM international conference on Multimedia* (pp. 761–764).

Kleinlein, R., García-Faura, Á., Luna Jimenez, C., Montero, J. M., Díaz-de María, F., & Fernández-Martínez, F. (2019). Predicting image aesthetics for intelligent tourism information systems. *Electronics, 8*(6), 671.

Kong, H. K., Liu, Z., & Karahalios, K. (2018). Frames and slants in titles of visualizations on controversial topics. In *Proceedings of the 2018 CHI conference on human factors in computing systems* (pp. 1–12).

Kong, H. K., Liu, Z., & Karahalios, K. (2019). Trust and recall of information across varying degrees of title-visualization misalignment. In *Proceedings of the 2019 CHI conference on human factors in computing systems* (pp. 1–13).

Konkle, T., Brady, T. F., Alvarez, G. A., & Oliva, A. (2010a). Conceptual distinctiveness supports detailed visual long-term memory for real-world objects. *Journal of Experimental Psychology: General, 139*(3), 558.

Konkle, T., Brady, T. F., Alvarez, G. A., & Oliva, A. (2010b). Scene memory is more detailed than you think: The role of categories in visual long-term memory. *Psychological Science, 21*(11), 1551–1556.

Krafka, K., Khosla, A., Kellnhofer, P., Kannan, H., Bhandarkar, S., Matusik, W., & Torralba, A. (2016). Eye tracking for everyone. In *Proceedings of the IEEE conference on computer vision and pattern recognition* (pp. 2176–2184).

Krizhevsky, A., Sutskever, I., & Hinton, G. E. (2012). Imagenet classification with deep convolutional neural networks. In *Proceedings of the 25th international conference on neural information processing systems - Volume 1, NIPS'12* (pp. 1097–1105). Red Hook, NY, USA: Curran Associates Inc.

Kuznetsova, A., Rom, H., Alldrin, N., Uijlings, J. R. R., Krasin, I., Pont-Tuset, J., Kamali, S., Popov, S., Malloci, M., Duerig, T., & Ferrari, V. (2018). The open images dataset V4: Unified image classification, object detection, and visual relationship detection at scale. *CoRR.*206137 http://arxiv.org/abs/1811.00982.

Kyle-Davidson, C., Bors, A., & Evans, K. (2019). Predicting visual memory schemas with variational autoencoders. In *BMVC 2019.*

Kyle-Davidson, C., Bors, A. G., & Evans, K. K. (2020). Generating memorable images based on human visual memory schemas. arXiv e-prints.

Lazebnik, S., Schmid, C., & Ponce, J. (2006). Beyond bags of features: Spatial pyramid matching for recognizing natural scene categories. In *2006 IEEE computer society conference on computer vision and pattern recognition (CVPR'06)* (vol. 2, pp. 2169–2178). IEEE.

Li, Y., Hou, X., Koch, C., Rehg, J. M., & Yuille, A. L. (2014). The secrets of salient object segmentation. In *Proceedings of the IEEE conference on computer vision and pattern recognition* (pp. 280–287).

Li, X., Yi, W., Chi, H. L., Wang, X., & Chan, A. P. (2018). A critical review of virtual and augmented reality (vr/ar) applications in construction safety. *Automation in Construction, 86*, 150–162.

Lin, T. Y., Maire, M., Belongie, S., Hays, J., Perona, P., Ramanan, D., Dollár, P., & Zitnick, C. L. (2014). Microsoft COCO: Common objects in context. In D. Fleet, T. Pajdla, B. Schiele, T. Tuytelaars (Eds.) *2014 European conference on computer vision (ECCV)* (pp. 740–755). Cham: Springer International Publishing. https://doi.org/10.1007/978-3-319-10602-1_48. https://doi.org/10.1007%2F978-3-319-10602-1_48.

Lowe, D. G. (2004). Distinctive image features from scale-invariant keypoints. *International Journal of Computer Vision, 60*(2), 91–110.

Lu, J., Xu, M., Yang, R., & Wang, Z. (2018). What makes natural scene memorable? In *Proceedings of the 2018 workshop on understanding subjective attributes of data, with the focus on evoked emotions* (pp. 9–15)

Lu, J., Xu, M., Yang, R., & Wang, Z. (2020). Understanding and predicting the memorability of outdoor natural scenes. *IEEE Transactions on Image Processing, 29*, 4927–4941. https://doi.org/10.1109/TIP.2020.2975957.

Lukavský, J., & Děchtěrenko, F. (2017). Visual properties and memorising scenes: Effects of image-space sparseness and uniformity. *Attention, Perception, & Psychophysics, 79*(7), 2044–2054. https://doi.org/10.3758/s13414-017-1375-9. https://doi.org/10.3758%2Fs13414-017-1375-9.

Ma, S., Wei, Z., Tian, F., Fan, X., Zhang, J., Shen, X., Lin, Z., Huang, J., Měch, R., Samaras, D., et al. (2019). Smarteye: Assisting instant photo taking via integrating user preference with deep view proposal network. In *Proceedings of the 2019 CHI conference on human factors in computing systems* (pp. 1–12).

Machajdik, J., & Hanbury, A. (2010). Affective image classification using features inspired by psychology and art theory. In *Proceedings of the 18th ACM international conference on Multimedia* (pp. 83–92).

Madan, C. R. (2020). Exploring word memorability: How well do different word properties explain item free-recall probability? *Psychonomic Bulletin & Review*, 1–13.

Mahowald, K., Isola, P., Fedorenko, E., Gibson, E., & Oliva, A. (2018). Memorable words are monogamous: The role of synonymy and homonymy in word recognition memory. PsyArXiv.

Mancas, M., & Le Meur, O. (2013). Memorability of natural scenes: The role of attention. In *2013 IEEE international conference on image processing* (pp. 196–200). IEEE.

Miller, G. A. (1995). Wordnet: a lexical database for english. *Communications of the ACM*, *38*(11), 39–41.

Monfort, M., Andonian, A., Zhou, B., Ramakrishnan, K., Bargal, S. A., Yan, Y., Brown, L., Fan, Q., Gutfreund, D., Vondrick, C., et al. (2019). Moments in time dataset: one million videos for event understanding. *IEEE Transactions on Pattern Analysis and Machine Intelligence*, *42*(2), 502–508.

Murray, N., Marchesotti, L., & Perronnin, F. (2012). Ava: A large-scale database for aesthetic visual analysis. In *2012 IEEE conference on computer vision and pattern recognition* (pp. 2408–2415). IEEE.

Newman, A., Bylinskii, Z., Haroz, S., Madan, S., Durand, F., & Oliva, A. (2018). Effects of title wording on memory of trends in line graphs. *Journal of Vision*, *18*(10), 837.

Newman, A., Fosco, C., Casser, V., Lee, A., Barry, Mcnamara, & Oliva, A. (2020). Multimodal memorability: Modeling effects of semantics and decay on video memorability. In *ECCV*.

Oliva, A., & Torralba, A. (2001). Modeling the shape of the scene: A holistic representation of the spatial envelope. *International Journal of Computer Vision*, *42*(3), 145–175.

Papoutsaki, A., Sangkloy, P., Laskey, J., Daskalova, N., Huang, J., & Hays, J. (2016). Webgazer: Scalable webcam eye tracking using user interactions. In *Proceedings of the twenty-fifth international joint conference on artificial intelligence-IJCAI 2016*.

Park, S., Aksan, E., Zhang, X., & Hilliges, O. (2020). Towards end-to-end video-based eye-tracking. In *European conference on computer vision* (pp. 747–763). Springer.

Perera, S., Tal, A., & Zelnik-Manor, L. (2019). Is image memorability prediction solved? In *Proceedings of the IEEE conference on computer vision and pattern recognition workshops* (pp. 0–0).

Qian, J., Chapin, A., Papoutsaki, A., Yang, F., Nelissen, K., & Huang, J. (2018). Remotion: A motion-based capture and replay platform of mobile device interaction for remote usability testing. *Proceedings of the ACM on Interactive, Mobile, Wearable and Ubiquitous Technologies*, *2*(2), 1–18.

Ramanathan, S., Katti, H., Sebe, N., Kankanhalli, M., & Chua, T. S. (2010). An eye fixation database for saliency detection in images. In *European conference on computer vision* (pp. 30–43). Springer.

Russakovsky, O., Deng, J., Su, H., Krause, J., Satheesh, S., Ma, S., Huang, Z., Karpathy, A., Khosla, A., Bernstein, M., et al. (2015). Imagenet large scale visual recognition challenge. *International Journal of Computer Vision*, *115*(3), 211–252.

Russell, B. C., Torralba, A., Murphy, K. P., & Freeman, W. T. (2008). Labelme: a database and web-based tool for image annotation. *International Journal of Computer Vision*, *77*(1-3), 157–173.

Rust, N. C., & Mehrpour, V. (2020). Understanding image memorability. *Trends in Cognitive Sciences*, *24*(7), 557–568. https://doi.org/https://doi.org/10.1016/j.tics.2020.04.001. https://www.sciencedirect.com/science/article/pii/S1364661320301030.

Saleh, B., Farhadi, A., & Elgammal, A. (2013). Object-centric anomaly detection by attribute-based reasoning. In *Proceedings of the IEEE conference on computer vision and pattern recognition* (pp. 787–794).

Sharif Razavian, A., Azizpour, H., Sullivan, J., & Carlsson, S. (2014). Cnn features off-the-shelf: an astounding baseline for recognition. In *Proceedings of the IEEE conference on computer vision and pattern recognition workshops* (pp. 806–813).

Shekhar, S., Singal, D., Singh, H., Kedia, M., & Shetty, A. (2017). Show and recall: Learning what makes videos memorable. In *Proceedings of the IEEE international conference on computer vision* (pp. 2730–2739).

Siarohin, A., Zen, G., Majtanovic, C., Alameda-Pineda, X., Ricci, E., & Sebe, N. (2017). How to make an image more memorable? A deep style transfer approach. In *Proceedings of the 2017 ACM on international conference on multimedia retrieval* (pp. 322–329).

Siarohin, A., Zen, G., Majtanovic, C., Alameda-Pineda, X., Ricci, E., & Sebe, N. (2019). Increasing image memorability with neural style transfer. *ACM Transactions on Multimedia Computing, Communications, and Applications (TOMM)*, 15(2), 1–22.

Sidorov, O. (2019). Changing the image memorability: From basic photo editing to gans. In *Proceedings of the IEEE/CVF conference on computer vision and pattern recognition (CVPR) workshops*.

Spearman, C. (1910). Correlation calculated from faulty data. *British Journal of Psychology, 1904–1920*, 3(3), 271–295. https://doi.org/10.1111/j.2044-8295.1910.tb00206.x.

Standing, L. (1973). Learning 10000 pictures. *The Quarterly Journal of Experimental Psychology*, 25(2), 207–222.

Szegedy, C., Liu, W., Jia, Y., Sermanet, P., Reed, S., Anguelov, D., Erhan, D., Vanhoucke, V., & Rabinovich, A. (2015). Going deeper with convolutions. In *Proceedings of the IEEE conference on computer vision and pattern recognition* (pp. 1–9).

Võ, M. L. H., Bylinskii, Z., & Oliva, A. (2017). Image memorability in the eye of the beholder: Tracking the decay of visual scene representations. bioRxiv. https://doi.org/10.1101/141044. https://www.biorxiv.org/content/early/2017/05/24/141044.

Wang, J., Yang, J., Yu, K., Lv, F., Huang, T., & Gong, Y. (2010). Locality-constrained linear coding for image classification. In *2010 IEEE computer society conference on computer vision and pattern recognition* (pp. 3360–3367). IEEE.

Wolfe, J. M., Horowitz, T. S., & Michod, K. O. (2007). Is visual attention required for robust picture memory? *Vision Research*, 47(7), 955–964.

Xiao, J., Hays, J., Ehinger, K. A., Oliva, A., & Torralba, A. (2010). Sun database: Large-scale scene recognition from abbey to zoo. In *2010 IEEE computer society conference on computer vision and pattern recognition* (pp. 3485–3492). IEEE.

Xiong, C., Ceja, C. R., Ludwig, C. J., & Franconeri, S. (2019). Biased average position estimates in line and bar graphs. Underestimation, overestimation, and perceptual pull. *IEEE Transactions on Visualization and Computer Graphics*, 26(1), 301–310.

Zarezadeh, S., Rezaeian, M., & Sadeghi, M. T. (2017). Image memorability prediction using deep features. In *2017 Iranian conference on electrical engineering (ICEE)* (pp. 2176–2181). IEEE.

Zhang, X., Sugano, Y., Fritz, M., & Bulling, A. (2015). Appearance-based gaze estimation in the wild. In *Proceedings of the IEEE conference on computer vision and pattern recognition (CVPR)*.

Zhou, B., Lapedriza, A., Xiao, J., Torralba, A., & Oliva, A. (2014). Learning deep features for scene recognition using places database. *Advances in Neural Information Processing Systems*, 27, 487–495.

Zhou, B., Lapedriza, A., Khosla, A., Oliva, A., & Torralba, A. (2017). Places: A 10 million image database for scene recognition. *IEEE Transactions on Pattern Analysis and Machine Intelligence*, 40(6), 1452–1464.

Zhu, J., Shen, Y., Zhao, D., & Zhou, B. (2020). In-domain GAN inversion for real image editing. In *European conference on computer vision (ECCV)*.

The Influence of Low- and Mid-Level Visual Features on the Perception of Streetscape Qualities

Gaby N. Akcelik, Kathryn E. Schertz, and Marc G. Berman

1 Introduction to Environmental Neuroscience

Psychologists, neuroscientists, sociologists, and urban planners alike have converged on investigating the influence of various environmental mechanisms on an individual's cognition and behavior (Berman et al. 2019b,a). The environment in this context refers to both the social environment (i.e the social contexts in which individuals interact in) and the physical environment (i.e. elements that make up an individual's surroundings, such as air, water, and built infrastructure). The physical environment breaks down into both natural and urban environments. The natural environment refers to the non-artificial aspects of our surroundings, such as greenspace, water, soil, land and air. The urban environment refers to artificial or man-made aspects of our surroundings, such as buildings, roads, pavements and streetlights.

One area of environmental neuroscience has focused on differences in cognition and behavior that seem to emerge after exposure to environments that vary along a natural-man made/built dimension. Previous studies have shown that an individual's exposure to and interaction with more natural environments, contrasted with built environments, leads to a variety of psychological and cognitive benefits such as improvements in working memory (Stevenson et al. 2018), a decrease in fear, aggression, and violent behavior (Kuo & Sullivan 2001; Schertz et al. 2019), an increase in wellbeing and health (Grahn and Stigsdotter 2003; Bowler et al. 2010), positive affect and mood (Hartig et al. 2011), energy (Kjellgren and Buhrkall 2010), self-esteem (Barton and Pretty 2010; McMahan and Estes 2015), concentration/focus (Bratman et al. 2015; Valtchanov et al. 2010; Berman et al. 2012),

G. N. Akcelik (✉) · K. E. Schertz · M. G. Berman
University of Chicago, Chicago, IL, USA
e-mail: gaby.akcelik@uchicago.edu; kschertz@uchicago.edu; bermanm@uchicago.edu

© The Author(s), under exclusive license to Springer Nature Switzerland AG 2022
B. Ionescu et al. (eds.), *Human Perception of Visual Information*,
https://doi.org/10.1007/978-3-030-81465-6_9

and stress reduction (Gladwell et al. 2012; Valtchanov et al. 2010; Hartig et al. 2014, 2011; Ulrich et al. 1991). Exposure to urban environments are documented to increase prevalence of at-risk mental states and psychiatric disorders (Lederbogen et al. 2011), incidence of crime (Schertz et al. 2019), incidence of social stress (Lederbogen et al. 2011), and an increase in global perceptual bias along with a decrease in selective attention (Cassarino and Setti 2016). Simultaneously, aspects of the urban environment, such as social cohesion, urban greenspace, architectural design, visual richness, and complexity, can elicit positive affect, and can even be more accessible and friendly to individuals experiencing dementia (Chavis and Wandersman 2002; Cassarino and Setti 2016; Mitchell and Burton 2006; Lecic-Tosevski 2019).

The mechanisms through which these benefits emerge, however, is an open question. The mechanisms that are theorized to elicit the benefits associated with nature are attention restoration theory, stress reduction theory, prospect-refuge theory, and perceptual fluency.

Attention restoration theory (ART) posits that stimuli present in natural environments require involuntary attention (i.e. attention that does not require active effort), allowing for an individual's voluntary attention (i.e. attention that requires active effort) to be replenished, which in turn results in an increase in performance on tasks that require one's voluntary attention (Kaplan & Kaplan 1989; Ohly et al. 2016). ART also posits that attention restoration from a natural environment encapsulates the following factors: being away (avoidance of what one is used to environmentally, e.g. "getting away from it all"), extent (content that can occupy one's mind enough so that directed attention can be replenished/restored), fascination (grabbing attention without any effort), and compatibility (whether or not an environment is compatible with the individual's intrinsic goals) (Herzog et al. 2003; Stevenson et al. 2018; Schertz & Berman 2019). Stress reduction theory (SRT) posits that an individual elicits a psychophysiological response dependent on environmental context, which is due to a human evolutionary affinity towards nature (Egner et al. 2020). For example, when placed in a natural environment, humans elicit a positive affective response that is associated with increased chances of survival in said environment because of this innate affinity for nature, which results in stress reduction (Egner et al. 2020). However, when placed in a non-natural environment, humans elicit a stress response that is associated with the idea that humans have not yet adapted to non-natural spaces, and are more likely to perceive these environments as hostile or threatening (Egner et al. 2020). Perceptual fluency states that both attention restoration and stress reduction are a result of visual processing ease: if both a natural and urban environment are nonthreatening, individuals can more fluently process the aspects of natural environments over urban environments, which suggests that visual aspects that are unique to natural environments are easier to process visually (Kaplan and Kaplan 1989; Joye and Van den Berg 2011). Prospect-refuge theory also discusses innate human preference, but in regard for a refuge (i.e. a space that suggests safety/protection) in an environment that allows for the ability to still observe the area for possible threats, which can elicit both positive affective responses and attention restoration in both natural and urban contexts (Egner et al. 2020; Joye and Van den Berg 2011).

Some of these effects of these various mechanisms could be due to the perception of the physical features of the natural environments. Some have theorized that these benefits are due to perceiving the different visual and acoustic features/properties of nature (Schertz and Berman 2019; Joye and Van den Berg 2011; Van Hedger et al. 2019a). Visual features are traditionally defined as low-level, mid-level, or high-level based on where they are thought to be primarily processed in the brain (Peirce 2015), with low-level features being processed posteriorly along the visual ventral stream and high-level features being processed anteriorly (DiCarlo and Cox 2007). As mid- and higher-level features are often used interchangeably in this body of literature, for the sake of this chapter, higher-level features will be referred to as mid-level features.

Low-level features are often noted as color features, like hue, brightness and color saturation, or spatial features, such as straight and non-straight edges, which end up combining together to form the physical aspects of a scene or objects within the scene. Additionally, other researchers may use different manipulations to measure low-level features, such as visual spatial frequency isolation, phase scrambling and amplitude scrambling of scenes (see Valtchanov and Ellard (2015) for further information). This chapter will define low-level features as color and spatial properties, such as straight edges, brightness and hue.

Conversely, mid-level features are objects that allow individuals to identify the context of the scene meaningfully (e.g. there are trees, a waterfall and rocks here, so this scene must be in a forest). However, while the distinction between low- and mid-level visual features can be identified neurally, their separation is less clear when examining the impact of these features on cognitive processes. This is due to findings which suggest that both low and mid-level features can carry semantic information that brings meaning to viewing a scene (Schertz et al. 2020; Berman et al. 2014; Kotabe et al. 2016; Oliva and Torralba 2006).

Therefore, this chapter will discuss how perceiving low-level and mid-level features of natural environments may contribute to their salubrious effects. Additionally, this chapter will cover the various types of low-level and mid-level features in scenes, as well as their effect on cognition in the sections that follow.

2 Low-Level Visual Features

2.1 Defining Low-Level Features

The consideration of low level features may provide insights into aspects of natural environments that differ from more built environments, that when processed, yield psychological benefits. To do so, a taxonomy of the low-level features that differ between the environments must be established. Identifying the various color and spatial properties when thinking about low-level features is key to understanding the specific aspects of low-level features that influence cognition.

There are many different ways to calculate low-level features, however, this chapter will address specifically how the Environmental Neuroscience Lab at the University of Chicago calculates low-level visual features. The color properties of low-level features are calculated using the Hue, Saturation and Value model using the built in functions in the MATLAB image processing toolbox (MATLAB and Image Processing Toolbox Release 2012b, The MathWorks, Inc., Natick, Massachusetts, United States), and are listed as follows: hue, standard deviation of hue, saturation, standard deviation of saturation, brightness, standard deviation of brightness (see Berman et al. (2014) for additional information about each color property). The spatial properties of low-level features are listed as follows: entropy, straight edge density and non-straight edge density (Please refer to Table 1 for definitions of each color and spatial property, and Fig. 1 for some examples).

Table 1 Low-Level Features and their definitions(Berman et al. 2014; Bertamini et al. 2016; Camgoz and Yener 2002)

Color features	
Hue	The color perceived by the dominant wavelength of light; comparing a stimulus to the similarities or differences in other stimuli that are categorized as red, green or blue
SDHue	The standard deviation of hue; accounts for an image's hue diversity
Saturation	The ratio of a dominant wavelength to other wavelengths present in light that gives us color
SDSat	The standard deviation of saturation; accounts for diversity in saturation in an image
Brightness	The measure of lightness or darkness in an image; also referred to as value or color value
SDBright	The standard deviation brightness; accounts for diversity in brightness of an image
Contrast	The difference between the darkest and brightest points/shades in an image
SdContrast	The standard deviation of contrast; accounts for diversity in varying levels of contrast in an image
Spatial features	
Entropy	A statistical measure of randomness to identify image texture, was quantified via intensity values of the pixels of an image
Straight Edge Density (SED)	The number of straight edges in an image in comparison to the size of the image itself
Non-Straight Edge Density (NSED)	The number of non-straight edges in an image in comparison to the size of the image itself
Fractal Dimension	The measure of structural patterns at different magnification scales (i.e. the degree as to which edge patterns repeat at these different scales)
Scaling	The average values of Edge Density and Fractal Dimension

Fig. 1 From Schertz and Berman (2019). A figure depicting the low-level features of a single scene. (**a**) representation of the original image; (**b**) visualization of scene brightness/color value; (**c**) visualization of scene color saturation; (**d**) visualization of straight edges and non-straight edges, in purple and green respectively; (**e**) visualization of hue. Reprinted from: Schertz, K. E., & Berman, M. G. (2019). Understanding nature and its cognitive benefits. Current Directions in Psychological Science, 28(5), 496–502. Copyright (2019), by SAGE Publishing/SAGE Journals. Reprinted with permission

2.2 The Effect of Low-Level Visual Features on Naturalness Ratings

Berman and collaborators (2014) examined which low-level visual features defined above were associated with perceived naturalness across a wide range of scenes. Naturalness perception was evaluated by asking participants to rate how natural they found a scene to be from a scale of 1 to 10 (Berman et al. 2014). Overall, this study found that perceptions of naturalness correlated with a higher amount of curved edges, and higher entropy, while images evaluated as non-natural correlated with a higher amount of straight edges, and color saturation within a scene (Berman et al. 2014). More specifically, a machine learning algorithm (in this case a linear discriminant) could be trained on these features to predict participant's perceived naturalness of the images with high accuracy (Berman et al. 2014).

This study had both human participants and a machine learning algorithm rate various scenes on how natural they perceived the scenes to be (Berman et al. 2014). Scenes that were associated with nature (e.g. a park, a nature trail) were rated as more natural, while scenes that contained more man-made structures (e.g. a corporate building, a campus lacking in greenspace, see Fig. 2) were rated as less natural (Berman et al. 2014). The machine learning algorithm in this study was able to reliably predict the naturalness ratings of various nature scenes via its low-

Fig. 2 An image (left) rated as low naturalness with high straight edges, high saturation, and high standard deviation of saturation, contrasted with an image (right) rated as high naturalness with high non-straight edges and high entropy. (Both from MIT SUN database; (Xiao et al. 2013))

level visual features—nature scenes contained an increase of of NSED, entropy, SDBright and hue which predicted high naturalness ratings, and less-natural and/or urban scenes had an increase in SED, saturation, SDSat, brightness and SDHue which predicted low naturalness ratings (Berman et al. 2014). Ultimately, this study supported that the presence of different features could influence one's perception of naturalness (Berman et al. 2014). Understanding how low-level visual features aid in the perception of naturalness renders the ability to manipulate these features to elicit the psychological benefits of nature in the construction and reform of architectural structures in urban centers (Berman et al. 2014).

2.3 The Effect of Low-Level Features on Aesthetic Preferences and Thought Content

An aesthetic preference, or a positive-affective response, toward naturalness and natural environments has previously been associated with the restorative benefits nature provides (i.e. if an individual aesthetically prefers nature, they are more likely to experience restoration) (Kotabe et al. 2017). While previous research has shown that the cognitive effects of nature may not depend on aesthetic preference (Berman et al. 2008; Stenfors et al. 2019) the mood benefits attained after interacting with nature do depend on aesthetic preferences (Meidenbauer et al. 2020). Building off of the Berman et al. (2014) study, Kardan et al. (2015), aimed to elucidate the relationship between the quantified spatial and color low-level visual features and an individual's aesthetic preference for natural vs urban images. In this study, individuals showed an aesthetic preference for images that carried a label of being more natural. This is inline with previous studies (Kaplan et al. 1972; Velarde et al. 2007). These features were green/yellow (lower) hues, diversity in color saturation (SDSat), defragmented-curvy surfaces/less presence of straight edges, (in objects such as shrubbery, waterfalls, rocks, and bodies of water), which were all implicated in predicting aesthetic preference (Kardan et al. 2015). The implications of this work lie in informing the design of built environments that are not only aesthetically pleasing, but also mimicking that of natural environments to elicit positive psychological and cognitive functioning in an individual (see Fig. 5 for an example).

Understanding and singling out the low-level regularities like presence of curvy lines/edges and color saturation in natural environments can certainly aid in the development of spaces that people would prefer to spend their time in, in addition to receiving all the positive benefits that naturalness provides (Kardan et al. 2015).

Identifying the low-level visual features that pertain to both aesthetic preferences and naturalness play a key role in moving one step closer to fully realizing which basic features are eliciting cognitive and psychological effects after interactions with natural environments (Schertz and Berman 2019). Both studies cover the particular spatial and color properties that pertain to naturalness and aesthetic preference, namely the presence of non-straight lines/edges vs straight lines/edges, color saturation diversity, and lower hues in the images shown to participants.

In natural environments, non-straight/curvy lines and edges are considered more chaotic and disorderly (Kotabe et al. 2017; Bertamini et al. 2016), however, curvy lines are associated with being friendly, or welcoming, and often are preferred by humans (Bar and Neta 2006; Silvia and Barona 2009; Bertamini et al. 2016). The general feeling around curvy lines and friendliness has been established in not only the artistic community(Bertamini et al. 2016), starting with Youtube user Triple-Q drawing Nintendo's Kirby and titling the video *Kirby is Shaped Like a Friend* (TripleQ 2014). This video triggered a series of memes (i.e. an idea, style, phrase that spreads from person to person within a culture; (Merriam-Webster n.d)), illustrating that fictional characters containing only curves/roundness are "shaped like friends" (e.g. Star Wars' BB-8 and R2-D2 droids are shaped like friends, see Fig. 3), while characters that have straight, abrupt and angular features are "not shaped like friends" (Bertamini et al. 2016), which are documented to be more aggressive, infuriating and unsettling (Bertamini et al. 2016).

In addition to potentially influencing perceptual judgements, visual features have also been shown to be associated with more complex processes, such as thought content. Work by Schertz et al. (2018) found that curves and non-straight edges are associated with thoughts about spirituality and life journey in free-response thought content (Schertz et al. 2018). Additionally, when participants were shown images with more non-straight edges, they were more likely to choose a word cloud reflecting the spirituality and life journey topic compared to being shown images with less non-straight edges. This study was replicated without overt semantic information present, by scrambling the images and only preserving edge content, which may indicate that these low-level features can be important independent of the higher level scene semantics, but also blurs the distinction traditionally given between high and low level visual features (Schertz et al. 2020). This research has the ability to inform on the design of built environments, by encouraging designers to intentionally consider the use of these low-level features that elicit positive feelings.

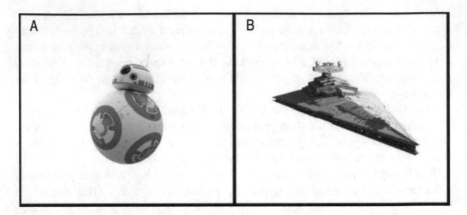

Fig. 3 A. BB-8 is *shaped like a friend* B. Imperial Star Destroyer is *not shaped like a friendThe use of the Star Wars^{TM} images in this figure are for educational purposes only—the authors do not own these images, and are operating under Fair Use educational purposes*

2.4 The Effects of Low-Level Visual Features on Disorder Perception

Curved lines are not always perceived positively though, as they do and can contribute to how disorderly an environment may be. Low level features were also theorized to play a role in how disorderly an environment/scene may be, which in turn could encourage complex, disorderly behavior in humans (see Wilson and Kelling (1982)). However, O'Brien et al. (2019) argued against Broken Windows Theory, by conducting a meta-analysis of how neighborhood disorder impacts health, essentially finding that neighborhood disorder has no impact on crime, or the perpetuation of unhealthy behavior, but that neighborhood disorder impacts mental health as well as overall health (O'Brien et al. 2019). In other words, disorder in an environment has been shown to be a stressor, which in turn impacts mental health, and does not promote any rule-breaking behavior (O'Brien et al. 2019).

Disorder in this context can be defined in different ways. Semantic or social disorder, much like a broken window, graffiti, or litter in this scenario could elicit an increase in stress, distress, substance abuse and depression (O'Brien et al. 2019; Kotabe et al. 2016). Pure visual disorder refers to the low-level features present in a scene that lead to the perception of disorder; this field of study also suggests that low-level features carry semantic information about how disorderly an environment is, and those features can have downstream effects on rule-breaking or disorderly behavior (Kotabe et al. 2016). Individuals exposed to disorderly environments result in a reduction of cognitive/executive control and an increase in negative affect (Kotabe 2014; Kotabe et al. 2016) in addition to an increase in rule breaking behavior (Wilson & Kelling 1982; Kotabe et al. 2016).

Disorder in the context of this chapter refers to how individuals perceive visual disorder, which, again, decomposes low-level features into spatial and color properties (Kotabe et al. 2016). When assessing differences in color and spatial properties as it relates to visual disorder and rule-breaking behavior (e.g. cheating on an exam), Kotabe et al. (2016) found that spatial properties contribute more to visual disorder than that of color. Furthermore, when presented with images (with no semantic information) exhibiting visual disorder, the average magnitude of aforementioned disorderly behaviors in individuals increased upwards of 87% (Kotabe et al. 2016). Additionally, these disorderly behaviors triggered by low-level disorder have a tendency to spread upon observation of others who are also partaking in these disorderly behaviors (Keizer et al. 2008); (Kotabe et al. 2016). Despite the fact that natural environments are often perceived as visually disorderly, they are aesthetically preferred, and do not elicit the aforementioned disorderly behaviors (Kotabe et al. 2016). Kotabe et al. (2017) investigated the various hypotheses that attempt to elucidate why nature is aesthetically preferred when in reality these scenes are visually disordered, finding the most support for the nature-trumps-disorder hypothesis, which states that aesthetic preference for naturalness overpowers the aesthetic aversion of disorder, rather than disordering being aesthetically pleasing in nature (Kotabe et al. 2017). The nature-trumps-disorder effect is most prominent when scene semantics and low-level features work hand in hand, rather than the absence of scene semantics and solely low-level visual features. In addition, Kotabe et al. (2017) came to the conclusion that scene semantics are necessary for the nature-trumps disorder effect, i.e., you can get the effect even if you just show people words about nature (e.g., the words: 'river', 'mountain', 'library', etc.) (Kotabe et al. 2017). You don't however, get this effect when you use scrambled stimuli that have the edge content, but no semantic content, hence why semantics are just sufficient enough to get the nature trumps disorder effect. That being said, the inclusion of low-level visual features in addition to the words about nature could amplify the nature-trumps-disorder effect (Kotabe et al. 2017).

3 Mid-Level Features

3.1 Defining Mid-Level Features

In addition to low-level visual features, mid-level visual features are an additional element that is key to understanding what aspects of the physical environment cause changes in behavior and cognition. Mid-level visual features are objects and/or physical attributes that carry semantic information of a particular scene or environment (e.g. the sky, buildings, walls, stoplights, trees etc) (Zhang et al. 2018); (Hunter and Askarinejad 2015). Mid-level visual features themselves are made from low-level visual features, and give meaning to a visual scene.

Hunter & Askarinejad (2015) formulated a list of physical attributes of environmental scenes that cover both spatial structure and contextual objects that

Fig. 4 *Scene Segmentation of a Google Street View image.* Using deep-learning semantic scene segmentation deeplabv3 by Google, this street view image was able to be segmented into different mid-level features such as the road, sidewalk, skycover, cars, etc.

exist within an environment that provide the most influence over preference and restoration when perceived, in order to inform on the creation of future built structures (e.g. skyline position, horizon line position, people presence, building distribution; Hunter and Askarinejad 2015, see for comprehensive list of qualities). These qualities can be used when constructing built environments to intentionally influence psychological and cognitive processes. This can be done by choosing qualities to minimize cognitively taxing visual features such as the presence of visual disorder, or in the auditory domain noise pollution in an urban environment, and account for the creation of structures that can elicit positive psychological effects for a restorative and aesthetically stimulating experience for pedestrians in urban centers.

With the rapid development of computer vision techniques for image recognition using deep learning methods (Hinton et al. 2012; He et al. 2016, 2017), researchers have started to use deep learning-based semantic scene segmentation techniques to extract mid-level features from images (see Fig. 4) in order to investigate the relationship between mid-level visual features and pedestrian perception of said features (Zhang et al. 2018; Rossetti et al. 2019). Zhang et al. (2018), predicted the ratings of six dimensions of human perception (safety, lively, beauty, wealthy, depressing, and boring), all of which were measured in the MIT Place Pulse dataset (https://pulse.media.mit.edu/) using deep convolutional neural networks (a model based in deep learning that is designed for processing layers/different aspects of images; He et al. 2016). A scene parsing model (an algorithm that segments and parses a whole image into different semantic categories, identifying the different parts and objects that make up an image, thus the extraction of mid-level features) was executed to identify 150 categories of objects in a given image (Zhao et al. 2017); (Zhang et al. 2018). Zhang and colleagues then ran a multivariate regression to determine the impact of these object categories on the aforementioned six perceptual qualities, illuminating a significant relationship between the perceptual qualities and mid-level features such as sidewalks, grass, walls, trees, cars and grass (Zhang et al. 2018). For example, sidewalks, cars, and roads were associated with the quality of lively, while trees and grass were associated with the beautiful, wealthy and depressing perceptual qualities (Zhang et al. 2018).

Rossetti et al. (2019) additionally used semantic scene segmentation techniques in order to observe the relationship between mid-level features and the six afore-mentioned perceptual qualities (Rossetti et al. 2019). A discrete choice model was conducted to explain the subjective perceptions as a function of the features extracted from views in the Pulse Place data set, and used the estimated model to create a perceptual map of Santiago, Chile (Rossetti et al. 2019). With that, images that conveyed more beauty had more vegetation, and more wealthy images had more vegetation present, with less sky cover (Rossetti et al. 2019). Less depressing images were associated with a more "open" concept, with more skycover, more pedestrian presence and less buildings (Rossetti et al. 2019). The perceptual maps also depicted more upper-income households were situated in the northeastern area of the city, and these areas were considered to be more lively, safe, wealthy and beautiful, and the surrounding middle-to-lower income families were correlated with the depressing, and boring perceptual qualities (see Fig 7 of Rossetti et al. (2019)). To confirm these perceptions surrounding low- vs higher-income neighborhoods, Rossetti and collaborators examined the relationship between perceived wealth and neighborhood income, vehicles per capita, and percentage of high income individuals at the street/traffic level (see Figure 8 of Rossetti et al. (2019)), which was found to be highly correlated with the aforementioned socioeconomic indicators. This implies that spatial socioeconomic variables can capture essential aspects of public and shared spaces in urban areas (Rossetti et al. 2019). These can inform local governments on pinpointing areas that need reform, as well as increasing access to greenspace (e.g. adding trees/green-cover) and increasing overall walkability of the area of interest (Rossetti et al. 2019).

3.2 The Effect of Mid-Level Visual Features on Cognition

An example of the influence of mid-level visual features on cognition is depicted by Ibarra et al. (2017) finding that several mid-level features play an important role in predicting aesthetic preference for natural environments (Ibarra et al. 2017). The study as a whole aimed to tease apart both low- and mid-level features from various scenes in order to elucidate the impact of these features, both separately and in conjunction on the variance of aesthetic preferences and judgements regarding naturalness (Ibarra et al. 2017). Generally, Ibarra et al. (2017) ultimately found that mid-level visual features containing context of a scene or an image are stronger predictors of aesthetic preference and naturalness than that of low-level features. Specifically, they also found that the mid/higher-level features played a mediating role in the relationship between low-level visual features and the variance of aesthetic preference and perceived naturalness in a mix of both natural and urban images(Ibarra et al. 2017). For example, the effect of brightness (a low-level feature) of an image is stronger when features like vegetation (a mid-level) are present on aesthetic preference, as the level of brightness in a natural space may allow the perceiver to take in more details of the vegetation of a scene, and discern the safety of the space around them (see Prospect-Refuge theory, Appleton 1996), which can impact one's preference for that image (Ibarra et al. 2017). Another example of the importance of context lies in the work of Van Hedger et al. (2019b), which posits that aesthetic preference for nature sounds over urban sounds depends on the context of the sound, and not innate preference for nature sounds. Participants were not given context on the origin of an ambiguous sound (i.e. whether this sound was from a natural or urban environment), which then led to the ambiguous sounds with more nature-related acoustic features to be more negatively rated in aesthetic preference (Van Hedger et al. 2019b).

Understanding that low-level features like hue or brightness in a scene can solely predict preference, and that objects/object design in that same scene can provide the perceiver enough context to inform on their preference can play a role in elucidating the salutary affective benefits from interacting with nature. However, the onset of benefit can be attributed to the perceivers' aesthetic preference for either natural or urban environments. The perceiver must highly prefer nature and natural scenes in order to actually reap the affective benefits of nature, as rating images (both nature and urban) as highly preferred is able to significantly predict affect change, regardless of whether the image was a natural or urban scene (Meidenbauer et al. 2020).

3.3   Low-Level and Mid-Level Features in Architectural Scenes

Some urban structures are built to mimic the aesthetics of nature, which would also harbor the visual features that are found in natural spaces to enhance pedestrian experience. In addition, architectural elements that mimic nature-like elements and patterns may be preferred over structures that look man-made (i.e. architecture that doesn't mimic natural elements in its structure, refer to Fig. 5 for an example) which may mimic the benefits of interacting with organic nature itself (see Figure 5) (Coburn et al. 2019; Kellert 2012; Berto 2005). Implementing, for example, a high density of curvier lines and edges, in built architecture in- and outdoors can boost the quality of health and aesthetic pleasure en mass (Coburn et al. 2019; Ibarra et al. 2017; Berman et al. 2014; Kardan et al. 2015). Figure 5 (Coburn et al. 2019) shows four panels of architecture that mimic elements of nature, which can elicit these benefits of nature. For example, panels A, B and C are reminiscent of the way trees and florals are structured (i.e. the structures are reminiscent of trees branching out into a canopy; floral and filigree are also present in these tree-like structures, which carry that semantic information that associates itself with nature), while panel D contains shapes that include geometric, proportional and self-symmetrical patterns that are evident in nature itself (Coburn et al. 2019). Figure 5 serves as a stark contrast to Fig. 6, which depicts architectural structures that are inorganic and synthetic, implementing more non-naturally occurring elements such as flat

Fig. 5 *From Coburn et al. (2019)*. Each panel shows a piece of man-made architecture that is inspired by natural and/or biological characteristics, which not only evoke the feeling of interacting with actual nature, but also can be preferred because of the aesthetic of naturalness. See (Coburn et al. 2019, Figure 1) for a further description of these natural man-made structures. Reprinted from: Coburn, A., Kardan, O., Kotabe, H., Steinberg, J., Hout, M. C., Robbins, A.,..., Berman, M. G. (2019). Psychological responses to natural patterns in architecture. Journal of Environmental Psychology,62, 133–145. Copyright (2019), Elsevier. Reprinted with permission

Fig. 6 *From Coburn et al. (2019)*. Each panel shows a piece of man-made architecture that is inspired by natural and/or biological characteristics, which not only evoke the feeling of interacting with actual nature, but also can be preferred because of the aesthetic of naturalness. See Coburn et al. (2019, Figure 1) for a further description of these natural man-made structures. Reprinted from: Coburn, A., Kardan, O., Kotabe, H., Steinberg, J., Hout, M. C., Robbins, A., ... Berman, M. G. (2019). Psychological responses to natural patterns in architecture.Journal of Environmental Psychology,62, 133–145. Copyright (2019), Elsevier. Reprinted with permission

surfaces and straight-rigid lines. This man-made design, influenced by aspects such as Euclidean geometry, seems to be reflective of economic development and overall elements of utilitarianism (i.e. substance over style; choosing 'substance' that is more efficient rather than a beneficial 'style' that is incompatible with the economic incentives that come with modern architecture) (Coburn et al. 2019; Joye 2007).

With psychologically salubrious design features established by researchers and architects alike, constructing these urban environments with the pedestrian's psychological and cognitive experience in mind could allow for an overall happier, healthier mass of individuals who can equally access the positive effects of nature that individuals who reside in more natural environments have readily accessible. With that being said, low-level and mid-to-higher-level features that exist within these organic and inorganic structures must be identified in order to inform the integration of nature-like characteristics into the built environment to elicit these en mass effects that could potentially improve mental health (Ibarra et al. 2017; Coburn et al. 2019).

Coburn et al. (2019) predicted that naturalistic color and spatial low-level features present in scenes involving architectural design would affect perceptions of naturalness and aesthetic preference (Coburn et al. 2019). In a series of experiments executed in this particular study, it was found that the low-level features of Scaling, sdSat and SdBright predicted naturalness ratings for interior and exterior architecture with little to no vegetation present in the scenes. Ultimately, this study found that more natural patterns in architectural structures had not only a higher naturalness rating, but also had a higher aesthetic preference (Coburn et al. 2019). Naturalistic aesthetics and patterns in these built structures seem to replicate results in Berman et al. (2014), and Kardan et al. (2015) for outdoor scenes, which show that low-level features in scenes can predict naturalness ratings and aesthetic preferences for naturalness (Coburn et al. 2019). In other words, these patterns of low-level features that are prevalent in natural landscapes/scenes can exist within man-made architecture, which makes some buildings look more natural than others, hence, garnering the aesthetic preference for them (Coburn et al. 2019). The study also found that scaling (see Fig. 1) and contrast patterns that mimic nature in architecture significantly predicted ratings of aesthetic preference, with perceptions of natural-like aesthetics acting as a mediator for this relationship, meaning that the naturalistic patterns present in these structures elicited aesthetic preference for the structures harboring said patterns (Coburn et al. 2019).

4   Street Psychology and Pedestrian Experiences in Urban Areas

While taking into account the impact of the visual features of different architectural structures on one's psychology, we also have to consider the importance of streetscapes in urban environments, and how pedestrians are experiencing these visual features at the street level. When observing streetscapes in different areas of major urban centres, one can conclude that polluted, unclean and aggressively-constructed architecture can be partially responsible for eliciting the psychological and cognitive maladies that are typically associated with urban environments. As mentioned, straight, angular features may elicit aggressive feelings, however, these types of spatial features are present in some constructions of buildings (a mid-level feature) in urban spaces. Additionally, when revisiting the Broken Windows theory and the recent O'Brien et al. (2019) study, mid-level features like a vandalized building or a graffitied window can provide semantic context that signals a pedestrian to note their level of neighborhood disorder, which can then cause negative impacts on mental and overall health (O'Brien et al. 2019; Wilson & Kelling 1982; Kotabe et al. 2016; Oliva & Torralba 2006).

The existence of these mid-level, semantic objects containing low-level features of disorder in built structures could contribute to any alimentary psychological and cognitive effects elicited by urban areas. Since we see low-level features play into visual disorder, mid-level features that provide a negative or even aggressive context (e.g. the broken window) and that visual disorder can perpetuate disorderly behavior amongst individuals, what does this mean for the pedestrian navigating streetscapes in urban centers, and how can we manipulate these features to elicit positive effects?

To answer this question, we must first account for how important streets are to urban environments, as they are not only a necessary public channel of foot and vehicle traffic, but also a means of people to interact with fellow pedestrians and the environment around them (Jacobs 1993). A pedestrian is an individual who travels via walking or any mobility-impaired individual using a wheelchair (Lo 2009). One must account for the importance of pedestrians' accommodations in the urban space, and how much influence they have on urban-planning and vice versa (Lo 2009). Walkability is a term used to describe how pedestrian-friendly one perceives an area to be, which ultimately influences a pedestrian's decision to exist and navigate the space within that area (Lo 2009; Ewing et al. 2006; Wang 2013). Good walkability of streets could encourage walking by offering comfort, safety and visual interest (Southworth 2005). Many urban design researchers identified urban design and perceptual qualities that were instrumental to walkability, (See Ewing et al. (2006) for an extensive list of design qualities on pedestrian experience; Handy 1992; Ewing et al. 1996; Ewing and Handy 2009). Ultimately, researchers have identified five design qualities of urbanity that have the potential to influence how the individual pedestrian perceives the 'streetscape' environment: imageability, transparency, human-scale, enclosure, and complexity (see Table 2). These design qualities predicted the ratings of six dimensions of human perception (safety, lively, beauty, wealthy, depressing, and boring). In addition, mid-level visual features with natural elements (e.g., green plants, trees) existing in urban environments increased positive pedestrian experiences, such as feelings of safety, liveliness and beauty, for example, trees can create a sense of enclosure (Rossetti et al. 2019). Understanding the impact of these perceptual and design qualities while also understanding how the visual features of the built environment affect the pedestrian experience is critical to our understanding of how to construct accessible built spaces that maximize restorative and salutary effects on a massive scale.

Table 2 *Excerpt from Ewing et al. (2006).* This table highlights and defines the five perceptual qualities that were operationally defined to contribute to walkability, thus allowing these aspects to be used to further understand pedestrian perceptions on the street level

Design qualities according to Ewing et al. (2006)	
Quality	Definition
Imageability	A quality that makes a place distinct, recognizable and memorable based on how physical elements are arranged. These elements could invoke emotions that lead to a lasting impression on a pedestrian
Transparency	A quality that is based upon the degree to which a pedestrian can perceive other pedestrians beyond physical elements in an area (e.g. can a pedestrian see human activity beyond the end of a street, beyond a wall or fence?)
Enclosure	A quality that refers to how streets and spaces are divided up by physical elements, such as walls or buildings
Human-Scale	A quality that refers to the size, texture and execution of physical elements that correspond to a pedestrian in size, proportion and walking speed
Complexity	A quality that refers to how diverse or visually rich an area is, such as number of buildings, different types of buildings, street furniture—essentially diversity and abundance of physical elements that make a space aesthetically interesting

While low- and mid-level features have such an impact on psychological and cognitive functioning, how does an individual approach quantifying these aspects when given an image? Previous studies used various computational, statistical methods to quantify low- and mid-level visual features from natural and urban images in order to elucidate the effect of these features on aesthetic preference and the perception of naturalness (Berman et al. 2014; Kardan et al. 2015; Ibarra et al. 2017; Coburn et al. 2019; Zhang et al. 2018; Rossetti et al. 2019). It is currently being investigated if different levels of visual features (both low- and mid-level features) can predict these streetscape qualities at the Environmental Neuroscience Lab at the University of Chicago.

This preliminary study focuses on observing pedestrian perceptions of low- and mid-level features of various streetscapes. Additionally, the study explores the impact of these visual features on walkability, preference, imageability, complexity, disorder, transparency, enclosure and human-scale ratings on both the sidewalk and road-view level using geo-tagged Google Street View images from the Chicago area. Participants rated each image based on the eight perceptual design qualities listed above, and both low- and mid-level features were extracted from each image using the Berman et al. (2014) method and a deep learning-based scene segmentation technique, respectively. Then multivariate regression analysis was conducted to analyze the contribution of low- and mid-level visual features to pedestrian's ratings of walkability, preference, imageability, complexity, disorder, transparency, enclosure and human scale. Preliminary results from this study suggest that NSED is positively correlated with levels of walkability, preference, imageability and enclosure, and negatively correlated with transparency and disorder, while SED is

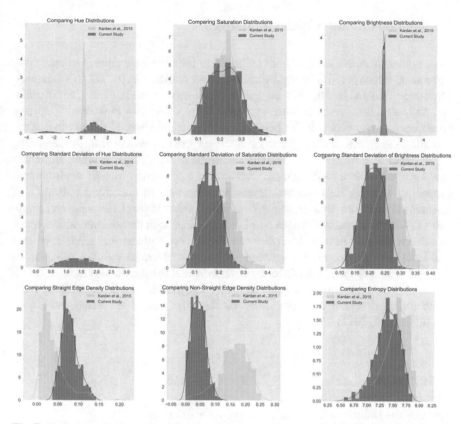

Fig. 7 *Preliminary Study vs Kardan et al. (2015).* Distributions of low-level features between image sets used in the Environmental Neuroscience Lab's preliminary study and the Kardan et al. (2015) study

positively correlated with walkability, preference, imageability, complexity, transparency and enclosure, and being negatively correlated with human-scale ratings.. Additionally, a mid-level feature like vegetation is positively associated with ratings of walkability, preference, imageability, humanscale and enclosure, while negatively correlated with ratings of transparency and disorder.

These findings seem to deviate from that of Kardan et al. (2015) in regard to the relationship between low-level features and aesthetic preference, particularly between SED and aesthetic preference scores, with SED preference negatively correlating with aesthetic preference ratings (Kardan et al. 2015). Considering both this preliminary study and the Kardan et al. (2015) study uses different sets of images, with the preliminary study using street-view images, and the Kardan et al. (2015) study using both natural and urban images, a possible explanation for this disconnect can possibly be found when comparing the distributions of low-level features between image sets (see Fig. 7).

5   Conclusion and Open Challenges

In summary, quantification of both natural and built environments is necessary to understand which low- and/or mid-level features contribute to the pedestrian experience, cognition and health when navigating these environments. This quantification and understanding which features can have these effects lie in reforming current urban centers to maximize the potential for the acquisition of the psychological benefits that nature elicits, whilst being in an urban environment. Additionally, the manipulation of low- and mid-level features in the design of urban structures could also be used to render a more walkable and pedestrian friendly environment. Currently, with big data sources, researchers are able to quantify a multitude of features of urban environments (such as low- and mid-level features) and relate them to other urban quantities such as health, crime, sociodemographics. However, these data do not allow us to derive the causal mechanisms that relate low- and mid-level features to these neighborhood factors. Because moving residents to different neighborhoods with different environmental features is not possible, future researchers will need to be creative in trying to uncover causal mechanisms from creative experimentation and/or using cutting-edge causal modeling techniques (Sugihara et al. 2012).

References

Appleton, J. (1996). *The experience of landscape*. Wiley Chichester.

Bar, M., & Neta, M. (2006). Humans prefer curved visual objects. *Psychological science, 17*(8), 645–648.

Barton, J., & Pretty, J. (2010). What is the best dose of nature and green exercise for improving mental health? a multi-study analysis. *Environmental science & technology, 44*(10), 3947–3955.

Berman, M. G., Jonides, J., & Kaplan, S. (2008). The cognitive benefits of interacting with nature. *Psychological Science, 19*(12), 1207–1212.

Berman, M. G., Kross, E., Krpan, K. M., Askren, M. K., Burson, A., Deldin, P. J., …Jonides, J. (2012). Interacting with nature improves cognition and affect for individuals with depression. *Journal of Affective Disorders, 140*(3), 300–305.

Berman, M. G., Hout, M. C., Kardan, O., Hunter, M. R., Yourganov, G., Henderson, J. M., …Jonides, J. (2014). The perception of naturalness correlates with low-level visual features of environmental scenes. *PloS one, 9*(12), e114572.

Berman, M. G., Kardan, O., Kotabe, H. P., Nusbaum, H. C., & London, S. E. (2019a). The promise of environmental neuroscience. *Nature Human Behaviour, 3*(5), 414–417.

Berman, M. G., Stier, A. J., & Akcelik, G. N. (2019b). Environmental neuroscience. *American Psychologist, 74*(9), 1039.

Bertamini, M., Palumbo, L., Gheorghes, T. N., & Galatsidas, M. (2016). Do observers like curvature or do they dislike angularity? *British Journal of Psychology, 107*(1), 154–178.

Berto, R. (2005). Exposure to restorative environments helps restore attentional capacity. *Journal of Environmental Psychology, 25*(3), 249–259.

Bowler, D. E., Buyung-Ali, L. M., Knight, T. M., & Pullin, A. S. (2010). A systematic review of evidence for the added benefits to health of exposure to natural environments. *BMC Public Health, 10*(1), 1–10.

Bratman, G. N., Daily, G. C., Levy, B. J., & Gross, J. J. (2015). The benefits of nature experience: Improved affect and cognition. *Landscape and Urban Planning, 138*, 41–50.

Camgoz, N., & Yener, C. (2002). Effects of hue, saturation, and brightness on preference: a study on goethe's color circle with rgb color space. In *9th congress of the international colour association* (Vol. 4421, pp. 392–395).

Cassarino, M., & Setti, A. (2016). Complexity as key to designing cognitive-friendly environments for older people. *Frontiers in Psychology, 7*, 1329.

Chavis, D. M., & Wandersman, A. (2002). Sense of community in the urban environment: A catalyst for participation and community development. In *A quarter century of community psychology* (pp. 265–292). Springer.

Coburn, A., Kardan, O., Kotabe, H., Steinberg, J., Hout, M. C., Robbins, A., . . . Berman, M. G. (2019). Psychological responses to natural patterns in architecture. *Journal of Environmental Psychology, 62*, 133–145.

DiCarlo, J. J., & Cox, D. D. (2007). Untangling invariant object recognition. *Trends in Cognitive Sciences, 11*(8), 333–341.

Egner, L. E., S"utterlin, S., & Calogiuri, G. (2020). Proposing a framework for the restorative effects of nature through conditioning: Conditioned restoration theory. *International Journal of Environmental Research and Public Health, 17*(18), 6792.

Ewing, R., & Handy, S. (2009). Measuring the unmeasurable:Urban design qualities related to walkability. *Journal of Urban Design, 14*(1), 65–84.

Ewing, R. H., et al. (1996). Pedestrian-and transit-friendly design.

Ewing, R., Handy, S., Brownson, R. C., Clemente, O., & Winston, E. (2006). Identifying and measuring urban design qualities related to walkability. *Journal of Physical Activity and Health, 3*(s1), S223–S240.

Gladwell, V., Brown, D., Barton, J. L., Tarvainen, M., Kuoppa, P., Pretty, J., . . . Sandercock, G. (2012). The effects of views of nature on autonomic control. *European Journal of Applied Physiology, 112*(9), 3379–3386.

Grahn, P., & Stigsdotter, U. A. (2003). Landscape planning and stress. *Urban Forestry & Urban Greening, 2*(1), 1–18.

Handy, S. L. (1992). Regional versus local accessibility: neo-traditional development and its implications for non-work travel. *Built Environment (1978-)*, 253–267.

Hartig, T., van den Berg, A. E., Hagerhall, C. M., Tomalak, M., Bauer,N., Hansmann, R., . . . others (2011). Health benefits of nature experience: Psychological, social and cultural processes. In *Forests, trees and human health* (pp. 127–168). Springer.

Hartig, T., Mitchell, R., De Vries, S., & Frumkin, H. (2014). Nature and health. *Annual Review of Public Health, 35*, 207–228.

He, K., Zhang, X., Ren, S., & Sun, J. (2016). Deep residual learning for image recognition. In *Proceedings of the ieee conference on computer vision and pattern recognition* (pp. 770–778).

He, K., Gkioxari, G., Dollár, P., & Girshick, R. (2017). Mask r-cnn. In *Proceedings of the ieee international conference on computer vision* (pp. 2961–2969).

Herzog, T. R., Maguire, P., Nebel, M. B., et al. (2003). Assessing the restorative components of environments. *Journal of Environmental Psychology, 23*(2), 159–170.

Hinton, G., Deng, L., Yu, D., Dahl, G. E., Mohamed, A.-r., Jaitly, N., . . . others (2012). Deep neural networks for acoustic modeling in speech recognition: The shared views of four research groups. *IEEE Signal Processing Magazine, 29*(6), 82–97.

Hunter, M. R., & Askarinejad, A. (2015). Designer's approach for scene selection in tests of preference and restoration along a continuum of natural to manmade environments. *Frontiers in Psychology, 6*, 1228.

Ibarra, F. F., Kardan, O., Hunter, M. R., Kotabe, H. P., Meyer, F. A., & Berman, M. G. (2017). Image feature types and their predictions of aesthetic preference and naturalness. *Frontiers in Psychology, 8*, 632.

Jacobs, A. B. (1993). Great streets: Monument avenue, richmond, virginia.

Joye, Y. (2007). Architectural lessons from environmental psychology: The case of biophilic architecture. *Review of General Psychology, 11*(4), 305–328.

Joye, Y., & Van den Berg, A. (2011). Is love for green in our genes? a critical analysis of evolutionary assumptions in restorative environments research. *Urban Forestry & Urban Greening, 10*(4), 261–268.

Kaplan, R., & Kaplan, S. (1989). *The experience of nature: A psychological perspective.* Cambridge university press.

Kaplan, S., Kaplan, R., & Wendt, J. S. (1972). Rated preference and complexity for natural and urban visual material. *Perception & Psychophysics, 12*(4), 354–356.

Kardan, O., Demiralp, E., Hout, M. C., Hunter, M. R., Karimi, H., Hanayik, T., ... Berman, M. G. (2015). Is the preference of natural versus man-made scenes driven by bottom-up processing of the visual features of nature? *Frontiers in Psychology, 6*, 471.

Keizer, K., Lindenberg, S., & Steg, L. (2008). The spreading of disorder. *Science, 322*(5908), 1681–1685.

Kellert, S. R. (2012). *Building for life: Designing and understanding the humannature connection.* Island press.

Kjellgren, A., & Buhrkall, H. (2010). A comparison of the restorative effect of a natural environment with that of a simulated natural environment. *Journal of Environmental Psychology, 30*(4), 464–472.

Kotabe, H. P. (2014). The world is random: a cognitive perspective on perceived disorder. *Frontiers in Psychology, 5*, 606.

Kotabe, H. P., Kardan, O., & Berman, M. G. (2016). The order of disorder: Deconstructing visual disorder and its effect on rule-breaking. *Journal of Experimental Psychology: General, 145*(12), 1713.

Kotabe, H. P., Kardan, O., & Berman, M. G. (2017). The nature-disorder paradox: A perceptual study on how nature is disorderly yet aesthetically preferred. *Journal of Experimental Psychology: General, 146*(8), 1126.

Kuo, F. E., & Sullivan, W. C. (2001). Aggression and violence in the inner city: Effects of environment via mental fatigue. *Environment and Behavior, 33*(4), 543–571.

Lecic-Tosevski, D. (2019). Is urban living good for mental health? *Current Opinion in Psychiatry, 32*(3), 204–209.

Lederbogen, F., Kirsch, P., Haddad, L., Streit, F., Tost, H., Schuch, P., ... others (2011). City living and urban upbringing affect neural social stress processing in humans. *Nature, 474*(7352), 498–501.

Lo, R. H. (2009). Walkability: what is it? *Journal of Urbanism, 2*(2), 145–166.

McMahan, E. A., & Estes, D. (2015). The effect of contact with natural environments on positive and negative affect: A meta-analysis. *The Journal of Positive Psychology, 10*(6), 507–519.

Meidenbauer, K. L., Stenfors, C.U., Bratman, G.N., Gross, J. J., Schertz, K. E., Choe, K. W., & Berman, M. G. (2020). The affective benefits of nature exposure: What's nature got to do with it? *Journal of Environmental Psychology, 72*, 101498.

Merriam-Webster. (n.d). Meme. *In Merriam-Webster.com dictionary.* Retrieved October 7, 2020, from https://www.merriamwebster.com/dictionary/meme

Mitchell, L., & Burton, E. (2006). Neighbourhoods for life: Designing dementiafriendly outdoor environments. *Quality in Ageing and Older Adults, 7*(1), 26–33.

O'Brien, D. T., Farrell, C., & Welsh, B. C. (2019). Broken (windows) theory: A meta-analysis of the evidence for the pathways from neighborhood disorder to resident health outcomes and behaviors. *Social Science & Medicine, 228*, 272–292.

Ohly, H., White, M. P., Wheeler, B.W., Bethel, A., Ukoumunne, O. C., Nikolaou, V., & Garside, R. (2016). Attention restoration theory: A systematic review of the attention restoration potential of exposure to natural environments. *Journal of Toxicology and Environmental Health, Part B, 19*(7), 305–343.

Oliva, A., & Torralba, A. (2006). Building the gist of a scene: The role of global image features in recognition. *Progress in Brain Research, 155*, 23–36.

Peirce, J. W. (2015). Understanding mid-level representations in visual processing. *Journal of Vision, 15*(7), 5–5.

Rossetti, T., Lobel, H., Rocco, V., & Hurtubia, R. (2019). Explaining subjective perceptions of public spaces as a function of the built environment: A massive data approach. *Landscape and Urban Planning, 181*, 169–178.

Schertz, K. E., & Berman, M. G. (2019). Understanding nature and its cognitive benefits. *Current Directions in Psychological Science, 28*(5), 496–502.

Schertz, K. E., Sachdeva, S., Kardan, O., Kotabe, H. P., Wolf, K. L., & Berman, M. G. (2018). Athought in the park: The influence of naturalness and low-level visual features on expressed thoughts. *Cognition, 174*, 82–93.

Schertz, K. E., Saxon, J., Cardenas-Iniguez, C., Bettencourt, L., Ding, Y., Hoffmann, H., & Berman, M. (2019). Neighborhood street activity and greenspace usage uniquely contribute to predicting crime. Preprint.

Schertz, K. E., Kardan, O., & Berman, M. G. (2020). Visual features influence thought content in the absence of overt semantic information. *Attention, Perception, & Psychophysics, 82*(8), 3945–3956.

Silvia, P. J., & Barona, C. M. (2009). Do people prefer curved objects? angularity, expertise, and aesthetic preference. *Empirical Studies of the Arts, 27*(1), 25–42.

Southworth, M. (2005). Designing the walkable city. *Journal of Urban Planning and Development, 131*(4), 246–257.

Stenfors, C. U., Van Hedger, S. C., Schertz, K. E., Meyer, F. A., Smith, K. E., Norman, G. J., ...others (2019). Positive effects of nature on cognitive performance across multiple experiments: Test order but not affect modulates the cognitive effects. *Frontiers in Psychology, 10*, 1413.

Stevenson, M. P., Schilhab, T., & Bentsen, P. (2018). Attention restoration theory ii: A systematic review to clarify attention processes affected by exposure to natural environments. *Journal of Toxicology and Environmental Health, Part B, 21*(4), 227–268.

Sugihara, G., May, R., Ye, H., Hsieh, C.-h., Deyle, E., Fogarty, M., & Munch, S. (2012). Detecting causality in complex ecosystems. *Science, 338*(6106), 496–500.

TripleQ. (2014). *Kirby is shaped like a friend*. Retrieved 2020-11-08, from https://www.youtube.com/watch?v=aPouHBYs6IY.

Ulrich, R. S., Simons, R. F., Losito, B. D., Fiorito, E., Miles, M. A., & Zelson, M. (1991). Stress recovery during exposure to natural and urban environments. *Journal of Environmental Psychology, 11*(3), 201–230.

Valtchanov, D., Barton, K. R., & Ellard, C. (2010). Restorative effects of virtual nature settings. *Cyberpsychology, Behavior, and Social Networking, 13*(5), 503–512.

Valtchanov, D., & Ellard, C. G. (2015). Cognitive and affective responses to natural scenes: effects of low level visual properties on preference, cognitive load and eye-movements. *Journal of Environmental Psychology, 43*, 184–195.

Van Hedger, S. C., Nusbaum, H. C., Clohisy, L., Jaeggi, S. M., Buschkuehl, M., & Berman, M. G. (2019a). Of cricket chirps and car horns: The effect of nature sounds on cognitive performance. *Psychonomic Bulletin & Review, 26*(2), 522–530.

Van Hedger, S. C., Nusbaum, H. C., Heald, S. L., Huang, A., Kotabe, H. P., & Berman, M. G. (2019b). The aesthetic preference for nature sounds depends on sound object recognition. *Cognitive Science, 43*(5), e12734.

Velarde, M. D., Fry, G., & Tveit, M. (2007). Health effects of viewing landscapes-landscape types in environmental psychology. *Urban Forestry & Urban Greening, 6*(4), 199–212.

Wang, K. (2013). Causality between built environment and travel behavior: Structural equations model applied to southern california. *Transportation Research Record, 2397*(1), 80–88.

Wilson, J. Q., & Kelling, G. L. (1982). Broken windows. *Atlantic Monthly, 249*(3), 29–38.

Xiao, J., Owens, A., & Torralba, A. (2013). Sun3d: A database of big spaces reconstructed using sfm and object labels. In *Proceedings of the ieee international conference on computer vision* (pp. 1625–1632).

Zhang, F., Zhou, B., Liu, L., Liu, Y., Fung, H. H., Lin, H., & Ratti, C. (2018). Measuring human perceptions of a large-scale urban region using machine learning. *Landscape and Urban Planning, 180*, 148–160.

Zhao, H., Shi, J., Qi, X., Wang, X., & Jia, J. (2017). Pyramid scene parsing network. In *Proceedings of the ieee conference on computer vision and pattern recognition* (pp. 2881–2890).

Who Sees What? Examining Urban Impressions in Global South Cities

Luis Emmanuel Medina Rios, Salvador Ruiz-Correa, Darshan Santani, and Daniel Gatica-Perez

1 Introduction

The online availability of large-scale urban imagery coming from social media or Google Street View, in combination with crowdsourcing-based image labeling and machine learning for visual recognition, are offering the possibility to build systems that can reason about a variety of urban phenomena (Salesses et al. 2013; Arietta et al. 2014; Dubey et al. 2016). In particular, understanding how people perceive and experience the urban environments we inhabit or visit—in aesthetics, affective, and social terms—is relevant for ubiquitous computing given the multiple connections between urban perception and personal and community well-being, e.g., the value of spending time in environments perceived as restorative (Florida et al. 2011; Rentfrow 2011; Lindal & Hartig 2013).

The state-of-the-art on machine recognition of urban perception (i.e., identifying if a place is perceived as safe, beautiful, or interesting) has essentially followed two stages: data labeling of perceived attributes by online crowdworkers who look at urban scenes (either volunteers (Salesses et al. 2013; Quercia et al. 2014) or

L. E. Medina Rios (✉)
EPFL, Lausanne, Switzerland
e-mail: luis.medinarios@epfl.ch

S. Ruiz-Correa
IPICYT, Mexico City, Mexico
e-mail: salvador.ruiz@ipicyt.edu.mx

D. Santani
Pepper Cloud, Singapore, Singapore
e-mail: dsantani@peppercloud.com

D. Gatica-Perez
Idiap Research Institute and EPFL, Martigny, Switzerland
e-mail: gatica@idiap.ch

© The Author(s), under exclusive license to Springer Nature Switzerland AG 2022   263
B. Ionescu et al. (eds.), *Human Perception of Visual Information*,
https://doi.org/10.1007/978-3-030-81465-6_10

remunerated workers Santani et al. 2015); followed by supervised learning methods that use such labels as ground-truth and attempt to generalize to unseen data (Naik et al. 2014; Ordonez & Berg 2014; Dubey et al. 2016). An increasing body of evidence is showing that blindly treating perceived attributes in this way can be problematic, and that research needs to account for the variety of contexts that affect human perception (Santani et al. 2017; Ma et al. 2017a, 2017b). Two fundamental issues in urban perception are: (1) how different kinds of observers might differ in their urban perceptions given their prior exposure to a place (i.e., locals vs. visitors) and thus produce different aesthetics or affective labels about the same scenes; and (2) what is the effect of these differences once they are implemented in machine inference systems. This is especially true when applying algorithms to world regions that are not well represented in digital terms, as is the case with many countries in the Global South (Shankar et al. 2017; DeVries et al. 2019). This also has important implications for urban analytic systems trained from crowdsourced data, given an (implicit or explicit) assumption in much of the current literature, namely that a model trained on a specific set of cities and human observers might generalize to other cities and to aesthetic or affective impressions by other people (Naik et al. 2014; Ordonez & Berg 2014; Dubey et al. 2016).

In the context of Global South cities, and using three cities in Mexico as a concrete case study, we address two research questions:

RQ1: Do local and non-local observers agree on the perception of urban dimensions in such cities? If not, what are the dimensions for which differences in perception are the largest, and what can explain such differences?

RQ2: Are there differences in the performance of machine inference systems trained to recognize urban scenes as locals perceive them, compared to how non-locals do? Are generic deep learning features equally effective for the two cases?

In this chapter, we address the above questions using the following approach. First, on a dataset of 1200 images collected from three cities in central Mexico, which correspond to different examples of urban density and economic activity, we collected a set of crowdsourced labels of urban impressions volunteered by young local inhabitants along six dimensions, namely *dangerous*, *dirty*, *interesting*, *pleasant*, *polluted*, and *pretty*. Local observers viewed and annotated images in an online setting comparable to the one used in our previous work (Santani et al. 2015), where we gathered impressions from Amazon Mechanical Turk (MTurk) workers.

Second, to characterize the content of the urban scenes under study, we extracted visual cues using both manual coding of high-level attributes derived from environmental psychology literature, and three versions of machine features extracted from convolutional neural networks (CNNs) pre-trained on large-scale scene data. This diversity of visual cues allows us to compare across representations of urban scenes: while manual cues correspond to semantic descriptors that one could expect to find in less privileged areas of cities worldwide (e.g. neglected vegetation), the CNN-derived features correspond to either scene types (e.g. alley) or object types (e.g. sky) present in urban images.

Third, we conducted a comparative analysis of urban perception by local and non-local online observers, using the impressions provided by the two groups of observers. Based on this analysis of crowdsourced labels, we find that non-local observers reach higher inter-observer agreement compared to local ones for most dimensions; and that these two groups disagree on what they report to perceive with respect to dimensions like danger and interest; namely, locals tend to perceive urban scenes as more dangerous than non-locals; while non-locals tend to see urban scenes as more interesting than locals. This result confirms, using 10 times more image data, a preliminary finding reported in our previous work Santani et al. (2017). Furthermore, we use additional sources of information, including open text provided by MTurk workers and in-situ discussions with local observers, to suggest plausible explanations for this finding.

Finally, we conducted a systematic evaluation of machine inference of urban perception variables in a regression setting. Using eight models corresponding to two sources of human labels (local and non-local) and four sources of visual cues, we find that (1) inference systems trained on impression labels provided by non-local observers result in higher performance (measured by the standard R^2 coefficient of determination) for three dimensions in the case of manual visual cues, and all six dimensions in the case of CNN features; (2) CNN features outperform manual cues for all the six urban perception dimensions for regressors trained on non-local labels, and (3) in contrast, manual visual cues outperform CNN features for all six urban dimensions when regressors are trained on labels by local observers. We discuss possible reasons for these trends, and also discuss about the implications of our findings for computing systems that use crowdsourced generation of subjective labels to analyze urban environments.

The chapter is organized as follows. Section 2 reviews related work and frames our work within the existing literature. Section 3 summarizes our methodology. Section 4 describes the image data and the protocol for collection of crowdsourced urban perception. Section 5 describes the methods used for manual and automatic extraction of visual cues from urban images. Section 6 presents the comparative analysis of urban perception by local and non-local observers. Section 7 presents and discusses the results of inferring urban perception. Section 8 discusses the implication of our findings. Section 9 provides final remarks.

2 Related Work

In this section, we review work related to perception of urban attributes using crowdsourcing, and machine recognition of urban perception from visual data.

2.1 Perception of Urban Attributes using Crowdsourcing

In environmental psychology, urban planning, and architecture, the visual assessment of landscapes (including urban ones) has used a suite of well-established methodologies (Kaplan et al. 1989; Daniel 2001), spanning the in-situ observation of environments (Russell & Pratt 1980), the use of on-street pedestrian surveys (Painter 1996), and the assessment of both real and synthetic urban imagery (Lindal & Hartig 2013). Online, geo-referenced imaging resources like Google Street View (GSV) have been more recently used as part of visual assessment tools of urban environments (Bader et al. 2015). Crowdsourcing research has also proposed to use GSV in combination with online crowdsourcing to collect labels of urban perception, making use of the large-scale nature of GSV and the potential availability of online workers who can observe images and provide their impressions (Salesses et al. 2013; Quercia et al. 2014). In the work by Salesses et al. (2013), a set of 4000 GSV images from four cities, two in the US (New York City and Boston) and two in Austria (Salzburg and Linz) were labeled with respect to three dimensions: *class* (later renamed as *wealth*), *safety*, and *uniqueness*. This dataset (dubbed Place Pulse 1.0) was labeled by online volunteers using a pairwise procedure, where pairs of images were relatively ranked with respect to each of these attributes. In the work by Quercia et al. (2014), following similar goals and techniques, a dataset of 500 GSV images from London were labeled for three attributes: *beauty*, *happiness*, and *quietness*. In the work by Dubey et al. (2016), a large dataset of pair-wise rankings for 100K GSV images from 56 large cities (Place Pulse 2.0) was sparsely labeled for six attributes: *beautiful, boring, depressing, lively, safe,* and *wealthy*. While the attributes used in these works have been adapted from existing environmental psychology literature, no systematic methodological justification for their choice was provided.

Most of the research described above has focused on cities in the US and Western Europe. This opens an opportunity to study cities in the Global South with similar approaches, as three quarters of the 100 largest populated urban areas worldwide are in the Global South (List of Largest Cities 2021). However, key factors need to be reconsidered. In many cities, online imaging resources like GSV might not have wide coverage. The use of phones as infrastructure to collect urban images becomes an attractive alternative in these cases (Ruiz-Correa et al. 2014). Furthermore, citizens from countries in the Global South do not often have the same access to online platforms to contribute annotations (e.g. Amazon's Mechanical Turk is not available to workers in most countries). This can pose significant limits to the collection of crowdsourced urban impressions from local inhabitants. Some work in these two directions (collecting crowdsourced impressions about Global South cities, and collecting urban impression labels specifically from locals) has been proposed in our previous work Santani et al. (2015, 2017) for the case of Mexico and by Candeia et al. (2017) for Brazil. Although not necessarily focused on urban perception as studied here, there has been considerable work on citizen participation for mapping and community-related purposes in Latin America (Offenhuber & Lee

2012; Balestrini et al. 2014; Caminos de la 2021; Connors 2014), Asia (Sturgis 2015), and Africa (Map Kibera 2021). The starting point for the work described in this chapter is the dataset from our previous work Santani et al. (2015). This consists of 1200 urban images collected in three cities in Central Mexico of diverse characteristics, for which we have additionally collected online impressions from local volunteers for six attributes, and which allows us to systematically compare the views of local inhabitants and AMT crowdworkers (*dangerous*, *dirty*, *interesting*, *pleasant*, *polluted*, and *pretty*.) As shown in Santani et al. (2015), these variables provide some coverage of the circumplex model of affect for environments (Russell & Pratt 1980).

2.2 *Situated Crowdsourcing and Local Knowledge*

Another related topic is situated crowdsourcing. This form of crowdsourcing exploits the availability of users to provide on-demand information via input devices like public displays embedded in the physical space (Goncalves et al. 2017). This view of crowdsourcing has seen interest in the last few years (Marshall et al. 2011; Heimerl et al. 2012; Goncalves et al. 2013, 2017) in the context of citizen participation and healthcare. Situated crowdsourcing requires available local contributors, who can respond to the needs of the task requester. Specifically to our research, some work has been done to understand the differences between local and non-local contributors with respect to performance in tasks that may need local knowledge. In the work by Goncalves et al. (2013), it was shown that situated crowdsourcing involving local contributors (university students interacting with large displays deployed on campus) was comparable to online crowdsourcing involving MTurk workers, in terms of task accuracy and task uptake rate, for tasks that did not require local knowledge (e.g., counting malaria infected blood cells in medical images). In other related work Goncalves et al. (2017), crowdsourced tasks that required local knowledge of the city were compared to more generic tasks. Some of the tasks involved photo taking. This work found that certain tasks requiring local knowledge were more attractive to the participants, as they gave them an opportunity to share such knowledge. In contrast to the above work, in which task performance can be objectively estimated given the fact-finding nature of the task (e.g. counting cells), we collect online judgments of urban impressions from locals and non-locals. In principle, many of these attributes have no unique ground-truth, so we can expect differences between the two types of observers, given their exposure to specific places.

2.3   Machine Recognition of Urban Perception Attributes

Approaches for automatic recognition of urban perception attributes have been proposed, using the datasets described in Sect. 2.1. The visual cues used in previous work have ranged from standard low-level descriptors, including color and a variety of texture features like Histogram of Oriented Gradients (HOG) (Dalal & Triggs 2005) and Scale-Invariant Feature Transform (SIFT) (Lowe 2004), to more recent CNN-derived features. In the work by Naik et al. (2014) and Ordonez and Berg (2014), recognition of the Place Pulse 1.0 urban perception attributes (*safety*, *uniqueness*, *wealth*) was done for New York City and Boston. In the work by Porzi et al. (2015), a study on automatic pairwise ranking of urban images was conducted for the *safety* attribute from the four cities of Place Pulse 1.0 using a CNN. This approach did not provide an automatically generated rating for a place, but rather compared pairs of places, which departs from the standard way of reasoning about place attributes in environmental psychology, in which places are independently rated (Russell & Pratt 1980). In the work by Arietta et al. (2014), a method that also used GSV images was proposed to automatically infer urban attributes (e.g. housing prices) from visual cues (HOG+color). In the work by Gebru et al. (2017), image data from GSV processed with CNNs to extract vehicle semantic descriptors (brand, model, and year) was used to find connections between neighborhoods in 200 US cities and income indicators (an attribute connected to the *wealth* dimension studied in previous work). Finally, in the work by Dubey et al. (2016), the Place Pulse 2.0 dataset was used to compare pairs of city scenes using a CNN for the six available urban perception dimensions. This approach thus follows the same idea of Porzi et al. (2015) of inferring relative rankings among pairs of places, reporting a pairwise accuracy of 73.5%. This is one of the few works reporting automatic inference of urban perception attributes on data from Global South cities, although the paper itself does not discuss the specific performance on such cities. A second exception is our previous work Santani et al. (2018), which presented an approach based on visual feature extraction using a pre-trained CNN, followed by a second regression module to infer urban perception attributes collected from AMT workers as presented in Santani et al. (2015).

We have used our previous work Santani et al. (2018) as starting point, and substantially extend the studied visual representations, which include both high-level descriptors of urban scene components manually generated by young observers, as well as three automated CNN-derived image representations. Furthermore, we study the effects of training CNNs with urban perception labels generated by local and non-local observers, and quantify the differences in performance obtained for each observer group. As we discuss later in the paper, this has important implications for AI systems for urban analytics trained from crowdsourced data, given the assumption in much of the current literature (Naik et al. 2014; Ordonez & Berg 2014; Dubey et al. 2016), that a model trained on a specific set of cities and human observers will generalize to other cities and to impressions by other people.

3   Methodology

Our methodology involves the following stages: selection of urban perception labels; collection of impressions; extraction of visual cues; and inference from visual cues. Each stage is summarized as follows.

Selection of Urban Perception Labels (Sect. 4)   Six attributes were chosen following the methodology in Ruiz-Correa et al. (2014) and Santani et al. (2017): *dangerous*, *dirty*, *interesting*, *pleasant*, *polluted* and *pretty*. These attributes describe the scene and environment in which the image dataset is based. Let us recall that the state of Guanajuato, as a tourist destination in Mexico, can elicit different responses from observers, from negative ones (e.g., concerns about streets with tag graffiti) to positive ones (e.g., enjoyment of the colonial architecture of some buildings, see Fig. 1 for examples). In the rest of the chapter, we use the terms *urban perception label* and *label* interchangeably.

Fig. 1 Samples from the image corpus. The shown images were selected randomly; each row represents a city. Top: Guanajuato; Middle: Silao; Bottom: Leon. For privacy reasons, images have a reduced resolution

Collection of Impressions (Sect. 4) To collect impressions of urban visual attributes, we use two approaches: (1) a crowdsourcing task where the annotators were local with respect to the cities presented in the image dataset; and (2) a crowdsourcing task in which the raters were part of a foreign-born population that did not know anything specific about the images they assessed.

Extraction of Visual Cues (Sect. 5) Two different methods to extract visual cues are used: CNNs and manual coding. First, CNNs are an example of what can be automatically extracted with current computer vision methods. Concretely, we use 3 different pre-trained CNNs (DilatedNet Semantic Segmentation: 150 features; GoogLeNet places205: 205 features; and GoogLeNet places365: 365 features) to extract visual cues at the object- or scene-level, based on the final layer of class probabilities using the Caffe Jia et al. (2014) framework. Before extraction, images were re-sized to 256×256 pixels and pre-processed by mean image subtraction. In contrast, manual coding provided by local observers, following a procedure adapted from the Block Environmental Inventory (BEI) (Perkins et al. 1992), is a way to explore specific high-level visual cues that are not included in the set of features extracted by the pre-trained CNNs. Throughout the chapter, we use the terms *visual cues* and *features* interchangeably.

Inference from Visual Cues (Sect. 6) The automatic inference methods produce continuous values for each inferred urban perception attribute. Specifically, we use Random Forests to implement a regression task in which the dependent variables are the urban perception labels and the independent variables are the visual features. To measure the performance of the regression task, we use the coefficient of determination (R^2). We use cross-validation with $k = 10$ folds and report the mean over these 10 runs.

4 Data: Images and Impressions

4.1 Image Dataset

We conduct our study on the image corpus generated in the Urban Data Challenge (UDC) explained in (Santani et al. 2015), where 7000 images were taken from a first-person perspective by young student volunteers with their smartphones in the state of Guanajuato (located in central Mexico with a population of about 6 million inhabitants, most of them urban (70%)). Students attended a public high-school in Guanajuato, the *Colegio de Estudios Científicos y Tecnológicos del Estado de Guanajuato* (CECYTE). This high school provides education on science, technology, and humanities to low-income youth living in Guanajuato City and surrounding areas. Students were altruistically motivated and eager to contribute to improve the understanding of their city. A partnership that included school authorities, teachers, parents, and a local research team supported the experiment.

From the collected images, 1200 were selected in groups of 400 images for each of the three cities that were chosen to collect the images: (1) Guanajuato City (170,000 inhabitants), which is a UNESCO world heritage site and whose economic activity relies mostly on tourism—a fact that makes local inhabitants care about the image of their city; (2) Leon City (1.6 million inhabitants, the seventh most populated metropolitan area in Mexico), which is an industrial and business center with factories specialized on leather and footwear products; and (3) Silao City (147,000 inhabitants), which is an industrial city, with industrial parks and automotive component companies due to the presence a major US car assembly plant. The images were collected in 2015 during daytime.

The volunteers participating in the image data collection tried to capture in pictures the characteristics of each of the three cities, documenting different neighborhoods and iconic places. Volunteers ventured in many of the neighborhoods of the city, except those in the suburbs of two of the cities (known to be unsafe). Please refer to Santani et al. (2015) and Ruiz-Correa et al. (2017) for a detailed explanation of the urban image collection process. Examples of the images taken can be seen in Fig. 1.

4.2 Impressions by Local Observers

In our experimental protocol, 120 additional student volunteers from CECYTE provided the local impressions (43 women and 77 men). At the time of the study, 80% were 16 years old, 15% were 17 years old, and 5% were 18 years old. To gather annotations, we followed a protocol similar to the one used in our previous work Santani et al. (2017). After conducting recruiting activities for a 1-month period, 120 volunteers were chosen from a school population of 1100 students. Each volunteer was required to have a signed parental approval and travel insurance to take part in the image labeling experiment. The experiment was conducted over a period of a month, in which groups of about 40 students visited computing facilities at IPICYT to perform the task. During the visit, students were given a meal and a guided tour to the computing facilities, after which they performed the labeling experiment. Data collected from volunteers during the experiment was anonymized, and personal information (age and gender) was only gathered for general statistics but not linked to each person's annotations.

The gathering of local impressions was conducted through a custom-built website, comparable in basic functionalities to the one used by MTurk workers (see next subsection). Six urban perception attributes were labeled during the experiment (*dangerous, dirty, interesting, pleasant, polluted* and *pretty*). In comparison to previous work, Salesses et al. (2013) labeled three attributes (*safety, uniqueness,* and *wealth*), two of which are also covered by our work with different names and in some cases inverted scale (*dangerous* for *safety*). Quercia et al. (2014) labeled three attributes (*beauty, happiness,* and *quietness*), one of which is also covered by

Table 1 Number and percentage of images containing potentially identifying place characteristics

Feature	Cities			Total	Percentage ($N = 1200$ images)
	Silao	Leon	Guanajuato		
People	168	291	70	529	44.08
Signs in Spanish	41	16	1	58	4.83

our work with a different name (*pretty* for *beauty*). Dubey et al. (2016) labeled six attributes (*beautiful, boring, depressing, lively, safe,* and *wealthy*), three of which are covered by our work with different names and sometimes inverted scale (*dangerous* for *safe*; *interesting* for *boring*; *pretty* for *beautiful*). In summary, three of our attributes have not been studied in these previous works (*dirty, pleasant, polluted*), while the other three have been studied. Besides the labels, students also labeled 10 high-level semantic descriptors following the procedure described in Sect. 5.2.

Each volunteer worked independently with a high resolution monitor to annotate 50 images. A team of three supervisors facilitated the process. On average, each volunteer spent 1.5 h to complete all annotations. Five annotations from independent observers were gathered per image, per label, and per semantic descriptor. A seven-point Likert scale was used to assess the urban perception labels (from 1: Strongly disagree to 7: Strongly agree). The online experiment followed the Code of Ethics and Conduct of the British Psychological Society.

In the online experiment, students were not given any information about the urban place being displayed. However, we acknowledge that some of the images contain identifying characteristics of the captured places, such as signs in Spanish as well as other details (e.g. flags) that might give away the location to some degree. It is known that people can pinpoint where a photo was taken Piasco et al. (2018). To quantify this issue, we manually annotated the 1200 image corpus for the following attributes: presence of people passing by, who could have dressing style characteristics more commonly expected in certain neighborhoods of a big city or in a small town (Matzen et al. 2017); and presence of signs in Spanish, which could help observers identify specific local businesses. Table 1 shows the number of images of our dataset that contain these attributes. While the presence of passersby is frequent (44% of the images), signs are substantially less common (4.8%.)

4.3 Impressions by Non-local Observers

Crowdsourcing of non-local impressions was conducted through Amazon's Mechanical Turk, in a process originally discussed in Santani et al. (2015). 146 US-based Master workers, with a minimum of 95% approval rate, were chosen to complete the corresponding HITs (Human Intelligence Tasks). Every HIT consisted of observing one image and providing impressions for each of the six urban perception labels. All annotations were done on a seven-point Likert scale (from 1: Strongly disagree to 7: Strongly agree), just as local observers did. The workers were not told about the source or location of the images, or about the cities in the study, to reduce potential bias. A number of 10 annotations were gathered per image and per label, making a total of 144,000 individual judgments.

Regarding demographics, 77 of the workers answered a post-task survey. For gender, 58% of respondents were women and 42% were men. For ethnicity, 80% of respondents were White/Caucasian, 12% Asian, 3% Hispanic/Latino, and 3% Black/African American. For age group, the distribution was as follows: 3% of respondents were 18–24 years-old, 32% were 25–34 years-old, 43% were 35–50 years-old, and 22% were 50+ years-old. Regarding residence, 18% lived in a big city, 18% in a small-to-mid-sized town, 45% in the suburbs, and 18% were rural. Finally, 23% of respondents reported visits to developing countries, and 44% of these respondents (i.e., 10% of the total workers) had visited Mexico. This last response was collected via free text (i.e., no written clues about the country where the images were taken were provided by the experiment.) In sum, the combination of low self-reported Hispanic/Latino ethnicity (3%) and the low number of people reporting previous visits to Mexico (10%) suggests that the MTurk workers who participated in our task qualify overall as non-local observers. More details about the online crowdsourcing task can be found in Santani et al. (2015).

5 Visual Cue Extraction

In this section, we describe the visual cues, both machine-generated features and manually labeled semantic descriptors used in the study.

5.1 Extraction of Visual Cues via CNNs

Using CNN architectures, we extract the following features:

DilatedNet Semantic Segmentation: 150 features This consists of 150 visual features resulting from applying deep learning techniques using a pre-trained semantic segmentation network called DilatedNet (Yu & Koltun 2016). The features include both indoor and outdoor generic elements such as wall, building, sky, floor, tree, etc. The images are described with the actual proportion of each of the features.

GoogLeNet places205: 205 Features This is based on the extraction of 205 visual cues using the final layer with class probabilities of a pre-trained CNN based on the GoogLeNet architecture trained on the places205 database (Zhou et al. 2014). This popular database, in its first version, allows to describe an image with place-related labels related to our image dataset, like alley, basilica, corridor, church, residential neighborhood, etc.

GoogLeNet places365: 365 Features The places365 database is an update of the places205 database and consists of around 1.8 million of training pictures. In this case, it uses the same CNN architecture (GoogLeNet), but trained on the new database (Zhou et al. 2017). This contains 365 visual features that were extracted by using the final layer with class probabilities. The features include almost the 205 from the places205 database and approximately 160 more, including categories like bazaar, downtown, flea market, house, industrial area, junkyard, park, promenade, etc. We decided to use both versions of the places databases to examine concrete benefits of using a more expressive vocabulary of scene labels during the automatic inference experiments.

5.2   Extraction of Visual Cues via Manual Coding and Local Annotation

While CNNs offer good performance in terms of extracting object-level and scene-level elements from the pictures, other high-level visual cues can evoke certain atmospheres. For example, how people can perceive danger is discussed in Blobaum and Marcel (2005) through the concept of perceived personal danger, i.e., the general fear of people to become a victim. More specifically, people walking at night might look at physical elements that can become an obstacle from escaping in case of danger (blocking elements or enclosed spaces), and also look at places with poor outdoor lighting. Other authors studied the relationship between tranquility and danger by conducting correlation analyses for natural and urban settings and three elements, namely nature, openness, and degree of care (Herzog & Chernick 2000). These three elements (nature, openness and care) are very general, yet one could relate them with semantic cues, e.g. *nature* can be related to the presence of visual cues such as plants, trees, or grass. *Openness* can be related to the presence of parks, plazas, or wide streets. Finally, *care* could be negatively related to visual cues such as litter on the street.

To manually extract a set of visual cues relevant to our dataset, we implemented a two-stage process. In the first stage, we defined a set of high-level visual cues. For this, we did a manual analysis based on a sample of images for two of the six labels, namely *dirty* and *dangerous*. We decided to focus on these two labels as they could correspond to visual concepts that are not sufficiently represented in existing databases used to train CNN models (Shankar et al. 2017). This procedure was based on a random sample of images for which attention was paid to understand specific visual cues, for example, understanding differences between tag graffiti (Fig. 2a) from artistic graffiti (Fig. 2b). This task was implemented by the first author, who was born and raised in Mexico, and therefore understands the context of the pictures. We then clustered the features defined from the above procedure using the *Block Environmental Inventory* (BEI) defined in Perkins et al. (1992), which uses three types of physical cues for *incivilities, vandalism and dilapidated*

(a) Tag graffiti   (b) Graffiti

Fig. 2 Examples of (**a**) tag graffiti and (**b**) artistic graffiti

houses; *signs of territorial functioning*; and *defensible space features*. Finally, we found 10 clusters of high-level visual cues that are part of the BEI and used them as part of the image annotation procedure described in Sect. 4.2. In alphabetical order, the semantic descriptors are: *deteriorated roads*; *lack of maintenance*; *lack of outdoor lighting*; *lack of security elements*; *littering*; *neglected vegetation*; *poor urban planning*; *unkempt houses/buildings*; *vacant lots*; and *vandalism*.

In the second stage, we gather the annotations of these 10 semantic descriptors in a binary way for all images (1 if the semantic descriptor appears in the image, and 0 otherwise) as part of the annotation process by student volunteers described in Sect. 4.2. Finally, for each picture and for each semantic descriptor, we aggregate the annotations to compute the mean over all annotators. The result is a number between 0 and 1 for each of the semantic descriptors, that can be seen as an empirical probability of the descriptor appearing in the picture. As mentioned earlier in this section, the process above was implemented only for two of the six attributes we analyze. However, as we show later, these manual cues have also explanatory power for some of the other labels.

6 Comparing Impressions Between local and Non-local Observers (RQ1)

In this section, we first present an analysis of the reliability of the collected impressions, followed by the presentation of their descriptive statistics; a comparison of the impressions for local and non-local observers; and a qualitative analysis of the collected impressions, which complements the quantitative analysis.

6.1 Annotation Quality: Inter-Rater Reliability

To measure the quality of the labels in terms of inter-rater reliability, we computed intraclass correlation (ICC) on each of the labels across the image corpus (Koo & Li 2016). Since each of the images is rated by a set of k annotators randomly selected from a larger population of K annotators (Santani et al. 2017), we chose the *One-Way Random-Effects Model* (Koo and Li 2016), known as *ICC(1,k)*.

The inter-rater agreement of the non-local observers was detailed in Santani et al. (2015). However, since we only consider 5 annotations per image for the local observers and to be fair in the comparison, we computed *ICC(1,k)* by randomly sampling 5 (out of 10) annotations, doing this 10 times and getting the mean and standard deviation over these 10 values. Results of the computed *ICC(1,k)* are reported in Table 2. Note that throughout this section, we will also use the results obtained in Santani et al. (2017), in which another set of 99 images from Guanajuato City was annotated. With respect to other previous work on crowdsourced urban perception (Salesses et al. 2013; Quercia et al. 2014; Dubey et al. 2016), note that the way in which the labels were obtained is different. The three works above used pair-wise comparisons, i.e., observers saw pairs of images and gave a relative ranking for the pair with respect to each attribute. In contrast, we collect individual ratings, where each image is assessed independently. This procedure allows to estimate measures of inter-observer agreement like ICC, unlike (Salesses et al. 2013; Quercia et al. 2014; Dubey et al. 2016), which do not report such measures of agreement.

According to Table 2, we see that for $k = 5$ annotators there is higher agreement among non-locals compared to locals. ICC values indicate moderate reliability (values between 0.5 and 0.75) for all labels except for *polluted* (Koo & Li 2016). Note that we use the term reliability in the usual sense in psychology (i.e., a measure of inter-observer agreement). For locals, three labels indicate moderate reliability: *interesting*, *pleasant* and *pretty*, while *polluted* is the label with the lowest agreement among raters. Label *pleasant* (resp. *pretty*) achieved the highest agreement among non-locals (resp. locals). Comparing the two groups for $k = 10$, we see a similar tendency as shown in Santani et al. (2017): non-local raters tend to agree more for

Table 2 *ICC(1,k)* scores, including standard deviation and mean values for the non-local case. Please note that the "–" indicates that the label was not included in the corresponding study

	Non-locals			Locals	
Label	$k = 5$ Mean $\pm$ SD	$k = 10$ Santani et al. (2018)	$k = 10$ Santani et al. (2017)	$k = 5$	$k = 10$ Santani et al. (2017)
Dangerous	0.62 ± 0.01	0.76	0.83	0.34	0.63
Dirty	0.65 ± 0.01	0.78	0.85	0.36	0.68
Interesting	0.54 ± 0.01	0.70	0.63	0.52	0.70
Pleasant	0.67 ± 0.01	0.79	–	0.56	–
Polluted	0.46 ± 0.02	0.64	–	0.28	–
Pretty	0.61 ± 0.01	0.73	0.83	0.58	0.80

most of the labels compared to local raters. Note that by definition, the ICC values are higher for larger k.

6.2 Descriptive Statistics

We follow the procedure described in Santani et al. (2017) to aggregate the values of the scores: the annotations rely on an ordinal scale (that also describes a ranking), and knowing that one of the statistics to get the central tendency of an ordinal scale is the median (Stevens 1946), we compute it on each of the 5 scores per image. Given these median scores, we compute the mean and the standard deviation per label using the image corpus.

Table 3 shows the descriptive statistics of the labels. All mean scores for both locals and non-locals, on the 1200 image corpus, show a trend towards disagreement, as values are below 4 on the seven-point Likert scale, which corresponds to *somewhat disagree*). Examining previous work, when comparing the two groups based on the 99 image corpus in Santani et al. (2017), we see that local observers overall tend to perceive the images as more *dangerous*, *dirtier* and *prettier*, while the non-local observers tend to perceive the images as more *interesting*. We find the same pattern in our data, except for the label *pretty*. Regarding *polluted* and *pleasant*, we see that locals perceive images as more *polluted*, while non-locals perceive them as more *pleasant*. A detailed comparison is presented in Sect. 6.3.

We also perform a Spearman's correlation analysis of the local and non-local median scores (Fig. 3a), and we get similar results as with the non-local people's study in Santani et al. (2018) (Fig. 3b): There are two groups of labels which are positively correlated among them and negatively correlated with the other group. These are *interesting*, *pretty*, and *pleasant* (referred to as positive labels in the rest of the analysis); and *dangerous*, *dirty*, and *polluted* (referred to as negative labels.) We see that correlation absolute values are generally higher for the non-local annotations than for the local ones.

Table 3 Means and standard deviations of the annotation scores for each label and group. Please note that the "–" indicates that the label was not included in the study

| Label | Non-locals | | Locals | |
	Mean ± SD Santani et al. (2018)	Mean ± SD	Mean ± SD	Mean ± SD Santani et al. (2017)
Dangerous	2.98 ± 1.00	3.19 ± 1.20	3.78 ± 1.45	4.43 ± 0.91
Dirty	3.16 ± 1.10	3.25 ± 1.26	3.53 ± 1.53	4.33 ± 1.24
Interesting	3.84 ± 0.90	4.14 ± 1.10	3.00 ± 1.54	3.55 ± 1.23
Pleasant	3.82 ± 1.00	–	3.08 ± 1.58	–
Polluted	2.89 ± 0.90	–	3.39 ± 1.38	–
Pretty	3.11 ± 1.00	3.25 ± 1.36	3.04 ± 1.65	3.47 ± 1.38

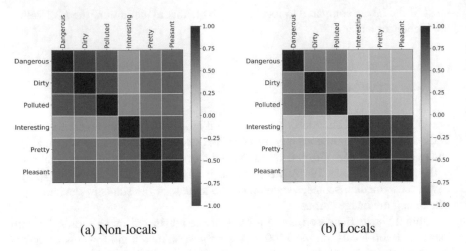

(a) Non-locals   (b) Locals

Fig. 3 Correlation matrix of the six urban perception labels for (**a**) non-locals, and (**b**) locals ($N = 1200$, $p < 0.05$ for all entries of the matrix)

Table 4 Tukey's HSD statistics. Lo and NLo stands for locals and non-locals. Values in bold are statistically significant with the indicated p-value. Note that the "–" indicates that the label was not included in the study used for comparison Santani et al. (2017)

Label	Group pair	Image corpus: 1200 images		Image corpus: 99 images Santani et al. (2017)	
		Mean difference	p-value	Mean difference	p-value
Dangerous	Lo-NLo	+0.79	**<0.001**	+1.24	**<0.001**
Dirty	Lo-NLo	+0.37	**<0.001**	+1.08	**<0.001**
Interesting	Lo-NLo	−0.85	**<0.001**	−0.59	**0.005**
Pleasant	Lo-NLo	−0.74	**<0.001**	–	–
Polluted	Lo-NLo	+0.50	**<0.001**	–	–
Pretty	Lo-NLo	−0.07	0.21	+0.22	0.24

6.3 Comparing Impressions Between Groups

6.3.1 Pair-Wise Analysis

We now compare the impressions between the two groups of observers. We want to understand if the mean difference of the labels between the two groups is statistically significant. We perform the Tukey's Honest Significant Difference (HSD) test, and present it in Table 4. Furthermore, to compare our findings, we also include the results of our previous work, which investigated such differences on a smaller, 99-image dataset (Santani et al. 2017). We complement this by plotting the distribution of the perception scores between the two groups of raters in Fig. 4.

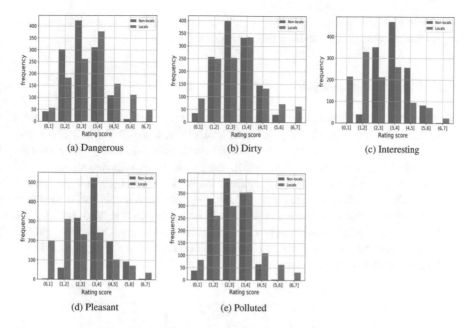

Fig. 4 Plots comparing the distributions of perception scores between non-locals (blue) and locals (orange). Only those labels whose mean difference in the Tukey's HSD test were statistically significant at $p < 0.05$ are included. (**a**) Dangerous. (**b**) Dirty. (**c**) Interesting. (**d**) Pleasant. (**e**) Polluted

Based on the statistics summarized in Table 4, we observe that:

1. Images were perceived as more *dangerous*, *dirtier*, and more *polluted* by the local observers compared to non-locals (local-to-non-local differences: +0.79, +0.37, and +0.50 in Table 4, respectively). This tendency was also seen in Santani et al. (2017) for *dangerous* and *dirty*. When looking at the individual median scores per image, we found that for locals, 73% of the images were rated to be more *dangerous*, 61% were rated to be *dirtier* and 75% were rated to be more *polluted*. For these three labels, one can see in Fig. 4 that they have a very similar distribution for locals along the Likert scale.

2. Images were perceived as more *interesting* and *pleasant* by the non-locals (local-to-non-local differences: −0.85, and −0.74 in Table 4, respectively). A similar result was also obtained in Santani et al. (2017) for the *interesting* attribute. When looking at the individual median scores per image (Fig. 4), we found that for non-locals 64% of the pictures were rated as more *interesting*, and 58% were rated as more *pleasant*.

3. Finally, we found that the range of perceptions for the label *pretty* is not statistically different between local and non-local people. (local-to-non-local difference: −0.07, in Table 4). A similar result was also obtained in Santani et al. (2017)

Overall, it is relevant that these results match several of our previous findings (Santani et al. 2017), while using 12 times more data.

6.3.2 Scatter Plot Analysis

The previous analysis is complemented by a scatter plot analysis. The scatter plots of the 5 statistically significantly different labels (based on the Tukey's HSD test) are shown in Fig. 5. Based on them, we confirm that for *interesting* and *pleasant*, many points are above the 45° line, which means that non-locals had a tendency to give higher scores to many images for these labels. In contrast, for *dangerous* and *polluted*, many points are below the 45° line, meaning that locals had a tendency to give higher scores to many images for these labels. In the next section, we will discuss two pictures with opposite scores for the two groups for two labels: *dangerous* and *interesting*. These pictures are identified with the tags *I-1* and *I-2* within the scatter plots shown in Fig. 5.

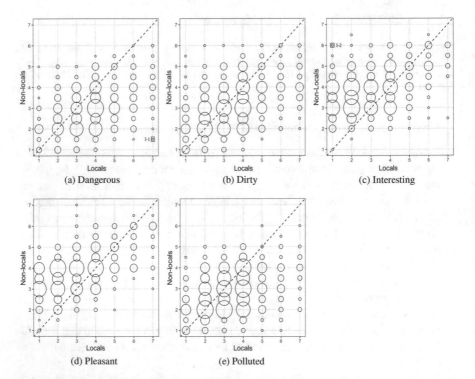

Fig. 5 Scatter plots showing the pair-wise annotator scores by locals and non-locals, for the 5 labels which statistically significant mean difference in Tukey's HSD test. Each circle corresponds to an image, with the size of the circle proportional to the number of observations. A 45° line is also shown in all the plots. Two dots are highlighted in the plots as I-1 and I-2, corresponding to Fig. 9. (**a**) Dangerous. (**b**) Dirty. (**c**) Interesting. (**d**) Pleasant. (**e**) Polluted

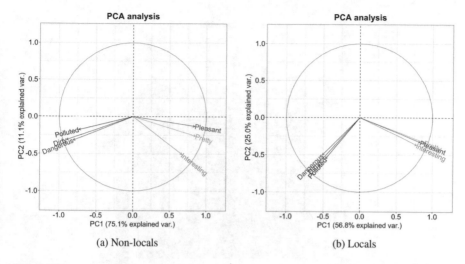

Fig. 6 PCA analysis on the aggregated median scores. The six variables are projected on the first two principal components for (**a**) non-local impressions; and (**b**) local impressions. Positive (resp. negative) variables are plotted in shades of green (resp. red)

6.3.3 Correlation Analysis

Finally, we perform a PCA analysis on the aggregated median scores for both locals and non-locals. Fig. 6 shows the projection of the labels on the two main principal components. We note that the results, while not exactly the same, are quite similar: the first two principal components explain over 80% of the variance, and the loading weights point to the same quadrants. We also see that *dangerous*, *dirty*, and *polluted* point to the negative side of the first principal component, while *pleasant*, *interesting*, and *pretty* point to the positive side. The first principal component seems to correspond to a valence-like dimension in the valence/arousal circumplex model of affect for environments proposed by Russell and Pratt (1980). If the first component is seen as valence, then the *dirty* and *dangerous* attributes are projected as negative, while *pretty* and *pleasant* are projected as positive (see Fig. 6). We corroborate this trend when we compute the correlation between the aggregated scores of both groups (Fig. 7): the same subset of labels (positive and negative) are positively correlated within the same subset, but negatively correlated with the opposite subset.

6.4 Qualitative Analysis of Impressions

During the data collection process, all non-local MTurk observers were asked to optionally provide comments about the images they labeled, as a means to document

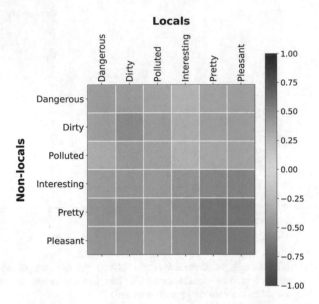

Fig. 7 Correlation matrix of the annotations of non-locals and locals ($N = 1200$, $p < 0.05$ for all entries of the matrix)

(a)   (b)   (c)

Fig. 8 Images that elicited diverging perceptions from local and non-local annotators. (**a**) The scene in image was perceived as dangerous by locals, less so by non-locals. (**b**) This scene was perceived as interesting by locals, and differently by non-locals. (**c**) This scene elicited comments by locals about being interesting, while it elicited other opinions by non-locals, e.g. about perceived safety

additional impressions of the depicted scenes. A subset of local observers was also asked to provide their comments on a small number of images. The qualitative analysis of these comments complements the statistical analysis of quality and pairwise differences of the annotations presented in Sect. 6.1. We provide five examples of images (Figs. 8 and 9) that evoked different impressions between locals and non-locals.

(a) Dangerous: I-1   (b) Interesting: I-2

Fig. 9 Images with large differences in perception between local and non-local annotators. (a) The scores for *dangerous* are 7 for locals and 1.5 for non-locals. (b) The scores for *interesting* are 1 for locals and 6 for non-locals. Reduced image resolution and pixelation have been used in (a) for privacy reasons. (a) Dangerous: I-1. (b) Interesting: I-2

A first example is shown in Fig. 8a. For the local annotators, the depicted site is perceived as dangerous, while for the non-locals it evokes other reactions. Locals seem to use specific visual cues to establish that the urban site depicted in the image is dangerous (stairs poor condition, lack of illumination, the presence of a water spill on the stairs, and exposed pipes.) More specifically, they argued that the stairs and walls are quite deteriorated and the presence of liquids make them slippery and difficult to use for children and the elderly: *"[Stairs are] dangerous because there is water and the steps are not well built, moreover, the space to pass is narrow"*, *"The steps on the alley look slippery due to [water] spills"* and *"The steps are short, people could run into the water pipes and fall down also due to the poor condition of the steps"*. Some annotators also express concern about vandalism and the lack of light in the space at night. *"[The alley] is dangerous because there are no light sources and very few people walk by"*, *"I think that this place is dangerous because it is a narrow alley and there is no light"* and *"Given the area and location, it looks like people gather to paint graffiti on the walls at night"*. MTurk workers, on the other hand, focused their comments on emotions that do not necessarily reflect a sense of danger: *"It makes me feel sad, oppressed and depressed, like the world is closing in on me in a non-physical sense"* or *"It makes me feel claustrophobic"*. Other comments are more linked to danger: *"Makes me feel as if I have turned down the wrong path into a back alley, or stairwell, that I should not have"* or *"It makes me feel cramped and like I might trip and fall"*.

A second example is shown in Fig. 8b. Local annotators perceive the site as interesting, in contrast with non-locals, who focus on visual cues that relate to other attributes. Local annotators say: *"[The place is interesting] because the street is wide and you have a view of the city"*, *"It looks interesting to me because of the structure and the steep ramp"*, *"It is interesting because of the view, the sunlight and it looks peaceful"*, *"This place looks interesting given the distribution of houses and the stone pavement"*, *"I like how it looks like and the trees make it look better"* or *"The place looks well maintained and pretty"*. Non-local annotators expressed a different view: They noted that: *"[the place] makes me feel like I should just keeping moving through if I found myself there"*, *"This area seems slightly isolated so it makes me feel slightly unsafe and weary"* or *"Looks like poor area where there is poverty"*.

A third example is shown in Fig. 8c. For some locals, the place is uninteresting: *"[The place] is boring, because it is only one alley with many steps"*, *"Boring, because it is only one alley with many steps"*, *"There are only stairs, I would not like living there, it will not be easy to walk or run"* or *"I like that the alley has many steps; by climbing up couple of steps to enter a house and I like the way to reach other houses through the alley"*. For others, *"the place is interesting because of the long and high stairs"*, and *"because the plants on the alley stand out"*. Non-locals focused on attributes leading to a different view: *"One structure in the background in what appears to be perfect condition. Then, along the stairs a building that does not appear to be in good repair"* or *"Lack of bars and graffiti types of things lead me to believe the criminal element in this neighborhood may be less than in some of the others, so the level of danger might be less"*. One non-local annotator observed that the place is *"Obviously from another time in history."*

As a final example, Fig. 9 shows two images that were selected as they had significant score differences across groups, for specific labels. Figure 9a is labeled as *I-1* in Fig. 5a; the scores for the *dangerous* label are 7 for locals and 1.5 for non-locals. This seems to be an outlier case. From our own inspection, it is not clear what kind of features are used by locals to perceived the place as dangerous, except perhaps the sidewalk that seems to blend into the street. We speculate that in a local context, background and prior experiences may play a key role. In contrast, and the basis of the visual cues present in the images, non-locals provide a low score that does not reflect a sense of danger. For Fig. 9b, labeled as *I-2* in Fig. 5b, the scores for the *interesting* label are 1 for locals and 6 for non-locals, respectively. In this case, the local score seems reasonable, given the visual cues present in the image. However, for non-locals, the site seems to be interesting. We speculate that annotators might have not previously seen a site like this, which may compel them to find out more about it.

This anecdotal evidence complements the quantitative analysis presented earlier in this section, and seems to confirm that the background and previous experience of observers play a crucial role when forming urban perceptions.

7 Inference from Visual Cues for Local and Non-local Impressions (RQ2)

The automatic inference methods produce continuous values for each inferred urban perception attribute. For the regression task, we first train Random Forest models using the annotation of each perception label as the dependent variable, and the datasets with visual cues based on CNNs (Sect. 5.1) and the one with semantic descriptors (Sect. 5.2) as the independent variables. We evaluate four models for each group of raters (locals and non-locals): (1) semantic segmentation features; (2) places205 features; (3) places365 features; and (4) semantic descriptors. Finally, we compare the obtained results with our previous work described in Santani et al. (2018), which uses a fully connected layer of a GoogLeNet CNN pre-trained on places205 database (CNN-FC) and non-local scores. This model is denoted by M0 in the rest of the section. The eight regression models are summarized in Table 5.

Model 1 (M1-1 and M1-2) This corresponds to the 150 automatically extracted semantic segmentation features. The results are shown in Table 6. The R^2 values range between 0.10 to 0.30. Furthermore, the results for the systems trained on non-local scores are better than those for the systems trained on local scores, in particular for *dangerous*, *dirty*, and *polluted*. We believe that this is partly due to the lower ICCs obtained for these attributes, as discussed in Sect. 6. Furthermore, the results with this model are below the results obtained with the CNN-FC in Santani et al. (2018). This can be partly explained by the fact that the number of features of the semantic segmentation is lower than the one for CNN-FC.

Model 2 (M2-1 and M2-2) This model corresponds to the automatically extracted places205 features. The results explain reasonably well the positively phrased labels (*pretty*, *interesting* and *pleasant*) as their R^2 values are above 0.25. We see the same pattern as the *model 1*, namely that the results obtained for non-local impressions are better than those for locals. On the other hand, the remaining three variables (*dangerous*, *dirty*, and *polluted*) cannot be inferred when using the local scores.

Table 5 Definition of the eight regression models used for inference, according to the choice of labels and visual representation

Model	Labels (locals or non-locals)	Visual cues (CNN or manual)
M1-1	Non-local	CNN DilatedNet semantic segmentation
M1-2	Local	CNN DilatedNet semantic segmentation
M2-1	Non-local	CNN GoogLeNet places205
M2-2	Local	CNN GoogLeNet places205
M3-1	Non-local	CNN GoogLeNet places365
M3-2	Local	CNN GoogLeNet places365
M4-1	Non-local	Manual semantic descriptors
M4-2	Local	Manual semantic descriptors

Table 6 Regression results. The values in bold represent the best result for a given label. All models use Random Forests. Models are defined in Table 5. M0 corresponds to the results obtained by using non-local scores and a fully connected layer of a GoogLeNet CNN pre-trained on places205 Santani et al. (2018)

Label	M0 R^2	M1-1 R^2	M2-1 R^2	M3-1 R^2	M4-1 R^2	M1-2 R^2	M2-2 R^2	M3-2 R^2	M4-2 R^2
Dangerous	0.38	0.28	0.35	**0.39**	0.32	0.08	0.13	0.16	0.18
Dirty	**0.37**	0.24	0.35	0.35	0.33	0.07	0.12	0.16	0.24
Interesting	**0.45**	0.28	0.41	0.41	0.19	0.14	0.26	0.24	0.28
Pleasant	**0.45**	0.31	0.42	0.42	0.37	0.18	0.26	0.26	0.32
Polluted	0.30	0.21	0.28	**0.32**	0.21	0.05	0.07	0.08	0.21
Pretty	**0.46**	0.29	0.43	0.42	0.33	0.15	0.27	0.25	0.33

Model 3 (M3-1 and M3-2) This model corresponds to the automatically extracted places365 features. In this case, the model with the scores generated by non-locals (M3-1) produced better R^2 values when compared to CNN-FC for the *dangerous* and *polluted* labels. As for the remaining labels, results were comparable to those of *model M2-1*. For the model trained on labels by locals, there is not much improvement when compared to *model M2-2*. The regression models trained on *dangerous*, *dirty*, and *polluted* local labels still get low R^2 values.

Model 4 (M4-1 and M4-2) This corresponds to the 10 manually annotated semantic descriptors. The results show that better R^2 is obtained using the annotations by non-locals. We speculate that since the non-local annotators lack contextual information about the cities where the images were taken, they rate mainly based on visual cues they perceive in the pictures as seen in Sect. 6. Although these results are lower than those obtained with both *M0* and *M3*, they are interesting as only 10 features were used in the regression task. For the case of the local scores, the R^2 of two of the negatively phrased labels (*dirty* and *polluted*) improved considerably. This suggests that when analyzing scenes from a local view, it is possible to achieve better inference performance if high-level visual elements, rather than object-level ones, are considered.

We remark that the results obtained with the local annotator scores are not as good as those produced by the non-locals. This could be explained by the finding that there is more disagreement among local annotators, particularly when scoring the negative labels (Sect. 6). Notice that this pattern is also visible in the correlation matrices (Fig. 3b and a).

In summary, we found that (1) inference systems trained on impression labels provided by non-locals result in higher performance numbers (measured by the standard R^2 coefficient of determination) for all six dimensions in the case of CNN features, and for three dimensions in the case of manual visual cues; (2) positively phrased attributes are inferred with higher R^2 than negatively phrased ones; and (3) for local labels, the three negative variables cannot be recognized at acceptable levels using CNN features, although the performance improved for the case of manual, high-level descriptors.

8 Discussion

In this section, we discuss some of the main findings of our work, and their implications.

Reliability of Local Annotations First, in contrast with our previous findings of Santani et al. (2017), which relied on a different cohort of local annotators, we found that the annotations generated by locals are less consistent (i.e., lower ICC values). Since the experimental procedure to gather the annotations was the same, we investigated which factors might have contributed to this lower inter-observer agreement. One possible explanation is that the population of locals is more heterogeneous. In our previous work Santani et al. (2017), the majority of participating volunteers (selected from a population of 600 students of CECYTE Guanajuato) lived in the downtown area. In contrast, the cohort participating in this study were from a new campus of the same institution, hosting 1100 students, a number of whom live in the suburbs. As life in the suburbs has differences with life in the downtown area, it is reasonable to think that the way urban spaces are perceived may differ to some degree. This hypothesis suggests the need to conduct a finer study that examines possible differences in perception across different sub-populations inhabiting a city.

Similarly, we need to consider gender differences (e.g. women vs. men). An example is the perception of danger. On one hand, there is an increasing sense on insecurity in many regions in Mexico Monroy-Hernández et al. (2013); on the other hand, gender violence is a prevalent phenomenon in the country (UN Women 2021). As a result, women tend to be cautious when walking outside. According to the members of our local research team, city alleys in Guanajuato that lack security elements are seldom used by women walking alone. We speculate that the perception of a dangerous place might differ between local men and women. As an alternative explanation, it is possible that some of the local participants had actually visited the locations they rated, and thus might have first-hand knowledge of the actual level of danger in those locations. These hypotheses would have to be tested as part of future work, since our experimental protocol considered anonymized data, i.e., personal information (age and gender) was only obtained for general statistics but was not linked to each person's annotations.

Comparing Local and Non-local Annotator Populations With respect to demographic comparisons with MTurk workers, recent work showed using a large-scale survey that the large majority of MTurk workers are from the US (75%), followed by India (16%), Canada (1.1%), Great Britain (0.7%), Philippines (0.35%), and Germany (0.27%). As for age, 20% of MTurk workers are born after 1990, 60% are born after 1980, and 80% are born after 1970. As for gender, 51% are women workers and 49% are men (Djellel Difallah & Ipeirotis 2018). This raises the question of how comparable our two populations of annotators are, and whether such differences might lead to biases. We acknowledge such possibility, yet remark that the unavailability of MTurk in Mexico limits direct comparisons of people working on the same platform. It is also worth considering the possibility that some of the US MTurk workers had Mexican heritage and thus are likely familiar with the urban scenes depicted in our corpus. While we cannot estimate this number accurately as we did not collect such data, we can provide partial evidence based on those MTurk workers who responded to our demographic survey ($N = 77$). As discussed in Sect. 4.3, only 3% of the respondents self-reported their ethnicity as Hispanic/Latino. Furthermore, only 10% of the respondents reported having visited Mexico. Another partial answer can be inferred from Djellel Difallah and Ipeirotis (2018), which reports that about 0.16% of MTurk workers are from Mexico. A 2018 estimate of the upper bound of the total number of MTurk workers is around 200,000 people, with about 2450 workers available at a given time (Djellel Difallah & Ipeirotis 2018). These numbers suggest a low probability that MTurk annotators are of Mexican origin.

Implications of Using Non-local or Local Annotations for Machine Learning
The generation of subjective urban labels exclusively from online crowdsourcing platforms like MTurk has the potential risk of inducing biases. This could in turn lead to machine learning systems that incorporate country- or population-specific perceptions, or that lack diversity. As previously mentioned, recent work found that 75% of MTurk workers are from the US (Djellel Difallah and Ipeirotis 2018). Furthermore, the majority of people in Mexico do not have access to work on platforms like MTurk due to a variety of factors, including platform restrictions, tax regulations, and lack of access to credit card services. Some of the challenges faced by crowdworkers have been discussed in Kittur et al. (2013), Kingsley et al. (2015). For these reasons, conducting future urban crowdsourcing experiments in Global South countries calls for the design of digital platforms adapted to the local conditions, the diversification of urban perception labels that reflect local views, and the use of culture-specific processes to effectively engage workers.

Practical Uses of Our Work Understanding the urban perception of local inhabitants in Global South cities clearly goes beyond scientific inquiry, which brings up the question on how to provide city officials with tools that leverage upon our findings. We can discuss two directions of the work presented here.

According to the United Nations Human Settlements Programme (UN Habitat 2021), 85% of the Mexican population will live in cities by 2030. For this reason and as a first direction, it is important to develop methods to understand how these increasing numbers of local inhabitants perceive and experience their environment, as part of participatory processes in collaboration with authorities to develop new public policy (Le Dantec et al. 2015). Since the beginning of our research, our team has been in close contact with city authorities in Guanajuato and Leon Ruiz-Correa et al. (2017), who were interested in understanding how youth perceive their city and what urban issues they considered more relevant. Over time, our team has shared tools with government officials from Guanajuato City and Leon City, Guanajuato's Youth Institute, the Institute of Legislative Investigations, the Leon's Teenagers House, and the Institute of Planning of Guanajuato State (Ruiz-Correa et al. 2018). This shows that the approach is valuable for city offices interested in youth.

In a second direction, contrasting differences of perceptions between locals and visitors has potential practical value for cities. According to the United Nations and the World Trade Organization, Mexico is consistently ranked as one of the ten most visited countries in the world. Understanding how visitors (both real and potential) perceive cities in Mexico, and what urban features are most important for them, could be studied through comprehensive urban perception studies to inform tourism strategies. Our team has also shared insights with government officials from Guanajuato's Tourism Observatory and Guanajuato's Tourism Ministry, with the goal of developing methods to explore how international tourists perceive urban spaces in touristic cities across Guanajuato state.

9 Conclusions

This chapter presented a study on urban perception by humans and machines, using images as input and six urban perception variables as inference targets. Our work used three cities in Mexico as a case study. We now summarize the answers to the two research questions we addressed.

Our first RQ inquired whether local and non-local observers agreed on the perception of urban dimensions in such cities. We found that non-locals reached higher agreement compared to locals for most dimensions; and that the impression scores of the two groups presented statistical differences for some of the dimensions. More specifically, locals had a tendency to score urban scenes as more dangerous than non-locals; in contrast, non-locals tended to score scenes as more interesting and pleasant than locals. We have discussed possible explanations for these findings. Future work involving a mixed-method approach (collecting additional online observations and interviews with observers) could refine some of the analysis presented here.

Our second RQ asked whether visual machine learning systems would result in comparable performance, when trained to infer subjective attributes of urban scenes with local or non-locals labels. Based on eight models trained on the two types of labels and four types of visual cues (three of them coming from standard CNN systems, and one obtained by manual coding), we found that systems trained with non-local labels produced higher performance. This result could likely follow from the higher inter-observer agreement obtained for the non-local labels. At the same time, this result highlights the importance of understanding the potential impact of systems deployed to recognize perceptual aspects in Global South cities, when these are learned from perceived labels generated by different groups of people, including local inhabitants and external observers.

The results of our work highlight the need for further studies about the influence of demographic and cultural diversity of crowdworkers on subjective label production, and about the implications of this on automation, through empirical analyses of systems that use crowdsourced subjective labels for machine learning in urban environments.

Acknowledgments L. Medina Rios acknowledges the support of Mexico's Consejo Nacional de Ciencia y Tecnología (CONACYT). S. Ruiz-Correa also acknowledges the support of CONACYT through project 247802. D. Gatica-Perez acknowledges the support of the Swiss National Science Foundation (SNSF) through the Dusk2Dawn Sinergia project. All authors thank the CECYTE Guanajuato community for their enthusiastic participation, and Yassir Benkhedda for technical support. We also thank the book editors for their valuable suggestions to improve the chapter.

References

Arietta, S. M., Efros, A. A., Ramamoorthi, R., & Agrawala, M. (2014). City forensics: Using visual elements to predict non-visual city attributes. *IEEE Transactions on Visualization and Computer Graphics, 20*(12), 2624–2633.

Bader, M. D., Mooney, S. J., Lee, Y. J., Sheehan, D., Neckerman, K. M., Rundle, A. G., & Teitler, J. O. (2015). Development and deployment of the computer assisted neighborhood visual assessment system (canvas) to measure health-related neighborhood conditions. *Health & Place, 31*, 163–172.

Balestrini, M., Bird, J., Marshall, P., Zaro, A., & Rogers, Y. (2014). Understanding sustained community engagement: A case study in heritage preservation in rural Argentina. In *Proceedings ACM Conference on Human Factors in Computing Systems* (pp. 2675–2684)

Blobaum, A., & Marcel, H. (2005). Perceived danger in urban public space: The impacts of physical features and personal factors. *Environment and Behavior, 37*(4), 465–486.

Caminos de la Villa, Argentina. Retrieved March 2021, from https://www.caminosdelavilla.org

Candeia, D., Figueiredo, F., Andrade, N., & Quercia, D. (2017). Multiple images of the city: Unveiling group-specific urban perceptions through a crowdsourcing game. In *Proceedings ACM Conference on Hypertext and Social Media, HT '17* (pp. 135–144).

Connors, W. (2014). Google, Microsoft expose Brazil's favelas. *Wall Street Journal*.

Dalal, N., & Triggs, B. (2005). Histograms of oriented gradients for human detection. In: *Proc. IEEE Conference on Computer Vision and Pattern Recognition* (p. 886–893).

Daniel, T.C. (2001). Whither scenic beauty? Visual landscape quality assessment in the 21st century. *Landscape and Urban Planning, 54*(1), 267–281.

DeVries, T., Misra, I., Wang, C., & van der Maaten, L. (2019). Does object recognition work for everyone? In *Proceedings of CVPR Workshop on Computer Vision for Global Challenges*

Djellel Difallah, E.F., & Ipeirotis, P. (2018). Demographics and dynamics of mechanical Turk workers. In *Proceedings ACM International Conference on Web Search and Data Mining*.

Dubey, A., Naik, N., Parikh, D., Raskar, R., & Hidalgo, C. A. (2016). Deep learning the city: Quantifying urban perception at a global scale. In *Proc. European Conference on Computer Vision* (pp. 196–212).

Florida, R., & Rentfrow, P. J. (2011). Place and well-being. In K.M. Sheldon, T.B. Kashdan, M.F. Steger (Eds.), *Designing positive psychology: Taking stock and moving forward*. Oxford University Press.

Gebru, T., Krause, J., Wang, Y., Chen, D., Deng, J., Aiden, E. L., & Fei-Fei, L. (2017). Using deep learning and Google street view to estimate the demographic makeup of neighborhoods across the united states. *Proceedings of the National Academy of Sciences, 114*(50), 13108–13113.

Goncalves, J., Ferreira, D., Hosio, S., Liu, Y., Rogstadius, J., Kukka, H., & Kostakos, V. (2013). Crowdsourcing on the spot: Altruistic use of public displays, feasibility, performance, and behaviours. In *Proceedings ACM International Joint Conference on Pervasive and Ubiquitous Computing* (pp. 753–762).

Goncalves, J., Hosio, S., Van Berkel, N., Ahmed, F., & Kostakos, V. (2017). Crowdpickup: Crowdsourcing task pickup in the wild. *Proceedings of the ACM on Interactive, Mobile, Wearable and Ubiquitous Technologies, 1*(3), 51:1–51:22.

Heimerl, K., Gawalt, B., Chen, K., Parikh, T., & Hartmann, B. (2012). Communitysourcing: Engaging local crowds to perform expert work via physical kiosks. In *Proceedings of the SIGCHI Conference on Human Factors in Computing Systems, CHI '12* (pp. 1539–1548).

Herzog, T. R., & Chernick, K. K. (2000). Tranquility and danger in urban and natural settings. *Journal of Environmental Psychology, 20*(1), 29–39.

Jia, Y., Shelhamer, E., Donahue, J., Karayev, S., Long, J., Girshick, R., Guadarrama, S., & Darrell, T. (2014). Caffe: Convolutional architecture for fast feature embedding. arXiv preprint arXiv:1408.5093.

Kaplan, R., Kaplan, S., & Brown, T. (1989). Environmental preference: A comparison of four domains of predictors. *Environment and Behavior, 21*(5), 509–530.

Kingsley, S. C., Gray, M. L., & Suri, S. (2015). Accounting for market frictions and power asymmetries in online labor markets. *Policy & Internet, 7*(4), 383–400.

Kittur, A., Nickerson, J. V., Bernstein, M., Gerber, E., Shaw, A., Zimmerman, J., Lease, M., & Horton, J. (2013). The future of crowd work. In *Proceedings ACM Conference on Computer Supported Cooperative Work* (pp. 1301–1318).

Koo, T. K., & Li, M. Y. (2016). A guideline of selecting and reporting intraclass correlation coefficients for reliability research. *Journal of Chiropractic Medicine, 15*, 155–163.

Le Dantec, C. A., Asad, M., Misra, A., & Watkins, K. E. (2015). Planning with crowdsourced data: Rhetoric and representation in transportation planning. In *Proceedings ACM Conference on Computer Supported Cooperative Work and Social Computing* (pp. 1717–1727).

Lindal, P. J., & Hartig, T. (2013). Architectural variation, building height, and the restorative quality of urban residential streetscapes. *Journal of Environmental Psychology, 33*, 26–36.

List of Largest Cities. Retrieved March 2021, from https://en.wikipedia.org/wiki/List_of_largest_cities

Lowe, D. G. (2004). Distinctive image features from scale-invariant keypoints. *International Journal of Computer Vision, 60*(2), 91–110.

Ma, X., Hancock, J. T., Lim Mingjie, K., & Naaman, M. (2017a). Self-disclosure and perceived trustworthiness of airbnb host profiles. In *Proc. ACM Conference on Computer Supported Cooperative Work and Social Computing.*

Ma, X., Neeraj, T., & Naaman, M. (2017b). A computational approach to perceived trustworthiness of airbnb host profiles. In *Proc. AAAI Int. Conference on Web and Social Media.*

Map Kibera, Kenya. Retrieved March 2021, from https://mapkibera.org

Marshall, P., Cain, R., & Payne, S. (2011). Situated crowdsourcing: A pragmatic approach to encouraging participation in healthcare design. In *5th International Conference on Pervasive Computing Technologies for Healthcare (PervasiveHealth)* (pp. 555–558).

Matzen, K., Bala, K., & Snavely, N. (2017). StreetStyle: Exploring world-wide clothing styles from millions of photos. arXiv preprint arXiv:1706.01869.

Monroy-Hernández, A., boyd, d., Kiciman, E., De Choudhury, M., & Counts, S. (2013). The new war correspondents: The rise of civic media curation in urban warfare. In *Proceedings of the 2013 Conference on Computer Supported Cooperative Work, CSCW '13* (pp. 1443–1452).

Naik, N., Philipoom, J., Raskar, R., & Hidalgo, C. (2014). Streetscore—predicting the perceived safety of one million streetscapes. In *2014 IEEE Conference on Computer Vision and Pattern Recognition Workshops* (pp. 793–799).

Offenhuber, D., & Lee, D. (2012). Putting the informal on the map: Tools for participatory waste management. In *Proceedings of the 12th Participatory Design Conference: Exploratory Papers, Workshop Descriptions, Industry Cases - Volume 2, PDC '12* (pp. 13–16).

Ordonez, V., & Berg, T. L. (2014). Learning high-level judgments of urban perception. In D. Fleet, T. Pajdla, B. Schiele, & T. Tuytelaars (Eds.), *ECCV 2014* (pp. 494–510). Springer.

Painter, K. (1996). The influence of street lighting improvements on crime, fear and pedestrian street use, after dark. *Landscape and Urban Planning, 35*(2), 193–201.

Perkins, D., Meeks, J., & Ralph, T. (1992). The physical environment of street blocks and resident preceptions of crime and disorder: Implications for theory and measurement. *Journal of Environmental Psychology, 12*, 21–34.

Piasco, N., Sidibea, D., Demonceaux, C., & Gouet-Brunet, V. (2018). A survey on visual-based localization: On the benefit of heterogeneous data. *Pattern Recognition, 74*, 74–109.

Porzi, L., Rota Bulò, S., Lepri, B., & Ricci, E. (2015). Predicting and understanding urban perception with convolutional neural networks. In *Proceedings of the 23rd ACM International Conference on Multimedia, MM '15* (pp. 139–148).

Quercia, D., O'hare, N., & Cramer, H. (2014). Aesthetic capital: What makes London look beautiful, quiet, and happy?

Rentfrow, P. J. (2011). The open city. In *Handbook of creative cities*. Cheltenham.

Ruiz-Correa, S., Hernandez-Huerfano, E., Alvarez-Rivera, L., Islas-Lopez, V., Ramirez-Sanchez, V., Gonzalez-Abundes, M., Hernandez-Castaneda, M., Carrillo-Sanchez, E., Hasimoto-Beltran, R., & Plata Ortega, I. (2018). Urbis: A mobile crowdsourcing platform for sustainable social and urban research in Mexico. In *Sustainable development research in Mexico (SDR'17)*. Springer World Sustainability Series.

Ruiz-Correa, S., Santani, D., & Daniel, G. P. (2014). Young and the city: Crowdsourcing urban awareness in a developing country. In *Proceedings Int. Conf. on Internet of Things in Urban Space*.

Ruiz-Correa, S., Santani, D., Ramirez-Salazar, B., Ruiz-Correa, I., Rendon-Huerta, F. A., Olmos-Carrillo, C., Sandoval-Mexicano, B. C., Arcos-Garcia, A. H., Hasimoto-Beltran, R., & Gatica-Perez, D. (2017). SenseCityVity: Mobile crowdsourcing, urban awareness, and collective action in Mexico. *IEEE Pervasive Computing, 16*(2), 44–53.

Russell, J., & Pratt, G. (1980). A description of the affective quality attributed to environments. *Journal of Personality and Social Psychology, 38*, 311–322.

Salesses, P., Schechtner, K., & Hidalgo, C. A. (2013). The collaborative image of the city: Mapping the inequality of urban perception. *PLOS ONE, 8*(7), 1–12.

Santani, D., Ruiz-Correa, S., & Daniel, G. P. (2015). Looking at cities in Mexico with crowds. In *Proceedings ACM Symposium on Computing for Development* (pp. 127–135).

Santani, D., Ruiz-Correa, S., & Daniel, G. P. (2017). Insiders and outsiders: Comparing urban impressions between population groups. In *Proc. ACM International Conference on Multimedia Retrieval*. ACM.

Santani, D., Ruiz-Correa, S., & Daniel, G. P. (2018). Looking south: Learning urban perception in developing cities. *ACM Transactions on Social Computing, 1*(3), 1–23.

Shankar, S., Halpern, Y., Breck, E., Atwood, J., Wilson, J., & Sculley, D. (2017). No classification without representation: Assessing geodiversity issues in open data sets for the developing world. In *Proceedings of NIPS Workshop on Machine Learning for the Developing World*.

Stevens, S. S. (1946). On the theory of scales of measurement. *Science, 103*(2684), 677–680.

Sturgis, S. (2015). Kids in India are sparking urban planning changes by mapping slums, Bloomberg CityLab.

UN Habitat. Retrieved March 2021, from https://unhabitat.org

UN Women, the long road to justice, prosecuting femicide in Mexico. Retrieved March 2021, from https://www.unwomen.org/en/news/stories/2017/11/feature-prosecuting-femicide-in-mexico

Yu, F., & Koltun, V. (2016). Multi-scale context aggregation by dilated convolutions. In *Proceedings Int. Conf. on Learning Representations (ICLR)*.

Zhou, B., Lapedriza, A., Khosla, A., Oliva, A., & Torralba, A. (2017). Places: A 10 million image database for scene recognition. *IEEE Transactions on Pattern Analysis and Machine Intelligence, 40*(6), 1452–1464.

Zhou, B., Lapedriza, A., Xiao, J., Torralba, A., & Oliva, A. (2014). Learning deep features for scene recognition using places database. In Z. Ghahramani, M. Welling, C. Cortes, N. D. Lawrence, & K.Q. Weinberger (Eds.), *Advances in neural information processing systems* (Vol. 27, pp. 487–495).

Printed in the United States
by Baker & Taylor Publisher Services